Cosmopolitan Communications
Cultural Diversity in a Globalized World

Societies around the world have experienced a flood of information from diverse channels originating beyond local communities and even national borders, transmitted through the rapid expansion of cosmopolitan communications. For more than half a century, conventional interpretations, Pippa Norris and Ronald Inglehart argue, have commonly exaggerated the potential threats arising from this process. A series of firewalls protect national cultures. This book develops a new theoretical framework for understanding cosmopolitan communications and uses it to identify the conditions under which global communications are most likely to endanger cultural diversity. The authors analyze empirical evidence at both the societal level and the individual level, examining the outlook and beliefs of people in a wide range of societies. The study draws on evidence from the World Values Survey, which covers 90 societies in all major regions worldwide from 1981 to 2007. The conclusion considers the implications of the authors' findings for cultural policies.

Pippa Norris is the McGuire Lecturer in Comparative Politics at the John F. Kennedy School of Government, Harvard University. Her work analyzes comparative elections and public opinion, gender politics, and political communications. Companion volumes by this author, also published by Cambridge University Press, include *A Virtuous Circle* (2000), *Digital Divide* (2001), *Democratic Phoenix* (2002), *Rising Tide* (2003, with Ronald Inglehart), and *Electoral Engineering* (2004).

Ronald Inglehart is Professor of Political Science and Program Director at the Institute for Social Research at the University of Michigan. His research deals with changing belief systems and their impact on social and political change. He helped found the Eurobarometer Surveys and directs the World Values Survey. Related books include *Modernization and Postmodernization* (1997); *Rising Tide* (2003, with Pippa Norris); and *Development, Cultural Change and Democracy* (2004, with Christian Welzel).

Politics and relations among individuals in societies across the world
are being transformed by new technologies for targeting individuals
and sophisticated methods for shaping personalized messages. The
new technologies challenge boundaries of many kinds – between news,
information, entertainment, and advertising; between media, with the
arrival of the World Wide Web; and even between nations. *Communication, Society and Politics* probes the political and social impacts
of these new communication systems in national, comparative, and
global perspective.

Titles in the Series:
C. Edwin Baker, *Media Concentration and Democracy: Why
    Ownership Matters*
C. Edwin Baker, *Media, Markets, and Democracy*
W. Lance Bennett and Robert M. Entmann, eds., *Mediated Politics:
    Communication in the Future of Democracy*
Bruce Bimber, *Information and American Democracy: Technology in
    the Evolution of Political Power*

Continued after the Index

Cosmopolitan Communications

Cultural Diversity in a Globalized World

PIPPA NORRIS
Harvard University

RONALD INGLEHART
University of Michigan, Ann Arbor

CAMBRIDGE
UNIVERSITY PRESS

CAMBRIDGE UNIVERSITY PRESS
Cambridge, New York, Melbourne, Madrid, Cape Town, Singapore,
São Paulo, Delhi, Dubai, Tokyo

Cambridge University Press
32 Avenue of the Americas, New York, NY 10013-2473, USA

www.cambridge.org
Information on this title: www.cambridge.org/9780521738385

First published 2009

Printed in the United States of America

A catalog record for this publication is available from the British Library.

Library of Congress Cataloging in Publication data
Norris, Pippa.
Cosmopolitan communications : cultural diversity in a globalized world / Pippa Norris,
Ronald Inglehart.
    p.   cm. – (Communication, society and politics)
Includes bibliographical references and index.
ISBN 978-0-521-49368-0 (hardback) – ISBN 978-0-521-73838-5 (pbk.)
1. Communication in politics.   2. Communication – Political aspects.
3. Communication – Social aspects.   4. Social change.   5. Social movements.
6. Political participation.   I. Inglehart, Ronald.   II. Title.   III. Series.
JA85.N66   2009
303.48'33 – dc22   2009004767

ISBN   978-0-521-49368-0 Hardback
ISBN   978-0-521-73838-5 Paperback

Contents

Tables and Figures

Tables

Figures

Acknowledgments

This book owes large debts to many friends and colleagues. The analysis draws on a unique database, the World Values Survey (WVS) and the European Values Surveys (EVS), conducted from 1981 to 2007. These representative mass surveys provide data from countries comprising almost 90 percent of the world's population and covering the full range of variation, from societies with per capita incomes as low as $300 per year to societies with per capita incomes a hundred times that high, and from long-established democracies with market economies to authoritarian states and former socialist states.

We extend our gratitude to the following WVS and EVS participants for creating and sharing this invaluable dataset: Anthony M. Abela, Q. K. Ahmad, Rasa Alishauskene, Helmut Anheier, José Arocena, W. A. Arts, Dziedzorm Reuben Asafo, Soo Young Auh, Taghi Azadarmaki, Ljiljana Bacevic, Olga Balakireva, Josip Balobn, Miguel Basanez, Elena Bashkirova, Abdallah Bedaida, Jorge Benitez, Jaak Billiet, Alan Black, Eduard Bomhoff, Ammar Boukhedir, Rahma Bourquia, Fares al Braizat, Thawilwade Bureejul, Harold Caballeros, Pavel Campeanu, Augustin Canzani, Marita Carballo, Henrique Carlos de O. de Castro, Pradeep Chhibber, Hei-yuan Chiu, Munqith Daghir, Jaime Diez-Medrano, Juan Diez-Nicolas, Karel Dobbelaere, Peter J. D. Drenth, Javier Elzo, Yilmaz Esmer, Ann Evans, T. Fahey, Nadjematul Faizah, Georgy Fotev, James Georgas, Mark Gill, Renzo Gubert, Linda Luz Guerrero, Peter Gundelach, Christian Haerpfer, Jacques Hagenaars, Loek Halman, Sang-Jin Han, Stephen Harding, Mari Harris,

Bernadette C. Hayes, Camilo Herrera, Virginia Hodgkinson, Nadra Muhammed Hosen, Desmond Hui, Kenji Iijima, Ljubov Ishimova, Wolfgang Jagodzinski, Aleksandra Jasinska-Kania, Fridrik Jonsson, Stanislovas Juknevicius, Jan Kerkhofs, S.J., Johann Kinghorn, Hans-Dieter Klingemann, Hennie Kotze, Hans-Peter Kreisi, Zuzana Kusá, Marta Lagos, Bernard Lategan, Abdel-Hamid Abdel-Latif, Carlos Lemoine, Noah Lewin-Epstein, Pei-shan Liao, Ola Listhaug, Jin-yun Liu, Augustin Loada, Brina Malnar, Mahar Mangahas, Mario Marinov, Carlos Matheus, Robert Mattes, Rafael Mendizabal, Joan Mico, Jon Miller, Felipe Miranda, Mansoor Moaddel, José Molina, Jotham Momba, Alejandro Moreno, Gaspar K. Munishi, Naasson Munyandamutsa, Neil Nevitte, Elone Nwabuzor, F. A. Orizo, Magued Osman, Merab Pachulia, Alula Pankhurst, Dragomir Pantic, Juhani Pehkonen, Paul Perry, Thorleif Pettersson, Pham Minh Hac, Pham Thanh Nghi, Gevork Pogosian, Bi Puranen, Ladislav Rabusic, Andrei Raichev, Angel Rivera-Ortiz, Catalina Romero, David Rotman, Rajab Sattarov, Sandeep Shastri, Shen Mingming, Renata Siemienska, John Sudarsky, Toru Takahashi, Tan Ern Ser, Farooq Tanwir, Jean-François Tchernia, Kareem Tejumola, Larissa Titarenko, Miklos Tomka, Alfredo Torres, Niko Tos, Jorge Vala, Andrei Vardomatskii, Malina Voicu, Alan Webster, Friedrich Welsch, Christian Welzel, Robert Worcester, Seiko Yamazaki, Birol Yesilada, Ephraim Yuchtman-Yaar, Josefina Zaiter, Brigita Zepa, Ignacio Zuasnabar, and Paul Zulehner.

Most of these surveys were supported financially by sources within a given country, but assistance for surveys where such funding was not available, as well as for central coordination, was provided by the National Science Foundation, the Bank of Sweden Tercentenary Foundation, the Swedish Agency for International Development, the Volkswagen Foundation, the Netherlands Foreign Ministry, and the BBVA Foundation. For more information about the World Values Survey, see the WVS Web site, http://www.worldvaluessurvey.org. The European surveys were conducted by the European Values Study group. For more information, see the EVS Web site, http://www.europeanvalues.nl/.

This study builds on our previous books based on the WVS, *Rising Tide: Gender Equality and Cultural Change Around the World* (2003), which examined changing attitudes toward gender roles, and *Sacred and Secular: Politics and Religion Worldwide* (2004), which analyzed the role of religion in the contemporary world. Some of the preliminary ideas of this study were first presented at professional conferences, including the Mid-West Political Science Association meeting in Chicago in March 2008 and the American Political Science Association annual meeting in Boston in August 2008, where we benefited from the useful feedback of discussants and colleagues. We also appreciated the opportunity to discuss these ideas at the CommGAP/World Bank and Harvard University Workshop on the Role of the Media in the Governance Agenda in May 2008. In addition, valuable feedback was generated during discussions with colleagues at the meeting of the World Values Survey Conference and General Assembly in Istanbul in September 2008, generously hosted by Yilmaz Esmer and Bahçesehir University. We have received support for the theme of this book in conversations over the years with many colleagues. We are also most grateful to Mark Franklin and Cees van der Eijk and all those who went out of their way to provide feedback on ideas for the research design or to read draft chapters and provide chapter-and-verse comments.

The support of Cambridge University Press has been invaluable, particularly the efficient assistance and continual enthusiasm of our editor, Lew Bateman, as well as the comments of the reviewers. We thank Jaime Diez Medrano for cleaning, documenting, and archiving the WVS and Martin Alonso at Harvard University for assistance in collecting aggregate datasets. Finally, this book would not have been possible without the encouragement and stimulation provided by many colleagues and students at Harvard's Kennedy School of Government and at the Department of Political Science and the Institute for Social Research of the University of Michigan.

Cambridge, Massachusetts,
and Ann Arbor, Michigan

INTRODUCTION

Is Cultural Diversity Under Threat?

In June 1999, Bhutan, the Himalayan Land of the Thunder Dragon, became the last nation on earth to switch on television. The king lifted the ban on the small screen as part of a radical plan to modernize his isolated mountain kingdom and boost the gross national happiness. The country had traditionally restricted tourism and emphasized spirituality and environmental protection over rampant capitalism. Suddenly, however, an idyllic and peaceful tantric Buddhist culture that had barely changed in centuries, with little access in rural areas to electricity or telecommunications, let alone the Internet, was bombarded by about four dozen cable channels, broadcasting mainly imported programs.[1] For cable subscribers, the nightly onslaught opened the world of Posh and Becks, of *Larry King Live* and *The Simpsons*, of the World Wrestling Federation and *American Idol*, of Bollywood soap operas, of music videos and reality TV, of *CNN* and *BBC World News*. The country plugged into the Internet the following year. All too soon reporters noted Bhutan's first wave of crimes – murder, fraud, drug offenses. Bhutan had suddenly crash-landed in the 21st century. Public concern quickly mounted over threats to the country's unique culture. The letters page in local newspapers featured columns of worried correspondence: 'Dear Editor, TV is very bad for our country; it controls our minds...and makes [us] crazy. The enemy is right here with us in our own living room. People behave like the actors, and are now anxious, greedy and discontented.'[2] Others expressed concern that a gulf had opened up between the old Bhutan and the new. One minister observed, 'Until recently, we shied away from killing insects, and yet now we Bhutanese are asked to watch people on TV blowing heads off with shotguns. Will we now be blowing each other's heads off?'[3] Television was widely blamed for a host of social ills, whether weakening spiritual values, undermining ancient traditions, inciting fraud, encouraging material consumerism, destroying family life, or provoking murder among a peaceable people. In response to public concern, in 2006 the government established a new ministry and regulatory authority to determine Bhutan's communication policy, including protecting vulnerable sectors of the public from the effects of excessive violence, obscenity, and drug taking.[4] But was the introduction of TV a major cause of these problems? Will access to modern information and communication technologies erode Bhutan's traditional Buddhist culture and its feudal society? Will wrestling displace the national sport of archery, will English be spoken instead of Dzongkha and Sharchop, and will jeans be worn instead of the *gho* and *kira*? Or are these concerns exaggerated?

Bhutan is perhaps the most dramatic recent example of a developing country adapting to an electronic invasion, but it is far from alone; most societies have experienced a flood of information from diverse channels originating far beyond local communities and national borders. Ideas and images are transmitted from society to society through terrestrial, cable, and satellite television and radio stations, feature films, DVDs, and video games, books, newspapers, and magazines, advertising, the music industry and the audiovisual arts, the digital world of the Internet, Web sites, Tivo, streaming YouTube videos, iPod players, podcasts, wikis, and blogs, as well as through interpersonal connections via mobile cellular and fixed-line telephony, social networking Web sites (like MySpace, Facebook, and Twitter), e-mail, VoIP (Skype), and instant text messaging. The world has come to our front door.

These profound changes are widely observed. But the consequences – especially the impact of the penetration of the mass media into geographically isolated cultures that were previously stranded at the periphery of modern communication grids – are far from clear. What happens to distant rural communities in Bhutan, as well as far-flung districts and remote provinces in Burkina Faso, Burma, and

Afghanistan, once the world connects directly to these places and the people living in them learn more about the world? In particular, will this process generate cultural convergence around modern values, and will national diversity be threatened?

Debate about the supposed peril arising from 'cultural imperialism,' 'Coca-colonization,' or 'McDonaldization' has raged for almost half a century. Nor is this a dated remnant of the cold war era; new protectionist cultural policies have been implemented during the past few years, including those by the United Nations Educational, Scientific, and Cultural Organization (UNESCO) and the European Union. At its heart, this book develops a new theoretical framework and provides systematic evidence to support the argument. We hypothesize that the expansion of information flowing primarily from the global North to South will have the greatest impact on converging values in cosmopolitan societies characterized by integration into world markets, freedom of the press, and widespread access to the media. Parochial societies lacking these conditions are less likely to be affected by these developments. Moreover, within countries, many poor sectors continue to lack the resources and skills necessary to access modern communication technologies. Important social psychological barriers further limit the capacity of the media to alter enduring values and attitudes. A failure to take account of the role of these sequential firewalls has commonly led to exaggerated assessments of the risks to national diversity. These conditions are not confined to the most hermetically sealed and rigidly controlled autocracies, such as Burma and North Korea, or to isolated villages and provincial communities off the mass communication grid in Tibet, Bhutan, and Mali; instead, these barriers are found in many parts of the world. This book outlines these ideas and then lays out the evidence, drawing on the World Values Survey, which covers 95 countries worldwide from 1981 to 2007. The mixed-method research design combines hierarchical linear models, cross-sectional time-series analysis, and selected qualitative case studies. The broad comparative framework and the wide-ranging evidence make it possible to test the core propositions empirically. The concluding chapter considers the implications for cultural policies.

Let us start by clarifying our central concepts and reviewing the controversy surrounding cosmopolitan communications and then outline how this book proceeds in more detail.

Why Cosmopolitan Communications Are Believed to Threaten Cultural Diversity

The starting point for our study is the observation that mass communications have been profoundly affected by the broader phenomenon of globalization – the process of expanding networks of interdependence spanning national boundaries, which follows the increasingly swift movement of ideas, money, goods, services, ecology, and people across territorial borders. Globalization is understood here to be multidimensional, encompassing *economic* aspects, such as the flow of trade, labor, and capital; *social* aspects, such as interpersonal contacts and mediated information flows; and *political* dimensions, including the integration of countries into international and regional organizations.[5] Strictly speaking, most mass communications are not and have not become *global* (meaning covering all parts of the world); rather, communications are in the process of becoming increasingly networked and exchanged across nation-states. These developments render territorial borders more permeable and open to external forces – making most places increasingly similar to bustling Heathrow, JFK, and Schiphol international airports and less like the isolated capitals of Pyongyang, Ashgabat, and Naypyidaw. In this study, globalization is understood to be a complex phenomenon that should not be confused with 'modernization,' 'Westernization,' or 'Americanization,' as the term is sometimes used.[6] By some measures, many smaller countries, such as Singapore, Malaysia, South Africa, Estonia, Hungary, and Israel, are more highly integrated into the world economy than is the United States.[7] Moreover, insofar as basic values are shifting, such countries as Sweden, the Netherlands, and Australia are more at the cutting edge of this process than the United States, although these changes are sometimes mistakenly dubbed 'Americanization.'[8]

Globalization is far from a novel phenomenon; it has occurred historically in periodic waves, whether driven by free trade, population migrations, military conquests, technology, or religious conversions.[9] Arguably both the Roman Empire and medieval Europe under Charlemagne represented earlier manifestations of this trend. The invention of the postal service, electronic telegraph, iron railway, and steamship during the industrial age connected once-distant lands. Networks of 19th-century traders, missionaries, soldiers, and diplomats linked peoples and places. Globalization has experienced eras of advance and retreat. Seen as an ongoing process, globalization is conceptualized as a work in progress rather than as an end state. But as we will demonstrate, the late 20th century witnessed a decisive acceleration in the scale, density, and velocity of interactions that cut across national boundaries.

Due to these developments, places that were once isolated and remote are now increasingly interconnected. Evidence of this phenomenon is all around us. As the authors sit in Massachusetts and Michigan, respectively, we follow real-time news of events in Darfur or Baghdad on our laptops and BlackBerries. Headlines about Barack Obama's victory instantly surged around the globe, connecting Kenyans celebrating in local villages with Americans rejoicing in Times Square. Travelers have access to Internet cafes in Bali, CNN in Doha Airport, or *Die Hard* movies in Beijing. Satellite TV from Al Jazeera and Al Arabia broadcasts reality television shows, music clips, and news images to 200 million Arab speakers from Morocco to Syria. People living in Belgium, the Netherlands, or Switzerland can receive dozens of foreign-language channels from Britain, Germany, Italy, and France on their cable TV. Mexican and Brazilian telenovelas are ubiquitous on Latin American television, as are American sitcoms in Canada, Australian soaps in Britain, British crime series in the United States, and Bollywood movies in South Asia. Reuters, Associated Press, and Agence France-Presse transmit foreign stories to newsrooms around the world. International markets are linked in real time by Bloomberg Business News, the Dow Jones, and related financial tickers. Telecenters in Bangalore and Toronto help Microsoft customers in London, Berlin, and Sydney. Cell phones and text messages instantly connect émigré Mexican, Chinese, and Turkish workers with news from relatives back home. Younger Americans and Europeans take all this for granted today, but it is striking to recall how rapidly it has transformed lives; the World Wide Web, born in 1989, is still in its adolescence.[10]

Multiple developments have expanded the volume and pace of information flowing across national borders. This process operates through the direct transfer of people – for example, through international travel, foreign tourism, and emigration. It happens through interpersonal communications, via the traditional flow of overseas postal mail, international phone calls, telegrams, and faxes, and more recently through person-to-person e-mails and text messages. Today the process also increasingly works through the diverse channels of mass communications. These include traditional printed publications (the overseas trade in newspapers, magazines, and books) and audiovisual media (the international market in radio and television news and entertainment programs, foreign videos, DVDs, movies and feature films, popular music, and transnational TV satellite and cable broadcasts), as well as the complicated flow occurring via more recent forms of digital information technologies, some of which blend the interpersonal with mass communications (typically via Web sites, online videos, blogs, virtual communities, interactive video games, and listserve e-mails).[11]

The concept of 'cosmopolitan' communications emphasizes the channels that increasingly bind people living in diverse communities and nation-states together. The word 'cosmopolitan,' which derives from the Greek word *kosmopolitês* (citizen of the world), refers to the idea that all humans increasingly live and interact within a single global community, not simply within a single polity or nation-state.[12] The conceptual distinction between cosmopolitans and locals has been part of the social sciences at least since Robert Merton developed it to study small-town America during World War II.[13] In recent years, the concept of cosmopolitanism has come back into vogue as an increasingly popular way to rethink processes of democracy for the purpose of extending these principles to international life. The idea of cosmopolitan democracy emphasizes that the principles of democracy should operate within states, but also among states and at the global level; one of the relevant issues is how citizens can organize collectively in civil society and have their voices heard in multilateral organizations beyond the boundaries of the nation-state.[14] In the same way, the idea of cosmopolitan communications can fruitfully be applied to conceptualizing the growing phenomenon of information flows that cut across state borders. Communications traditionally were far more provincial and territorial – binding together friends and neighbors living in local villages, towns, and regions through social meetings and voluntary organizations, local newspapers, community radio stations, and face-to-face interpersonal connections. The change over time should not be overstated; links between national elites have always been maintained through international networks, through, for example, foreign correspondents, diplomatic missions, and UN agencies and bureaus. Mobile populations have always traveled back and forth across territorial national borders, whether as footloose tourists, colonists, students, exiles, expatriate employees, labor migrants, rootless nomads, or members of diaspora communities spread over multiple states. In the contemporary era, however, connections among peoples living in different nations have often become far more cosmopolitan, with multiple information networks linking the lives of strangers from distant lands. The idea of 'cosmopolitan communications' is understood here, most simply, to be the way that we learn about, and interact with, people and places beyond the borders of our nation-state. This concept is thus far broader and more comprehensive than the idea of 'transnational' media – referring to specific communication channels and sources that are designed to reach a multinational audience, exemplified by BBC World, CNN International, Reuters, and Al Jazeera.[15]

From National to Cosmopolitan Communications

Multiple factors contributed to the growth of cosmopolitan communications.[16] In many nations, broadcasting and telecommunications were deregulated. Protectionist trade barriers were lifted. Access to the mass media widened. Innovative technologies permeated societies. Multinational media corporations expanded their empires. As a result, nations have often increasingly encountered a rising tide of ideas and images imported from abroad.

During the height of the modern era of national communications, spanning the period from the rise of radio broadcasting in the early 20th century until at least the early 1980s, with a few exceptions public service corporations throughout continental Western Europe enjoyed a monopoly on the airwaves. Broadcasting operated as a nationally owned public utility monopoly, with the distribution of radio and then television licenses overseen by the postal, telegraph, and telephone authorities. Public broadcasting corporations were subject to periodic review in the issuance and renewal of licenses, modeled after the BBC. They often operated following principles of impartial balance across all major parties, with a mission to educate and entertain, although some, such as French and Greek TV, were more closely aligned with the state. The rationale for this system included spectrum scarcity and the need to provide a universal service in the public interest, as well as the powerful role of broadcasters. There were some important variations in this pattern, however; Britain, Australia, and Japan operated a dual public service and commercial system from the 1950s onward, while the United States and Luxembourg favored private enterprise. Meanwhile, state broadcasters directly controlled the airwaves in Central and Eastern Europe, and most developing countries operated a mix of public service and state broadcasting. During this era, most local, regional, and national newspapers, magazines, and book publishers were usually domestically owned, with legal regulations often limiting the extent of foreign investment. Some major publications were widely distributed on the international market, but this revenue was usually subsidiary to domestic sales. In Europe, the major national production companies in the creative industries and the performing arts were also often run as public corporations. The operating costs of national opera companies, theatrical productions, and musical performances were commonly subsidized by the nation-state, as part of its cultural heritage, in common with national museums, art galleries, and archeological historical sites.

Of course, this process should again not be exaggerated; cultural trade on international markets was important for certain sectors, even during the golden years of the national era. The motion picture industry has always been heavily reliant on overseas sales for generating revenues; such sales have been important for Hollywood but especially for production companies based in countries with a limited domestic audience.[17] The recording music industry based in the United States, Europe, and Japan was also highly export oriented, and this was especially true for major players such as EMI, Sony, and Bertelsmann.[18] Many news outlets with limited resources for overseas bureaus and correspondents have also always relied heavily on Western news agency wire services for international news and foreign affairs coverage, with distant correspondents networked by telegraph, submarine cable, teletype, and wireless and communication satellites.[19] Books, periodicals, magazines, and newspapers have always relied on a proportion of their revenues from overseas sales. The trade in television programs is also long established, and U.S. exports were particularly important, as Tunstall reminds us, when broadcasting systems were first being set up in many countries during the late 1950s and 1960s and insufficient facilities existed for domestic productions.[20] Once established, however, in most places the broadcasting and newspaper industries were usually home owned, nationally regulated, and designed primarily to serve a domestic audience; the British Broadcasting Corporation, *Le Figaro*, and *Arbeitsgemeinschaft der öffentlich-rechtlichen Rundfunkanstalten Deutschlands* (German ARD) reflected their local origins, as distinctive as the Paris Opera, the Drury Lane theater, or Die Berliner Philharmoniker.

The liberalization of public service broadcasting and telecommunication monopolies, which occurred in many countries during the 1980s and 1990s, led to the rapid proliferation of more loosely regulated commercial or privately owned TV and radio channels and telecommunication companies. The new channels of commercial broadcasting also fueled the expansion of mass advertising and encouraged the growth of transnational advertising and market research companies. The print sector has also been affected by growing foreign ownership of newspapers and multinational publishing companies, as well as by cross-media ownership that seeks vertical integration across delivery platforms, linking books, magazines, and newspapers with movies, videos, DVDs, and advertising.

Technological developments have also played a major role in this process, shaping the way business, society, and governments work, function, and interact throughout the world, bringing multiple changes to everyday life.[21] The rapid expansion of access to new information and communication technologies from the mid-1990s onward and media convergence across platforms accelerated the pace of interchanges across state boundaries through the panoply of electronic mail and text messaging, mobile phones, online Web sites and blogs, and related developments.[22] Television broadcasting was transformed by the growth of satellite broadcasting and cable programming, and there were important innovations in digital technologies associated with the rise of the Internet, mobile cell phones, and multimedia convergence. Today multiple sources of entertainment, news, and information vie for attention in the most media rich environments – from feature films to YouTube videos, from headlines on the BBC World Service to CNN, and from blogs to networked e-mails – only some of which are locally or nationally based. These profound developments have had the greatest impact in advanced industrial societies, where many people have adopted the paraphernalia of laptops, Wi-Fi, iPods, and BlackBerries. But digital technologies such as data-connected smartphones have also spread to emerging economies in the developing world, including some remote rural villages, but especially to those of the relatively affluent middle classes living in cities such as Mumbai, Johannesburg, and Doha.

These combined trends have torn down protection and thrown open national markets to a flood of imported products, as documented in Chapter 3, providing opportunities for multinational multimedia production and distribution conglomerates. Although, as exemplified by 10 of the most important players, these are not exclusively based in the United States, all are located in a handful of larger postindustrial societies; these conglomerates include Time Warner, Viacom, Disney, the BBC (United Kingdom), Sony (Japan), News Corporation (United States–Australia), Bertelsmann (Germany), Associated Press, Reuters (United Kingdom), and General Electric. Despite some important second-tier hubs operating within particular geolinguistic regions, such as Bollywood, Al Jazeera, or TV Globo, the international trade in cultural goods and services flows mainly from a few major production conglomerates based in the global North to audiences in the rest of the world. The rise of cosmopolitan communications can therefore be traced back to the deregulation of mass communications, technological innovations, and trade liberalization, processes that started in most advanced industrialized societies during the 1980s, before this transformation eventually swept through the rest of the world in subsequent decades.[23] These changes have resulted in the expansion of all major media sectors, including transnational TV networks, international news wire services, the market for feature films, television programs, and publications, advertising agencies, recorded popular music, and the Internet.

The Impact of Cosmopolitan Communications on the Audience

These basic developments have been widely observed, but what have been the consequences for national cultures? This question has sparked intense debate, and for more than half a century theorists have offered a range of conjectures; the alternative viewpoints are illustrated schematically in Figure 1.1.[24] Perhaps the most popular view anticipates a gradual process of cultural convergence around Western values

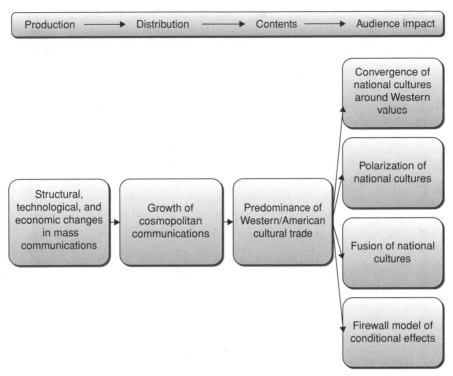

FIGURE 1.1. Theories About the Impact of Cosmopolitan Communications.

worldwide; the predominance of American and other Western media conglomerates in the production of cultural exports is expected to erode the diversity of traditional values, indigenous languages, and local practices found in societies importing these products. Other observers challenge these claims, however, emphasizing that many highly traditional societies in the Middle East, Africa, and Asia have actively rejected foreign ideas and images imported through Western media – from liberal sexual mores to notions of individualism, secularism, and free market capitalism – intensifying culture wars around the world. Still others claim that we are experiencing fusion, whereby cultural artifacts from many different places are exchanged, merged, and reinvented in a world bazaar. These interpretations, illustrated in Figure 1.1, predict alternative long-term effects of cosmopolitan communications, ranging from assimilation to rejection or amalgamation.[25]

In contrast to all these arguments, the more skeptical perspective developed in this study suggests that, due to the existence of important firewalls, many indigenous values, social attitudes, and core beliefs embedded within national cultures are far more impervious to the impact of cosmopolitan communications than is generally believed. The direct experience of globalization does have clear effects, as we will demonstrate, as does the mass media. Nevertheless, the influence of cosmopolitan communications has a less radical or transformative impact on deep-rooted societal differences than is often assumed. As is often the case with important new phenomena, the effect of these developments has been exaggerated. Important changes clearly *are* occurring, but we expect cultural diversity to persist. Let us examine the theoretical arguments in the literature. We will then outline our core argument and the reasons we remain highly skeptical of many of the sweeping claims that are commonly made.

The L.A. Effect: Cultural Convergence?

The most popular view of the past half century remains cultural convergence around Western values, or the 'homogenization' scenario, which can also be termed the 'L.A. effect' since so many of the consequences are thought to arise from the products generated by Hollywood and Silicon Valley. The core contention is that greater exposure to foreign news and popular entertainment, imported mainly from multinational corporations based in the United States or from other major Western producer countries, will gradually undermine, dilute, or even eradicate the variety of national identities, distinctive beliefs, cultural practices, and traditional lifestyles found around the world. Cultural convergence has often been regarded as 'Americanization' or 'Westernization,' although these notions are much too simple to capture the multinational complexity of this phenomenon. This argument is not confined to developing societies by any means; it is often expressed in European debates, such as French concerns about imported American entertainment and news. Nevertheless, if the claims of convergence are true, previously isolated traditional cultures located in peripheral geographic areas in the global South, exemplified by Bhutan, seem most vulnerable to these developments.

This idea is hardly novel; these arguments echo concerns about the dominance of Western journalism and news agencies expressed at the height of the mid-20th-century era of decolonization.[26] Theories of cultural imperialism, popularized during the 1960s and 1970s by Johan Galtung and Herbert Schiller, claimed that the mass media were powerful tools used by neocolonial Western powers to exert hegemonic control over the ideas, habits, and traditions found in weaker developing states and peripheral societies.[27] Thomas McPhail dubbed this phenomenon 'electronic colonialism' and emphasized the dangers of Americanization: 'All of the US multimedia empires, along with their extensive advertising networks, project and encourage US tastes, values, mores, history, culture and language around the world.'[28] This view was reinforced during the 1970s by Tapio Varis's analysis of the continued imbalance of the traffic in television programs and supported by Jeremy Tunstall's *The Media Are American*.[29] These ideas contributed to the contentious New World Information Order debate in the early 1980, a process that divided UNESCO and left an enduring rift in the organization.[30] It should not be thought that these concerns have faded with the passage of time; during the 1990s, echoes of these historic fights continued to be heard by commentators who dubbed American predominance of audiovisual trade 'Coca-colonization' (Howes), 'Dallasification' (Liebes and Katz), 'McDonaldization' (Ritzer, Barber), or 'McDisneyization' (Ritzer and Liska).[31] Most commentators have usually regarded cultural convergence with concern, although Joseph S. Nye, Jr., suggests that American predominance in the market for cultural products represents a more positive and benevolent development, as 'soft power' can supplement the power of military might and economic resources in U.S. foreign policy.[32] American observers believe that the diplomatic use of communications is an important tool that the United States can use to strengthen the spread of American and Western liberal ideas, such as the value of democratic governance, respect for human rights, and support for free markets.[33]

These arguments are not merely academic; their legacy has also been influential during the past decade among policymakers in the international community; indeed, political support has revived these ideas, providing the intellectual rationale for the implementation of new protectionist regulations, import quotas, tariffs, license fees, and subsidies. In 2005 UNESCO secured international agreement for the Universal Declaration on Cultural Diversity, addressing the concern that global communications may be capable of undermining, or even destroying, local customs and traditions, minority native languages, and indigenous lifestyles in developing societies.[34] The sponsors, France and Canada, gathered the support of 148 countries, with only the United States and Israel voting against the convention. Although the convention legitimates domestic legal measures protecting local creative industries, the implications for world trade remain unclear.[35] Protectionist measures have also been passed by the European Union, including most recently the 2007 Audiovisual Media Services Directive, designed to provide a regulatory framework promoting European-produced programming (and limiting American television program imports) within EU member states.[36] In recent decades, the World Trade Organization (WTO) reached an agreement to liberalize trade in multiple economic sectors; since 1995, for example, average tariffs have fallen by one-third in member states.[37] Real growth in trade has surged by around 7–9% worldwide during the past decade, affecting all regions and national income groups, with particularly strong export-led growth in emerging markets such as China, India, and Brazil. The world has negotiated trade agreements on everything from textiles and minerals to banking and manufactured products; nevertheless, sensitivities have limited attempts to further liberalize trade in cultural goods and services.

But are the widespread popular fears about the potential impact of cultural convergence, arising from the imbalance in world markets, actually well founded? The *consequences* of these changes for the audience, and for society in general, may be far from straightforward.[38] Most importantly, the convergence thesis rests, rather unreflectively, on the implicit supposition that people submissively assimilate, and even emulate, ideas and images transmitted directly by mass communications. Audiences are viewed as essentially passive, absorbing Western ideas and values, along with fashions and lifestyles. The simplest version of the argument implies a powerful and direct media effect based on a straightforward 'stimulus–response' psychological model. Whether the globalization of mass communications actually has these effects on the audience, however, remains to be demonstrated. For many reasons, as discussed at length in this book, deeply imbedded cultural values and attitudes in each nation may prove relatively impermeable to these processes.

Despite the intensity of the theoretical debate, until recently little direct evidence has been brought to bear on these issues.[39] In part, this neglect has arisen from the limited availability of systematic and reliable cross-national survey data on cultural values as well as media habits. It may also be attributed to ideological and methodological limitations, inadequate comparative theorizing, and the individualistic bias in the social psychological study of media behavior. Whatever the reasons, it is obviously risky to jump directly from observations about the American or Western trade imbalance in cultural markets to claims about the effects of this process on the public. It is especially danger-ous when these ideas are used to justify restrictive cultural policies and the regulation of the mass media. It is true that today, compared with earlier decades, many more people living in Paris, Tokyo, and Johannesburg have access to the headlines on CNN International or BBC World, to watch a Hollywood blockbuster, or to use Google or YouTube. When they do so, it is indeed possible that they may grad-ually assimilate the ideas and images they are exposed to by these sources, eventually leading to long-term cultural convergence. Alter-natively, they could choose to react against any messages, reinterpret their meaning, or simply ignore them.

The Taliban Effect: Cultural Polarization?
The cultural convergence argument has attracted many critics over the years. In particular, an alternative scenario is provided by the polarization argument, or 'Taliban effect.' This view does not dispute the core changes in media landscapes, including the changing eco-nomic structure of the mass media and the direction and volume of trade in international cultural markets. Rather than emulation, how-ever, theorists such as Pearse envisage a process of active rejection by traditional societies, so that the growth of cross-border informa-tion flows may spark growing culture wars between the global North and South. For example, some observers argue that a backlash against imported Western entertainment and news, along with the values of secularism, individualism, and consumerism, has encouraged a revival of tribal loyalties and ethnic identities in the Middle East and South-east Asia, directly fueling rage against the United States.[40] Accord-ing to this view, traditional societies consciously attempt to distance themselves and to protect their cultures from the foreign values, ideas, and images commonly conveyed by imported Western and Ameri-can media.[41] The tensions between convergence and polarization have

been popularized in vivid metaphors by Benjamin Barber as the rivalry between McWorld and Jihad, while Thomas Friedman has drawn the contrast between the Lexus and the Olive Tree.[42] Although the role of mass communications is not central to the argument, the idea of value-based polarization is also reflected in Samuel Huntington's provocative thesis, which predicts a clash of civilizations between the West and other cultures.[43] In the polarization scenario, exposure to the 'other' is believed to provoke active measures to reject foreign threats. This process can also been termed the 'Taliban effect,' which refers to one of the most extreme examples of a regime trying to exert rigid control on all media in order to reduce foreign influences. After it had gained control of Afghanistan in the mid-1990s, the Taliban banned TV and cinema, as well as many types of painting and photography, cassette players, VCRs, musical instruments, and video tapes, and demolished thousands of historical statues and artifacts.

In support of the polarization argument, cultural theorists suggest that audiences reinterpret the contents of messages imported from foreign media, thereby remaking their meaning in particular local contexts and undermining their intended effects.[44] From this perspective, people have the capacity to actively criticize, resist, and reject media messages, just as they can read between the lines of official state propaganda, especially if the messages reflect culturally unacceptable values, attitudes, and forms of behavior. They are considered capable of deconstructing meanings and generating resistance to the spread of a uniform Western or American culture. For example, a study of audiences in various European countries that watched similar popular forms of entertainment imported from the United States (Dallas) found that people constructed diverse frameworks of meaning from this shared experience.[45] Moreover, some theorists of this perspective argue that in highly traditional or socially conservative cultures, greater familiarity with Western values carried in popular entertainment and news about the world can trigger unintended effects, catalyzing new culture wars between the forces of modernization and reaction. Opposition to globalization manifests itself in popular street protests based on cultural issues (exemplified by Muslim demonstrations in Pakistan against the Danish publication of cartoons of Mohammed) and in consumer boycotts against imported cultural products or the development of local alternatives (illustrated by the popularity of Mecca

Cola in the Middle East or the slow-food movement in Europe).[46] The collapse of the Doha world trade negotiations in July 2008 over agricultural protectionism, after seven years of talks, also signaled the limits of this process. Political and environmental concerns may increase support for antiglobalization forces; such concerns are stimulated by rising public apprehension about global warming, the loss of jobs in rich countries, food safety and security, the growing cost of extended supply chains associated with rising oil prices, and transportation costs. The International Network for Cultural Development was formed in 1998 as an advocacy nongovernmental organization (NGO) to fight economic globalization and to promote multicultural expression, indigenous arts and crafts, and local diversity.[47]

Although the polarization thesis provides an interesting and plausible perspective, its relevance to the audience has not been subjected to rigorous scrutiny or evaluated against systematic evidence from public opinion surveys. Too often there is a tendency for theorists to jump from patterns of conflict that have been widely observed to casting blame on the media messenger for these developments. Hence, the spread of transnational media and cross-border information flows, exemplified by the popularity of Al Jazeera and Al Arabia, is used to explain tensions between the forces of radicalism and the status quo within Arab states, without demonstrating the connection in any systematic way, rather than attributing these developments to other underlying causes. Do people living in countries such as Egypt, Burkina Faso, and Ethiopia, who are regularly exposed to the cross-border flow of information and popular entertainment, absorb or reject the modern values contained in foreign cultural products? Does this process influence sexual mores, consumer attitudes, or trust in other nations? So far, these questions have not been addressed by systematic testing against a wide range of empirical evidence.

The Bangalore Effect: Fusion?

Another interpretation has also emerged – the fusion or 'hybridization' thesis, which can also be referred to as the 'Bangalore effect.' Theorists of this perspective suggest that easier and faster communications among societies generate a creative global mélange that mixes genres, programs, and contents derived from different times or places.[48] Through this process, creative ideas are exchanged in different countries, but these are then remade and re-exported. As a result, the very concept of an indigenous (and American) cultural product becomes unclear. 'Glocalization' encourages a blending of diverse cultural repertoires through a two-way flow of global and local information generating cross-border fertilization, mixing indigenous customs with imported products. This process is thought to generate original fusions of music, design, and fashions, which are neither uniquely ethnically traditional nor industrial-modern.[49] From this perspective, Asians in London's Brick Lane, Hispanics in New York's Queens, and pied noirs in Paris's XVIIIe arrondissement are neither wholly Western nor purely the product of immigrant cultures but a mixture of both. McDonald's and similar American fast-food restaurants are certainly popular, but according to this view they are outnumbered by the diverse ethnic cuisines, whether Italian, Chinese, Thai, Indian, Japanese, or Mexican, that have spread to cities throughout the world, including those in the United States. The process can be dubbed the 'Bangalore effect,' reflecting the global reach of the financial services and information technology companies based in that city.[50] American customers seeking technical support for computer products are routinely connected to Bangalore call centers, in a geographically meaningless space.

A fusion culture emphasizes that modern mass communications involve a two-way exchange worldwide, generating complex currents and eddies, seen more as a global bazaar with counterflows than a simple form of neocolonial dominance. California fusion cuisine typically amalgamates eclectic dishes – Asian, Mediterranean, and Latin American – with local farmers' market produce. It is neither wholly local nor wholly global. Another typical fusion product is mash-up music, made by sampling, remixing, and combining distinct pop songs. The fusion interpretation suggests that although American companies predominate in the production, distribution, and sales of popular TV entertainment and feature films, these products have absorbed genres, formats, and program ideas from diverse sources – the Dutch Big Brother, British Pop Idol, and Hong Kong action flicks. Thus, the quintessentially American center of information technology, Silicon Valley, has a huge component of Asian scientists and entrepreneurs. With open borders, the United States has become the largest consumer market for information and communication, as well as the most successful exporter of cultural products and services. But like the popularity of Chicago pizza, Amsterdam *rijsttafel*, or London chicken tikka masala, the cultural goods that emerge are neither wholly indigenous to each country nor wholly foreign, but a fusion. Thus, McDonald's itself now offers croissants and Asian noodles. Pushed to the extreme, there is no such thing as cultural authenticity; rather, there are a variety of creative mélanges drawn from diverse sources.[51]

Important regional markets have also emerged, facilitating local exchanges and counterflows, such as Bollywood films in South Asia, Mexico and Brazilian popular TV in Latin America, Chinese video software on Wal-Mart shelves, and South Korean television dramas broadcast in other Asian countries. International Web sites, advertising messages, consumer products, and newspapers are other examples of cross-border goods and services that are tailored to fit local markets and interests. Fusion can occur because global media companies adapt their products to local communities, using indigenous images and accents to sell imported brands. National media companies may also import but then adapt global products, dubbing feature films into domestic languages or adding subtitles. And audiences may transform imported cultural products by adapting them to local needs and conditions.[52] Understanding these issues is complicated by the fact that diverse reactions to the same phenomena may be occurring simultaneously among different social sectors; for example, the affluent and educated urban elite living in developing countries may come to share similar ideas and attitudes with their counterparts living in Europe or North America due to the spread of mass communications, while at the same time this process may generate greater polarization between elites and more conservative groups living in traditional rural communities in the same societies.

Plan of the Book

Part I
In the light of this debate, the next chapter outlines the firewall theory at the heart of this book, identifies the core testable empirical propositions that flow from our theory, explains the book's research design, and outlines the sources of evidence. Chapter 3 examines the international market for cultural goods and services, including the

volume and direction of exports and imports across national borders, as well as trends over time. We analyze evidence for the trade in audio-visual services, the flow of news information, and the role of new information and communication technologies. We demonstrate that cultural exchange is more commonplace among core societies, based mainly in the global North, that have rich and dense networks of connectivity. By contrast, peripheral societies, which are not as closely connected, are heavily concentrated in the global South. The evidence demonstrates the leading share of the international market in cultural trade held by the United States – and the way that this share has grown, not shrunk, in recent years. But the chapter also demonstrates the limits of trade integration for poor societies.

Chapter 4 investigates the extent to which deep-rooted poverty and lack of economic development remain major barriers to accessing the mass media; to this end, it examines the regular use of newspapers and magazines, television and radio broadcasts, and the Internet or e-mail. The chapter also looks at how this usage varies among and within societies worldwide. The comparative framework focuses on some of the leading media-saturated postindustrial countries, such as the United States, Sweden, Germany, and Japan; some middle-income nations and emerging economies, such as Brazil, India, and China, where public access to all forms of electronic and printed communications has been rapidly growing; as well as some of the least developed societies, where isolated rural communities have minimal access to the news media, such as Burkina Faso, Rwanda, and Ethiopia. There are also substantial disparities in the use of news between the information-rich and -poor within countries. Information and communication technologies (ICTs) have spread most widely among more affluent households in high- and middle-income countries, but substantial gaps in media access remain, not simply in new ICTs. Evidence from international statistics gathered by UNESCO, the International Telecommunication Union (ITU), and related agencies enables us to compare the patterns of access around the world and to consider whether the digital divide has gradually closed over time. The WVS helps to monitor patterns of mass communications at the individual level and to explain the underlying reasons for disparities in access. Case studies from Mali and South Africa illustrate the contrasts in greater depth.

Chapter 5 compares and classifies societies worldwide using a new Cosmopolitanism Index based on identifying the external and internal barriers to the free flow of information. The most cosmopolitan societies, such as Denmark, Estonia, and Switzerland, are characterized by widespread public access to multiple media channels and sources, limited trade barriers to cultural imports, and few major restrictions on the independence of journalists and broadcasters. These societies are at the forefront of the globalization process and are integrated with many other countries through strong communication, economic, and political networks. Certain emerging economies and developing nations, such as the Czech Republic, South Africa, and Argentina, are increasingly integrated into cosmopolitan networks. By contrast, in provincial societies, such as Burma, Iran, Syria, and Vietnam, the state continues to exert considerable control over news and public affairs, restricting both cultural imports and freedom of the press. These countries are also poorly integrated into global markets in trade and communication networks, and the public has restricted access to mass communications. Provincial societies also include emerging economies such as China and Russia, which are integrated with world trade markets but restrict information flows at home. Other cases, such as Mali, Indonesia, and Ghana, are newer democracies with considerable media freedom but with relatively weak integration into global markets and communication networks, underdeveloped communication infrastructures, and relatively limited public access to the mass media. We classify the societies in the countries under comparison according to the Cosmopolitanism Index and illustrate the typology with selected case studies.

Part II

The second part of the book tests the firewall theory. This theory predicts that individual use of the news media will have a *direct* effect on individual values. In addition, it predicts that a *cross-level interaction* effect will also be apparent, as external and internal barriers to information flows in each society will interact with individual patterns of news media use. In particular, the theory predicts that, in the most cosmopolitan societies, even after other social characteristics are controlled for, people who are most regularly exposed to information from the media will differ significantly from those who remain more isolated from mass communications. Our study tests the impact of exposure to the mass media on the strength of national identities and cosmopolitan orientations; values and attitudes toward markets and the state; orientations toward religion, gender equality, and traditional standards of morality; and attitudes toward democracy, self-expression values, and human rights. In all cases, other individual-level characteristics associated with use of the media, including education, income, gender, and age, are controlled for.

Chapter 6 opens this part of the book by examining whether those most exposed to news and information are less nationalistic and more cosmopolitan in their orientations than others, as expected, and how this pattern varies in open and closed societies. Commentators such as Anthony Giddens have argued that globalization is leading to the 'end of the nation state.'[53] Regular exposure to more information about other societies and the world via the news media should contribute to this process. Yet skeptics doubt whether identification with the nation-state has been seriously weakened among the mass public, even in the European Union, and whether an emerging 'cosmopolitan identity' is sufficiently powerful to replace the visceral tribal appeals of nationalism. In Anthony Smith's view, for example, we are witnessing the growth of regional blocs, where nation-states remain the primary actors, not the emergence of a new world order that transcends states.[54] To consider these issues, this chapter examines whether regular users of the news media differ significantly in the strength of their national identities, support for the organizations of global governance, and attitudes toward national or multilateral solutions to policy problems.

Chapter 7 explores the impact of the news media on attitudes toward the free market and the role of government intervention in the management of the economy. This issue is particularly important for the former Communist states and Latin American societies that have followed the policies of the Washington consensus, deregulating and privatizing the public sector, liberalizing trade, and shrinking the role of the state. Mass communications are expected to have encouraged support for economic liberalism by emphasizing mass consumerism, individualism, and capitalism, especially through advertising as well as through the values conveyed by popular entertainment and financial news exported from affluent postindustrial societies. A body of research has explored factors leading to public support for free trade and economic integration.[55] This chapter goes further to examine the role of mass communications in this process, in particular whether those groups that do and do not regularly use the news media display distinctive economic values that underly preferences concerning the role of markets and the state.

Chapter 8 examines whether media users have distinctive orientations toward traditional moral values and religion. Previous work by the authors has demonstrated a consistent gap between postindustrial and developing societies in traditional moral values, attitudes toward marriage and divorce, tolerance of homosexuality, and support for gender equality in the roles of men and women.[56] A wealth of evidence from the WVS also demonstrates that rich and poor societies differ substantially in patterns of religious values and practices.[57] What is the impact of mass communications on these processes? The convergence thesis suggests that popular entertainment or news information reflecting Western values, when imported into traditional cultures, will probably accelerate the process of value change – for example, by encouraging greater tolerance of sexual liberalization and more secular behavior. Alternatively, the polarizing thesis reflects the views of other commentators who argue that Western popular entertainment has generated a backlash in developing societies, particularly in the highly conservative Arab states, by emphasizing explicit sexuality, gratuitous violence, consumerism, and a celebrity culture; denigrating respect for historical traditions, established customs, and religious authorities; and undermining the importance of family, marriage, and honor. From this perspective, the spread of the global media may have contributed to culture wars. Chapter 8 explores the empirical evidence for these arguments by contrasting the groups on the basis of their use of mass communications.

Chapter 9 analyzes support for democratic ideals, self-expression values, and human rights. The logic of the convergence view is that greater familiarity with democratic practices and human rights as conveyed by the media will result in the spread of these ideas, thereby encouraging reform movements and human rights activists in previously closed societies and autocratic regimes. Access to international news and information about democratic societies abroad should be a particularly potent mechanism for spreading demands for political rights and civil liberties at home. At the same time, where the news media are largely controlled by powerful governing elites, or through state ownership of broadcasting, overt censorship, intimidation of independent journalists, or related mechanisms, mass communications can be used as a mechanism of state control and propaganda. We examine the evidence for these claims and attempt to determine whether those with and without access to mass communications, who live in countries ruled by very different regimes, such as Russia, Ukraine, and Poland, differ in their political orientations and support for the regime.

In Chapter 10, utilizing aggregate indicators to classify more than 90 societies in terms of the Cosmopolitanism Index, we examine the degree to which cultures actually have converged over time. The WVS has been conducted in five waves since the early 1980s, and by comparing trends over time in selected attitudinal indicators we can test whether national cultures have gradually converged in the most cosmopolitan societies.

Finally, Chapter 11 summarizes the main results and considers the consequences for understanding theories about the impact of mass communications on cultural diversity, as well as the broader implications for cultural policy. Proponents of the globalization of mass communications regard it as a potential means of strengthening awareness about other countries and promoting international understanding around the world, as well as spreading the principles and practices of democratic governance and human rights. They advocate neoliberal free market policies that dismantle trade restrictions, cut tariff barriers, and loosen media ownership regulations in order to maximize the free flow of information and trade across national borders. Critics who view this process with alarm see cultural diversity under threat, due especially to the predominance of American or Western multinational corporations in audiovisual trade. They favor protectionist cultural trade policies, including the use of tariffs and quotas to regulate and limit the import of audiovisual services, and subsidies designed to preserve domestic creative industries and cultural pluralism. Protectionist sentiments are strongest in developing nations, as exemplified by debates within UNESCO, but they can also be found among affluent postindustrial societies; the European Union, for example, remains divided between those member states favoring more competitive markets within Europe and others, led by the French, seeking to protect

Europe's creative economy against the Americanization of popular culture.[58] There are also deep divisions over these issues among theorists in the social sciences. Chapter 11 discusses whether interventions designed to protect national cultures against foreign influences are appropriate, or whether the free flow of information and the maintenance of open borders are more desirable policies.

2

Theoretical Framework

Many voices can be heard in the dispute over the consequences of cosmopolitan communications. The empirical evidence on this issue remains mixed; the results are inconclusive, and there are plausible counterclaims to each argument. The popular debate is based largely on theoretical speculation about the possible consequences of the widely observed structural and economic changes in the production and distribution of mass communications, rather than on a careful empirical examination of how public opinion is actually changing in the light of survey evidence. As in Bhutan, the people in developing societies exposed to imported American or Western television, movies, and news often encounter values, practices, and ways of life that conflict with those traditionally found at home. But it remains unclear from the existing research whether, and under what conditions, this process erodes traditional aspects of distinctive national cultures. Do cosmopolitan communications accelerate the assimilation of modern values in traditional societies, as argued by the convergence thesis? Or do they trigger a backlash among those who feel most threatened by this process, as the polarization thesis proposes? Do they produce a fusion culture, with strands borrowed from different places and societies? Or as the firewall model suggests, are deeply rooted attitudes and values relatively robust in the face of mass communication flows? At this point, the answers to these questions are not clear. The evidence thus deserves rigorous scrutiny.

This chapter explains the theory at the heart of this book, the testable empirical hypotheses derived from this argument, and the research strategy for analyzing the core propositions. Our research design is simple to explain. To examine the direct effect of media use on social values, as a first step we use individual-level survey evidence to analyze the attitudes and values of representative samples of citizens, comparing those who do and do not regularly use the mass media and controlling for many other characteristics of the audience. The individual-level comparisons focus on the potential impact of media exposure on national identities, the economic values of consumer capitalism, traditional moral values concerning sexuality and gender equality, and support for democracy and human rights. But our theory suggests that the effect of media use will differ for those living in cosmopolitan societies and those living in provincial societies. We develop a Cosmopolitanism Index based on the extent of internal and external barriers to cross-border information flows. We then apply this to classify the 90 countries included in the World Values Survey. Hierarchical linear models, in particular multilevel regression analyses, are used to disentangle the impact of societal-level media environments, individual-level social characteristics, and cross-level interaction effects. In addition, we examine longitudinal evidence of the degree of cultural change over time, comparing the impact of global media on cosmopolitan and parochial societies. Finally, selected qualitative case studies, contrasting countries with relatively similar cultural traditions and levels of development but with differing media environments, illustrate the core findings in greater depth.

Theoretical Framework: The Firewall Model

The scenarios we outlined in the preceding chapter differ sharply in how they depict the future; but they all focus on developments in the structure and ownership of the media industry, changes in international trade in cultural markets, and the accelerated pace and volume of cross-border information flows. They all assume that the expanded volume of cultural imports from major producer countries will have a strong and direct impact on the domestic audience, for good or ill, by altering indigenous national values and beliefs. In this regard, although the alternative perspectives appear to differ, in fact they actually share remarkably similar premises. All are rooted in an implicit belief in powerful media effects, and they diverge only in the predicted direction of change.

We challenge these popular views and argue that more nuanced claims about the way that the public responds to cosmopolitan communications would be more realistic. Our theory suggests that national cultures remain diverse and relatively enduring. In particular, the firewall model presented in this book implies that the impact of cosmopolitan communications on national cultures is moderated by a series of intervening conditions. At the societal level, the degree of trade integration determines whether countries are incorporated into global markets. The level of media freedom influences the availability of news and information within any country. And levels of economic development shape investment in modern communication infrastructures and thus access to the mass media. These factors are closely interrelated, so they are used to develop a Cosmopolitanism Index, which is defined, operationalized, and then applied to classify countries around the world. Moreover, within each society, two further important firewalls operate primarily at the individual level, namely poverty, whereby a lack of socioeconomic resources and skills hinders access to mass communications, and social psychological learning processes, reflecting the socialization filters involved in the acquisition and transmission of core attitudes and enduring values. This framework, understood to be a sequential process, is illustrated schematically in Figure 2.1. These firewalls, individually and in combination, help protect national cultural diversity from foreign influences. The mass media do have important effects – as we shall demonstrate – but the consequences of cosmopolitan communications seem to be more limited than usually assumed.

Trade Integration: Barriers to Cultural Markets

We accept that the world market for the trade of cultural goods, news information, and audiovisual services has expanded dramatically in volume, pace, and reach in recent decades. Chapter 3 examines trends in the market for cultural goods and services around the world since the early 1970s. We analyze three dimensions of this phenomenon: the cultural trade of *audiovisual services* (television programs, feature films, and recorded music); the *news flow* arising through printed newspapers

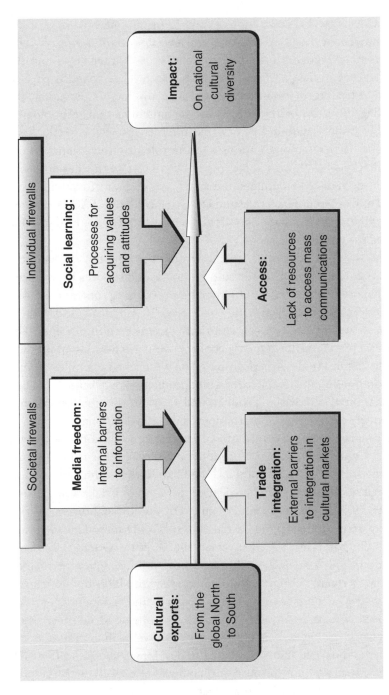

FIGURE 2.1. The Firewall Model of Cosmopolitan Communications.

and magazines, TV news and current affairs, and news wire services; and interconnections arising through *new information and communication technologies*, including complex cross-border flows and the convergence of media arising via the Internet. The expanded pace of transborder information flows is due to many factors, including the growing diffusion of information and communication technologies, notably radio, satellite TV, and the Internet, as well as reductions in trade barriers among nations and the role of transnational media corporations.[1] Although some intangible aspects of this development cannot be reduced to dollars and cents, as one indicator, the United Nations Conference on Trade and Development (UNCTAD) estimated that global trade in creative goods and services almost doubled in value during the past decade alone.[2]

The strongest potential influence from cosmopolitan communications occurs if the market for cultural goods and services is produced and exported primarily by multimedia production companies based in Western postindustrial nations – especially America – and if these products are imported into societies with divergent cultural values. The evidence presented in Chapter 3 confirms the concentration of production in cultural trade. American-based or Western-based multinational corporations dominate the ownership, production, marketing, and dissemination of audiovisual products and news information sources that are widely exchanged on international markets, including films, television programs, music, transnational satellite news stations, news wire services, and related cultural products and services. Far from decreasing, the audiovisual trade of the United States, the leading exporter in this market, has expanded in recent decades. Among the leading media groups worldwide, for example, ranked by audiovisual turnover, 7 of the top 10 are based in the United States: Walt Disney, Time Warner, News Corporation, NBC Universal, the DirecTV Group, CBS Corporation, and Viacom.[3] Other important producer nations include Britain, Germany, Canada, and France, each with large domestic markets, as well as a major slice of world exports among networks of trade partners. With a few exceptions, such as Bollywood in South Asia, Nollywood in Nigeria, and Mexican telenovelas in Latin America, smaller audiovisual industries based in developing societies often lack the infrastructure and resources to compete effectively with the production values required to manufacture and sell cultural products in the world market. Coproductions help, but once-flourishing film industries in many countries, such as Russia and Italy, are now struggling to attract sufficient investment in production, distribution, and marketing and to recoup costs through overseas sales.[4]

The economic and organizational structure of the mass media as an industry has been transformed in recent decades by the deregulation and privatization of state and public service broadcasting, which has greatly increased the number of commercial television and radio channels available in many societies, and by the rise of the Internet and multimedia digital technologies. Greater competition among multiple privately owned television channels swept away the traditional monopolies that used to exist in many countries having state-controlled or public service broadcasters. Since the early 1990s, in many societies, one or two TV channels have often been replaced by dozens.[5] The deregulation of broadcasting generated a flood of new television commercial or privately owned stations, which typically often seek to fill hours of broadcasting by programming low-cost imported popular entertainment, with endless reruns of American TV sitcoms and drama series, Hollywood movies, animation, popular music, and reality or game shows, with advertising messages reflecting consumer values.[6] In countries with a limited domestic market, lacking the capacity or finances to generate their own programs, this expansion fueled the demand for imported TV. Public service television and radio have come under growing pressure to adapt to this new media landscape and to justify their role and subsidy, given the range of alternative choices available to the audience.[7] In addition to these transformations in the broadcasting landscape, as shown in Chapter 3, transnational news channels such as CNN International and BBC World are now widely available in many parts of the globe; U.S.- and European-based news wire services – Reuters, the Associated Press, and Agence France-Presse – continue to be the predominant sources of international news for many media outlets worldwide; Hollywood retains its predominance in the international movie market; and foreign ownership of newspapers and magazines has increased in recent decades.[8] New information from Web sites and the Internet has opened the floodgates further and expanded the cultural role of major software corporations and Web sites, also based in the United States, exemplified by Microsoft, Google, and YouTube.

At the same time, it is necessary to qualify the overly simple view that the transfer of cultural goods and service flows one way, from the global North (or the United States) to South. First, as the fusion thesis emphasizes, the market for producing and distributing cultural goods remains complex, and regional hubs are emerging for specific sectors in certain middle-income economies, such as India, Mexico, China, and Brazil. The rapid growth of major emerging economies, and the shift from agriculture to manufacturing and the service sector, are expected to increase the capacity of these countries to produce and export audio-visual goods to other nations with shared languages and cultural ties. Moreover, many of the most successful American-produced TV programs reflect genres that originated elsewhere, whether *Big Brother*, *Pop Idol*, *The Office*, or *Survivor*, with local spin-offs popular in many countries, so that, as with American pizza, tacos, or hot dogs, it is increasingly difficult to identify what is distinctively 'American' about these cultural products.

Equally important, the integration of economies into world markets, along with trade in cultural goods and services in the creative economy, remains far from equal around the globe. Many of the least developed nations are largely excluded from world markets, functioning neither as producers nor as major consumers of cultural goods and services. Lack of development among low-income societies, ironically, counteracts the impact of global communications on national cultures.[9] The poorest societies have not yet developed the mass markets that sustain foreign investment in their broadcasting, telecommunication, and publishing infrastructures. External barriers to the flow of information across national borders arise from multiple sources, including protectionist trade policies, tariffs, and broadcasting regulations – for example, governing foreign and domestic media ownership, imports, standards, copyrighting, intellectual property, licensing, and contents. States can also intervene actively by subsidizing domestic industries – for example, by leveling license fees for state-controlled and public service broadcasting, providing financial assistance for the performing arts, or offering tax breaks to reduce the cost of newsprint or newspaper distribution. The strictest protectionist trade barriers are imposed in closed societies, such as Cuba, Uzbekistan, Saudi Arabia, and Burma, but it should not be thought that these practices are confined to autocratic regimes, by any means, as many democracies also seek to protect and subsidize their national cultural industries.

Poverty and Development: Access to Mass Communications

In recent decades, technological innovations have transformed access to interpersonal and mass communications throughout many parts of the world. This social revolution accelerated after the emergence of innovative digital technologies in the mid-1990s, from the personal computer (PC) and Internet to data-accessible smart mobile cell phones. But these changes have had the greatest impact in affluent postindustrial nations, especially among affluent households and the young tech-savvy generation, and, to a lesser extent, in many middle-income emerging market economies such as South Korea, Taiwan, South Africa, and Brazil. A substantial digital divide remains today, preventing poor segments of the population within affluent societies, as well as many of the world's least developed countries, from gaining access to traditional mass media, as well as to new digital information and communication technologies.

The extent of these disparities, documented in detail in Chapter 4, is often underestimated by observers based in media-rich nations. Television penetration illustrates these disparities; for example, UNESCO estimates that worldwide, only about one-quarter of all households have a television set today.[10] TV penetration has reached saturation levels in advanced industrialized societies; almost all households in these countries (97%) have a TV set. Emerging economies such as Turkey, China, and Mexico have made rapid gains in acquiring these consumer durables; about 84% of all households in lower-middle-income societies have TVs, up by 20% from the preceding decade. By contrast, among low-income societies, on average only 15% of all households have a TV set, and even today less than 5% of homes have access to TVs in countries such as Uganda, Burma, Rwanda, and Ethiopia. Radios are far more widely available in poor nations, reaching more than 40% of all households worldwide. Community radio is a particularly important source of local information, music, and news in many developing societies. Innovative low-cost windup and solar-powered radios reduce the need for batteries. Another important trend has been the rapid spread of mobile cellular telephones, with access soaring in developing nations from 3.2% of people subscribing in 1999 to up to one-third (32.4%) in 2006.[11] Fixed telephone lines almost doubled in developing societies during the same period, from 7.6 to 13.9%. Growing levels of literacy and primary schooling, the latter prioritized as one of the key UN Millennium Development Goals, has also expanded the market for newspapers, books, and magazines in many poor nations. Recent years have seen the dramatic growth of digital information and communication technologies associated with the rise of computers and the Internet, facilitating the use of text messaging, e-mail, and Web sites, which diffused even further through smart cellular mobile phones and communal technology kiosks.

Chapter 4 demonstrates that, despite these developments, the gap *between* rich and poor nations in terms of access to all major forms of information and communication resources remains substantial, as does the digital divide *within* societies.[12] The World Bank estimates that in 2005 there were more than 10 times as many mobile telephone subscribers in high-income countries as there were in low-income countries. While television sets are present in almost all households in Europe and the United States, only one in seven households has a TV in low-income nations.[13] In 2006, less than 5 of every 100 Africans used the Internet, compared with an average of 50% among the inhabitants of the G8 countries.[14] In developing societies, access to printed media (daily newspapers, magazines, and books) is limited by enduring problems of illiteracy and the cost of these products, as well as by language barriers. All these factors combine to generate severe information poverty in poor nations, making these societies and especially their rural populations increasingly peripheral to communication networks.[15] The least developed and poorest countries are often the ones that are most isolated from modern ICTs, and thus cut off from the knowledge economy, without the telecommunication infrastructure needed for landline telephones in many homes and businesses. Many rural areas in these societies lack a regular supply of electricity, and where reliable power is available, limited access to television sets and computers restricts connectivity via television and the Internet. Community radio remains a vital source of information in poor areas, and the spread of access to mobile cellular technologies in rural villages has been an important development. But in many poor societies, access to mediated news and information from television, national daily newspapers, and the Internet and World Wide Web remains limited. Unless access to these technologies becomes widespread in developing countries, mass communications may reach the affluent and educated elite living in urban areas, but it will fail to penetrate the national culture directly. It is not clear how Western cultural imperialism can wipe out cultural diversity in poor societies such as Ethiopia, Mali, and Burkina Faso, where much of the rural and illiterate population has little or no regular access to newspapers, television, or movies, let alone the Internet. The impact of individual learning from cross-border news information may be significant, but if exposure is confined to a small group of elites – for example, if CNN International is watched only by diplomats, government officials, and the expatriate community, this process will not have a direct impact on the general public or the collective national culture.

Freedom: Internal Barriers to Information

In addition to the external barriers, limits on freedom of the press restrict access to information internally within any society, just as open markets are limited by tariffs, taxes, and import quotas that protect commercial trade. It is not clear how cultural imperialism can exert a strong impact in places such as Burma, Uzbekistan, or North Korea, where the regimes use a variety of techniques to deny citizens access to foreign news organizations and to rigidly control information flows (inward and outward) across their national borders. The Chinese suppression of news about the Tibetan uprisings in March 2008 and the Burmese military junta's strict control of information about the devastating cyclone Nargis a few months later exemplify these practices. Even in liberal countries, such as those in the European Union, there are regulations restricting the import of non-European entertainment. Internal restrictions on information flows arise from limits on freedom of the press, including laws governing freedom of expression and information (such as penalties for press offenses); patterns of intimidation and violations of press freedom affecting journalists and the mass media (such as imprisonment and harassment of reporters); and the nature of state intervention in the media (such as state monopolies of broadcasting or the use of official censorship). The relationship between the state and the news media in any society is important and is shaped by issues of ownership, regulation, and control. In the most cosmopolitan media environments, such as those of India, Canada, and

the Netherlands, there are open markets, deregulation of telecommunications, and freedom of information concerning what is broadcast,
published, or transmitted. By contrast, protectionist barriers are far
stronger in restrictive communication systems, characterized by policies ranging from state control of the newspaper and broadcasting
sectors, overt government censorship, stringent import controls, and
repression of foreign news, at one extreme, to less draconian restrictions on foreign ownership of the mass media and protectionist policies regulating what can be imported and distributed, at the other.
Chapter 5 develops the Cosmopolitanism Index at the societal level,
representing the permeability of nations to cross-border information
flows, and operationalizes this according to a society's participation
in global markets, level of economic development, and freedom of the
press. This index is applied in order to classify all the countries under
comparison and is illustrated with case studies.

Learning: Individual Social Psychological Barriers to Learning

The cultural convergence thesis assumes that as audiences in different
societies become more exposed to imported music and television programs, foreign movies, and Internet Web sites, they gradually absorb
and emulate the modern ideas, images, and values embedded in these
products, which eventually results in the erosion of national diversity.
We suggest that these arguments underestimate the external barriers
to cultural trade across national borders, the lack of internal freedom
of the press found in many societies, and the significant developmental restrictions on public access to communication technologies, all of
which limit the direct impact of cross-border information flows. But let
us ignore these barriers for the moment, on the reasonable grounds that
freedom of information and open borders for cultural trade have gradually been gaining hold in many countries, accompanied by the growth
of democracy and civil liberties and compounded by the difficulties
of controlling digital information. Over time, public access to mass
communication technologies is gradually becoming more widespread,
even in the poorest nations – for example, through innovative micro-
financing projects that distribute mobile cell phones to Asian villages and low-cost computers to African schools. Nevertheless, even
if all these structural barriers gradually diminish or even vanish over
time, there are still good reasons to question whether exposure to

cross-border information flows is capable of exerting powerful effects on the general public.

Extensive research on media effects, public opinion, and social psychology suggests that what individuals learn from direct exposure to mass communications is far more complex, subtle, and limited than is generally assumed. Significant social psychological barriers restrict what we absorb from information conveyed by the media. The debate over the threat arising from cross-border media, cultural imperialism in the developing world, and the Americanization of European culture has rested largely on selected anecdotes, xenophobic assumptions, and cold war ideological diatribes rather than systematic empirical research concerning how mass media actually affects citizens. Evidence-based studies of the effects of imported communications – usually based on American and European public opinion – have yielded mixed and inconclusive results.[16] Contrary to popular accounts, existing research does not provide much support for the assumption of a massive shift in domestic public opinion that can be attributed to the role of the foreign media. Indeed, the most extensive body of social psychological research currently available on the impact of mass communications – examining the general capacity of the media to alter the way we think and act in any context – casts serious doubts on popular assumptions about the strong impact of cross-border communication flows on public opinion and social values. The mass media are only one avenue for learning about the world; the images and ideas of Hollywood, CNN, and Google may not exert as great an influence as other important socialization agencies that transmit enduring cultural values throughout the formative years of childhood and adolescence. Socialization processes include all the factors and agencies whereby values, attitudes, roles, skills, and patterns of behavior are transmitted from one generation to the next. An extensive body of literature has demonstrated that we learn from the home and family, the school, the workplace, the local community, and religious organizations, as well as from the direct experience of growing up in rich or poor societies.[17] Personal contact with people from other societies has increased through travel, telecommunications, and population migrations. Core values, such as strong feelings of national identity, traditional attitudes toward morality, and orientations toward authority, acquired during the formative years of early youth, may prove relatively enduring. Will television and the Internet destroy thousands of years of Bhutanese culture and religious teachings? Does watching *Die Hard*, *Desperate Housewives*, and CNN really threaten French culture in the land of Molière, Degas, and Sartre? Should TV images of Western lifestyles be blamed for provoking outraged anti-Western protests in the Middle East and violent hatred of America? We will present reasons and evidence to doubt these claims.

To understand how cross-border information flows could potentially influence individual citizens and erode collective national cultures, it helps to recall the different steps in the mass communication process outlined earlier. We need to distinguish the contents of mass communications that are exported across national borders from processes of audience reception by which messages are received and their meaning interpreted, as well as the subsequent direct impact of this process on audiences within each county and the more diffuse impact on society as a whole.[18] Over the years, these last steps have been debated in a large body of research literature, with conflicting findings concerning the strength and significance of the media's social psychological effects on citizens.

Before the emergence of direct evidence from social surveys and experiments, the earliest 'propaganda' model suggested that the mass media were capable of exerting a powerful direct impact on public opinion.[19] Thus, when the U.S. Congress passed the Radio Act of 1912, it restricted foreign ownership of radio stations out of a concern that, during wartime, foreigners would transmit information to enemy forces or jam American military communications. As commercial radio stations became popular, the U.S. Congress was also concerned that foreigners would broadcast subversive propaganda.[20] During World War II, German and Japanese propaganda was widely feared by the Allies as capable of shaping public opinion, both at home and abroad. The classic underlying model assumed a 'hypodermic needle' or 'stimulus–response' effect, where the messages that were seen or heard from foreign media directly altered public attitudes and behavior at home.[21] The first rigorous social science research conducted on media effects during the 1940s, however, soon reversed this thinking by emphasizing the limits of these techniques. Classic experimental studies on American soldiers, by Hovland and colleagues, proved that the series of U.S. military training films, *Why We Fight*, was relatively ineffective in altering attitudes and behavior.[22] The Columbia school headed by Katz and Lazarsfeld pioneered some of the first systematic surveys using random samples of the electorate in the 1940 Erie County studies in order to examine the influence of campaign communications on voting behavior.[23] They also reported limited media effects, in this case the capacity of newspaper coverage and campaign radio broadcasts to alter enduring partisan orientations or to determine American voting choices. These seminal studies influenced generations of social scientists and generated a broad consensus that attempts to use mass communications alone tended to be unsuccessful in either converting cultural attitudes or changing behavior, at least in the short term.

Consequently, a consensus emerged during the 1960s and 1970s that the main impact of the mass media was that of reinforcing existing preferences, rather than that of persuasion or change. Media effects seemed to be weak, especially when compared with the influence of enduring partisan and social cues on voting behavior and political participation. These much stronger influences were developed through personal ties and face-to-face communications within the family and local community. Traditional socialization theories during these decades suggested that enduring and resilient cultural values, attitudes, and ways of behaving are learned in one's formative years, particularly from parents and siblings within the home, from role models such as teachers, local leaders, and spiritual leaders in the community, and from social networks of neighbors and friends. People's values are also shaped by their firsthand experiences, such as growing up in conditions of affluence or poverty. Socialization theories acknowledge that the mass media also contributes to what we learn, in childhood and later life, by reinforcing preexisting dispositions, but that it is not the most important source of deep-rooted values and ways of life.[24] Additional research questioned the conventional way that we assess the impact of the mass media; for example, the 'uses-and-gratification' school emphasized that selective attention to mediated messages is used to reinforce cultural attitudes, so that even when a correlation is established between media exposure and attitudes, the direction of causality may reflect the fact that people choose to watch, read, or listen to sources of information that are congruent with their prior values.[25] Moreover, constructivist theories and cultural studies emphasize that people are capable of selectively discarding media messages that conflict with their core values, especially if they mistrust the information source, thereby actively resisting, deconstructing, criticizing, and reinterpreting their original meaning.[26]

Nevertheless, debate about these issues has continued, and countercurrents have emerged in the literature to challenge the conventional minimal-effects view. Cultivation theory, proposed in 1982 by Gerbner and colleagues, argued that the ubiquity of regular or habitual television viewing over many years generated a distorted view of reality that encouraged a commonality of outlooks and values.[27] Although many social psychologists emphasized limited media effects, the cultural imperialism school of Schiller and Galtung assumed that foreign media are capable of exerting an overwhelming impact on developing countries, reinforcing the power of Western states and capitalist predominance in relationships of neocolonial dependency.[28] The minimal-effects perspective came under the most sustained and convincing challenge, however, in the extensive social psychological literature on mass communications that started to emerge in the early 1990s.[29] Contemporary communication theories propose a complex series of specific psychological effects arising from media consumption. In particular, an extensive research literature has emphasized the role of the mass media in 'agenda setting' (shaping public concerns and policy priorities), 'framing' (cueing the meaning and interpretation of events), and 'priming' (providing evaluating criteria with which to judge outcomes).[30] The mass media was also recognized by social psychological theories as shaping various aspects of knowledge and cognitive beliefs, attitudes and values, as well as behaviors.

The revision of mass communication theories was encouraged by methodological developments that became increasingly effective in capturing relatively modest and subtle media effects. This included improvements in multiwave and longitudinal panel survey design to capture dynamic effects over time, more fine grained measures of media exposure and attention, and the use of experimental designs and qualitative focus groups, widening the repertoire of methods available for studying mass communications.[31] The bulk of this research has focused on within-nation studies, particularly in the United States and Western Europe. By contrast, far less research has been devoted to exploring the effects of mass communications by means of systematic cross-national comparisons, especially in order to examine this process under different social contexts and regime types.[32] There continues to be debate within the research literature about which of the new concepts and theories are most useful, but recent work highlights the dangers of the oversimplified assumptions that underlie much of the policy and journalistic debate, which jump directly from the unquestionably important structural changes in the production, marketing, and distribution of the media industry, and equally important changes in the contents of information and communication, to their presumed social psychological effects on the general public.

Core Theoretical Propositions

The theoretical controversy over the impact of cosmopolitan communications on national cultures remains unresolved and many questions remain unanswered. Although the convergence thesis emphasizing American/Western hegemony or cultural imperialism remains popular, this view has been challenged by others who see polarization or fusion as a more plausible scenario. In contrast to all of these views, the firewall model posits that these developments will have a far more limited impact and that the diversity of deep-rooted cultural values will persist, despite exposure to the most recent wave of globalization, because of a series of conditions that mitigate the impact of cross-border information flows.

The previous literature analyzing the impact of globalization on public opinion, reviewed in subsequent chapters, has generated mixed findings. For example, an extensive body of longitudinal survey research has explored identities within the European Union. The European Union provides an exceptionally strong test of the impact of globalization. It is an ambitious effort to integrate diverse countries into a single market and to break down economic, political, and psychological boundaries between member states. These studies provide little support for the view that European integration – despite the expansion of the role, size, and powers of the European Union, the emergence of a single market, the free flow of migrant workers and travel, and the erosion of barriers to cross-border cultural trade and communications within Europe – has generated a strong sense of European identity among its citizens, even in countries that have been members of the European Union for 50 years.[33] But research has also examined the relationship between media use and the strength of national identities in the United States and Europe, concluding that those of the younger generation use traditional national news media less frequently than their elders and that they are also less attached to the nation-state than their elders.[34] These are suggestive findings, but it remains to be established whether patterns of media use are causally related to the strength of national identities and whether this relationship is conditional on the structure of the communication system and the openness of societies to external influences. Other scholars who have explored the impact of the flow of U.S. popular entertainment into Europe have generally concluded that this process has not led to a systematic Americanization of worldviews or the wholesale adoption of 'Western' values.[35] Any analysis must carefully disentangle the direction of causality; those who prefer to watch Hollywood movies, CNN, or American-produced TV entertainment may well be those who were already favorably predisposed toward U.S. popular culture.[36] Despite much popular speculation, social scientists and policymakers still lack sufficient reliable generalizations based on the analysis of empirical evidence from many different societies and contexts to determine with any certainty the consequences of the expanding role of cosmopolitan communications.[37]

To consider these issues, on the basis of arguments developed in subsequent chapters, we propose a series of plausible propositions that can be tested against the empirical evidence. These propositions are based on the individual-level analysis of the direct impact of media use on public opinion, variations by types of mass media, contrasts among social sectors, and the interactive effects of media use within cosmopolitan and provincial societies.

    1. Hypotheses concerning the social sectors that use the news media within countries

Use of the media is expected to vary among social sectors within each country (H1.0), and our theory also generates several testable sub-propositions at the individual level, which we analyze using survey data in Chapter 4. In particular, news media use should be greatest among well-educated, affluent households and those familiar with the English language, and it should vary between women and men, and among age groups. Education should also be particularly significant

(H1.1), as schooling provides the cognitive skills to understand and absorb complex information about the society and the world, as well as being closely related to patterns of literacy, all factors facilitating media use. Household income (H1.2) is closely related to educational achievements and social status, and this is also predicted to facilitate access to mass communications, providing, for example, the financial resources for buying TV and radio sets, for purchasing services such as cable, satellite, and pay TV, and for Internet subscriptions. Those with affluent lifestyles often have more leisure time to use the mass media. Income is also closely related to occupational class, although income provides a more appropriate and consistent comparison of status and wealth across diverse types of societies and economies.

The generational gap is expected to influence news media access (H1.3); most previous research conducted in postindustrial societies has suggested that use will be greater among those who are middle aged or older. Given the rapidly changing patterns of education and literacy in fast-developing societies, however, it remains to be seen whether this pattern holds in these nations. When young people access the media, moreover, this may have particularly important consequences for processes of value change. Socialization theories emphasize that cultural orientations are acquired during childhood, adolescence, and early adulthood, through role models provided by parents, teachers, and authority figures, as well as through general observation and direct experience. The mass media is expected to function as one of the socializing agents that can shape values and attitudes during a person's most formative years. If they regularly access the mass media, the effects of this process should therefore have a stronger impact on the younger generation, as they are expected to have more fluid attitudes and values than their parents and grandparents. In addition, young people have adapted most thoroughly to the digital world of blogs, iPods, YouTube, and MySpace. In terms of gender, research in postindustrial societies suggests that men are likely to be more regular news media users than women, reflecting broader cultural and structural differences in men's and women's lives (H1.4). Languages are also expected to be important; in particular, (H1.5) knowledge of English is predicted to be a significant predictor of media use, especially access to the Internet. We make this prediction even though much news and information is usually available in many local languages within each country,

imported popular audiovisual entertainment is often translated with
dubbing or subtitles, and UNESCO estimates that the amount of non-
English-language content on the Internet is expanding.[38] By comparing
those accessing different sources of information, Chapter 4 examines
the social characteristics of users within particular countries.

H1.0: Use of the news media will differ among social sectors.

H1.1: Use of the news media will be greater among those who are
well educated.

H1.2: Use of the news media will be greater among high-income
groups.

H1.3: Use of the news media will be greater among those who are
middle-aged or older.

H1.4: Use of the news media will be greater among men than
women.

H1.5: Use of the news media will be greater among those who are
fluent in English.

2. Hypotheses about the direct impact of news media use on public
opinion

Building on this foundation, the second set of propositions concerns the direct impact of individual exposure to the news media on
social, economic, and political values and attitudes, controlling for the
prior social characteristics of media users. By focusing on 'cultural
values,' we seek to examine the priorities and concerns that people
have for themselves, their families, their communities, their nation,
and the world.[39] For example, should children be raised to respect
traditional sources of authority, the need for self-discipline, and the
importance of hard work? Or should they be encouraged instead to
value creativity, self-expression, and self-fulfillment? At the societal
level, should emerging economies such as China and Brazil seek to
pursue basic agricultural and industrial development, thereby raising
the standard of living for the poor, or when there is a trade-off, should
they give higher priority to policies generating sustainable environmental protection? Should governments favor policies designed to maximize social welfare and economic equality, or should they encourage
greater entrepreneurial activity and individual initiative? These types
of choices tend to reflect fundamentally divergent values – that is, relatively enduring orientations that shape broader orientations toward

the world. We will use the WVS to examine the extent to which access to the mass media affects these and other dimensions of public opinion, such as individual-level feelings of national pride, orientations toward civic engagement and political activism, and attitudes toward democracy and government.

If the convergence thesis is correct, exposure to images of and ideas about other societies derived from the news media should foster more cosmopolitan orientations among media users by encouraging greater tolerance as people learn about foreign lifestyles and other societies, gradually reducing support for nationalism (H2.1). We examine this dimension by comparing the strength of national identities, attitudes toward the institutions of global governance, and tolerance of foreigners among individual users and nonusers of the media. Mass communications and commercial advertising, with its materialist and individualistic values, could also potentially alter views about the role of government and the value of economic competition; leading theorists such as Herbert J. Schiller, Edward S. Herman, and Robert W. McChesney have argued that global media corporations provide advertising, entertainment, and news designed to spread the values of consumer capitalism and thus serve as 'missionaries' for global capitalism.[40] To examine evidence for this thesis, we compare those who do and do not use the news media to see whether these groups diverge in their ideological orientations toward the role of markets and the state (H2.2). Exposure to the news media may also influence moral values and attitudes toward gender equality, sexuality, and religion by accelerating the acceptance of more liberal and secular views (H2.3). Finally, exposure to Western news and information can be expected to reinforce civic engagement by expanding information and awareness about public affairs and opportunities for activism, and to increase support for the principles of democratic governance and human rights, especially in states where such practices are lacking (H2.4). Within given societies, we compare the attitudes and values of people who do and do not make regular use of the news media. In Chapters 6–9 we expect to find significant contrasts at the individual level between these groups, controlling for such characteristics as age, gender, education, and income, which are typically associated both with access to mass communications and with processes of underlying value change.

H2.1: Exposure to the news media will foster more cosmopolitan orientations and greater tolerance to foreign lifestyles.

H2.2: Exposure to the news media will encourage favorable attitudes toward global capitalism.

H2.3: Exposure to the news media will shape more liberal and secular attitudes toward gender equality, sexuality, and religion.

H2.4: Exposure to the news media will reinforce civic engagement.

3. Hypotheses about the direct impact of different types of media

In addition, the typical characteristics of media users vary with respect to TV or radio news, newspapers, and the Internet, and as some of these types of mass communications are more cosmopolitan than others, their cultural effects can be expected to differ. The Internet is the most international media under comparison; although many popular online sources of information are local or national, the Internet generates the lowest barriers to connecting directly to global networks and news sources. The Internet is also the medium that states find most difficult to restrict. Techniques of censorship, blocking of Internet providers, and content filtering are employed by the most repressive regimes, including Pakistan, Burma, and China, to restrict Internet traffic into and out of the country.[41] In most countries, however, states and Internet service providers impose relatively few controls on online content, compared with other mass media. Use of the medium also eradicates the traditional spatial barriers to information; users can read and compare stories from online newspapers, multimedia news Web sites, or journalistic blogs originating from New York, London, Delhi, or Qatar.

Compared with the Internet, television and radio news is more commonly based on domestic broadcast networks and filtered through the prism provided by local, regional, and national reporters and journalists, even though many more people now have access to transnational news broadcasts from satellite networks such as MSNBC and CNN International. The contents of television and radio are also more closely regulated and managed through broadcasting authorities. With the exception of a handful of titles, such as the *Economist* or *Herald Tribune*, the majority of newspapers, magazines, and other printed publications are still designed to generate sales and advertising revenues primarily from a domestic readership.[42] Even transnational magazines that are sold widely around the world, such as *Vogue*, *Elle*, and *Cosmopolitan*, print editions with contents, images, and advertising tailored to each national or regional market. Foreign newspapers and imported magazines have always been sold on newsstands and made available in libraries, but access has also become far easier and cheaper with the rise of the Internet. Giant multinational corporations such as News Corporation and Bertelsmann have increased their involvement in the publishing sector in many countries through growing foreign investment, mergers or outright takeovers, and regional partnerships. In the light of these considerations, Chapter 10 examines the contrasts by type of media. We predict (H3.1) that the impact of cosmopolitan communications will be strongest among regular users of the Internet and e-mail, and (H3.2) that it will be weaker among regular readers of newspapers and radio or TV news.

H3.1: The impact of cosmopolitan communications will be strongest among regular users of the Internet and e-mail.

H3.2: The impact of cosmopolitan communications will be weaker among regular newspaper readers and radio or TV news users.

4. Hypotheses concerning the interactive effects of media exposure in provincial and cosmopolitan societies

All of the preceding hypotheses can be tested using individual-level survey data. But our model specifies that each society's external and internal barriers to information flows will interact with individual patterns of news media use. Consequently, we hypothesize that a *cross-level interaction* effect will also be apparent; the firewall model implies that (H4.0) the impact of exposure to the mass media on cultural values will be strongest in the most cosmopolitan societies. In particular, the expansion of cosmopolitan information flows will have the strongest effect on national cultures under certain conditions: (H4.1) in the most globalized societies, with few significant external barriers to cultural imports; (H4.2) in societies with internal media freedom; and (H4.3) in affluent societies with widespread public access to media technologies. People who are heavy media users, and who live in cosmopolitan societies – such as Switzerland, Norway, Belgium, and Hungary – that combine integration into international cultural markets, freedom of the press, and the growing affluence that facilitates public access to the mass media, are expected to be the most strongly influenced by cross-border communications flows. By contrast, people living in provincial countries that are relatively closed externally to foreign cultural imports, with limited internal media freedom and limited media access – such as Myanmar, Rwanda, and Togo – are expected to be relatively immune to the effects of cosmopolitan communication flows. Successive models comparing media users living in different types of society enable us to pinpoint any cross-level interaction effects. Multilevel regression models (which are a part of hierarchical linear models, or HLMs) are the most suitable for examining individual-level, national-level, and cross-level interaction effects, as described in detail in Technical Appendix C at the end of the book.

H4.0: The impact of exposure to the mass media on cultural values will be strongest in the most cosmopolitan societies.

H4.1: The impact of exposure to the mass media on cultural values will be strongest in societies integrated into global markets and communication networks.

H4.2: The impact of exposure to the mass media on cultural values will be strongest in societies with internal media freedom.

H4.3: The impact of exposure to the mass media on cultural values will be strongest in economically developed societies, where many people have widespread access to media technologies.

5. Hypotheses concerning societal-level trends in cultural convergence over time

Finally, if cultural convergence is indeed occurring, evidence of this phenomenon should be observable using time-series data. The WVS has been conducted in five waves since 1981. As described later in this chapter, longitudinal analysis at the individual level is complicated by the fact that the questions concerning media use have changed over time, as well as by discontinuities in country coverage in the WVS. Nevertheless, certain identical items have been included in 11 countries over successive waves of the survey from 1981–1983 to 2005–2007. This facilitates the direct comparison of changes in national cultures over a quarter of a century. The convergence thesis implies (H5.0) that values should prove relatively similar today and that they should have gradually converged most clearly over time in persistently cosmopolitan societies with the most open borders to information flows, such as Norway, the United States, Britain, and Japan. By contrast, more parochial contemporary societies, such as Mexico, Argentina, and South Africa, should remain more diverse in their cultural values today and should not display growing convergence over time. We can test these propositions empirically by comparing variance today among contemporary societies contained in the most recent wave of the WVS, as well as analyzing value changes over time among countries during the last quarter of a century, since the start of the WVS.

H5.0: Cultural convergence over time will be the greatest among the most cosmopolitan societies.

H5.1: The most cosmopolitan contemporary societies will display the greatest similarities in cultural values today.

H5.2: The most parochial societies will display the greatest divergence in cultural values today.

H5.3: Over time, cosmopolitan communications will reduce divergence among national cultures.

Data and Evidence

Our research design classifies cosmopolitan and provincial societies according to their external and internal barriers to cross-border information flows. Within each type of society, we compare those who do and do not have regular access to news and information from television and radio, newspapers, and the Internet. We analyze the values and attitudes of these groups, controlling for other characteristics, such as age, gender, income, and education, that typically differentiate news users. Through multilevel analysis, we test the strength and the direction of any *individual-level* effects arising from media use, any *national-level* effects arising from living in different types of society, and any *cross-level* effects arising from use of the media in each type of society.

Evidence from the World Values Survey

Individual-level evidence about exposure to mass communications and cultural values in a wide range of societies is derived from analysis of

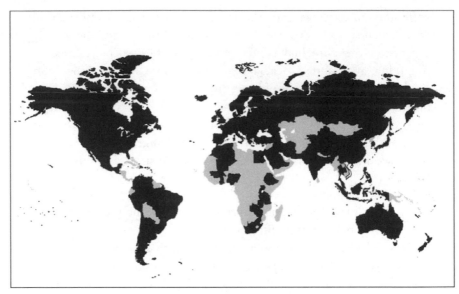

FIGURE 2.2. Countries Included in the Values Surveys, 1981–2007.

the WVS; a global investigation of sociocultural and political change gathered cross-nationally comparable data in five waves from 1981 to 2007. The WVS project has undertaken representative national surveys of the basic values and beliefs of the publics in more than 90 independent countries, containing over 88% of the world's population and covering all 6 inhabited continents (see Figure 2.2). It builds on the European Values Survey, first carried out in 23 countries in 1981. A second wave of surveys was completed in 43 countries in 1990–1991. A third wave was carried out in 55 nations in 1995–1996, and a fourth wave, in 70 countries, took place in 1999–2001. The fifth wave, covering 56 countries, was conducted in 2005–2007.[43] The WVS includes some of the most affluent market economies in the world, such as the United States, Japan, and Switzerland, with per capita annual incomes of more than $40,000, together with middle-income countries, including Mexico, Slovakia, and Turkey, as well as poor agrarian societies, such as Ethiopia, Mali, and Burkina Faso, with per capita annual incomes of $200 or less. In total, 11 nations have been included in all five waves of the survey since 1981, facilitating a consistent comparison of long-term trends during the past quarter of a century (see Table B.2 in Technical Appendix B for the list). A broader range of 27 nations was included in both the 1990 and 2005 surveys, allowing comparisons over the past 15 years.

As Table 2.1 and Figure 2.3 illustrate, there are also significant variations in levels of human development in the countries under comparison, as monitored by the Human Development Index of the United Nations Development Program (UNDP), combining per capita income with levels of education, literacy, and longevity. Some nations, such as Malta, Luxembourg, and Iceland, have populations below 1 million, while at the other extreme both India and China have populations of well over 1 billion people. The survey covers relatively old democracies, such as Australia, India, and the Netherlands, relatively new democracies, including El Salvador, Estonia, and Taiwan, and autocracies, such as China, Zimbabwe, Pakistan, and Egypt. The transition process varies markedly: some nations have experienced a rapid consolidation of democracy during the 1990s; today the Czech Republic, Latvia, and Argentina currently rank as high on political rights and civil liberties as Belgium, the United States, and the Netherlands, which have long traditions of democracy.[44] The survey also includes some of the first comparative survey data from several Muslim states, including Arab countries such as Jordan, Iran, Egypt, and Morocco, as well as from Indonesia, Iran, Turkey, Bangladesh, and Pakistan. The most comprehensive coverage comes from Western Europe, North America, and Scandinavia, where public opinion surveys have the longest tradition, but countries are included from all world regions, including sub-Saharan Africa.

The WVS and EVS have included some media items, monitoring the regular use of a daily newspaper and the frequency of TV viewing, since the first wave in 1981. This facilitates some comparisons over time, but longitudinal analysis is complicated by the fact that these items were not carried consistently in all countries or in all subsequent waves of the survey. Television use was included in the third and fourth waves in a few countries where more detailed cases made it possible to examine change over time, including that in developing societies in South Africa, Bangladesh, Peru, and Pakistan and in contemporary postindustrial nations such as Spain, Sweden, Norway, and the United States. The richest battery of items monitoring news media use was introduced in the most recent survey in 2005–2007, however, so this book draws primarily on the fifth wave, covering

TABLE 2.1. Countries in the World Values Survey, Ranked by Contemporary Levels of Income

High-Income Societies ($15,000+)	GDP per Capita, PPP, 2006 (World Bank, 2007)	Human Development Index, 2005 (UNDP, 2007)	Medium-Income Societies ($2,000–$14,999)	GDP per Capita, PPP, 2006 (World Bank, 2007)	Human Development Index, 2005 (UNDP, 2007)	Low-Income Societies ($1,999 and Below)	GDP per Capita, PPP, 2006 (World Bank, 2007)	Human Development Index, 2005 (UNDP, 2007)
1 Luxembourg	$54,779	0.944	Korea Rep.	$13,865	0.921	Macedonia, FYR	$1,940	0.801
2 Norway	$40,947	0.968	Greece	$13,339	0.926	Guatemala	$1,771	0.689
3 Japan	$40,000	0.953	Slovenia	$12,047	0.917	Bosnia and Herzegovina	$1,741	0.803
4 Andorra	$38,800		Portugal	$11,124	0.897	Egypt, Arab Rep.	$1,696	0.708
5 United States	$38,165	0.951	Trinidad and Tobago	$10,268	0.814	Albania	$1,604	0.801
6 Iceland	$35,782	0.968	Saudi Arabia	$9,910	0.812	China	$1,595	0.777
7 Switzerland	$35,696	0.955	Malta	$9,618	0.878	Azerbaijan	$1,576	0.746
8 Denmark	$32,548	0.949	Argentina	$8,695	0.869	Serbia and Montenegro	$1,455	
9 Ireland	$31,410	0.959	Czech Republic	$7,040	0.891	Morocco	$1,439	0.646
10 Sweden	$31,197	0.956	Uruguay	$6,987	0.852	Armenia	$1,284	0.775
11 Taiwan	$29,500		Estonia	$6,945	0.860	Philippines	$1,175	0.771
12 Singapore	$27,685	0.922	Mexico	$6,387	0.829	Georgia	$1,071	0.754
13 United Kingdom	$27,582	0.946	Hungary	$6,126	0.874	Ukraine	$1,040	0.788
14 Finland	$27,081	0.952	Chile	$5,846	0.867	Indonesia	$983	0.728
15 Austria	$26,110	0.948	Latvia	$5,683	0.855	India	$634	0.619
16 Canada	$25,562	0.961	Poland	$5,521	0.870	Pakistan	$623	0.551

Rank	Country	GDP (PPP)	Index	Country	GDP (PPP)	Index	Country	GDP (PPP)	Index
17	Netherlands	$25,333	0.953	Croatia	$5,461	0.850	Vietnam	$576	0.733
18	Germany	$24,592	0.935	Venezuela	$5,427	0.792	Moldova	$492	0.708
19	Belgium	$24,541	0.946	Lithuania	$5,247	0.862	Bangladesh	$454	0.547
20	France	$23,899	0.952	Slovak Republic	$5,126	0.863	Nigeria	$439	0.470
21	Australia	$23,372	0.962	Malaysia	$4,623	0.811	Zimbabwe	$409	0.513
22	Cyprus	$22,699	0.903	Brazil	$4,055	0.800	Zambia	$365	0.434
23	Italy	$19,709	0.941	Iraq	$3,600		Tanzania	$335	0.467
24	Israel	$18,367	0.932	Turkey	$3,582	0.775	Kyrgyz Republic	$326	0.696
25	Spain	$16,177	0.949	South Africa	$3,562	0.674	Ghana	$300	0.553
26	New Zealand	$15,458	0.943	Dominican Republic	$2,694	0.779	Uganda	$274	0.505
27				Russian Federation	$2,621	0.802	Rwanda	$268	0.452
28				Thailand	$2,549	0.781	Burkina Faso	$267	0.370
29				Peru	$2,489	0.773	Mali	$250	0.380
30				Romania	$2,443	0.813	Ethiopia	$155	0.406
31				Colombia	$2,317	0.791			
32				Bulgaria	$2,256	0.824			
33				Jordan	$2,193	0.773			
34				El Salvador	$2,173	0.735			
35				Algeria	$2,153	0.733			
36				Belarus	$2,070	0.804			
37				Iran, Islamic Rep.	$2,029	0.759			

Note: The 93 countries in the World Values Survey (1981–2007) are classified and ranked by GDP per capita in purchasing power parity (PPP), 2006.

Source: World Bank Development Indicators (2007).

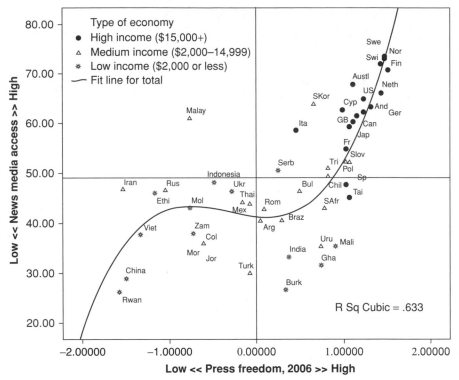

FIGURE 2.3. Societal Mean Levels of News Media Access by Levels of Press Freedom and Type of Economy. Societal mean levels of news media access, aggregating the 100-point combined scale (WVS, 2005–2007). Levels of press freedom (2006), standardized z-scores from Freedom House. Type of economy categorized by levels of per capita GDP in purchasing power parity (World Bank, 2007).

more than 50 societies. This dataset allows us to compare a wide range of countries from all major cultural regions, as well as democratic and autocratic regimes that vary in their levels of freedom of the press and cultural trade protectionism, with China, Vietnam, and Russia having some of the world's most restrictive policies controlling the flow of information across their national borders. The fifth wave of the survey collected evidence about the regular use of mass communications, including the print media (newspapers, magazines, and books), broadcast mass media (radio and TV news and public affairs), the new media (Internet and e-mail), and personal communications (talking with friends or colleagues). The study analyzes the impact of access to these various types of mass communication, as dependent variables, on multiple dimensions of cultural change, including feelings of national identity, attitudes toward markets and the state, attitudes toward traditional moral values, and support for democracy and human rights. Aggregate data at the societal level are used to compare the pattern of media freedom, global information flows, and the openness of cultural trade in all contemporary independent nation-states worldwide, drawing on standard international indicators from such sources as UNESCO, UNCTAD, the ITU, Reporters sans Frontières (Reporters without Borders), and Freedom House.

Monitoring Use of the News Media

To examine these issues, for the individual-level analysis we draw on the fifth wave of the WVS, which measured the regular use of daily newspapers, radio or TV news, magazines, books, and the Internet or e-mail 'to learn what is going on in your country and the world.' Regular use of each of these sources was registered as a simple dichotomy, providing a comparative indicator of news exposure, although providing no information about the intensity of use (e.g., how many hours people watched or listened to news), levels of interest and attention (e.g., whether people read stories about politics or economics), the type of newspaper or TV station (public service or commercial TV), or levels of exposure to the wide range of other types of mass communications (such as popular TV entertainment or movies). Since people commonly spend only a small proportion of their time listening to or watching news, compared with the hours they devote to other types of TV or radio programs, this measure is likely to provide a conservative estimate of any effects that are detected from exposure to the mass media, and broader indicators could possibly detect stronger effects. At the same time, if significant effects are detected from regular exposure to news, these can be regarded as an indirect proxy for media habits (people who regularly watch or listen to the news are likely to use radio and TV for other types of programs as well). These data allow us to construct an overall news media use scale, generated by summing self-reported weekly use of newspapers, radio or TV news, the Internet, books, and magazines as information sources, with the mean 5-point score standardized to 100 points for ease of comparison. Principal-component factor analysis (not reproduced here) showed that all of these items were strongly intercorrelated, producing a balanced scale with a normal distribution. As previous studies have reported, the analysis confirms that far from being distinctive, patterns of Internet use continue to be significantly associated with use of other forms of news media, a pattern with important implications for the interpretation of the digital divide.[45] Table 2.2 shows the WVS estimates of regular (at least weekly) use of these media, showing disparities that can also be observed through aggregate statistics.

Overall, as numerous studies have found, among all the media under comparison, radio and TV news was the most popular, with 88% of respondents reporting that they use this resource to obtain information on a regular basis.[46] Television and radio news was ubiquitous in affluent societies, but even in the poorest places, such as Rwanda, India, and Burkina Faso, about two-thirds of the population reported getting information regularly from these sources. Newspapers were also used regularly by the majority of respondents, although the overall average proportion of users (57%) disguises marked disparities between countries such as Norway and Sweden, where 9 out of 10 people use newspapers regularly, compared with less literate and poorer societies such as Mali and Morocco, where one-third or less of the respondents use them. The contrasts were equally striking for access to the Internet and e-mail; overall about one-third of respondents (30%) reported using these as information sources, similar to the proportion of those who reported using magazines (34%) and books (32%).

As illustrated in Figure 2.3, most of the countries with the highest media use – located in the top third of countries ranked on this scale – were affluent postindustrial societies, including the Nordic countries (Sweden, Norway, and Finland), where newspaper use was particularly high, smaller European welfare states (Switzerland, the Netherlands, and Germany), and Anglo-American countries (Australia, the United States, Britain, and Canada); there was a slightly lower use of newspapers and the Internet in Italy, France, and (especially) Spain. These disparities among economies of the Organization for Economic Cooperation and Development (OECD) confirm previous studies, and they can be attributed at the macrolevel to the structure and distribution of the newspaper industry (national or regional, broadsheet or tabloid), as well as to public policies – for example, the Scandinavian use of heavy newspaper subsidies to maintain media pluralism.[47] As one of

TABLE 2.2. Use of Media Sources for Information, 2005–2007

	Daily Newspaper (%)	Radio/TV News (%)	Internet/e-Mail (%)	Magazine (%)	Books (%)	No Use of Any of These Media (%)	Media Use, 100-Point Scale
Sweden	94	98	71	61	44	0	73
Norway	92	99	75	61	38	0	73
Switzerland	91	95	62	57	53	0	72
Finland	89	97	57	69	42	1	71
Australia	85	98	54	57	48	0	68
Netherlands	75	97	67	55	38	1	66
United States	71	91	67	51	44	2	65
South Korea	75	94	65	37	47	1	64
Andorra	85	94	49	48	40	1	63
Cyprus	76	90	36	71	39	1	63
Germany, West	86	96	44	51	35	0	62
Canada	72	96	53	44	42	2	61
Malaysia	87	92	37	46	43	1	61
Britain	72	93	49	48	42	2	60
Germany, East	79	97	35	49	39	1	60
Japan	90	98	46	36	27	1	59
Italy	71	95	40	51	36	0	59
France	62	95	38	47	33	2	55
Poland	56	97	28	45	35	2	52
Slovenia	63	90	35	51	23	2	52
Trinidad	81	93	21	23	38	3	51
Serbia	73	89	29	31	30	3	51
Chile	64	93	34	27	28	3	49
Indonesia	53	91	21	33	41	3	48
Spain	63	91	27	32	25	5	48
Russia	54	94	21	31	35	1	47
Ukraine	61	92	11	39	29	2	46
Bulgaria	63	97	19	28	28	2	46

(continued)

TABLE 2.2 *(continued)*

	Daily Newspaper (%)	Radio/TV News (%)	Internet/ e-Mail (%)	Magazine (%)	Books (%)	No Use of Any of These Media (%)	Media Use, 100-Point Scale
Ethiopia	53	79	18	35	38	6	46
Taiwan	56	90	34	27	18	5	45
Iran	51	85	19		32		44
Thailand	50	91	14	27	39	2	44
Mexico	48	89	22	27	33	7	44
Moldova	55	90	20	26	24	3	43
South Africa	60	82	14	34	25	9	43
Romania	51	94	14	32	22	4	43
Turkey	60		22	16	22		42
Brazil	36	86	24	28	28	4	41
Argentina	47	90	21	23	21	4	40
Zambia	43	72	18	24	33	19	38
Vietnam	39	95	10	21	23	3	38
Jordan	42	86	17	13	22	8	36
Colombia	31	89	17	20	21	8	36
Morocco	31	87	27	17	15	10	36
Mali	32	71	22	32	31	11	35
Uruguay	30	90	19	15	22	7	35
India	52	61	9	22	22	30	33
Ghana	23	82	9	11	33	13	32
China	23	75	11	17	19	19	29
Burkina Faso	19	66	8	16	22	19	27
Rwanda	10	63	12	11	25	16	26
TOTAL	57	88	30	34	32	5	49

Note: Proportion who reported using each of these media sources 'to learn what is going on in their country and the world . . . during the last week.' The 100-point media use scale is generated by summing self-reported regular use of each of these five sources of information (newspaper, radio/TV news, magazine, books, and the Internet/e-mail). The scale counts each source as a simple 1/0 dichotomy, where each source is weighted equally, and the mean score is standardized to 100 points for ease of interpretation. In total, 60 nation-states (and 51 societies, as East and West Germany had separate samples) monitored news media use in the fifth wave of the WVS. In two cases, mean substitution was used to estimate the mean national media use scale for missing items not asked in Turkey (radio/TV use) and Iran (magazine use).

Source: World Values Survey (2005–2007).

60

the authors noted in an earlier study, 'The newspaper market varies greatly by country due to such factors as long-standing historical and cultural traditions in each region; levels of social development in terms of education, literacy, and income; the news industry's organization, economics, production and distribution system; and the overall structure of public subsidies, government regulations, and national levels of democratization.'[48]

Even among relatively affluent nations, the digital divide in access to new ICTs in the Mediterranean region and Scandinavia has been widely observed; for example, two-thirds to three-quarters of all respondents reported using the Internet or e-mail regularly in Norway, Sweden, the United States, and the Netherlands, compared with 4 out of 10 Italians and around one-quarter of all Spaniards.[49] Although these patterns are familiar, it is also striking that some East Asian societies rank among the top third of countries in media use, including Malaysia and South Korea (where governments have aggressively promoted investment in ICT infrastructure and skills to develop knowledge societies), and Japan (the latter due to maintaining large subscriptions of major daily newspapers, rather than particularly high Internet or e-mail usage), although other East Asian tigers such as Taiwan lagged behind these countries.

Various types of societies and regimes can be found among the countries in the middle ranks of media use, although many of these are emerging middle-income economies with moderate levels of literacy and education. Finally, the poorest and least developed countries with low literacy levels, including Rwanda, Mali, Zambia, Burkina Faso, and Ghana in sub-Saharan Africa, also tend to have the lowest levels of public access to the news media, although it is noteworthy that according to these estimates, both India and China also rank low on media access. Another way to make the comparison is to examine the proportion of respondents who reported that they did not regularly use any of these sources of media information; among the countries ranked lowest overall, 1 in 10 reported no regular use of any of these sources in Morocco and Mali, one-fifth reported no use in China, Burkina Faso, and Zambia, while one-third reported no use in India. In Chapter 5 we will discuss the reasons for these differences and analyze the factors contributing to disparities in access to ICTs.

Monitoring Television Watching

We can compare general use of television across 69 societies during the 1980s and 1990s. The WVS measured the number of hours that people spent watching television. Surveys that break down viewership figures in much finer detail, such as those conducted in the United States by the Pew Research Center for People and the Press, show that television news and current affairs are important, but represent only a relatively modest proportion of the overall time devoted to watching TV.[50] By contrast, far more time is devoted to popular entertainment, such as drama series, movies, comedies, game and reality shows, and similar fare. The WVS monitored TV habits in 16 postindustrial nations in 1981–1983, expanding coverage to 50 societies from many parts of the world in the second wave and including 17 societies (many in the Middle East) in the third wave. The survey asked, 'Do you ever watch television? If yes, how much time do you often watch television during an average workday?'

The result of the comparison, shown in Table 2.3, confirms that use of TV has become almost ubiquitous in many places, including post-Communist Europe and most affluent postindustrial societies. In a dozen countries, including Britain, the United States, and Canada, more than one-third of all respondents report spending at least three hours per day watching television. By contrast, the survey includes 11 developing countries, such as India, Mexico, and Zimbabwe, where at least in the middle or late 1990s, one-fifth to one-half of all respondents reported never watching TV. These estimates are out of date today, given the growing availability of TVs in many of these societies, but some important disparities remain, and the comparison allows us to test the effects of television watching among viewers and nonviewers in earlier waves of the survey. The societal disparities in access to television, as well as the contrasts observed in the use of a wider range of news media sources, provides a suitable 'most different' comparison with which we can test the impact of these patterns on cultural values.

Mixed Methods

Any single approach, taken in isolation, has limits. Consequently, this study opts for a mixed research design, combining the virtues of pooled

TABLE 2.3. *Use of Television and Frequency of Viewing*

	Wave	Does Not Watch TV (%)	1–2 Hours per Day (%)	2–3 Hours per Day (%)	More than 3 Hours per Day (%)
Moldova	1994–1999	0.5	51.5	28.5	19.6
Iceland	1981–1984	0.9	66.8	24.4	8.0
Belarus	1994–1999	1.0	32.1	32.8	34.1
Lithuania	1994–1999	1.0	41.6	29.7	27.6
Armenia	1994–1999	1.2	15.2	25.4	58.3
Azerbaijan	1994–1999	1.2	14.0	32.5	52.3
Japan	1994–1999	1.3	36.0	35.3	27.4
Estonia	1994–1999	1.3	41.8	31.9	25.0
Macedonia, Republic of	1994–1999	1.4	21.5	28.9	48.1
Sweden	1994–1999	1.7	78.7	11.7	8.0
Latvia	1994–1999	1.7	44.4	32.8	21.0
Norway	1981–1984	1.7	67.0	21.5	9.8
Sweden	1981–1984	1.8	72.0	16.3	9.9
Germany, West	1981–1984	1.8	59.3	26.4	12.4
United States	1981–1984	2.0	35.0	21.0	42.0
Ukraine	1994–1999	2.1	52.3	30.8	14.9
Great Britain	1981–1984	2.1	31.9	24.9	41.1
Northern Ireland	1981–1984	2.2	34.6	26.3	36.9
Australia	1994–1999	2.3	40.9	26.7	30.1
Italy	1981–1984	2.7	55.0	24.1	18.2
Norway	1994–1999	2.7	58.5	25.8	13.0
Canada	1981–1984	2.8	43.6	18.3	35.3
Taiwan	1994–1999	2.9	49.7	23.6	23.9
Bosnia and Herzegovina	1994–1999	2.9	28.6	38.3	30.2
Denmark	1981–1984	3.0	65.1	21.5	10.4
Spain	1999–2004	3.1	44.8	30.7	21.5
United States	1994–1999	3.4	41.7	27.4	27.5
Spain	1981–1984	3.9	50.6	24.9	20.6
Saudi Arabia	1999–2004	3.9	33.8	37.3	25.0
Netherlands	1981–1984	3.9	61.1	21.2	13.8
Romania	1994–1999	4.5	33.1	33.3	29.0
Chile	1994–1999	4.6	45.6	26.9	22.9
Hungary	1994–1999	4.8	50.0	26.5	18.7
Spain	1994–1999	4.9	44.4	31.9	18.9
Egypt	1999–2004	4.9	45.3	28.2	21.6
New Zealand	1994–1999	5.1	39.8	35.5	19.6

(continued)

TABLE 2.3 *(continued)*

	Wave	Does Not Watch TV (%)	1–2 Hours per Day (%)	2–3 Hours per Day (%)	More than 3 Hours per Day (%)
Belgium	1981–1984	5.2	48.1	28.0	18.7
Russian Federation	1994–1999	5.3	29.6	31.7	33.5
Switzerland	1994–1999	5.5	67.9	19.1	7.6
Indonesia	1999–2004	5.6	41.9	28.4	24.0
Algeria	1999–2004	5.7	36.2	28.4	29.7
Uruguay	1994–1999	5.7	34.8	29.8	29.7
Argentina	1999–2004	6.0	41.7	29.1	23.2
Brazil	1994–1999	6.1	47.0	17.1	29.8
Argentina	1994–1999	6.2	49.9	25.3	18.7
Bulgaria	1994–1999	6.2	20.6	37.3	36.0
Peru	1999–2004	6.2	45.4	28.0	20.4
Ireland	1981–1984	6.4	34.5	19.1	39.9
Malta	1981–1984	6.4	55.6	19.1	18.9
Poland	1994–1999	6.5	46.4	27.4	19.7
Croatia	1994–1999	6.6	39.9	32.3	21.2
Puerto Rico	1994–1999	7.3	40.8	24.1	27.8
France	1981–1984	7.3	52.7	24.3	15.7
Iraq	1999–2004	7.6	35.0	30.6	26.9
Puerto Rico	1999–2004	8.1	45.5	25.4	21.0
Germany	1994–1999	8.4	47.4	28.3	15.8
Serbia and Montenegro	1994–1999	8.5	42.5	26.3	22.7
Venezuela	1994–1999	9.1	36.6	25.4	28.9
Colombia	1994–1999	9.9	55.4	19.2	15.4
Bangladesh	1999–2004	10.2	47.5	36.5	5.8
Czech Republic	1994–1999	10.3	34.0	31.8	23.9
Peru	1994–1999	10.3	45.5	24.0	20.2
Slovenia	1994–1999	11.1	61.4	18.3	9.2
Dominican Republic	1994–1999	11.6	53.4	20.2	14.8
China	1994–1999	11.9	47.8	25.9	14.5
Morocco	1999–2004	12.2	45.1	20.6	22.1
Slovakia	1994–1999	12.3	40.3	29.9	17.5
Jordan	1999–2004	12.3	37.9	22.9	27.0
South Africa	1999–2004	12.3	36.5	26.4	24.8
Philippines	1994–1999	12.6	57.5	16.4	13.5
Albania	1994–1999	13.5	58.8	22.6	5.1
El Salvador	1994–1999	14.1	52.0	14.7	19.3
Nigeria	1999–2004	19.6	34.5	21.1	24.9

	Wave	Does Not Watch TV (%)	1–2 Hours per Day (%)	2–3 Hours per Day (%)	More than 3 Hours per Day (%)
Pakistan	1994–1999	20.1	9.2	59.2	11.5
Pakistan	1999–2004	21.2	50.5	21.0	7.3
Nigeria	1994–1999	21.6	37.5	21.8	19.0
Uganda	1999–2004	22.9	47.9	16.8	12.4
Finland	1994–1999	23.8	35.2	25.2	15.8
South Africa	1994–1999	24.5	36.3	20.0	19.3
Bangladesh	1994–1999	29.2	53.8 ·	13.5	3.5
India	1994–1999	35.8	51.6	11.3	1.3
Mexico	1994–1999	49.2	29.1	11.9	9.7
Zimbabwe	1999–2004	53.0	26.4	9.5	11.1

Note: The question asked was 'Do you ever watch television? If yes, how much time do you often watch television during an average workday?' Responses were monitored in 69 societies.
Source: Values Surveys (1981–2004).

survey data in more than 90 nations with rich and detailed narrative studies of contrasting paired cases.[51]

A large-N pooled dataset is used to establish the overall picture. The variables used here, including the construction of the Cosmopolitanism Index, are described in Technical Appendix A. The countries and surveys included in the study are listed in Technical Appendix B. The use of HLMs, in particular multilevel regression analysis, is described in detail in Technical Appendix C. In brief, the firewall theory predicts that individual use of the news media will have a *direct* effect on individual values. In addition, it predicts that a *cross-level interaction* effect will also be apparent, as external and internal barriers to information flows in each society will interact with individual patterns of news media use. To operationalize these factors, we use the key models in the second section of the book, which involve measurement at two distinct levels. A representative sample of individual respondents (Level 1) is nested within national-level contexts (Level 2). The WVS was conducted among representative samples of the adult population in each nation-state. Given the use of multilevel data, HLMs are most appropriate for analysis, including multilevel regression analysis.[52] Level 1 in our core models includes the following *individual-level* measures: male gender (0/1), household income using a 10-point scale, age (in years), the education scale, and the media use 5-point scale (or each of the separate dummy variables for use of newspapers, radio or TV, and the Internet). Level 2 includes the following *national-level* variables: the standardized KOF Globalization Index, the standardized Freedom House Press Freedom Index, and the standardized level of economic development (per capita GDP [2006] in purchasing power parity). *Cross-level* interactions are also included, as the effects of media use are expected to be moderated by the level of cosmopolitanism in each country. To measure the joint effects of media use at the individual level, while taking account of the environment at the national level, models include the Cosmopolitanism Index × media use. A more detailed description of the multilevel regression methods employed can be found in Technical Appendix C.

In addition, in Chapter 10 we use HLMs to estimate the direct changes over time, utilizing the social values and attitudes contained in successive waves of the WVS conducted since 1981. We classify nations included in the survey according to the annual Cosmopolitanism Index estimated for the year closest to that of the survey. We can then examine the degree of change in cultural values among cosmopolitan and parochial societies. Chapter 10 draws on cross-sectional time-series panel data, consisting of repeated observations (each wave of the survey) on a series of random units (the countries included in the WVS). The analysis of panel datasets through regression faces certain important challenges, and the interpretations of the results are quite sensitive to the choice of specification issues, alternative models, and diagnostic tests.[53] Ordinary least-squares (OLS) regression estimates assume that errors are independent, normally distributed, and with constant variance. Panel data violate these assumptions and raise potential problems of heteroscedasticity, autocorrelation, robustness, and missing data. In particular, autocorrelations are generated because, with time-series data, the same countries are observed repeatedly and the additional observations do not provide substantially new information. The danger of OLS analysis is that the beta coefficients will remain unbiased but the disturbance terms from the errors (i.e., omitted variables) are likely to be correlated. In other words, if OLS regression models are used, the significance of any coefficients may be inflated, generating Type II errors, suggesting that significant relationships exist when in fact they do not. Various techniques have been designed to handle panel datasets, including OLS linear regression with panel-corrected standard errors and the use of robust regression.[54] In this study, we extend the use of generalized linear models (HLM). Our multilevel regression models include both subjects (countries) and repeated variables (waves) with correlated residuals within the random effects.

Finally, we use selected narrative paired case studies to illustrate the underlying causal mechanisms at work, taking account of historical developments and processes of cultural change within given nations.[55] Cases allow researchers to develop theories, to derive hypotheses, and to explore causal mechanisms. This approach is particularly useful with outliers that deviate from the generally observed pattern. The case comparisons examine societies that are similar in certain important regards, such as sharing a cultural tradition and level of socioeconomic development, while differing in their media environments. Chapter 4 compares cases that exemplify cosmopolitan and parochial societies. Among the African democracies included in the WVS with relatively open and pluralistic media environments, Mali represents one of the poorest societies in the world with limited public access to the mass media, whereas South Africa has a well-developed communication infrastructure and global networks. These contrasts are explored further in Chapter 5. Among parochial societies, Syria exemplifies a society that has minimal freedom of the press and is relatively isolated from global markets. In contrast, China, a rapidly industrializing society that has recently joined the WTO, has growing affluence due to extensive international trade but also sets serious limits on internal freedom of expression and publication. Case studies must always be sensitive to problems of selection bias, and it is difficult to determine the extent to which broader generalizations can be drawn from the particular countries.[56] Nevertheless, the combination of cross-national large-N comparisons with selected cases is a strong design that maximizes the potential benefits of each approach. If the two contrasting approaches point to similar conclusions, our confidence in the robustness of the findings will increase.

Conclusions and Qualifications

This research design allows us to test the impact of mass communications using a broad range of countries and multiple techniques. We anticipate that any direct effects arising from the use of the mass media will be most evident among individuals who make regular use of newspapers, television, radio, and the Internet. By comparing the social values, attitudes, and beliefs of the media audience with others living in the same society, we can see whether these groups differ significantly. By nesting the analysis within different types of environments, we can examine broader contextual and interactive effects. We hypothesize that the impact of *cosmopolitan* communications can best be tested by analyzing the interaction between media use at the individual level and the type of society. Information flows arising from media sources are expected to have the greatest tendency to facilitate cultural convergence in the most cosmopolitan societies, characterized by free trade cultural policies, widespread media access, and freedom of information. This process advances the analytical framework and research agenda to a much greater extent than earlier studies.

Nevertheless, some important qualifications of and limits to this research design should be acknowledged. In particular, with this approach we cannot detect any more *diffuse* long-term effects arising from mass communications – for example, whether advertising, television, and movies convey broader images and ideas that gradually percolate throughout society. People do not have to see glossy images of Levis or Nikes to want to buy these products. People who watch or read about the news often discuss the events and headlines with family members, friends, colleagues, and neighbors. Through social networks, news gradually trickles down to others in the community (the 'watercooler' effect). Interpersonal discussion is likely to be a particularly important source of information in societies with low levels of literacy and with an oral culture. Nevertheless, diffuse long-term indirect effects on society as a whole are the most difficult, if not impossible, to attribute with any degree of reliability to mass communications per se. We can certainly speculate about the way that images or ideas in advertising, news headlines, or popular entertainment shape societal attitudes and values beyond the audience, but it is not clear how this process can be established empirically.

Another major challenge arises from attempts to establish the direction of causality between use of the media and social values. Prior interests may plausibly drive media use; for example, an interest in international affairs may well encourage people to surf the Internet for news about events abroad. At the same time, regular media use may plausibly shape social attitudes and values; for example, regularly accessing foreign news Web sites may well facilitate learning about other people and places. The difficulty of determining the direction of causality is not unique to this study; indeed, it plagues all cross-sectional survey analyses seeking to establish the impact of media use. The WVS monitors public opinion among different samples of respondents taken at roughly five-year intervals. Experimental 'pre–post' research designs and panel surveys of the same respondents over time are the most effective techniques used to disentangle causality, in that they control for prior media selection biases. Unfortunately, both techniques are also challenging to implement on a cross-national basis. It is also often difficult to generalize from the results of specific social psychological experiments conducted among small groups and atypical populations, such as college students, to discern broader patterns in society as a whole. The approach taken in this study cannot ultimately control for self-selection biases in the audience, but any *direct* effects arising from the use of the mass media should be evident most clearly in the contrasts found between the audience and the nonaudience.

The available survey measures of media use are also limited. At the individual level, the fifth wave of the WVS monitored the regular use of daily newspapers, news broadcasts and in-depth reports on radio or TV, printed magazines, books, the Internet and e-mail, and the viewing of television entertainment, as well as personal discussions with friends or colleagues. The questionnaire items concerning media use are presented in Technical Appendix A. As general measures designed to cover multiple societies and media systems, these are inevitably restricted in their precision. We lack any survey evidence about the potential impact of many other types of global communication flows – for example, the role of imported feature movies, video games, or popular music. Nor can we identify the specific contents and messages that people are exposed to when they access the mass media, such as the types of Web sites that people typically use, or whether they read tabloid or broadsheet newspapers, or whether they watch public service or commercial TV stations. It is possible that attitudes toward the United States are shaped more directly by other forms of mass entertainment, such as the images conveyed by Hollywood blockbusters, than by CNN nightly news or by TV dramas and game shows.

Nor can we monitor the extent of exposure and attention to the news media – for example, how frequently people read newspapers or watch TV news, or for how long people have used the Internet. The distinction between radio and television news is also poorly captured by the questionnaire, as are differences between the use of e-mail and the World Wide Web. These issues and many others must be left to further comparative research, which can replicate some of the core propositions developed in this study by exploring media contents and audience reception in finer detail. What we can examine in this book, however, is whether regular users of the most common types of mass media differ significantly from those who do not use these sources of information.

Moreover, individual-level surveys of media use ideally should be supplemented by information about media contents. We lack data about what people were watching or reading when they used the news media or television in general, and thus the extent to which individuals were exposed to particular types of cross-border information flows. For example, European Audiovisual Observatory monitors the extent to which European public service and private TV stations feature American movies, drama, and entertainment, the results showing substantial variations in European societies. Within countries, people could choose to watch mostly domestically produced TV, or alternatively those with cable or satellite access could tune into CNN, EuroNews, or Sky TV. To monitor viewing habits with any degree of precision requires far more fine grained audience research surveys, such as those provided by Nielsen Audience Research. The picture becomes even more complicated if we try to monitor the degree of attention individuals paid to international news in the print sector or radio, as well as to nondomestic content via the Internet. In addition, ideally we need a measure of exposure to nondomestically produced contents that operates across all channels of mass communications; for example, people could watch a high proportion of American movies on cable TV while also regularly tuning in to local or national news. In the absence of any precise measure of media contents or individual-level patterns of exposure, we assume that people living in societies that are most cosmopolitan are generally more likely than others to encounter cross-border information flows from a variety of sources. Our research design provides only a conservative indicator of any impact, and again experimental research would make it possible to explore these issues with control over the precise contents of the messages.

These are all important qualifications, and we will return to them in more detail, considering their consequences for the interpretation of the overall results, in the concluding chapter. In the meanwhile, to start to build the empirical evidence concerning the core argument, we go on in the next chapter to analyze the international market that determines the exchange of cultural goods and services.

PART I

FIREWALLS

3

Markets

Arguments about the potential threat of cosmopolitan communications to national cultures are based on structural developments in the production and distribution of mass communications. Globalization, it is often argued, has expanded the volume of cultural trade in the international market for cultural goods and services. In this chapter, we start by examining the evidence for these claims. The pattern of cultural trade is complex and no one indicator covers all dimensions, so we will examine the overall trends during recent decades by drawing on international statistics from the World Trade Organization (WTO), the United Nations Educational, Scientific, and Cultural Cooperation Organization (UNESCO), the United Nations Conference on Trade and Development (UNCTAD), and the European Audiovisual Observatory.[1] We focus attention on three aspects of cosmopolitan communications: the balance of trade in *audiovisual services* (television programs, feature films, and recorded music); the flow of *news information* through printed newspapers and magazines, TV news and current affairs, and news wire services; and interconnections through *new information and communication technologies*, including complex cross-border flows and media convergence via the Internet. The evidence is most systematic and reliable for the balance of audiovisual trade, and less comprehensive information is available for monitoring the other types of exchanges, although we can piece together some information from indirect proxy indicators.

The evidence presented in this chapter points to certain key conclusions. First, most audiovisual cultural exports have been, and continue
to be, generated by a few major producer countries located in the global
North, as many other studies have reported. Moreover, the United
States, the leading exporter in this market throughout the postwar
era, has not only maintained but substantially expanded its share of
audiovisual trade in recent decades. Other important producers include
Britain, Germany, Canada, and France, each with large domestic markets and a major slice of world exports to networks of trade partners
linked by neocolonial ties, expatriate communities, and shared languages. Increasingly dense cross-border communications bind many
advanced industrialized economies tightly together. The Netherlands,
Belgium, Austria, and Switzerland are some of the world's most globalized societies today, with cable and satellite channels providing direct
access to German, French, Italian, Dutch, and English-language television stations, as well as dubbed or translated American-produced
TV programs, music, and movies, while foreign newspapers, imported
books, magazines, advertising, and high-speed broadband connections
to e-mail and online international Web sites are all widely available.
The existence of rapidly growing connections across national borders
provides preliminary evidence that cultural convergence, around an
American or Western set of values, could potentially occur, as many
theorists have long claimed, if other conditions are met. This pattern
reinforces the importance of further careful investigation of this phenomenon's consequences.

Before we can accept that this process will lead to cultural convergence, however, this interpretation needs important qualifications.
Trade patterns remain complex, the exchange is far from one way, and
important regional hubs and counterflows are emerging among producers located in certain middle-income economies, as the fusion thesis emphasizes.[2] Chinese-manufactured video games flood Wal-Mart
shelves in Iowa. Bollywood produces more films per year than the
United States. Bangalore phone centers advise software customers in
New York. Latin American telenovelas are popular in Spain. Cape
Verde and Mali musicians can be heard on world music stations in
London and Paris. News about Darfur and Iraq is broadcast on American television evening news. Crafts and arts products from Bali, Delhi,
and Kashmir are sold on eBay. Malaysia and Singapore have some of
the most globalized economies in the world. There are also major

questions about what constitutes an 'American' product: U.S. popular culture often imports popular formats and creative ideas from abroad, and companies co-finance productions with partners overseas, in a complex exchange, before then manufacturing and re-exporting products. The process is analogous to franchising branches of Pizza Hut in Italy, Taco Bell in Mexico, and Starbucks in Brazil. With its entertainment-oriented leisure industry, diverse multiethnic population, consumer economy, and open borders, the United States is the world's largest importer of many cultural goods and services, as well as the leading exporter. America may be so successful in selling popular entertainment and news abroad because it is a multiethnic immigrant society with a fusion culture that borrows foods, fashions, fads, and TV formats from around the world.[3] These multifaceted counterflows give some support to the fusion scenario.

At the same time, the integration of economies into world markets, along with the balance of trade in cultural services in the creative economy, remains far from equal around the globe. Observers in America or Europe often overlook the fact that the people of many of the world's poorest nations are largely excluded from access to this marketplace, both as consumers and as producers. The density and pace of information flows remain strongest among advanced industrialized economies. Integrated networks bind together the economies, peoples, and states of the expanding European Union into a single market, while a common language and historical connections bind the United States with Canada and Britain. There are also strong communication links between OECD countries and fast-growing middle-income nations, such as the Philippines, South Korea, Brazil, and the Czech Republic. By contrast, far weaker ties of cultural trade and international communications connect the richest and poorest nations around the world. As a result, the expanded volume of cultural trade and cross-border information flows continues to have only a limited impact in many geographically isolated developing societies and poor communities located in the global South. In many poor countries, the public remains relatively isolated from cross-border information flows, because of limited access to mass communication and information technologies, protectionist barriers to foreign imports, and internal restrictions on what can be seen or read in the press. Accordingly, in some of the least developed societies, such as Mali, Ethiopia, and Bangladesh, people living in rural communities still acquire most of their information, values, and beliefs about events in their society and the world from personal contacts with parents and siblings, teachers, spiritual leaders and community chiefs, friends, neighbors and colleagues, and traditional social networks within their neighborhood, as well as from their direct experience of living conditions in these societies, rather than from cross-border information flows. Lack of integration into world markets suggests the need for considerable caution in generalizing about cultural convergence; ironically, globalization itself is not a fully worldwide phenomenon.

Moreover, even in cosmopolitan societies, the existence of dense cross-border information flows that originate primarily in the global North does not, by itself, determine the social psychological consequences of this process and its impact on public opinion. Although it seems plausible that cultures may be exposed to a common set of (Western or American) values and norms, it may still be true that most people fail to assimilate these ideas if they acquire deep-rooted and enduring values, beliefs, and practices during their formative years in childhood and adolescence from many primary sources, role models, and experiences besides the mass media. The media competes with many other socialization agencies. Cultural theorists argue that critical readers and viewers deconstruct and reinterpret the meaning of messages received from the mass media, and they may reject values and attitudes conveyed by these sources if they feel they are inappropriate or that the media fails to provide trustworthy and credible information. Theories suggest that the influence of mass communications is subtle, complex, and indirect; it would be rash to jump directly from evidence about the imbalance of cultural trade to assume its effects on the audience. Systematic empirical analysis is needed to investigate whether viewers, readers, and listeners with regular access to mass communications, who live in cosmopolitan societies permeable to information flows, within and from outside their national borders, actually differ significantly in their attitudes, values, and beliefs from those who do not.

What Has Changed in the Trade in Cultural Goods and Services?

In examining the evidence supporting these claims, we will first focus on the market in creative industries. UNCTAD has classified creative

FIGURE 3.1. Types of Creative Industries. *Source:* Adapted from UNCTAD's classification of creative industries. UNCTAD. 2008. *Background Paper: Secretary-General's High-Level Panel on the Creative Economies and Industries for Development.* TD(XII)/BP/4.

industries into several distinct sectors, as illustrated in Figure 3.1. Heritage goods, including museums, traditional festivals, crafts, archives, libraries, and art galleries, are an important and growing sector, especially for sustainable development and attracting revenue from travel and tourism. The performing arts sector includes performances of live music, theater, dance, and opera, which can also be important for drawing visitors. Visual arts constitute the sector concerned with paintings, sculptures, and antiques. Cultural protectionism and the regulation of exports tend to be particularly strong with respect to distinctive symbols and artifacts representing a society's heritage and legacy. The commercial aspects of the creative economy encompass services such as architecture, advertising, and research and development, as well as the modern visual design involved in the manufacture and production of furniture, interior design, decorating, fashion, and jewelry. Finally, the three commercial sectors that have been most strongly represented in debates about cultural trade concern the provision of audiovisual services (including the production and dissemination of feature and documentary motion pictures, musical recordings, as well as television and radio broadcasting of news and entertainment over terrestrial, cable, and satellite), new media (a diverse category involving the rapidly evolving range of digitalized contents transmitted through broadband, Wi-Fi, and the Internet, including Web sites, computer software, and video games), and publishing (including newspapers and periodicals, books, journals, and related printed contents). Although it is useful to distinguish between these categories, in practice they often merge, with online newspapers and video downloads, for example, delivering traditional media through new technologies.

Moreover, analysis is complicated by the limited availability, harmonization, and reliability of international data on culture. National statistical offices, led by initiatives in UNESCO, OECD, and the European Union's Eurostat, have recently been revising the collection of official data on employment in the creative economy and public participation in cultural activities, but existing cross-national indicators are fragmented and they lag behind the transformation of ICTs.[4] Official trade statistics usually document the flow of manufactured goods across national customs borders, such as exports or imports of printed newspapers and published magazines, musical instruments, radio and TV sets, and heritage artifacts such as artworks and antiques. National trade data are then collected and presented in standardized format by international agencies, such as UNCTAD and the WTO. Official national statistics also monitor telecommunication services, with electronic messages transmitted by landline and cellular telephone, telex, telegram, and posted mail, collected worldwide under the auspices of the ITU. Official statistics on the individual or household distribution of ICTs, including the availability of landline and cellular telephones, PCs, fax machines, Internet hosts, Internet bandwidth, Internet costs, and the number of Internet subscribers, is also available from census and household surveys for many countries around the world.

The reliability of these data depends on standardized classifications used by national statistical offices and the accuracy of records maintained by customs offices; there are some important systematic biases, as records are often incomplete in some of the least developed nations.

Nevertheless, national statistics are monitored and harmonized by international bodies and conventions. By contrast, the most relevant indicators of the production, distribution, and exchange of audiovisual services, including trade in feature films and television programs, are captured only incompletely at present in national statistics. Most of the evidence is contained in proprietary private sector databases, often with limited geographic coverage, collected by commercial market research companies. The field of cultural services is complex, and the responsibility for collecting data is dispersed among many bodies. Cross-national surveys such as the Eurobarometer have sought to measure social uses of the Internet and participation in the creative economy in more detail within the European Union, and there are numerous international indices of Internet access. But there are few systematic cross-national data that monitor worldwide trends in the growing and complex inflow and outflow of digital news and online information across national borders, such as how many readers and viewers download news and information from online television, radio, or newspapers, Weblogs, and social networking sites based in other countries. The number of printed newspapers and published magazines that are imported captures only a microcosm of information flows in this sector today, given the easy availability of most publications via the Internet. The growing availability of faster broadband connections means that access to online music, radio, video, and television programs is also rapidly expanding, regardless of country of origin, bypassing conventional cross-border trade statistics.

Social scientists have sought to examine changing patterns of information and communication flows by piecing together a range of alternative indicators and methodologies covering different sectors. This includes content analysis of the international or foreign news coverage carried in a sample of the world's major newspapers, wire services, and television news programs during a particular period.[5] The proportion of broadcasting programs produced domestically or abroad has been analyzed by a comparison of the hours of television broadcasting schedules, such as within the European Union.[6] Commercial data available on the film industry include the costs of film production, marketing, distribution, box office ticket sales, and secondary merchandizing, analyzed by revenues in the country of origin and overseas. Market research, household surveys, and time-budget diary studies have examined cultural activities, such as attendance at movies, art galleries, and live performances.[7] Detailed case studies have documented the organizational structure, ownership, and finances of the main transnational communication corporations and their growth in recent decades.[8] Other indicators include patterns of telecommunication traffic, financial data on the inflow of tourism and public attendance at cultural heritage sites, and commercial market research on advertising and marketing revenues.[9] Finally, in addition to the distribution and location of Internet hosts and subscribers, the direction of online information flows has been monitored through analysis of inbound and outgoing hyperlinks connecting Web sites.[10] These all represent important sources of information about the exchange of cultural expression across national borders, but unfortunately many existing indicators are limited in their scope, standardization, geographic coverage, and sampling periods. The results should also be aggregated across diverse subsectors to provide a comprehensive and systematic comparison of the total volume and direction of total communication and information flow around the world.

To obtain a more comprehensive picture, let us examine what we know about the overall volume of trade in cultural goods and services, and then focus on indicators comparing the exchange of information through three sectors: the audiovisual trade in television, movies, and music; the news flow in journalism among countries; and the exchange of digital information through ICTs.

The Total Volume of Trade in Cultural Goods and Services

The analysis of trade in cultural goods and services, based on UNCTAD data, indicates that although some emerging economies are becoming important exporters within their region, the global production and distribution of mass communication products are concentrated in just a few postindustrial societies. In 2002, for example, UNESCO estimated that the value of exports of cultural products and services was $45 billion in high-income economies, compared with just $329 million in low-income countries.[11] Among individual countries, the top three exporters in 2002 were the United Kingdom (exporting $8.5 billion worth of cultural goods), the United States (exporting $7.6 billion), and Germany (exporting $5.8 billion). Among emerging economies, China was an important player in cultural exports (totaling $5.3 billion), especially in visual arts and audiovisual media (notably video games). Despite its highly protectionist cultural policies, France was also a major force, exporting $2.5 billion in cultural goods. By contrast, cultural exports earned only $347 million for Russia, $284 million for India, $56 million for South Africa, $38 million for Brazil, and $6 million for Saudi Arabia. The combined export revenue of these five major countries was less than that of the United Kingdom alone. In developing societies, exports of cultural goods exceeded imports, while the reverse was true of advanced industrialized societies.[12] As a result of the global imbalance in cultural trade, developing societies at the periphery of these trade networks import far more information and popular entertainment from the North than they export.

Audiovisual Trade in Television, Movies, and Music

One major reason for this disparity in information flows is that a handful of countries continue to predominate in the production, dissemination, and marketing of audiovisual goods and services (including film, broadcasting, music, television, and radio), with trade concentrated disproportionately in the United States, Canada, Germany, France, and Britain. The trade in audiovisual services and fees includes the value of the production of motion pictures, radio and television programs, and musical recordings, where the sum of all exports and imports is calculated as a proportion of GDP (measured in purchasing power parity [PPP] in constant 2000 international dollars). Figure 3.2 illustrates the average audiovisual trade from 1990 to 2006, compared with the total volume of trade in all goods and services, calculated from data provided by the WTO. The pattern clearly illustrates the leading role of the United States in audiovisual trade, followed at some distance by Germany, Canada, France, and Britain. By contrast, China predominates worldwide in the overall trade in goods and services, but little of this revenue derives from this sector. The music industry, for example, was worth an estimated $31 billion in 2002, through sales of records, CDs, tapes, and related products. The United States and Europe dominate, representing three-quarters of world sales, while the African music market represents less than 1%.[13] High-income countries accounted for 94% of global exports of recorded media.

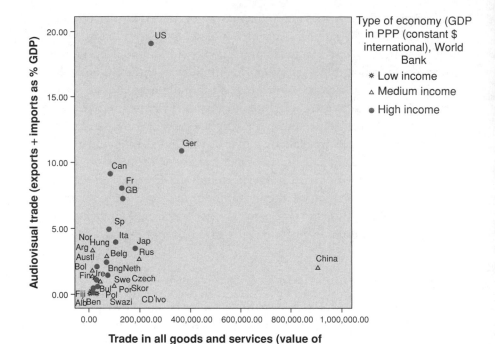

FIGURE 3.2. Comparing Trade in All Goods and Services with Trade in Audiovisual Services. Trade in audiovisual services and fees related to the production of motion pictures, radio and television programs, and musical recordings. This is calculated in the summed mean values of annual exports and annual imports from 1990 to 2006 as a proportion of GDP in constant (2000) international dollars. Total trade in all goods and services was calculated by the same method. The type of economy is categorized from per capita GDP (in PPP) in constant (2000) international dollars. 'Low income' corresponds to less than $1,999; 'medium income,' $2,000–$14,999; 'high income,' $15,000+. *Sources:* Data on audiovisual trade were provided by the Statistical Office of the World Trade Organization. Data on trade in all goods and services are from Arthur S. Banks Cross-National Time-Series dataset. GDP values are from World Development Indicators (World Bank).

Feature films are another major audiovisual sector, generating an estimated $25 billion in revenues worldwide in 2006.[14] Here, Hollywood continues to dominate the industry, producing about 600–700 new releases a year. By contrast, throughout its entire history, Africa is estimated to have produced only around 600 films.[15] Bollywood is a striking exception to the usual pattern in the developing world, with the Indian film industry turning out 800–900 movies a year. But this production caters mainly to domestic demand, plus some exports to the Indian diaspora abroad, attracting relatively modest foreign audiences or export revenues. Moreover, a longitudinal study of the international economic market for movies during the past three decades found that Hollywood films have gradually become even more dominant globally, crowding out movies from other places and leaving a more concentrated market.[16] British movies have also expanded their market share. By contrast, despite the historical renown of directors such as Sergei Eisenstein, Federico Fellini, Kurosawa Akira, and Rainer Fassbinder, the export of films from Russia, Italy, Japan, and Germany has declined.[17] The 25-member European Union produces about 700–800 feature films per annum, more than the United States alone, but this figure is somewhat misleading, as the industry is heavily concentrated in the major players, France, Germany, Spain, Italy, and Britain (respectively), with most other member states generating very few movies per year.[18]

Broadcasting of popular television entertainment may represent the most important part of the audiovisual sector, feeding the growth of commercial television stations during the past decade through the expansion of terrestrial, satellite, and cable channels. Extensive research published since the early 1970s has consistently reported the leading position of the American audiovisual industry in the world.[19] This predominance has grown within Europe during recent decades, fueled by the deregulation and privatization of public service television, which occurred in most European societies during the 1980s, and the expansion of new commercial TV channels in Europe that import a high proportion of popular American-produced and -financed entertainment, fiction, drama series, and sitcoms, as well as movies, as a cheaper alternative to domestic production.[20] The contents of European TV have become increasingly American, despite attempts to hold back the tide through the European Union's 1989 Television without Frontiers directive requiring that European channels reserve at least half of their transmission time for European work, excluding the time allocated to news, sports events, games, advertising, teletext, and teleshopping services.[21] The European Audiovisual Observatory, which monitors the trade in television broadcasting programs between the European Union and North America, reported that the substantial

EU trade deficit on television programs doubled from 1995 to 2000.[22] Estimates suggest that the average proportion of imported American programs broadcast on European television represented about one-tenth of all hours of European TV broadcasts during the early 1980s, but this proportion doubled to about one-fifth by the following decade.[23] If we restrict the comparison to television entertainment alone (including fiction, drama series, feature films, and made-for-TV movies), however, it has been estimated that by 1990 about half of all the hours of European television broadcast were occupied by programs imported from America.[24] By 2001, the total proportion of American programs had risen even further, to occupy on average about 70% of all European program schedules. In some countries the proportions are far higher: U.K. channels are the most heavily dependent on American-originated material, so that by 2001, 88% of fiction programming imported into the United Kingdom and 93% of feature films were either entirely American or American coproductions.[25] The Irish and Danish channels also broadcast a high proportion of non-European programs, with the most European programming shown in France, Finland, and Switzerland. Most of the imported programs are drama series and soaps (43%), followed by feature-length films (35%), animation (16%), and made-for-TV films (6%). By contrast, the internal market for European-produced entertainment television and feature films has remained relatively stable and modest, constituting about 15% of the total volume of imported broadcast programs by EU member states.

Some important qualifications should be added to put these figures in context. In particular, counting the total hours of imported programs, much domestic television entertainment in Europe is imported from the United States. But local audiences often prefer to watch domestically produced programs, which may have high audience shares and program ratings.[26] There are also differences by type of channel, with the heaviest share of U.S. imports shown on commercial channels rather than among public service broadcasters.[27] Moreover, the most popular news and current affairs programs on radio and television are often produced locally and nationally, with events interpreted from strongly divergent domestic viewpoints, even if the audiovideo materials used in these broadcasts are derived from international and foreign news sources and despite the growing availability of transnational news and current affairs programs via satellite and cable broadcasts, such as Sky News, CNN, and BBC World.[28]

Looking beyond Europe, developments in recent decades have exacerbated the worldwide disparity in audiovisual trade, including patterns of convergence among satellite, cable, telecommunication, and Internet media technologies; a series of corporate mergers and acquisitions concentrating resources in large transnational media behemoths; and communication policies of liberalization, deregulation, and commercialization that have transformed state-owned telecommunications and public service broadcasting and expanded the number of private channels and niche broadcasting stations.[29] We can compare the balance of trade in audiovisual services worldwide, illustrated in Figure 3.3, by analyzing the average log value of exports and imports in this sector from 1990 to 2006, measured as a proportion of GDP in constant PPP dollars. It is apparent that the United States enjoys a net positive trade balance, exporting a far greater share of audiovisual services than it imports. By contrast, Britain, Canada, and France have a high volume of trade but a net trade balance in their import and export of these services. Some affluent countries such as Japan, Spain, and Germany, as well as some middle-income nations such as South Korea and Brazil, have a net trade deficit, importing far more than they export during these years. The countries in which audiovisual imports are the lowest include some of the poorest developing nations worldwide, such as Swaziland, Benin, Bangladesh, Mali, and Madagascar, with restricted television markets and limited film distribution, which are relatively isolated from this trade.

Moreover, an examination of trends over time in Figure 3.4 illustrates the growing market share of American audiovisual trade since the early 1990s, measured by the value of audiovisual trade as a proportion of GDP (in constant international dollars PPP). It is apparent that the gap between the United States and other major exporting countries has widened during this era, with the value of trade also growing, albeit at a slower rate, for Germany, France, Britain, and Canada. One important reason for this pattern is the size of the domestic TV and movie market in the United States. For example, worldwide box office receipts for movies generated an estimated $25.8 billion in 2006, the U.S. box office generating one-third of the total revenue ($9.49 billion).[30] The size of the domestic market encourages

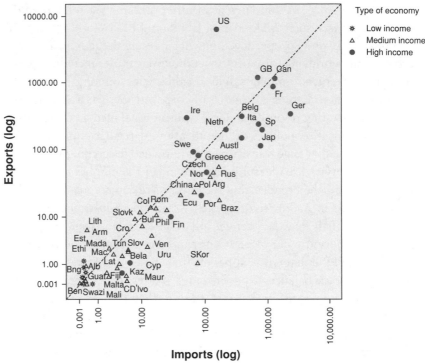

FIGURE 3.3. Western Predominance in Audiovisual Trade. Trade in audiovisual services and fees related to the production of motion pictures, radio and television programs, and musical recordings. This is calculated in the mean value of annual audiovisual exports from 1990 to 2006 as a proportion of GDP (in PPP) measured in constant (2000) international dollars. Annual audiovisual imports were calculated by the same method. The type of economy is categorized from per capita GDP (in PPP) in constant (2000) international dollars. 'Low income' corresponds to less than $1,999; 'medium income,' $2,000 to $14,999; 'high income,' $15,000+. The scales are logged. The dashed diagonal line represents the balance of trade, with countries falling below the line having a negative trade balance and countries above having a surplus. *Sources:* Data on audiovisual trade were provided by the Statistical Office of the World Trade Organization. Data on trade in all goods and services are from Arthur S. Banks Cross-National Time-Series dataset. GDP values are from World Development Indicators (World Bank).

American investment in the audiovisual industries, supporting production quality and generating low-cost films and TV programs that are competitively priced for the international market.[31] Britain has also been relatively successful in selling television to countries abroad,

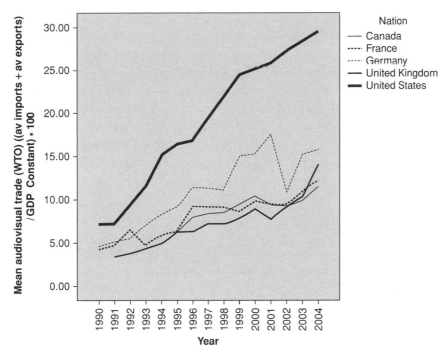

FIGURE 3.4. The Growing Predominance of American Audiovisual Trade. Trade in audiovisual services and fees related to the production of motion pictures, radio and television programs, and musical recordings. This is calculated in the mean value of annual audiovisual exports from 1990 to 2006 as a proportion of GDP (in PPP) in constant (2000) international dollars. Annual audiovisual imports were calculated by the same method. This graph shows the top five trading nations. *Source:* Data on audiovisual trade were provided by the Statistical Office of the World Trade Organization.

including the United States.[32] Globalization and technological developments have reinforced and strengthened the international reach and resources of major media conglomerates based in the United States, led by Disney/ABC, Westinghouse/CBS, AOL/Time Warner, News Corporation/Fox, Viacom International, Yahoo, Microsoft, Apple, Google, and General Electric. The global reach of multimedia corporations is exemplified by Rupert Murdoch's News International, which owns a chain of major newspapers and magazines in many countries, including the *Wall Street Journal*, the *New York Post*, the *Times* in the United Kingdom, and the *Australian*, as well as Fox cable television and Twentieth Century Fox in the United States, BSkyB satellite in Europe, and

Star satellite broadcasting in Asia. The company has approximately U.S. $64 billion in assets and total annual revenues of about U.S. $30 billion.[33] The international market for television programs has risen, driven in recent decades by the expansion of access to cable and satellite stations, alongside deregulation and privatization of state and public service television channels. The rapid expansion in the number of commercial television channels available, due to privatization and deregulation of state media, and the need for these channels to fill programming hours cheaply has enhanced America's lead in cultural trade.[34]

News Flows and Journalism

One area that has always been considered particularly important for international information flows is the news industry and journalism, including printed newspapers and published magazines, as well as television and radio news and current affairs programs. The imbalance in international news coverage is not a novel phenomenon; during the 1950s and 1960s, the earliest systematic content analysis of international stories carried by the world's press emphasized the disparities of news flows around the globe; most coverage focused on advanced industrialized societies, with relatively little reporting of peoples, countries, and events in the developing world.[35] This pattern was first documented when major newspapers were the main channel of international news. Subsequent research conducted during the era of the 1970s and 1980s, when broadcast television news and current affairs became the most widespread communication channel, confirmed the persistent lack of coverage of the developing world.[36] Since then, the rise of transnational TV channels such as CNN International, BBC World, and BSkyB News, as well as new technologies for collecting information and reporting, might be expected to have altered this pattern, but in fact a series of studies conducted during the 1990s has confirmed the continuing asymmetrical flow of news coverage around the globe. Research has compared the volume and direction of news flows carried in newspaper reporting, television reporting, and wire services, concluding that most journalistic attention is still given to affluent postindustrial countries, with relatively little coverage of developing societies.[37] For example, a recent study compared international news carried in a sample of newspapers and broadcast news in 38 countries during the mid-1990s and concluded that media coverage generally reflected the world's power structure, with the United States being given the most attention, followed by France and the United Kingdom.[38]

The global imbalance in news flows has been attributed to many factors. Foreign ownership of newspapers and magazines has increased in recent decades; many Western European media groups have invested heavily in major publishing companies in Eastern Europe.[39] As mentioned, Rupert Murdoch's News Corporation has multiple newspaper holdings in many countries.[40] Bertelsmann, a German-based company with an annual turnover of €18.8 billion, is similarly diversified across several media markets; it controls RTL Group, the number one European broadcaster; Random House, the world's largest book-publishing group; Gruner + Jahr, Europe's biggest magazine publisher; and BMG, which holds a joint venture stake in Sony BMG Music Entertainment, the second-largest music company in the world.[41]

Most importantly, the three major international news wire services – Reuters, the Associated Press (AP), and Agence France-Presse – are the source of much of the overseas news carried in radio, television, and newspapers, especially in developing societies. Companies based in Britain, the United States, and France, respectively, own and control these services.[42] The American-based AP serves thousands of daily newspapers, 5,000 radio and television outlets, and online Web sites in 121 countries, providing news, photographs, graphics, and audio and video services.[43] The AP is a nonprofit cooperative owned by its 1,500 U.S. daily newspapers, with more than 4,000 employees (including 3,000 journalists) operating in more than 240 bureaus in 97 countries worldwide. The AP distributes news in four languages, and the contents are translated into many more languages by international subscribers. Associated Press Television News provides video footage to many broadcasters throughout the world. The demise in 1993 of its traditional rival, United Press International, left the AP as the only nationally oriented news service based in the United States.[44] A similar service is provided by Reuters, a London-based news agency. With 2,400 editorial staff members, journalists, photographers, and camera operators located in 196 bureaus, Reuters serves about 4,000 clients in 131 countries. Reuters Holding makes its main profit today by

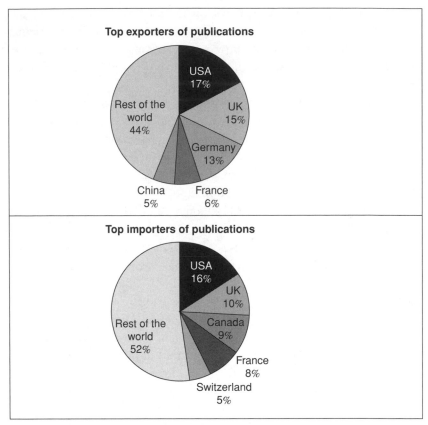

FIGURE 3.5. World Trade in Published Newspapers, Magazines, and Books, 2004–2007. The figures represent the share of the total value of world exports and imports in published products by the top five producer countries, averaged 2004–2007. *Source:* Estimates from UN Comtrade statistics.

supplying financial and investment information. Reuters Television is one of the world's largest TV news agencies, trading in footage that is used by major outlets such as CNN and BBC. It covers current affairs, financial news, sports, and showbiz; it also offers ready-to-air packages and provides a rolling news broadcast to its subscribers.

Like the role of news agencies, the worldwide trade in printed publications is heavily lopsided (see Figure 3.5), with the United States exporting newspapers and magazines worth around $880 million per annum and the United Kingdom exporting about $744 million per annum, compared with imports into each country of around $300 million. The United Kingdom also enjoys a healthy trade surplus for published books, exporting $1.8 billion (the second-highest level of any country worldwide) while importing $1.2 billion. By contrast, most developing societies are net importers of printed publications, and their imports of newspapers and magazines have increased during the past decade.[45] Nor is this simply a matter of the popularity of the English language or the size of these countries; Mandarin Chinese is widely spoken, but the value of imported newspapers and magazines in China is 10 times that of the exports, and similar trade imbalances are evident in Russia. Mexico and Saudi Arabia both spend twice as much on imported newspapers and magazines as they gain from newspaper exports.[46] Content analysis, the role of news wire services, and the world trade in published products all suggest that peoples, countries, and events in affluent postindustrial societies continue to be given disproportionately greater attention in the printed and electronic news than do poor nations.

New Information and Communication Technologies

The Internet adds another layer of complexity to these information flows. As a highly decentralized medium, with far lower costs for equipment and access than newspapers or television, it is well suited to supporting a large number of dispersed Web sites, blogs, and online social networks linking local communities, irrespective of geographic location. The new media also facilitates the production and transmission of digital video films, music, news, and advertising. Moreover, many computer hardware components and software products are produced in developing and middle-income nations, such as India, China, and Brazil. Nevertheless, the headquarters of the major transnational corporations in the computer industry – such as Microsoft, Google, and Apple – are located on the Pacific West Coast. During the mid-1990s, when the World Wide Web was starting to become more widely available, the contents were heavily dominated by postindustrial societies, especially the United States.[47] Since then, there is evidence of far greater diversification of contents, reflecting rapid diffusion of access.

Certain counterflows to trade patterns can also be observed, since information and communication channels have diversified in recent decades, especially through the simultaneous growth of online information and news sources. Multiple local sites of information are now available on the Internet, given the lower start-up and production costs

for the thousands of blogs, community and NGO Web sites, and online
videos posted around the world. Online news sites typically contain a
mix of international and domestic stories. Moreover, some emerging
economies have also expanded cultural trade within regional markets,
generating counterflows.[48] The growth of regional broadcasting has
been facilitated by the development of digital technologies and satellite networks, such as Sky TV in Europe, Star in Asia, and Al Jazeera
and Al Arabia as pan-Arabic media, which can tailor the contents of
international news, advertising, entertainment, and information to fit
the interests and cultural sensibilities of the people living within these
areas.[49] Regional hubs have facilitated a proliferation of multilingual
and multifaceted media contents and a North–South or East–West
contraflow in cultural trade.[50]

Numerous metrics are available to gauge the evolving geography
of the Internet and the diffusion of information and communication
technologies, including the distribution of telephone densities, PCs,
hosts, Web sites, and blogs, as well as indicators of connectivity for
governments, schools, hospitals, and rural areas.[51] But these are less
effective at monitoring the strength of networks and the complex interaction and volume of information traffic among countries using new
ICTs. One of the best ways to do this is to estimate the geographic
location of international hyperlinks, including outgoing linkages that
connect a Web page to another source located in another country and
incoming links that connect a source from another country to a Web
page. A study compared 174 countries in 1998 on this basis, finding
that postindustrial societies had the densest networks of hyperlinks,
both outgoing and incoming.[52] The direction of the information flow
can be calculated for each country and region, and the ratio between
the two can be compared, as is done for disparities in the value of cultural trade. The imbalances were particularly strong for poor regions;
in particular, sub-Saharan Africa had 10 times as many incoming as
outgoing links, while Southeast Asia had 20 times as many. In these
countries, information on the Internet flowed mainly from North to
South, with poor societies importing information from outside their
borders. By contrast, there was a relatively even balance of outgoing and incoming links on Web sites based in Europe and North
America.

Another indicator concerns the languages of online users and Web
sites, including the marked predominance of English during the early

years of the World Wide Web. Indicators of the linguistic contents of Web sites remain imprecise, but Global Research has been tracking the evolution of the non-English-speaking population that is online.[53] Countries are classified by the size of linguistic groups, and this figure is multiplied by the number of Internet users in each country to estimate the overall languages of those online. The results suggest that in the mid-1990s, when the World Wide Web was first becoming widely available, about 80% of all users were English speaking. By 2005, this proportion had dropped to only one-quarter of those online, while the proportion of Chinese, Japanese, or Spanish speakers had substantially increased. These estimates are only approximate, but they suggest a gradual broadening and diversification of the online population, a pattern that is consistent with the spread of access to new information and communication technologies in many middle-income nations, as examined in subsequent chapters. Despite these trends, relatively little online content is available in many of the world's languages, and English remains disproportionally represented among the online population: an estimated 300 million out of 1 billion Internet users.

Discussion and Conclusions

The evidence considered in this chapter confirms that the flow of information, including the expanding volume of trade in cultural goods and services, is predominantly from the global North to the South, as many observers have emphasized. In the trade in audiovisual services, including TV, film, and music, the United States has reinforced its preeminent market share of exports during recent years, expanding its lead over its closest rivals: Germany, the United Kingdom, France, and Canada. The market for cultural goods and services is fragmented and complex, involving a variety of sectors, but a few postindustrial societies continue to predominate in the manufacture and export of cultural goods and services, notably the United States, Germany, France, Britain, and Canada. Moreover, the audiovisual trade imbalance between the global North and South has widened during recent decades, despite the emergence of important regional hubs and contraflows among certain media sectors in some emerging economies.[54] Systematic evidence of trade in printed newspapers, magazines, and books suggests that a few major countries in North America and Western Europe also continue to dominate the export market here; in 2004–2007, half the total value of the world trade in publications was generated by exports from just four countries: the United States, the United Kingdom, Germany, and France. The exchange of information via the Internet is vast, complex, and difficult to identify, but the available data from analysis of the inflow of Web links also suggests a substantial imbalance between the global North and South.

The evidence examined here suggests that the direction and flow of global trade in cultural goods and services has expanded in recent decades, reinforcing the predominance of the United States and other major producer nations in this market. Proponents of cultural convergence may see this as reason to fear that an L.A. culture is sweeping the world, imposing the images and ideas of American capitalism and undermining national diversity. It is clear that many middle-income and emerging economies are net importers of American or Western culture. Billboards, TV screens, movie theaters, and newspaper headlines from Jakarta to Mumbai, Manila, Johannesburg, Moscow, Shanghai, Doha, and Santiago reflect imported images and ideas, and contain cultural messages about individualism, women's equality, and liberal sexuality that are at odds with the more conservative values of traditional societies. Emerging economies that import many audiovisual products and services – such as South Korea, Brazil, and Argentina – are potentially the most receptive to these developments. Yet at the same time the reach of these developments is limited, as a substantial gap persists between rich and poor nations. Small advanced industrialized economies, such as Belgium, Switzerland, and Sweden, are the most densely involved in communication ties with other societies. Certain emerging and middle-income economies, such as Turkey, Chile, Poland, and China, are becoming increasingly integrated with the rest of the world. The flow of cultural goods operates at four levels: local, national, world regional, and global. Traditional information and communication flows operate within the local community, through face-to-face interaction in the workplace, village meetings, and political rallies, supplemented by cell phones and text messaging at a distance, as well as through local newspapers, neighborhood Web sites, and community radio. Access to national daily newspapers, radio stations, and television channels facilitates information flows within the borders of the nation-state, connecting major metropolitan hubs with more distant provinces and rural villages. National broadcasting channels, in particular, are often viewed as an important component of nation building, especially in plural multicultural states. Public service broadcasters in many developing societies saw their role as providing programming that promoted socioeconomic development and cultural integration. Continental markets add another layer of complexity, which is especially important for regional hubs in some leading emerging economies such as Mexico, China, and South Korea. This pattern has led some observers to note that developing societies can potentially resist the dominance of the North and even generate a contraflow in cultural products.[55] The expansion in access to new ICTs also complicates the picture, providing new connections between the global and local. Nevertheless, like many other trade flows, the worldwide export and import of cultural goods generally reflects the disparities of power and wealth around the planet. Information continues to flow asymmetrically from Northern core to Southern periphery, and there is evidence that the predominance of the United States has expanded in recent decades.

Nevertheless, the people of many low-income societies and those living under restrictive regimes remain relatively isolated from global economic, social, and political networks. The impact of cultural trade and global information flows on poor countries remains limited, in large part because their domestic markets are restricted and relatively few people have access to modern forms of mass communications, for reasons discussed in the next chapter. Globalization has the greatest capacity to facilitate cultural convergence in cosmopolitan societies that have opened their borders to information flows, although even in this context there remain grounds for skepticism about the claimed effects of Americanization or Westernization. Whether global media actually do have the capacity to erode or transform national cultures remains to be seen. To explore these issues further, the following chapter examines the extent of public access to mass communication and information technologies. We can then look at the impact of global communications on cultural values in cosmopolitan and provincial societies.

4

Poverty

Mali has democratic institutions and few restrictions on the free press. The International Research and Exchanges Board (IREX) used the Media Sustainability Index to compare three dozen sub-Saharan African nations in 2006–2007. Mali ranked fourth highest in freedom of the press, just behind South Africa, Namibia, and Ghana.[1] IREX reports that legal protection of free speech is enforced, licensing of broadcast media is fair and competitive, and laws designed to prevent crimes against journalists are rigorously enforced. Even today, however, most of the population has limited opportunities to learn about the rest of the world. Mali is one of the least developed societies in West Africa, one of the poorest parts of the globe, and it is a land-locked country overlapping the Sahara, with poor transportation and few visitors. Public service TV and radio stations (ORTM) compete with more than 200 commercial and community radio stations. CNN, TV5Monde, and RTL are available on cable TV, along with sports and movies. Beyond those of the urban middle class, however, relatively few homes pick up these signals; only one in seven households has a TV set.[2] The telecommunication sector was partially privatized in 2002. A population of 12.3 million has access to 82,500 mainline and 1.5 million mobile cell phones, representing 12 phones per 100 people. One of the first African national dial-up Internet services was established in Mali in 2001, and it includes public access from a Bamako café and some hotels. The remote and dusty desert city of Timbuktu is home to ancient manuscripts and books, and also has a UNESCO-sponsored local telecenter, a pilot project offering public access to telephones, facsimile and Internet communications, and an official Internet Web site.[3] Nevertheless, today less than 1% of Malians (100,000) use the Internet.[4] There is a market for state-owned and privately owned newspapers and magazines, mostly published in French, such as the daily papers *L'Aurore*, *Le Republicain*, and *L'Independent*, concentrated in the capital of Bamako, but more than half the population remains illiterate. Subsistence farmers living in isolated towns and villages along the Niger River constitute almost three-quarters of the population and are largely cut off from the rest of the world.[5] Since the early 1990s, therefore, the underlying conditions of democratic governance, respect for human rights, and freedom of expression have favored the development of a flourishing independent news industry in Mali, but people's lives continue to be relatively untouched by 21st-century mass communications.

South Africa is a far more cosmopolitan society that has become an integral part of the modern globalized world. It has some similarities with Mali: both countries have about the same physical size, and both became democratic in the early 1990s. There the similarities end. As Table 4.1 indicates, South Africa is a middle-income economy with far higher levels of literacy, and communication and information technologies are much more widely available than in Mali. In major cities, such as Johannesburg and Cape Town, the media landscapes are similar to those in more affluent postindustrial societies. People can choose from an array of news and information sources, including daily newspapers, public service radio, programs, commercial news and talk radio programs, online sources, Web sites and e-mail, and the evening TV news, documentaries, and current affairs programs. More than half of all households possess a TV set, and public service, commercial, and pay TV are available in multiple languages. SABC, the public service broadcaster, comprises four television channels – three of them free-to-air, and the fourth, pay TV. The free-to-air channels (paid for by license fees and advertising) attract more than 17.5 million adult viewers daily, reaching 89% of the total adult TV-viewing population. SABC is committed to educating, informing, and entertaining, the Reithian trilogy, and to providing multicultural, multiracial, and multilingual programs for various sectors, regions, and age groups.[6] SABC Africa broadcasts across the continent and SABC News

TABLE 4.1. *ICTs in Mali and South Africa*

	Mali	South Africa
Physical size, total, million square miles	1.2	1.2
Population, millions, 2006 (World Bank)	13.9	47.4
Per capita GDP in U.S. $ PPP, 2007 (World Bank)	$250	$3,562
Literacy, % (World Bank)	46.4	86.4
Urban, % (World Bank)	31.0	59.8
Press Freedom Index, 100 points (Freedom House)	76	73
Globalization Index, 100 points (KOF, 2008)	40	63
Telephones		
Fixed telephone lines, total 2006 (ITU)	82,500	4.7 million
Cellular telephones subscribers, total 2006 (ITU)	1.5 million	39.7 million
Total telephones per 100 people, 2007 (ITU)	12	94
Radios		
Radio broadcast stations	AM 1, FM 230 (27 regional and government stations, and 203 private stations), shortwave 1 (2001)	AM 14, FM 347 (plus 243 repeaters), shortwave 1 (1998) SABC – state broadcaster with 20 regional and national services in 11 languages YFM 702 Talk Radio
Radio sets, total 2004 (ITU)	1.6 million	11.3 million
Radio sets per 100 people, 2004 (ITU)	12	24

	Mali	South Africa
Television		
Television broadcast stations	2 (plus repeaters) and 2 cable channels (2007) ORTM – state broadcaster; Multi Canal – cable multichannel; Tele-Kledu – cable multichannel	556 (plus 144 network repeaters) (1997) SABC – state broadcaster, 3 national TV networks, 2 pay-TV channels; e.tv – free-to-air commercial network; M-Net – pay TV
Households with a television set, %, 2000–2004	14.5	56.8
Newspapers		
Newspaper circulation, %, 2004 (UNESCO)	n/a	29.6
Newspaper titles, 2004 (UNESCO)	9	18
Internet		
Internet hosts, 2007 (ITU)	28	1.1 million
Internet users, total 2007 (ITU)	100,000	3.96 million
Internet users per 100 people, 2007 (ITU)	0.81	8.35
Computers per 1,000 people, 2005 (World Bank)	3.3	84.6

International, a 24-hour news channel, is available in several countries. The country is well integrated into global markets in cultural trade; in 2002 UNESCO estimated that South Africa exported about U.S. $57 million worth of cultural products (such as books, newspapers, recorded media, and audiovisual media) and imported about $309 million worth.[7] The 29th Durban International Film Festival featured more than 70 South African feature films, documentaries, and shorts, as well as movies from many other countries.[8] Internet use remains relatively low, but South Africa has 10 times as many users per capita as does Mali. The World Economic Forum's 2007 Network Readiness

Index ranked South Africa 51st out of 127 countries, ahead of such countries as China, Greece, Russia, and Mexico.[9] This level of connectivity provides major urban areas, where the majority of people live, with 24/7 access to real-time headlines from SABC, CNN International, and Google news. Fewer communication resources can be found in the rural areas and shantytowns of South Africa, but radio is a popular and cheap resource for news, music, and commentary. On average, there is almost one telephone per person, and a modern well-equipped telecommunication sector provides a reliable domestic and international service. In short, South Africa is a cosmopolitan society that is fully integrated into global communication networks.

There are striking differences between these media landscapes. As we shall demonstrate, the evidence indicates that Mali is not an exceptional case; similar patterns of information poverty exist in many of the world's poorest societies.[10] UNDP estimates that half a billion inhabitants – almost one-tenth of the world's people – live in the 25 nations characterized by low human development.[11] A lack of connectivity limits the capacity of global communications to reach isolated communities. The cultural convergence thesis assumes that the use of ICTs has gradually percolated down to almost all contemporary societies. This thesis assumes that exposure to Western- or American-produced popular entertainment and news information will gradually transform indigenous values in developing societies and thereby threaten traditional ways of life. If television and the Internet gradually penetrate previously isolated communities – even remote places such as Timbuktu – then logically this process could potentially undermine local cultures. But the argument underestimates the persistence of enduring patterns of social exclusion and the growing gap between rich and poor parts of the world in terms of access to nearly all types of ICTs. The products of the combined forces of leading multinational media corporations – the brand-name products typical of the Disney Corporation, Sony, and Microsoft – have flooded the market in OECD nations, but they have not yet penetrated the poorest societies, such as Mali, to any great extent. This is not a novel claim; during the past decade, numerous studies have highlighted the global digital divide in Internet connectivity and the broader phenomenon of information poverty – generally viewing it as negative.[12] What has been neglected in previous discussions, however, is the role of these well-known and growing disparities in limiting the capacity of global communications to touch lives in isolated societies.

What evidence supports this argument? This chapter documents patterns of access to ICTs. We start by considering the reasons for growing concern about the global digital divide, and we compare trends in the diffusion of the Internet and telecommunications, as well as levels of access to television sets, radios, and newspapers.[13] To understand some of the underlying reasons for these cross-national disparities, we compare media access across countries with different levels of economic development, establishing relative and absolute levels of inequality.[14] In addition, even within affluent nations, substantial disparities exist among social sectors in terms of both access to ICTs and regular use of the news media as an information resource. We draw on the 2005–2007 World Values Survey to estimate the size of these differences and to analyze the extent to which these gaps are shaped by four factors: *socioeconomic resources* (occupational class, household income, work status, and household savings); *cognitive and linguistic skills* (measured by education and the language used at home); *demographic characteristics* (including gender, age, and urbanization); and *motivational factors* (such as political interest and trust in the press and television). The conclusion summarizes the results and offers an interpretation of them.

Two key findings emerge. First, cross-national comparisons suggest that generalizations about the perceived threat of global communications to cultural diversity in the developing world are often exaggerated, and a more cautious interpretation of developments would be appropriate. *Societal-level* barriers to accessing information remain substantial. In particular, the diffusion of ICTs has been strong among the relatively well off sectors living in middle-income emerging economies, such as in South Africa, Taiwan, Mexico, and Hungary. These nations are characterized by free trade across national borders, democratic governments, and freedom of the press, as well as rapidly growing public access to a diverse array of modern communication technologies. At the same time, patterns of exclusion from access to ICTs persist in many of the world's low-income societies. There is not simply a digital divide in Internet access but a broader and more enduring phenomenon that does not seem to be fading away. Levels of access to the Internet, telephones, television, and even radio have been characterized by a deepening inequality between rich and poor countries during recent decades, not by gradual convergence.

Second, as others have reported, substantial information gaps remain among sectors and individuals living *within* societies. The individual-level models suggest that the primary drivers of patterns of media use to obtain news and information about society and the world include the cognitive skills that come with education, the material resources required to purchase TVs, computers and Internet access, and motivational interest. The news audience does not reflect the general population; there is a clear skew toward educated and affluent segments. This imbalance is clearest with respect to users of the Internet and newspapers, media with the highest demands for cognitive skills and literacy, while the audience for radio or TV news is slightly broader, although still socially biased toward the haves versus the have-nots. Before examining the impact of attention to news on attitudes and values, we therefore need to control for the demographic and social characteristics of the audience. These models will help to identify some of the most important variables that will be incorporated into the analysis of potential media effects in subsequent chapters.

Concern over the Digital Divide and Information Poverty

What first catalyzed growing concern about gaps in access to information in recent years? As use of the Internet surged during the middle to late 1990s, it became evident that many developing countries – and the poor people within these societies – were being left behind in this process and were thus excluded from the potential benefits of what has been termed the 'information society' or the 'knowledge-based economy.'[15] The Internet was launched in 1969, under the U.S. Defense Advanced Research Projects Agency research project, in order to transfer interlinking packet networks between computers.[16] This initiative facilitated file sharing and e-mail, but early access was limited to elite circles of scientific researchers, financial institutions, and commercial users located in the United States. The Internet evolved within the technological community over the next two decades, but widespread use among the general public took off only after the invention of hypertext in 1989, the launch of the first point-and-click Web browsers with embedded graphics a few years later (Mosaic in 1993,

Netscape in 1994, Internet Explorer in 1995), and thus the birth of
the World Wide Web. Globally the Internet population proliferated
from an estimated 3 million users in 1994 to more than 330 million by
the mid-2000s.[17] ITU figures indicate that in 2007, less than a decade
after the creation of hypertext, roughly 1.4 billion people – representing one-fifth of the world's population – were using the Internet.[18]

The early Internet era generated immense optimism, and a good
deal of hyperbole, about the capacity of technology to transform the
way people communicate, live, work, consume, network, and social-
ize. This raised concern about the digital divide, which excluded some
from partaking of the fruits of this new era. Numerous studies suggest
that ICTs contribute to economic growth, particularly by integrating
societies and businesses into the global marketplace for commodities,
manufactured goods, and services, raising levels of productivity in the
service sector, and providing new sources of employment, income, and
wealth.[19] They represent a development tool that can enable enter-
prising firms and local communities to address economic and social
challenges with greater efficiency; in poor villages and isolated rural
communities, for example, access to local telecenters or cell phones can
provide essential information about storm warnings and crop prices
for farmers.[20] Local governments connected electronically to official
records can help villagers locate medical information, birth and marriage certificates, and legal documents for land claims.[21] Moreover,
the broader potential of ICTs for strengthening innovative forms of
good governance, democratic participation, and civic engagement has
attracted considerable interest; for example, ICTs can be used for electoral administration and management, for connecting transnational
and local networks of NGOs working in civil society, as well as for
facilitating government consultation processes, public debate in the
'blogosphere,' and the interaction of virtual communities.[22] Much
effort has also gone into enlarging the deployment and use of specific software applications that address public sector challenges, such
as the efficient and effective delivery of public services in health care
and schooling, as well as more transparent and competitive processes
of contract procurement in local government.[23]

A loose coalition of agencies and bureaus of the United Nations
became involved in this issue, including divisions within UNESCO,
UNDP, the United Nations Department of Economic and Social Affairs

(UNDESA), the World Bank, and the ITU. These organizations collaborated with bilateral donors, national and local stakeholders, philanthropic foundations, and NGOs; they also developed private and public partnerships in conjunction with technology companies, including Microsoft, Google, Cisco, and Sun Microsystems.[24] Various programs were designed to expand the technological infrastructure and to strengthen skills, to facilitate access and network readiness, and to shrink the global disparities in Internet connectivity. Concern about the digital divide generated a series of reports that called for governments, corporations, and the nonprofit sector to address inequalities in access to ICTs. In 1998, UNESCO argued that economic divisions between the global North and South were exacerbated in a situation where most of the world's population lacked access to a telephone, let alone a computer, leaving poor societies increasingly at the periphery of communication networks.[25] The following year, the UNDP *Human Development Report* warned that productivity gains due to ICTs would widen the economic gap between the most affluent nations and those that lacked the skills, resources, and infrastructure to invest in the information society: 'The network society is creating parallel communications systems: one for those with income, education and literally connections, giving plentiful information at low cost and high speed; the other for those without connections, blocked by high barriers of time, cost and uncertainty and dependent upon outdated information.'[26] The 1999 *World Development Report* issued by the World Bank emphasized that OECD nations were benefiting from substantial productivity gains through ICTs and expanding their exports in global markets, and that emerging economies, such as Taiwan, Malaysia, Brazil, and India, had the capacity to leverage themselves profitably into niche ICT products and services. At the same time, the report warned that many poor societies lagged far behind in Internet access; they lacked the investment resources, telecommunications, computing infrastructure, and skill capacity to benefit from new ICTs, which could cause them to fall farther behind economically in the long term.[27] At the Lisbon Council in 2000, EU heads of states and government pledged to turn the European Union into the world's leading knowledge-based economy and to ensure that no citizens were excluded from the information society.[28] Heads of state at the G8 meeting a few months later in Okinawa echoed similar concerns.[29] World leaders came together to address this issue in a series of international meetings culminating in the World Summit on the Information Society (WSIS) meeting in Geneva in 2003 and Tunis in 2005.[30] The WSIS charter pledged to create an inclusive and development-centered information society 'where everyone can create, access, utilize and share information and knowledge, enabling individuals, communities and peoples to achieve their full potential in promoting their sustainable development and improving their quality of life.'[31] The charter established specific development targets for ICT infrastructure and access at national, household, and individuals levels, which were designed to be met by 2015, as well as concrete indicators of progress. To measure performance indicators and goals, the WSIS spurred new work on developing and monitoring internationally agreed-upon information and communication statistics.[32]

After the dot-com bubble burst in 2001, international stock markets punctured the inflated value of many start-up Silicon Valley ventures, and skepticism has grown about the developmental benefits of costly investments in ICTs rather than in basic infrastructure such as agriculture and health care.[33] In recent years it has become fashionable to dismiss the importance of addressing the digital divide, on the grounds that the social and global gaps will gradually fade away as costs fall, technologies become more user friendly, and markets do their work.[34] Other urgent problems have also recently grabbed the international headlines, from the security challenges of terrorism and internal conflicts, to the environmental threat of climate change, the economic effects of soaring oil prices, and problems of food security. Since 2001, the changing international agenda has lowered the priority of ICT development. On balance, however, the bursting of the dot-com bubble and other subsequent developments have facilitated a more realistic and dispassionate analysis of what ICTs can, and cannot, do. The digital divide attracts less attention in the news headlines, but many development and telecommunication agencies within the international community, such as the ITU, as well as many governments and civil society organizations, not only continue to support interventions that address social exclusion and expand Internet connectivity, but seek to strengthen the independent media sector and professional standards in news journalism.[35] It is therefore important to examine trends in access to ICTs over time and to analyze the reasons for any persistent and growing global disparities in order to identify the implications of future trajectories.

Cross-National Trends in Access to Information

Is there evidence that social and global inequalities in access to information are gradually lessening over time, as mass communications continue to diffuse – or do substantial disparities continue to exist, or even deepen? In analyzing trends and attempting to understand their implications, we need to go beyond the issue of the digital divide in Internet access and use. This represents an important issue, but it is only the most recent manifestation of the broader phenomenon of information poverty.[36] Across and within societies, as we shall show, enduring and widespread disparities exist in access to all forms of information and communication technologies, including the audio-visual sector (radio, television, and films), telecommunications, and the print sector, as well as dial-up and broadband connections to the Internet. Moreover, today it makes little sense to focus only on the digital divide in computing technology, because industries that once were regarded as distinct sectors are increasingly converging into multimedia enterprises; iPhones access DVD movies, the *New York Times* video can be watched on Tivo-enabled televisions, and cell phone snaps of breaking events appear on network TV. Indeed, even the conventional notions of 'news' and 'the news media' or 'access to the Internet,' once clear-cut, have fuzzier boundaries today.

To address these issues and clarify trends, we will start by comparing national indicators based on official statistics, standardized by international agencies such as UNESCO, the ITU, OECD, Eurostat, and the World Bank, based on time-series data for all countries where data are available. These sources have certain important limitations, however, including systematic bias in missing data, the need to determine the relevance of measurements to availability or use, and the necessity of finding the most appropriate unit of analysis for comparison.

Missing data are most prevalent in the least developed economies. For example, a third of these societies have no recent official statistics on the proportion of households that have a radio or TV set.[37] Missing data can arise from the absence of a recent official household or market research survey that monitors ownership of consumer durables. National statistical offices in the least developed economies often lack the capacity and resources to conduct reliable and comprehensive household surveys and censuses, and surveys are also problematic in fragile post-conflict states that contain a highly mobile population of displaced persons and refugees. As a result, estimates of the worldwide distribution of ICTs contain a systematic bias in missing data, potentially inflating these estimates.[38] Rapid changes in the use of ICTs make it important to have up-to-date annual estimates, and decennial population censuses are insufficient for this purpose. Some major ICTs indicators are now more than five years out of date or suffer from poor reliability and incomplete time series. UN agencies, including UNESCO, are currently taking steps to improve the international comparability and accuracy of statistical indicators for ICTs, but these initiatives will take time to bear fruit.[39] There have also been attempts to generate comprehensive multidimensional indicators. For example, since 2001 the World Economic Forum has published a composite Network Readiness Index for 127 countries, providing benchmarks to monitor the economic environment, technological infrastructure, and patterns of usage.[40] Given the serious limits of missing data in many developing countries, however, and systematic biases that can arise from their exclusion, more reliable and comprehensive coverage is provided by the analysis of separate indices.[41]

In addition, there is greater emphasis on gathering ICT statistics that measure the availability of technological products than on collecting more complex data on their use and impact. While counting the number of radio or television sets or personal computers in households is relatively straightforward, it is more difficult to assess levels of use – for example, whether Internet access is available at work, at home, or elsewhere, such as public libraries, cafés, or community telecenters. Some people have 24/7 Wi-Fi and fast broadband connections; others may access a particular Web site once a week or once a month. Some may use the Internet intensively every day for research and education, e-mail and file sharing, financial transactions, online gaming, and entertainment, while others may send an occasional text message. Are all these people equally 'Internet users'? The convergence of ICTs and the rapid development of new functions for ICTs complicate the measurement and comparisons over time. For example, YouTube was invented in a Menlo Park garage in February 2005; just a few years later, in a Fall

2007 survey, almost half of all American Internet users (48%) reported
that they had used YouTube or other video-sharing Web sites. This
figure rose to almost three-quarters (70%) of the younger generation
(those less than 30 years old).[42] The reliability of surveys on the access
and use of ICTs has improved over time, but we are still a long way
from standardizing these measures.

The unit of analysis should also be considered; for example, official records document the number of subscriber identity module (SIM)
cards that are issued by the telecommunication industry for mobile cell
phone accounts or the number of cell phones sold, but this does not
tell us the number of individual users.[43] Many people may have multiple SIM cards, exchanging them to gain coverage in different areas or
countries, or separate mobiles for use at home and at work. Convergence across sectors has also complicated the estimates of trends; for
example, official statistical offices maintain records of newspaper sales
and circulation figures, but this does not take account of the millions
of online readers. The number of television sets per household is also
a poor proxy for the number of viewers, not simply because of time-
displacement technologies such as VCRs and Tivo, but also because of
cross-national variations in social patterns of TV viewing and in the
average size of households.[44]

Bearing these important qualifications in mind, we can nonetheless
say that the international data provide the best available estimate of
trends over time and comparisons across countries and global regions.
For a cross-check, however, we can compare the estimates provided
from official statistics by international agencies with the aggregated
national-level results from self-reported media use available in the fifth
wave of the WSV, carried out in 2005–2007. If the estimates from
both sources are strongly correlated, this will increase our confidence
in the estimates. Conversely, if they differ substantially, we will need
to consider the potential reasons for the disparity.

Trends in Access to the Internet
Has access to the Internet gradually broadened to include most of the
population in developing societies, or do deep-rooted inequalities persist? During the 1990s, many who were aware of the digital divide
envisaged the necessity of distributing personal computers and wired
broadband connections (DSL, cable) so that people could gain access to

the Internet and e-mail; they thus foresaw the need for reliable electricity sources, keyboard skills and computer literacy, landline telephone infrastructure, and the like. But recent years have witnessed important technological innovations in this field that have reduced some of the technological hurdles to information access in poor societies and bypassed some of the obstacles. These include wind-up radios, solar-powered batteries, wireless connectivity (Wi-Fi, Wi-Max), $100 rugged laptops, Internet cafés, community telephone and Internet centers, and cell phones with data services, e-mail, and text messaging.[45] All of these developments may help to close the global digital divide. At the same time, some observers suggest that the core inequalities in access to information have persisted and may even have deepened.[46] Postindustrial societies and emerging economies that invested heavily in advanced digital technologies have reaped substantial gains in productivity. This may encourage them to build on their success and expand this sector of the economy even more. And it remains the case that, beyond isolated pockets of innovation, many of the poorest societies in the world continue to lack the basic infrastructure and resources to connect their rural populations to global communication networks and markets.

Despite a substantial surge in access to mobile cell phones with data services, the available evidence on the distribution of Internet users suggests that the relative gap between rich and poor societies worldwide has widened in recent years. Figure 4.1 illustrates the trends in access to the Internet from 1990 to 2007, based on data from the ITU measuring the average number of users per 100 inhabitants in each society. The graph compares high-, medium-, and low-income economies worldwide, based on per capita levels of GDP, with data from the World Bank measured in constant international dollars PPP. The graph illustrates the restricted size of the online population from 1990 until 1996, when use suddenly began to accelerate steadily and rapidly in high-income nations, continuing in the series until 2007, when the majority of the population living in these countries was online. Nevertheless, substantial variations remain even among these nations; for example, within the European Union, only one-fifth of all households in Bulgaria and Romania were connected to the Internet in 2007, compared with more than three-quarters of all households in the Netherlands, Sweden, and Denmark.[47] The graph shows that the

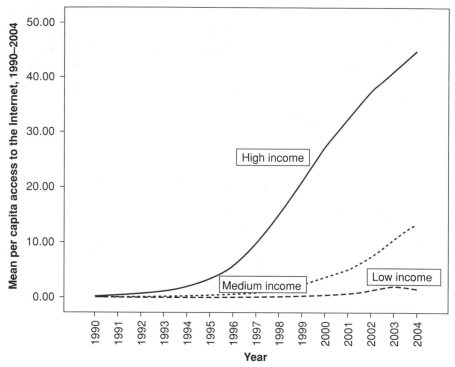

FIGURE 4.1. The Global Gap in Access to the Internet, 1990–2004. Societies worldwide are classified by per capita GDP in constant international dollars PPP. 'Low income' corresponds to less than $1,999 per capita income; 'medium income,' $2,000–$14,999; 'high income,' $15,000+. *Sources:* International Telecommunication Union; World Bank, *World Development Indicators,* 2008.

diffusion of the Internet among middle-income economies accelerated later than in richer nations, and most of these societies continue to lag far behind in Internet connectivity. By 2007, the latest year for which figures are available, just more than one-quarter of the population (29%) was online in middle-income societies, whereas almost twice that proportion of the population (58%) was online in high-income societies. In rapidly growing, emerging markets that are large consumers and producers of ICT goods and services, such as Brazil, China, Russia, South Africa, and India, the spread of Internet access and e-mail has been most extensive among the professional urban middle classes, often through data services via smart mobile cell phones rather than traditional computers.[48]

TABLE 4.2. *Indicators of Information Gaps Between Rich and Poor Societies*

	Low-Income Societies (i)	Middle-Income Societies (ii)	High-Income Societies (iii)	Gap Between Low- and High-Income Societies (i)–(iii)
Percentage of Internet users				
1997	0.06	0.81	9.74	9.68
2007	6.27	28.69	58.78	52.51
Percentage of all telephone, including cellular, subscribers				
1975	4.22	68.08	38.27	34.03
2007	31.20	97.48	152.54	121.34
Number of television sets per 100 people				
1975	0.19	7.60	30.79	30.60
2003	6.40	24.50	59.58	53.18
Number of radios per 100 people				
1975	5.26	19.63	64.04	58.78
1999	17.99	39.69	82.60	64.61
Newspaper circulation per 100 people				
1975	1.10	8.96	31.05	29.95
1999	1.22	8.11	25.71	24.49

Note: Societies worldwide are classified by per capita GDP in constant international dollars PPP. 'Low income' signifies less than $1,999 per capita income; 'medium income,' $2,000–$14,999; 'high income,' $15,000+.

Sources: Arthur S. Banks, Cross-National Time-Series Dataset, 1815–2007; World Bank, World Development Indicators, 2008.

By contrast, despite these trends, people living in the least developed societies around the world, such as Mali, continue to lack Internet access, including connectivity via computers with fast broadband connections as well as data service cell phones. The starkest contrasts are in Africa and Asia. Thus, the ITU estimates that fewer than 5 of every 100 Africans used the Internet in 2006, compared with 1 of every 2 people living in the G8 nations.[49] As Figure 4.1 illustrates, according to ITU estimates, Internet use has expanded only modestly in low-income societies during recent years, increasing from 0.06% of the population in 1997 to 6% a decade later. This is a large proportional increase, but the absolute level remains low. As shown in Table 4.2, the size of the global gap can be calculated to summarize the difference in the proportion of Internet users in low- and high-income societies; although the relative size of the gap diminished, the absolute size quintupled, from almost 10 percentage points in 1997 to 53 points in 2007. Access is gradually growing in most poor nations; places such as Mali are not untouched by these developments, but they lag far behind the rapid rate of diffusion of PCs, laptops, and smartphones with fast wireless and LAN broadband connections common in most affluent postindustrial nations, along with the related digital technologies through iPods, Tivos, personal digital assistants (PDAs), and similar devices.

To gain some insight into whether these estimates are reliable, we can compare the ITU data on the proportion of Internet users in a country in 2007 with the proportion of self-reported users of the Internet from the fifth wave of the WVS. In the survey, people were asked: 'People use different sources to learn what is going on in their country and the world. From each of the following sources, please indicate whether you used it last week or did not use it last week to obtain information . . . Internet, email.' The results of the comparison for the 51 countries where information is available from both sources, illustrated in Figure 4.2, show a striking correlation between the two series ($R = .864$, significant at $p < .001$, cubic $R^2 = .783$). The cubic regression slope is illustrated, with virtually all countries falling within the 95% confidence interval. The scatter plot confirms that the affluent societies show much higher use of the Internet, although a few of the relatively affluent medium-income countries, such as Malaysia, Slovenia, and South Korea, also fall into this category. Most middle-income countries, such as Brazil, Thailand, and South Africa, show moderate Internet access. Finally, the poorest countries show low levels of Internet use, although there are differences within this category, such as those between Morocco, India, and Burkina Faso. Given the differences in the methodology used by the ITU and the WVS, and in light of our discussion about the complexity of assessing Internet use, the strong correlation between the results from these two sources increases our confidence in these estimates.

Access to Landline and Cellular Telephones

Access to the Internet used to be limited by the availability of PCs and the need for dial-up connections through landline telephones. This represented a major bottleneck; in particular, state-controlled telecommunication monopolies in Central and Eastern Europe, Africa, and

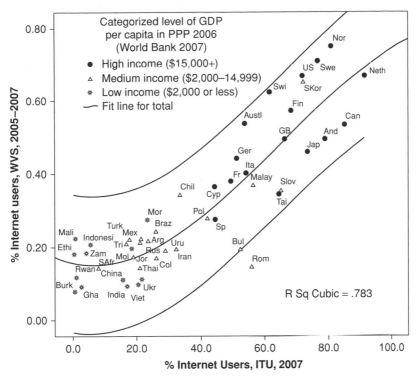

FIGURE 4.2. The Proportion of Internet Users Estimated from the International Telecommunication Union and World Values Survey. Societies worldwide are classified by per capita GDP in constant international dollars PPP. 'Low income' corresponds to less than $1,999 per capita income; 'medium income,' $2,000–$14,999; 'high income,' $15,000+. *Sources:* International Telecommunication Union; World Values Survey (2005–2007).

Asia often failed to provide universal services to many remote rural areas, and the demand for landlines lagged far behind supply.[50] Today Wi-Max and Wi-Fi connections have reduced the need for landline connections for Internet access, and the surge in the use of mobile cell phones, many of which provide data services, has been dramatic. Nevertheless, although mobile cell phones have reduced the barriers to Internet use and although they represent a cheaper technology, they have not totally eliminated global inequalities in Internet access or in telephony. The global disparities between rich and poor societies show a familiar pattern, with affluent countries expanding connectivity at the fastest rate. Figure 4.3 shows the trends in the per capita number of

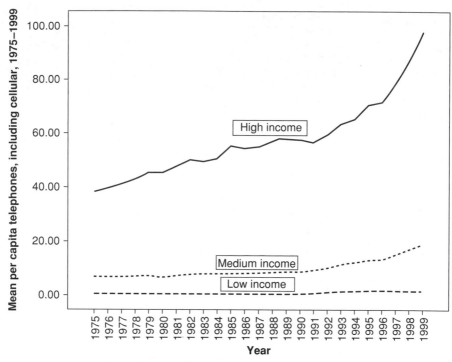

FIGURE 4.3. The Global Gap in Telephone Access, Including Cellular, 1975–
1999. Societies worldwide are classified by per capita GDP in constant international dollars PPP. 'Low income' corresponds to less than $1,999 per
capita income; 'medium income,' $2,000–$14,999; 'high income,' $15,000+.
Sources: Arthur S. Banks, *Cross-National Time-Series Dataset, 1815–2007*;
World Bank, *World Development Indicators, 2008*.

total telephone subscribers from 1975 to 1999, the latest available year
for the annual time series, combining both fixed landline and mobile
cellular subscribers. The comparison shows the substantial disparities
between high- and low-income economies, which gradually widened
during the 1970s and 1980s and then expanded rapidly during the
1990s.

   Since then, however, these disparities may be changing, as the number of fixed telephones lines in OECD countries largely stabilized from
2000 to 2006, while the number of landlines grew in developing societies.[51] Moreover, the spectacular growth in mobile cellular phones
has transformed the market. The 2008 World Summit on the Information Society report indicated that there were 3.3 billion mobile

subscribers at the end of 2007 – an increase of more than a billion users during the two years since 2005.[52] India, Brazil, Russia, and China each added many millions of users. Mobile cell phones are important for interpersonal communication and for extended social networks, especially in developing societies that lack the infrastructure for reliable and affordable landline telephones. Cell phones with data services facilitate e-mail, SMS texting, gaming, music, photos, videos, and mobile access to Web sites, bypassing the need for keyboard skills and expensive computing equipment. With small screens and limited speeds, however, they are most useful for obtaining brief information updates on the Internet – for example, checking the weather, bank accounts, flight departures, social networks, e-mail, or map directions – and they are still not as flexible, effective, or fast as PCs and laptops for surfing the Internet for extended periods of time. Nielsen Mobile, tracking usage in 16 countries, found that in mid-2008, nearly 40 million Americans (16% of all U.S. mobile users) used their handset to browse the Web, twice as many as in 2006, as higher-speed connections and unlimited data packages spread.[53] The United Kingdom, Italy, and Russia were the next highest in usage. But in Indonesia, Taiwan, India, and New Zealand, for example, less than 2% of mobile subscribers used their phone handset to surf the Web. Moreover, Nielsen Mobile found that while PC users surfed about 100 individual Web sites per month, mobile users visited about 6 domains. The most popular Web sites were Yahoo Mail, Google Search, and the Weather Channel. Data connection speeds will be faster with third-generation connections, once network footprints for this service expand. It is also difficult to determine the exact number of individual customers who have mobile phones, since many people have duplicate SIM cards, as noted earlier.[54] The ITU estimates that mobile penetration is now more than 100 percent in Europe. Nevertheless, even with the aggressive surge in cell phones, global disparities in access persist. In 2007, in the poorest countries, such as Burundi, Ethiopia, Sierra Leone, and Niger, less than 3% of the population subscribed to a mobile phone.[55] On average, in 2007 there were 152 telephone subscriptions per 100 people in high-income societies (including fixed and mobile accounts at home and work), compared with 31 in low-income societies. Again, poor developing countries have indeed expanded their telephone connectivity, but they started from a very low base, and the absolute

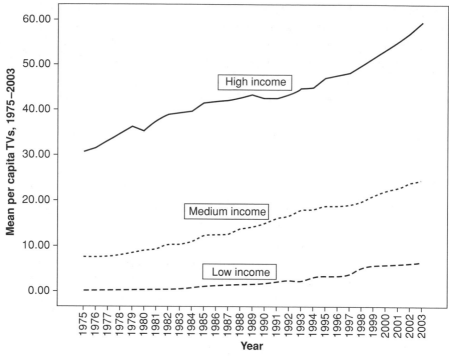

FIGURE 4.4. The Global Gap in Access to Television, 1975–2003. Societies worldwide are classified by per capita GDP in constant international dollars PPP. 'Low income' corresponds to less than $1,999 per capita income; 'medium income,' $2,000–$14,999; 'high income,' $15,000+. *Sources*: Arthur S. Banks, *Cross-National Time-Series Dataset, 1815–2007*; World Bank, *World Development Indicators, 2008*.

gap between rich and poor nations has grown over the past three decades.

Access to Radio, Television, and Newspapers

How do these trends compare with the diffusion of radio and television sets (whether connected via terrestrial, cable, or satellite signals), as well as the circulation and sales of newspapers? Figure 4.4 illustrates comparable trends from the mid-1970s until 2003 in the per capita distribution of television sets. Because television is an older technology, it might be expected that the diffusion rate should be flatter over time than that of new ICTs, and indeed this is what the trend indicates. In high-income societies, from 1975 to 2003 the average proportion

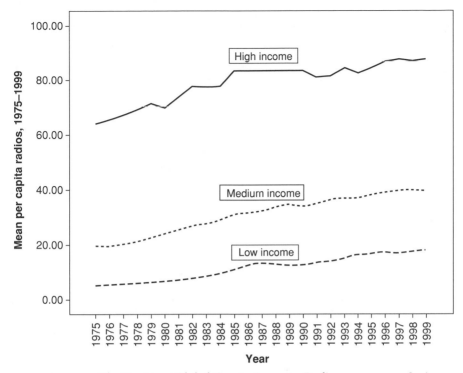

FIGURE 4.5. The Persistent Global Gap in Access to Radio, 1975–1999. Societies worldwide are classified by per capita GDP in constant international dollars PPP. 'Low income' corresponds to less than $1,999 per capita income; 'medium income,' $2,000–$14,999; 'high income,' $15,000+. *Sources:* Arthur S. Banks, *Cross-National Time-Series Dataset, 1815–2007*; World Bank, *World Development Indicators, 2008.*

of television sets roughly doubled, from 31 TVs for every 100 people in the population to 60. Middle-income societies saw a tripling of the per capita number of TV sets, rising from 8 to 24 per 100 people in the population. But both absolute and relative inequalities in access persisted; in low-income societies, there were only 6 television sets per 100 people. The absolute global gap (summarizing the difference between the proportion of television sets in low- and high-income societies) almost doubled from about 30 percentage points in 1997 to 53 in 2007.

Listening to the radio is one of the most important ways that people in developing societies learn about the world. Figure 4.5 shows that with this old electronic technology, the rate of diffusion is less dramatic

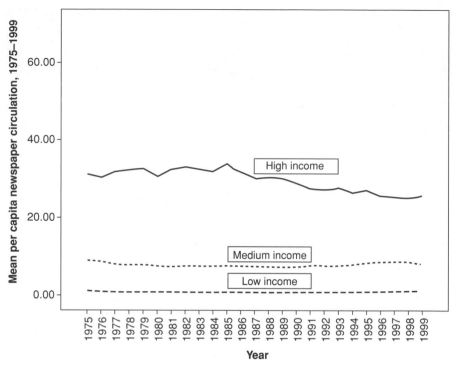

FIGURE 4.6. The Eroding Global Gap in Access to Newspapers, 1975–1999. Societies worldwide are classified by per capita GDP in constant international dollars PPP. 'Low income' corresponds to less than $1,999 per capita income; 'medium income,' $2,000–$14,999; 'high income,' $15,000+. *Sources:* Arthur S. Banks, *Cross-National Time-Series Dataset, 1815–2007*; World Bank, *World Development Indicators, 2008*.

than that of TVs, telephones, or the Internet. In high-income societies, there is an increase in the number of radios as a proportion of the population, but this rise stabilized in the 1990s as the market became saturated, with roughly 83 radios per 100 people. From 1975 to 1999 the proportion of ratios tripled in medium-income societies, from 7 to 25 per 100 people. A modest rise in the availability of radios also occurred in low-income societies, but according to the latest figures, on a per capita basis, almost five times as many radios are available in rich as in poor societies.

UNESCO gathers statistics on the number of outlets and the distribution, circulation, and sales of printed daily newspapers and periodicals. When the data are standardized on a per capita basis, the trends illustrated in Figure 4.6 show that this is the only media where there has been a growing convergence between high- and low-income societies. But this is not because of a significant expansion of readership or circulation figures in the low- or medium-income countries; it reflects an erosion of newspaper circulation figures in the high-income countries ever since the mid-1980s (predating the rise of online newspapers on the Internet). Even with this closure, the gap in newspaper circulation between rich and poor nations remains substantial. Multiple readers may compensate somewhat for the contrasts in sales and circulation, but on a per capita basis, 1 newspaper per 100 people is sold in low-income countries, compared with 26 per 100 in rich countries. Rising levels of literacy in developing societies have not substantially increased sales of daily papers. Comparisons of the distribution of published books and periodicals show similar disparities.

Individual-Level Inequalities in Access to Information

In addition to these cross-national disparities, a related and even more complex form of inequality exists; even within affluent postindustrial economies, such as the United States, some citizens have far greater access to and use of information sources than others. Even among those with access, people differ significantly in their regular exposure and attention to mass communications and news sources, and this pattern usually reflects social and demographic groups within each country. The 'social information gap' refers to individual-level disparities that are closely associated with socioeconomic resources (measured by household income, household savings, work status, and occupational social class), cognitive skills (measured by education and language), demographic characteristics (age and gender), and motivational factors (such as interest and trust in the media). During the early 1970s, the 'knowledge gap' was first noticed by scholars, whereby a group of well-educated people, who already have more information than others, acquire more information from the media, and by contrast, those with a low level of education, who already know less than others, acquire less information.[56] Educational and socioeconomic differences are thereby thought to be reinforced over time, not mitigated, by attention to the news media.

Broader patterns of selective exposure to news are not simply linked to education and social class, however, as there are also generational and age-related patterns of news consumption. For example, cell

phones with data services and wireless handheld PDA devices are particularly common among the younger generation in the United States.
These devices facilitate on-the-go texting and e-mail communications,
sharing digital photos, and viewing YouTube videos, Accuweather
forecasts, or GPS maps, in coffee shops, airports, and traffic jams. But
this does not necessarily mean that members of the younger generation have become heavy consumers of online news from traditional
media sources, such as CNN and the *New York Times*.[57] Readership
of newspapers is usually found to be skewed toward the older population, as has viewership of television, due to the sedentary nature of
this activity. A comparative study of newspaper readership in European societies since the early 1970s showed that social background
continued to be an important predictor of who does and does not regularly read the newspaper, although educational and gender differences
diminished gradually over time.[58] The same study demonstrated that
the social profile of those who watch the news in Europe also widened
over the same period, as the audience expanded in size. Race-related
patterns of news consumption have also been widely documented in
the United States, while there are continuing debates about the role
of race and ethnicity in determining the contemporary use of the
Internet.[59]

Most of the recent evidence concerning these issues has been derived
from studies of Internet access in postindustrial societies, especially
the United States and Europe. During the 1990s, for example, the
U.S. Department of Commerce generated a series of reports, *Falling
through the Net*, drawing attention to patterns of exclusion among
African-American and rural communities.[60] It was claimed that some
of these social gaps had closed over time, although this interpretation
was subsequently challenged by other studies.[61] Similar concerns about
the digital divide became common in other affluent postindustrial
societies; for example, the OECD and the European Union reported
parallel social disparities in computer and Internet access, reflecting
differences in income, social class, and employment status, education, generation, ethnicity/race, gender, and urbanization.[62] Debate
during the 1990s focused on whether the social gaps in the online
population would become a permanent feature of information societies, with social and employment status determined by levels of technological connectivity and skills, or whether these differences in the

online population would gradually fade away over time or 'normal-ize,' as costs fell and the technology became more user friendly – for example, once text messaging and Web browsers became cheaper and more widely available through smart cell phones.[63] Tracking surveys conducted by the Pew Internet and American Life Project since 2000 have documented a gradual closure of the gender gap in Internet use in the United States, but the persistence of a 10-point gap between black and white populations and a massive 55-point generational gap between those under 30 and those over 65.[64] Scattered research has explored similar disparities in other countries, but it remains to be seen whether they reflect a general pattern.[65]

We therefore need to explore not just patterns of Internet access but also the reported use of the broader range of news media. Identifying the most effective public policies for overcoming the global and social information gaps, and predicting future trends, require a careful examination of the underlying drivers of these gaps. What are the most plausible explanations of these disparities? During the past decade, research in the scholarly literature and in the policy community has focused on understanding the economic, political, and sociological reasons for lack of connectivity to new ICTs.[66] Here a helpful analyti-cal strategy is to distinguish between explanations of the digital divide in access to new ICTs (typically focused on indicators such as the distribution of Internet hosts and users, the availability of hardware such as laptops, PCs, and smartphones, and the price and availability of broadband or wireless connectivity) and explanations concerned with broader patterns of information inequality across a wide range of media sources.[67] If global inequalities are confined to access to new ICTs, the most appropriate explanation (and the most effective policy interventions) might rest on factors closely related to this medium. Thus, one might focus on the cost of computer hardware, software, and Internet service connection charges; the telecommunication infrastruc-ture supporting dial-up, broadband (such as DSL, cable, fiber), and third-generation wireless (Wi-Fi, Wi-Max) connections; the regulatory environment in telecommunications and bottlenecks arising from gov-ernment policies and lack of market competition; the computing and literacy skills necessary for people to use these technologies effectively, creating, for example, their own community Web sites, networks, and blogs; and the predominance of English-language contents, which characterized much of the World Wide Web during the early years, limiting access by non-English speakers.[68]

But if a lack of connectivity to ICTs closely reflects disparities that persist across and within societies in access to other, more traditional mass communication channels – including radio and television sets, newspapers, magazines, and books, and telephones – then this suggests that the causes are not specific to the medium itself.[69] One doesn't need keyboard or literacy skills to switch on a radio or TV. Instead, information inequalities in poor societies may be attributed to more deep-rooted problems of economic development, such as endemic poverty, low levels of education and cognitive skills, not to speak of a lack of a reliable electricity supply, which would also hinder access to traditional mass media such as television.[70] Major utilities supplying power grid and transmission lines often fail to serve remote areas; in Ethiopia, for example, less than 1% of the rural population and only 13% of all households have access to electricity.[71] The growth in population is outstripping the growth in connections, leading to an increase in the proportion of Ethiopians without electricity. Half the population cannot read. Innovative projects, such as distributing $100 laptops, free wind-up radios, and solar-powered flashlights, will not solve these basic developmental problems. Unless broader social and economic inequalities are addressed, it will remain difficult for the flow of information and news about the world to penetrate beyond elites in poor societies and to affect public opinion more generally. It may well be the case that journalists, politicians, diplomats, and business leaders in Dubai, Kuala Lumpur, and Addis Ababa are densely networked via laptops and smartphones, and receive information about world affairs from headline stories on CNN International, Google News, and BBC World. But this does not mean that poorer people in these countries will have affordable access to these resources.

How do we explain these disparities? To examine these issues, for the individual-level analysis we draw on the fifth wave of the WVS, which monitored the regular use of a variety of news and information sources in 51 societies. As discussed in Chapter 2, these data allow us to construct an overall summary media use scale, generated by summing self-reported weekly use of newspapers, radio or TV news, the Internet, books, and magazines as information sources 'to learn what is going on in your country and the world,' with the mean 5-point score standardized to 100 points for ease of comparison. This evidence allows us to compare four types of individual-level factors that account for use of the news media in high-, medium-, and low-income societies. Demographic characteristics include age (in continuous years) and gender. Socioeconomic resources include household income, household savings, work status, occupational class, and urbanization. Cognitive skills are measured by highest educational qualification and language (whether English is used at home). And motivational factors are indicated by political interest and trust in newspapers and television. Technical Appendix A provides a description of the coding and construction of all variables.

The results in Table 4.3 demonstrate that among these individual-level factors, education is one of the strongest predictors of news media use, being significant across all societies, with the strongest impact in low-income societies. This relationship is to be expected because education is closely related to literacy, which is essential for reading the newspaper and using the Internet, and also provides the cognitive skills and background knowledge that help people process complex information about current events and public affairs in the news. After education, household income proved a strong and significant predictor across all types of society; as already observed, money is necessary to buy TVs and radio sets and to access cable, satellite, and pay-TV services, as well as to subscribe to the Internet and buy newspapers on a regular basis. More affluent households are more likely to be able to afford these services than less affluent ones. Among the demographic predictors, the age effect proved significant and negative across all types of economies, reflecting the fact that those in the younger generations were more likely to use the news media than were older people. The gender gap was reversed by type of economy, with women predominating in the news media audience in the rich countries, but men predominating in poorer societies. Social class, however, demonstrated a more complex pattern; it played a significant role in predicting news use in medium- and low-income nations, but not in more affluent societies. This pattern suggests that the class disparities in use of the news media are greatest in countries where access is relatively limited, but that once access diffuses throughout the population, class differences in use of the news media may fade. Finally, both political interest and trust in the news media had a significant effect in all societies,

TABLE 4.3. *Explaining Individual-Level Patterns of Media Use in High-, Medium-, and Low-Income Societies*

	High-Income Economy				Medium-Income Economy				Low-Income Economy			
	B	S.E.	Beta	Sig.	B	S.E.	Beta	Sig.	B	S.E.	Beta	Sig.
Demographic characteristics												
Age (years)	−0.041	.012	−.029	***	−0.040	.001	−.062	***	−0.172	.012	−.090	***
Gender (male = 1)	−1.81	.369	−.036	***	1.145	.023	.013	n/s	1.23	.372	.022	***
Socioeconomic resources												
Income	1.08	.078	.112	***	2.05	.005	.114	***	1.59	.089	.121	***
Work status	3.07	.409	.061	***	1.05	.028	−.037	***	−0.472	.432	−.008	n/s
Professional/managerial	−0.047	.546	.000	n/s	4.15	.047	.076	***	8.57	.692	.095	***
Other nonmanual class	−0.265	.511	−.004	n/s	6.06	.045	.095	***	9.61	.751	.091	***
Skilled manual class	−1.552	.535	−.023	**	0.819	.030	.048	***	2.69	.603	.032	***
Cognitive skills												
Education	2.67	.097	.234	***	4.04	.007	.307	***	5.25	.087	.436	***
Language (English = 1)	−1.10	.428	−.019	**	9.84	.040	.100	***	16.88	2.17	.049	***
Motivational attitudes												
Political interest	5.49	.203	.205	***	2.79	.012	.084	***	2.64	.186	.093	***
Trust in newspapers and TV	0.519	.139	.027	***	0.779	.007	.080	***	−0.377	.112	−.022	***
Constant	27.7				2.10				5.52			
Adjusted R^2	.177				.256				.348			
No. of respondents	16,222				24,822				16,347			

Note: The results of individual-level OLS regression models with the 5-point media use scale (combining use of newspapers, radio/TV, Internet, books, and magazines for information) as the dependent variable. All models were checked by tolerance tests to ensure that they were free of multicollinearity problems. See Technical Appendix A for details about the measurement, coding, and construction of all variables. *p = .05; **p = .01; ***p = .001.

Source: World Values Survey (2005–2007).

and in the expected direction, with high levels of interest and trust being linked with high media use – with one exception: in low-income nations, the relationship between trust and media use was reversed. The overall fit of the models indicated by the adjusted R^2 suggests that social and demographic characteristics (especially education, income, and occupational class) proved the strongest predictors of news use in low-income societies, whereas these factors played less important roles in high-income societies.

How does this pattern vary by type of media? Table 4.4 shows similar models for the use of newspapers, radio/TV, and the Internet, adding level of economic development (per capita GDP measured in PPP) as a further control and using logistic regression due to the binary dependent variables. The results confirm the importance of education and the cognitive skills associated with it: education had a significant and strong impact on all types of media use, especially newspapers and the Internet. Figure 4.7 illustrates this pattern graphically; in each case the most highly educated exhibit the highest news media use, but the disparities between high- and low-income groups are particularly strong in poor societies. By contrast, in relatively affluent societies, there is a flatter educational profile for newspaper readers and the TV or radio news audience. The age profile, illustrated in Figure 4.8, shows the pattern that has been widely observed for affluent societies: while newspapers and TV or radio news draw on an older readership, Internet use is skewed toward the younger generation. But in low-income societies, the younger generation is more likely to access all forms of news media information than the older age groups, including newspapers and TV or radio news as well as the Internet. This suggests that the rapidly rising levels of primary and secondary schooling, literacy, and access to higher education that accompany human development in poor societies have probably strengthened the cognitive skills, and thus media use, of those in the younger generation more than their parents and grandparents. Familiarity with the English language was also linked with use of the Internet and newspapers, but not with audiovisual media, which are more likely to be available in local languages. The material resources of household income and savings were also related to use of all types of media, while social class was significant across most categories, with higher class being particularly closely linked with greater use of newspapers and the Internet. Men

TABLE 4.4. *Explaining Individual-Level Patterns of Use of Newspapers, Radio/TV, and the Internet, All Societies*

	Newspapers			Radio/TV			Internet		
	B	S.E.	Sig.	B	S.E.	Sig.	B	S.E.	Sig.
Economic development									
Log per capita GDP in PPP	0.346	.007	***	0.255	.010	***	0.600	.009	***
Demographic characteristics									
Age (years)	0.007	.001	***	0.014	.001	***	−0.041	.001	***
Gender (male = 1)	0.264	.019	***	−0.004	.029	n/s	0.286	.022	***
Socioeconomic resources									
Income	0.111	.006	***	0.046	.007	***	0.149	.005	***
Professional/managerial	0.377	.034	***	0.234	.057	***	0.437	.034	***
Other nonmanual class	0.535	.033	***	0.361	.056	***	0.409	.032	***
Skilled manual class	0.297	.026	***	0.325	.042	***	−0.190	.032	***
Cognitive skills									
Education	0.247	.005	***	0.186	.007	***	0.311	.006	***
Language (English = 1)	0.191	.037	***	0.077	.064	n/s	0.255	.035	***
Motivational attitudes									
Political interest	0.266	.010	***	0.205	.015	***	0.206	.012	***
Trust in news media	0.057	.006	***	0.115	.009	***	−0.045	.008	***
Constant	−5.8			−2.74			−7.49		
Nagelkerke R^2	.272			.114			.410		
% correctly predicted	71.4			89.6			78.9		
No. of respondents	58,301			57,570			57,177		

Note: The results of individual-level binary logistic regression models with each of the indicators for use of newspapers, radio/TV, and Internet, as the dependent variables. All models were checked by tolerance tests to ensure that they were free of multicollinearity problems. See Technical Appendix A for details about the measurement, coding, and construction of all variables. *p = .05; **p = .01; ***p = .001.

Source: World Values Survey (2005–2007).

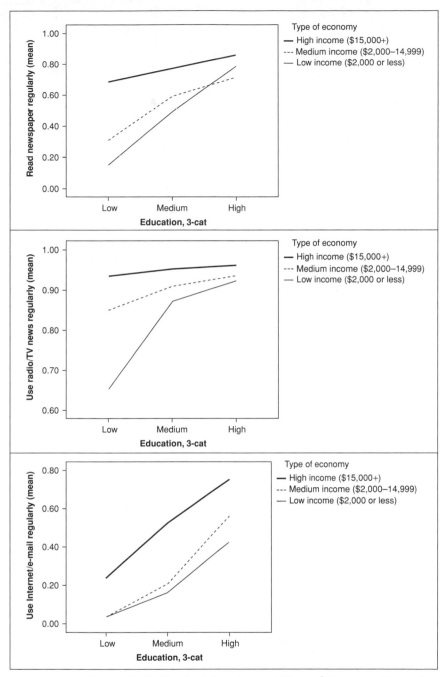

FIGURE 4.7. News Media Use by Education and Type of Economy. Type of economy is classified by per capita GDP in PPP (World Bank, 2007). Regular use of newspapers, radio/TV, and the Internet/e-mail media for information is based on the World Values Study (2005–2007).

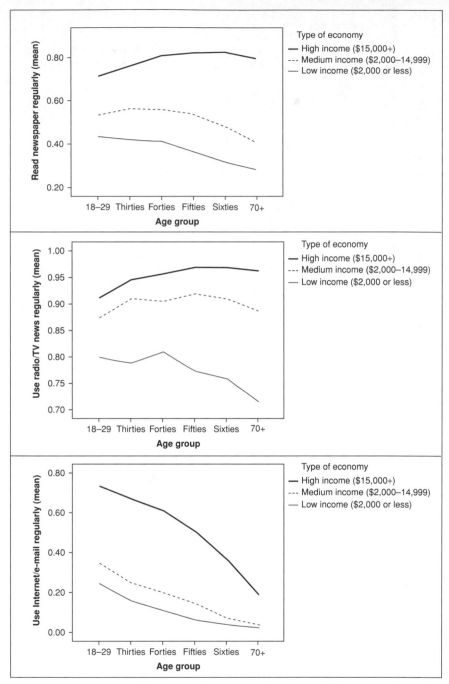

FIGURE 4.8. News Media Use by Age Group and Type of Economy. Type of economy is classified by per capita GDP in PPP (World Bank, 2007). Regular use of newspapers, radio/TV, and the Internet/e-mail media for information is based on the World Values Study (2005–2007).

were more likely than women to use newspapers and the Internet, while there was no gender gap in the use of TV or radio. Finally, political interest was significant, and trust in newspapers and TV was linked with the use of these media. The overall fit of the model suggests that these social characteristics are better at predicting who will be Internet and newspaper users, while radio and TV attracted a broader and more socially diverse audience. The general pattern suggests that the social profile of newspaper readers and Internet users is relatively similar in terms of resources, motivation, and skills, with the most important difference in affluent nations linked with age. The strong similarity across use of these two media suggests that similar factors are driving usage in both cases, and that we do not need to focus on factors that are unique to the Internet, such as the cost or availability of broadband Internet service providers, keyboard skills, or the availability of computers.

Discussion and Conclusions

Inequalities in access to information are important for many reasons. In this book, we focus on how they affect the impact of global communications on cultural change. Our core model hypothesizes that inequalities in access to information operate in a sequential filtering process, and in this way serve as one of the main factors that limit the impact of global communications on national cultures (see Figure 2.1). In earlier chapters, we discussed how given states actively restrict what can be seen or read; the autocracies that Reporters sans Frontières rates worst in terms of freedom of the press, such as Eritrea, Belarus, and North Korea, control state monopolies of TV broadcasting and newspapers, repress independent reporters, journalists, and bloggers, and use software filters to censor online Web sites and Internet service providers.[72] Less draconian protectionist barriers at national borders also act as bottlenecks on cultural imports through common practices such as trade tariffs, customs regulations, and telecommunication policies.

This chapter has demonstrated that even in cosmopolitan societies with permeable trade borders and widespread respect for freedom of expression, the impact of foreign ideas and information can also be severely curtailed if patterns of social exclusion limit equitable and affordable access to the channels of mass communications. Isaiah

Berlin emphasized the classic distinction between negative and positive liberty.[73] Negative liberty represents constraints on the individual that explicitly restrict certain fundamental freedoms and human rights – for example, where states actively curtail opportunities for expression, movement, or assembly. Legal and constitutional guarantees of freedom of the press are a necessary condition for facilitating a pluralist and independent news media industry, but this is insufficient by itself to ensure equitable and inclusive access to mass communications. Positive liberty, on the other hand, requires active interventions so that people have the opportunity to achieve their goals. In this regard, communication policies, NGOs, and private–public partnerships implement programs that are designed to remove important obstacles to accessing information, such as a lack of investment in the telecommunication infrastructure, a lack of affordable equipment, or a lack of cognitive and technical skills. Thus, many countries specify that telecommunication companies have an obligation to provide universal service, spreading the costs of connectivity across all customers, so that remote areas are guaranteed affordable service. Licensing policies requiring national broadcasters to provide a certain proportion of programming in minority languages, or for specific cultural regions and groups, also reflect these principles. In the same way, policies designed to overcome problems of exclusion from information and communication technologies require active intervention to address these issues.

In affluent countries with a pluralistic free press and with open borders to cultural imports – such as the United States, Australia, and Sweden – there continue to be significant inequalities in the extent to which various groups and social sectors are connected to new ICTs. Marked disparities with respect to age, class, and education characterize access to PCs, the Internet, mobile cell phones, PDAs, and related electronic devices. But the digital divide is not a new phenomenon; as we have seen, these patterns reflect broader disparities in access to traditional media channels, including television, radio, landline telephones, and daily newspapers and magazines. In poor societies, community radios are an important resource, especially in rural areas, and subscriptions to mobile cell phones with data services are rapidly growing in popularity. Nevertheless, widespread illiteracy limits the circulation and readership of the press outside the educated professional middle classes in major cities. Household ownership of TVs also remains restricted, and there is an even smaller market for paid sub-scriptions to cable and satellite services. Relatively few fixed landline telephones are available, and service is often expensive and unreliable. Despite the recent surge in the use of data-enabled wireless mobile cell phones, access to the Internet remains even more restricted. Lack of media access insulates many traditional national cultures from modern values – whether one considers exposure to them good or bad.

The evidence considered in this chapter leads to three main con-clusions. First, in *absolute* numbers, recent years have seen a remark-able surge in access to ICTs, especially in postindustrial societies. The worldwide expansion of the online population has obviously been most striking; the first working prototype for the World Wide Web was built in 1990; today, an estimated 1.4 billion people use the Internet.[74] There has also been rapid growth in the adoption of mobile cell tele-phones; today the ITU estimates that there are about 3.3 billion mobile cell phone subscribers, in a world of about 6.7 billion people.[75] Cell phones expand social networks and communications, and those with data services facilitate flexible access to e-mail, text messaging, and the Internet. Major emerging markets, such as Malaysia, Russia, China, Brazil, and India, have registered some of the most substantial gains in connectivity, but growth has also been relatively rapid across Africa. In affluent postindustrial societies and in many emerging middle-income economies, such as South Africa, there has been an expansion in the availability of many other related ICTs, including landline telephones, household radios and TVs, facsimile and DVD machines, personal and laptop computers, as well as dial-up, broadband, and wireless Internet connections.

Second, despite these important developments, we demonstrate that, far from gradually closing, the *absolute* gap in levels of access to mass communication and information technologies, which divides the richest and poorest societies, has expanded in recent years. Advanced industrialized economies have pulled farther ahead of the rest of the world in information access, as they started the technology race with greater financial resources for investment in high-tech industries, a deeper and wider pool of people with technical and scientific skills, and an established telecommunication infrastructure. The public has relatively little access to ICTs in the least developed and poorest coun-tries in Africa and Asia. Nevertheless, many of the new digital ICTs have become widely available only during the past decade, and in the longer term, patterns of technological diffusion, societal development, and generational turnover may help to close the global and social information divides. But there is little evidence that can be gleaned from available international statistics that this process is already under way, even with access to old media such as radio, TV, and newspapers. In recent decades, the poorest nations have not been catching up; they have been falling farther behind.

Finally, social inequalities in access to ICTs have persisted in recent years, and most show no signs of diminishing, even within the richest nations, such as the United States, Sweden, and Australia.[76] Many recent technological accounts imply that information gaps are confined to the use of PCs and the Internet, but the evidence indicates that these inequalities apply to other kinds of media exposure and reflect deep-seated social inequalities based on cognitive skills, socioeconomic resources, and motivational attitudes. The models presented here help to identify some of the most important variables, including education, income, and age, that will be incorporated in subsequent analyses of the strength of media effects on social and political attitudes and values.

On the basis of these observations, we conclude that the perceived threat of global communications on cultural diversity in developing societies has often been exaggerated, and a more cautious interpretation of developments is more appropriate. If modern ideas and images from Google, Disney/ABC Television, or the Murdoch newspaper empire do not actually reach poor people living in isolated places such as Timbuktu and Thimpu – regardless of the effects of state restrictions on freedom of expression, trade barriers, or social psychological filters – the multinational media corporations are unlikely to pose an immediate threat to traditional lifestyles, values, or beliefs in these communities. It is possible that there could be indirect effects, as ideas gradually percolate down from the more affluent and educated groups with access to ICTs, until they eventually penetrate the society at large. One does not need media access to be aware of the messages reflected in billboards and posters, and deregulation of broadcasting in recent decades has generated a substantial increase in the number of commercial radio stations. In the long term, processes of economic development gradually expand public access to the mass media throughout societies, and this process can be accelerated, as shown by the rapid social shifts that have transformed communications in cities with concentrations of high-tech industries, such as Bangalore, Seoul, and Shanghai. But the persistence of substantial global and social inequalities in access to information during recent decades has been underestimated. It reflects deep-rooted disparities in resources. And it suggests that the claims about the threat of either cultural convergence or polarization may have been overstated.

5

Classifying Societies

We have examined evidence of the extensive and growing international market for the exchange of audiovisual goods and news information services. Global trade in creative goods and services almost doubled in value during the past decade and now accounts for more than 7% of the world's gross domestic product.[1] This expansion was fueled by many factors, including the diffusion of ICTs, reductions in trade barriers, and the marketing and distribution of cultural exports by transnational media corporations. The United States and Europe are the dominant producer nations on the supply side; although China's role is expanding in some sectors, developing countries generated less than 1% of global cultural exports. But which countries are fueling the demand for these products? To explore the reasons for these patterns, this chapter develops a Cosmopolitanism Index that measures the permeability of societies to inward information flows. The term 'cosmopolitan communications' is conceptualized to represent the degree of information flowing across national borders, which includes the extent to which people interact today within a single global community and the extent to which these networks remain localized and parochial.[2] The terms 'cosmopolitan' and 'parochial' are employed here descriptively without any normative judgment about either type of society. Cosmopolitan communications are understood to reflect openness toward ideas and information derived from divergent cultures, as well as a growing awareness of other places and peoples, including their languages, habits, and customs. Greater understanding and broader knowledge about other countries are generally viewed as desirable, but they can also be seen as reflecting a superficial familiarity with world cultures and a loss of identity. There are some recognized advantages to being deeply immersed in dense communication networks rooted in one particular local community. In practice, all contemporary societies reflect a mix of local and global information sources, and there are important variations among social sectors within countries. But there is also a recognizable continuum stretching from one extreme, the most isolated and parochial societies at the periphery of communication networks, exemplified by rural and illiterate groups living in Myanmar (Burma), North Korea, Syria, and Rwanda, to the other extreme, consisting of highly educated groups in Switzerland, Luxembourg, and Sweden, which are densely interconnected with information flows from the rest of the world.

The idea of cosmopolitan communications is operationalized here in terms of three closely related aspects. External barriers include the degree to which national borders are open or closed, whether imports of cultural goods and services are limited by tariffs, taxes, or domestic subsidies, and the extent to which there are restrictions on the movement of people through international travel, tourism, and labor mobility. To compare the extent to which countries are integrated into international networks, we draw on the KOF Globalization Index. This provides comprehensive annual indicators of the degree of economic, social, and political globalization in 120 countries around the world since the early 1970s.[3] Limits on media freedom restrict news and information within societies; they do so through the legal framework, which governs freedom of expression and information (e.g., penalties for press offenses); intimidation, which affects journalists and the news media (e.g., imprisonment, deportation, and harassment of reporters); and state intervention in the media (e.g., state monopolies of broadcasting, political control over news, and official censorship). The most isolationist regimes seek to control domestic public opinion through rigid censorship of any channels of external information, controlling state broadcasting and limiting access to foreign news. To measure the free flow of news and information internally within each society, we draw on annual estimates of media freedom developed by Freedom House.[4] Finally, the preceding chapter demonstrated that economic underdevelopment is also an important barrier to information; poor nations generally lack modern communication infrastructures, such as an efficient telecommunication sector and a well-developed multichannel broadcasting service, and large sectors of the population in these countries often do not have the resources or skills to access media technologies. To compare national levels of media access, we monitor differences in economic development, measured by per capita GDP in PPP. Economic development is closely correlated with patterns of media access. In combination, these three factors make up the Cosmopolitanism Index, which is operationalized, tested for reliability, and then applied to compare and classify societies. Selected case studies illustrate the contrasts between the most cosmopolitan and provincial societies, illustrating the underlying reasons for the patterns.

Comparing News Media Systems

Students of mass communications have long been interested in developing typologies useful for comparing media environments across diverse societies, although no consensus has been established in the research literature, in sharp contrast to the standard conceptual frameworks that have become established elsewhere in comparative politics to classify, for example, party systems or electoral systems, types of power-sharing or power-concentrating democracies, and types of presidential-parliamentary executives. Perhaps the best-known typology that compares macrolevel news media systems was established during the cold war era by Siebert, Peterson, and Schramm in their classic *Four Theories of the Press*.[5] The authors suggested that media systems around the world could be divided into four main categories, each reflecting different normative values: a libertarian press, emphasizing the importance of the press as a free marketplace of ideas without state interference or regulation; a socially responsible press, reflecting many of the core values embodied in public service broadcasting; authoritarian systems, in which journalists were kept subservient to the state for the sake of maintaining social stability and cohesion; and the Soviet Communist model, in which the press served as a collective agitator on behalf of the party (and thus the working class). This classification was widely used in earlier decades, but it has become outdated, particularly since the demise of the Soviet Union. More recently, two ideal types of media system have been identified and compared across postindustrial societies: the market-oriented commercial broadcasting industry, which developed in the United States and throughout much of Latin America (following the libertarian ideal), and the public service model of broadcasting (following the social responsibility ideal), which traditionally dominated contemporary Western Europe and Scandinavia. Increasingly, however, since the deregulation of state-controlled television, many countries have evolved toward a mixed or dual system, such as that used in Britain, which combines both forms of broadcasting.[6] Moreover, the simple distinction between market-oriented and state-oriented media systems, as well as between commercial and public service broadcasting, conceals important differences within each category.[7] Even the notion of 'the press' as an institution is now outdated, given the great diversity of mass media outlets and information sources, such as online blogs, discussion forums, and viral videos. Other theorists have subsequently expanded or modified the Siebert et al. typology – for example, by adding a development model of the press – although no consensus has emerged about the most useful classification.[8]

On the basis of their recent cross-national research, Hallin and Mancini proposed a revised classification of the structure of media systems found in advanced industrialized societies.[9] The authors distinguished four criteria: the extent to which countries differ in the development of media markets (especially for newspapers); the strength of linkages between parties and the media; the degree of journalistic professionalism; and the nature of state intervention in the media system. Given these criteria, among Western countries the typology identified an Anglo-American (liberal) model (which the authors suggested was found in the United States, Canada, and Britain), a Mediterranean (polarized pluralism) model (found in Italy, Spain, and France), and a democratic-pluralist model (found in Austria, Norway, and the Netherlands). The Hallin and Mancini framework is a useful development, but it has been challenged. The authors classify the British dual commercial–public service media system as Anglo-American, for example, but McQuail points out that Britain may have far more in common with the Northern European model, given the strong role of BBC public service broadcasting, rather than with the more commercially dominant American television market.[10] Moreover, as other observers have noted, the traditional distinction between commercial and public service television has become diluted, with convergence caused by the deregulation, commercialization, and proliferation of channels now available in European societies, as well as the spread of transnational media conglomerates.[11] A broader worldwide comparison that goes beyond the role of the news media in postindustrial societies and established democracies is necessary to deal with the issues involved in this study. A more comprehensive classification must include the remaining state-controlled television systems within contemporary autocracies, such as China and Vietnam, and severe limits on freedom of expression, independent journalism, and human rights, such as in Zimbabwe, Syria, and North Korea; it must also take account of whether journalists have a distinctive function in transitional autocracies and emerging democracies.[12] Apart from conceptual issues, it is difficult to apply the Hallin and Mancini typology to media environments worldwide with any degree of reliability and consistency – for example, to classify developing societies in terms of the professionalization of journalism or to gauge the strength of the linkages between parties and news media outlets.

Many other metrics are now available for comparing and evaluating media systems, including both categorical and continuous measures.[13] An alternative approach has classified rights to freedom of expression contained in written constitutions and determined whether countries have passed freedom of information laws.[14] These measures are an important part of an open society, but they were not used in this study because the factor that is crucial to freedom of the press is the implementation of such rights or legislation, rather than their existence as a legal formality. The Kyrgyz Republic, Russia, and Colombia have freedom of information laws, for example, and Uzbekistan's constitution guarantees freedom of speech and the press, but this does not mean that in practice journalists are safe from imprisonment or intimidation in these countries or that these regulations have proved effective in promoting partisan balance in the news, freedom of expression and publication, or transparency in government. Moreover, freedom of information is only one dimension of any media environment, and while often closely linked with freedom of speech and freedom of the press, these are not equivalent concepts. Others have examined and classified the structure of the news industry in different countries around the world, including state and private ownership of the major television channels and newspapers.[15] It would be naive, however, to assume that private ownership necessarily guarantees greater freedom of the press and pluralism than does well-regulated public service television. On balance, we believe that continuous measures are often preferable to categorical classifications, because unless there are extremely transparent coding processes and judgment rules, the dividing line for the latter often generates relatively arbitrary judgments by the researcher. We are also seeking comprehensive indices that facilitate reliable comparisons over time and across a wide range of societies.

Consequently, we compare societies using the Cosmopolitanism Index, conceptualized as the permeability of national borders to cross-border information flows. We constructed this composite measure by combining three well-established indicators: those measuring media freedom, economic development, and globalization.

Classifying and Comparing Media Freedom

The first core component of the Cosmopolitanism Index is the extent to which countries have internal freedom of information. To measure this, we classify countries using Freedom House's annual Press Freedom Index. An NGO, Freedom House was founded on a bipartisan basis more than 60 years ago to promote democracy. The annual Press Freedom Index, probably the best known of the available media indicators, is widely used by policymakers, academics, and journalists.[16] It is also the most appropriate for our purposes, because it measures the extent to which countries restrict the flow of information within their national borders. The Freedom House index provides the most comprehensive coverage of countries around the world, and the longest time series, since Freedom House began conducting its media freedom survey in 1980. Since 1994 Freedom House has published its assessments using a 100-point scale.

The Freedom House index is designed to measure the extent to which the free flow of news is influenced by legal, political, and economic environments. The *legal environment* category encompasses 'both an examination of the laws and regulations that could influence media content as well as the government's inclination to use these laws and legal institutions in order to restrict the media's ability to operate.' In this category Freedom House assesses several issues, such as legal and constitutional guarantees of freedom of the press, penalties for libel and defamation, as well as penal codes, the independence of the judiciary, and other factors. The *political environment* category reflects 'the degree of political control over the content of news media.' This includes the editorial independence of the media, intimidation and threats to journalists, access to informational sources, and repressive actions such as arrests, imprisonment, physical violence, and assassinations. Finally, the issues included in the *economic environment* category are related to 'economic considerations that can influence the media's activities.' Within this category, Freedom House evaluates the existence of competitive pressures leading to biased press reports and investigations, the extent of sponsoring, subsidies, and advertisement, and the effect of such pressures on press coverage and content, the impact of bribery by self-interested actors on what is published, and the structure and concentration of media ownership.

Both the legal and economic categories vary from 0 (complete freedom) to 30 (lack of freedom), while the political subindex ranges from 0 to 40. A country's overall freedom of the press score is simply the sum of the scores in each of the subcategories. The assessment of freedom of the press by Freedom House distinguishes between the broadcast and print media, and the resulting ratings are expressed as a 100-point scale for each country under comparison. The index is based on expert ratings derived from overseas correspondents, Freedom House staff members, and international visitors; from the findings of human rights and freedom of the press organizations, of specialists in geographic and geopolitical areas, of governments and multilateral bodies; and from a variety of domestic and international news media.[17] For an intuitively clearer interpretation, we reverse the Freedom House index, so that a larger number represents greater freedom of the press. Moreover, the coefficients are standardized around the mean (*z*-scores).

Before we go any farther, it is important to check whether the Freedom House index is reliable and unbiased, or whether there is any systematic skew toward an American journalistic culture or liberal notions of freedom of the press. To do so, we can compare the Freedom House index with the Worldwide Press Freedom (WPF) Index, produced annually by Reporters sans Frontières.[18] The nonprofit Reporters sans Frontières, based in Paris, works to reduce censorship, oppose laws restricting press freedom, and support journalists. Their 100-point scale reflects the degree of freedom journalists and news organizations enjoy in each country and the efforts made by the state to respect and ensure respect for this freedom. The Reporters sans Frontières' annual WPF Index provides measures since 2002 and covers a more limited range of countries.[19] The organization compiled a questionnaire containing 52 criteria for assessing the freedom of the press in each country each year. It includes a wide range of violations that directly affect journalists (such as murders, imprisonment, physical attacks, and threats) and news media (censorship, confiscation of issues, searches, and harassment). It registers the degree of impunity enjoyed by those responsible for such violations. It also takes account of the legal situation affecting the news media (such as penalties for press offenses, the existence of state monopolies in certain areas, and the existence of regulatory bodies), the behavior of the authorities toward the state-owned news media and the foreign press, and the main obstacles to the free flow of information on the Internet. The WPF Index is meant to reflect not only abuses attributable to the state, but also those by armed militias, clandestine organizations, or pressure groups that can pose a real threat to freedom of the press – for example, intimidation of investigative journalists by drug cartels. The survey questionnaire was sent to partner organizations of Reporters sans Frontières, including 14 freedom of expression groups on five continents, as well as to the organization's 130 correspondents around the world, journalists, researchers, jurists, and human rights activists. A 100-point country score was estimated for each country under comparison. Based on the 2005 score, the 168 countries included in the WPF Index were then ranked. The scale was standardized around the mean and the direction reversed, so that a higher ranking represents greater freedom of the press.

Because journalistic cultures differ and notions of freedom of the press are contested, the European origins and base of Reporters sans Frontières provides a cross-check against the Washington-based Freedom House metric. As others have noted, these two measures differ in their methodologies, conceptualization, and operationalization; nevertheless, they are strongly related, which increases our confidence in

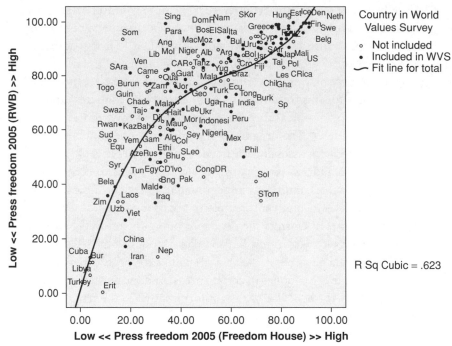

FIGURE 5.1. Comparing Media Freedom, 2005. The ratings of press freedom
for 2005 were provided by Freedom House and Reporters sans Frontières
for the countries included in the fifth wave of the WVS, 2005–2006. The
100-point scores were reversed and standardized around the mean (z-scores).
Sources: Freedom House. *Freedom of the Press, 2006: Table of Global Press
Freedom Ranking,* www.freedomhouse.org; Reporters sans Frontières. *Annual
Worldwide Press Freedom Index, 2005* (September 2004–September 2005),
www.rsf.org.

the reliability of their estimates.[20] To test for reliability, both indices
were compared in the countries included in the World Values Survey.
The results, illustrated in the scatter plot in Figure 5.1, show a strong
correlation between the two measures ($R = .762$, $N = 159$, significant at $p < .001$, cubic $R^2 = .623$, significant at $p < .001$). There
are some outliers, such as Somalia and the Philippines, for which the
organizations disagree slightly in their estimates. The two indices differ
in their design and methods, but the two organizations report similar
estimates, which increases our confidence in the reliability of the underlying measures.[21] Many countries scoring the highest in their internal
openness, according to both these indicators, are highly developed

nations such as the Netherlands and Sweden, as would be expected in view of the well-established linkages between wealth and democracy.[22] But other countries classified as having relatively free media environments by both organizations, such as Hungary, Mali, Trinidad and Tobago, Taiwan, Ghana, Poland, Burkina Faso, and Uruguay, are far less affluent. The countries ranked as having the most restrictive internal barriers by both organizations, in the bottom left corner of the scatter plot, include China, Cuba, Eritrea, Libya, and Turkmenistan, with Ethiopia, Colombia, and Russia classified as less extreme but still restrictive. Given the advantages of providing a longer time series and more comprehensive global coverage, the Freedom House Press Freedom Index was adopted to compare countries. The nations included in the WVS are skewed toward the open media environments, but there are enough restrictive cases to permit comparison.

Comparing Integration into Global Markets

The second core component of the Cosmopolitanism Index is the extent to which countries are integrated into global communication networks. As discussed earlier, globalization is understood to be a multidimensional phenomenon that includes access to international communication networks, but also broader interconnections among nation-states, integrating peoples, resources, money, alliances, ecology, goods, services, ideas, and laws.[23] An extensive literature has examined specific components of this phenomenon, but the pace and extent of change often differ substantially according to the aspect examined – for example, in the timing of waves of population migration following the disintegration of fragile states or outbreaks of armed conflict; the dismantling of trade barriers after regional and bilateral trade agreements; and the adoption of new advances in consumer digital technologies or innovative social functions of the Internet, such as Facebook, YouTube, and text messaging. An attempt to develop an integrated and comprehensive multidimensional index of globalization, that of A. T. Kearney for *Foreign Policy*, combines indicators of economic integration through trade and finance, the diffusion of technological connectivity, levels of personal contact, and the engagement of states in international organizations.[24] This ranking is useful, but unfortunately it is restricted to measuring annual trends since 1999 in about

70 countries, which means that it cannot be used for a worldwide comparison over a longer time period.

For the second dimension of the Cosmopolitanism Index, this book draws instead on the 2008 KOF Index of Globalization, constructed by the Swiss Economic Institute, which provides consistent time-series annual data for a broader range of 120 nations from 1970 to 2005.[25] This 100-point index is based on two dozen variables, designed to gauge three dimensions: *social* globalization (the spread of personal contact, information flows, and cultural proximity); *economic* globalization (the actual long-distance flows of goods, investment capital, and commercial services, as well as restrictions through import barriers, taxes, and tariffs); and *political* globalization (measured by integration with international intergovernmental organizations, the number of embassies based in a country, and national engagement in UN peace missions). The KOF index measure of social globalization monitors potential information flows that are available in any country through mass and personal communications, including trends in the proportion of Internet users, cable television subscribers, access to radio receivers, outgoing telephone traffic, international letters, international tourism, and trade in newspapers and periodicals (in percentage of GDP) since 1970. One important caveat is necessary: the KOF index utilizes a comprehensive set of statistical indicators derived from official sources and standardized by international agencies, but unfortunately these data are missing for many states, especially low-income countries that lack the institutional capacity to record and collect reliable statistics. The comparative framework includes 120 nations, but coverage is systematically skewed toward more affluent economies. As a result, the index tends to overestimate the degree of globalization worldwide. Given this qualification, the index is best used for gauging annual trends over time within countries.

Using these data enables us to analyze whether there has been a steadily rising tide of economic, social, and political globalization around the world in recent decades, as many observers suggest, and to identify which states and continents have been leaders and laggards in this process. The comparison of the overall trends in the KOF index illustrated in Figure 5.2 confirms that the level of globalization throughout the world has increased dramatically, as many accounts have argued.[26] The economic and social indices showed the steadiest

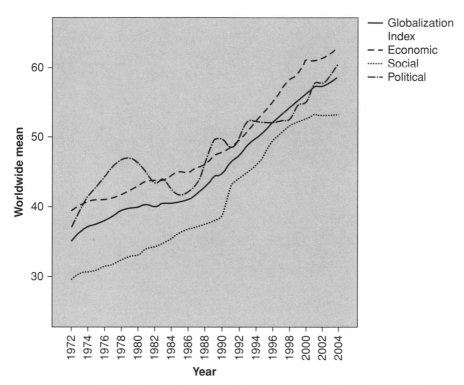

FIGURE 5.2. Rising Trends in Globalization, 1972–2004. *Source:* KOF Globalization Index (2008).

pattern of growing interconnections since the early 1970s, while the indicators of the political dimension displayed slightly greater fluctuations over time. In the period from 1972 to 2004, the overall 100-point KOF index rose on average worldwide from 36 to 56 percentage points, representing a two-thirds increase. The overall pattern shows a gradual rise from the early 1970s to the late 1980s, followed by an accelerated surge during the past fifteen years. International agreements leading to the reduction of trade barriers and tariffs have opened markets, while the spread of technological communications has contributed to denser social networks, and the growth of the institutions of multilateral governance and regional organizations during this era has encouraged states to become increasingly interconnected.

At the same time, however, the impact of globalization, and thus the openness of borders to external information flows, have been far

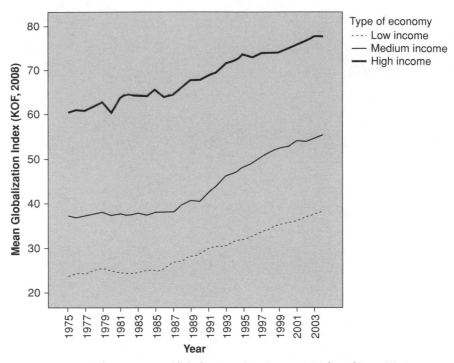

FIGURE 5.3. The Persistent Globalization Gap Between Rich and Poor Nations, 1975–2004. The type of economy is categorized according to per capita GDP (in PPP) in constant (2000) international dollars. 'Low income' corresponds to less than $1,999; 'medium income,' $2,000–$14,999; 'high income,' $15,000+. *Source:* GDP from World Development Indicators (World Bank); KOF Globalization Index (2008).

from even around the world. Figure 5.3 illustrates how globalization has affected different types of economies (classified by levels of GDP in PPP measured in constant [2000] international dollars). Low-income economies, which depend largely on exports of raw primary commodities, have become increasingly integrated into international markets since the early 1990s. Economic studies indicate that societies have attracted greater international investment and flows of foreign capital following state reforms, leading to liberalization, deregulation, and privatization, the dismantling of trade barriers, and the reduction or removal of protectionist tariffs. More open developing societies have generally attracted greater inward investment and increased trade flows, which have generated economic growth.[27] Several developing nations have grown substantially through export-led strategies; today

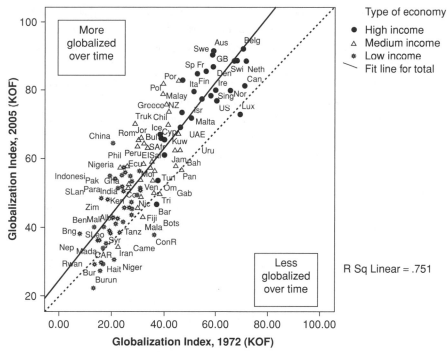

FIGURE 5.4. Changes in Globalization over Time, 1972–2005. The type of economy is categorized according to per capita GDP (in PPP) in 2006 measured in international dollars. 'Low income' corresponds to less than $1,999; 'medium income,' $2,000–$14,999; 'high income,' $15,000+. The solid line represents the regression best fit. The dashed diagonal line represents the 'no change' position. *Source:* GDP from World Development Indicators (World Bank); KOF Globalization Index (2008).

European and North American supermarkets are regularly supplied with a wide range of fresh imported goods flown around the world, from Kenyan produce to Colombian flowers or Thai shrimp. Among the middle-income emerging economies, China lifted trade barriers and negotiated entry into the WTO in 2001, and it has rapidly become the global leader in the export of manufactured goods, a strategy that has lifted large sectors of its urban population out of poverty, while India has benefited from the rapid expansion of service technology, call centers, and offshore commerce.[28] Nevertheless, despite these important cases, a substantial 35-point gap in the KOF Globalization Index divides high- and low-income economies today, and no narrowing of this gap has occurred during the past three decades (see Figure 5.4).

Poor societies have become more integrated into the global economy and global communication networks during this era, but they
have not caught up with the level of integration found in most rich
societies.

To compare changes among the leaders and laggards in more detail,
Figure 5.4 illustrates the position of countries included in the KOF
Globalization Index in 1972 and in 2005. Countries falling on the diagonal line experienced no change over this period. As the scatter plot
shows, most countries (such as China, Poland, and Sweden) fall above
the diagonal line, indicating that they have become more globalized
during the past three decades. The countries that were most globalized
in 2005 include many of the relatively small advanced industrialized
countries and service economies, such as Belgium, Austria, Sweden, the
Netherlands, and Switzerland, which are leaders in this process. The
A. T. Kearney index suggests similar patterns.[29] This confirms more
impressionistic evidence, such as the internationalization of Brussels,
Geneva, The Hague, Stockholm, and Vienna, the home of many international NGOs and many multilateral organizations for the European
Union, NATO, and UN bureaus and agencies. The process of European integration during these decades, including the development of a
single market and the institutions of European governance within the
borders of the European Union, has contributed to the interconnections of member states that are at the top of the Globalization Index. It
is notable that although one-sixth of the U.S. GDP is currently earned
from the export of goods and services, plus income from foreign investment, the United States is not at the forefront of globalization, in part
because the size of the American economy ensures a large domestic market for its goods and services. Most leaders in globalization
are smaller, high-income, advanced industrialized societies but some
middle-income economies, including Portugal, Poland, Malaysia, and
Turkey, are also relatively globalized. Among low-income nations and
emerging economies, China, the Philippines, Indonesia, and Pakistan
all stand out as increasingly interconnected with the rest of the world
by ties of trade, communications, and multilateral governance. Finally,
the countries that are most isolated from these networks include many
of the poorest nations on the African subcontinent, such as Ethiopia,
Rwanda, Madagascar, Burundi, and the Central African Republic, as
well as other low-income nations, such as the isolated kingdom of

Nepal, the closed regime of Iran in the Middle East, and the fragile state of Haiti in the Caribbean.[30]

The geographic spread of globalization is shown in more detail in Figure 5.5. The KOF Globalization Index was divided into low- and high-globalization countries, and the results of the classification are compared, showing snapshots in 1990 and 2005 (recall the earlier qualification that many poor nations are not included in the index). The transformation of the world during these years is readily apparent from the available data; in 1990, the major states that were most globalized included postindustrial economies in North America and Western Europe, as well as Australia, New Zealand, Singapore, Malaysia, Japan, South Korea, Chile, and Venezuela. But by 2005, globalization had swept through most of Central and Eastern Europe, Latin America, and the Caribbean, Southeast Asia, as well as Asia Pacific and parts of southern and western Africa. This process has not yet transformed most of Africa, however, or the Middle East and central Eurasia, which pinpoints the location of the disparities already observed between rich and poor economies. We can conclude that most nations have experienced a dramatic increase in the volume, density, and speed of cross-border interconnections during recent decades. Globalization has been encouraged by the lowering of trade barriers and tariffs under international agreements, the spread of travel and tourism, international migration, expanding access to interpersonal and mass communications, and the integration of countries into the institutions of global and regional governance, as many observers have noted.[31] At the same time, the reach of the globalization process has been limited, and many of the poorest societies in the world have been largely excluded from world markets, as have some autocratic states.

Development and Lack of Media Access

The last core component of the Cosmopolitanism Index is the extent to which countries have widespread public access to communication networks. Limits on communications arise from underdeveloped communication infrastructures, as already documented. This process operates at the societal level and also at the individual level. If only a few affluent segments of the public regularly watch the television news or

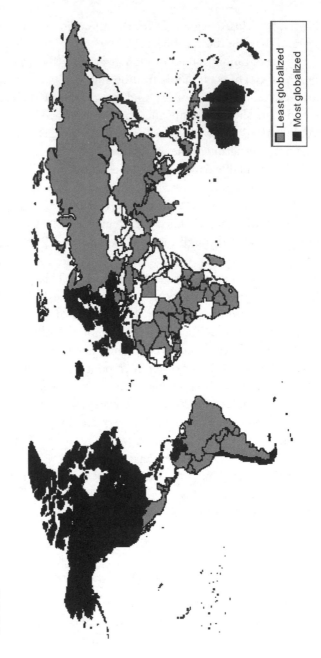

1990

Least globalized
Most globalized

2005

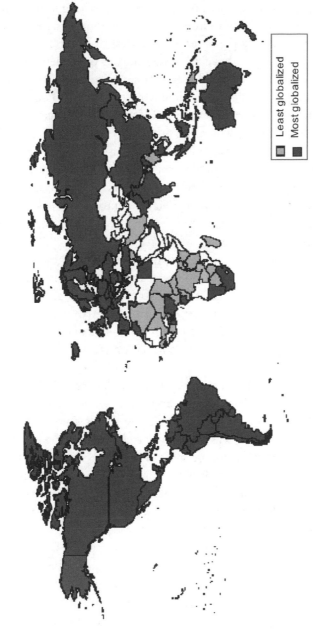

FIGURE 5.5. The Expansion of Globalization, 1990–2005. The KOF Globalization Index 100 points are divided into least (0–49) and most globalized (50–100) nation-states.

Least globalized

Most globalized

read newspapers, then even if this process has a strong impact on these individuals, it is unlikely to affect public opinion or the national culture more broadly. On the other hand, widespread public access to the news media is likely to have a broader impact on societal values and attitudes. Many international statistics have attempted to harmonize indicators of media access, including work by UNESCO on newspaper circulation figures, the availability of TV sets, and access to radios, as well as by the ITU, which monitors the telecommunication infrastructure. These measures are helpful for illustrating the disparities in access discussed in the preceding chapter. Nevertheless, the standard indicators are often incomplete across country coverage, as well as limited in their ability to provide reliable annual estimates.

Given these problems, the third component of the Cosmopolitanism Index incorporates estimates of per capita GDP in PPP, expressed in international dollars, which provides a standard indicator for levels of economic development. These statistics are almost universally available on an annual basis as a reliable time series and are strongly correlated with the available statistics from the Arthur S. Banks Cross-National Time-Series dataset of 1972–2007 on media access. Table 5.1 shows the strong and significant correlation ($R = .742***$) between levels of economic development (GDP in PPP, expressed in constant international dollars) and the media access scale (combining the proportion of households with TVs and radio sets, newspaper circulation, and Internet users) derived from the Banks dataset. Moreover, economic development was strongly correlated with the annual KOF Globalization Index during the same period ($R = .806***$). The Freedom House Press Freedom Index (1994–2006) was also significantly correlated with economic development ($R = .547***$) as well as with the KOF Globalization Index ($R = .574***$) and the Banks media access scale ($R = .470***$).

Reliability analysis is a suitable procedure for estimating the internal consistency of any composite scaled measure. The standardized indicators for media freedom, the Globalization Index, and economic development generated a strong Cronbach's alpha (.855), suggesting a high degree of internal consistency in the scale, and the alpha weakened if any separate component was excluded. When the three indices were subjected to principal-component factor analysis with varimax rotation, as shown in Table 5.2, the test could extract only a single

TABLE 5.1. *Correlations with the Cosmopolitanism Index*

		Economic Development (GDP in PPP, Constant International $) (World Bank)	Media Access (Banks)	Media Freedom (Freedom House)	Cosmo-politanism Index
Media access (Banks)	Pearson correlation	.742			.866
	Sig. (2-tailed)	.000			.000
	N	4,255			700
Media freedom (Freedom House)	Pearson correlation	.547	.470		.797
	Sig. (2-tailed)	.000	.000		.000
	N	1,764	1,995		1,283
Globalization Index (KOF 2008)	Pearson correlation	.806	.716	.574	.912
	Sig. (2-tailed)	.000	.000	.000	.000
	N	3,305	3,759	1,308	1,283

Note: Media freedom, representing internal openness to information flows, is measured by the Freedom House Press Freedom Index (*z*-scores). Integration into global networks, representing external openness to information flows, is measured by the KOF Globalization Index (*z*-scores). There were 14 cases in which information was not available for the KOF index; in these cases, countries were classified on the basis of the regional mean for the KOF index. The level of economic development is measured by per capita GDP in PPP in constant international dollars (World Bank). The Cosmopolitanism Index combines the indices for economic development, media freedom, and globalization. For comparison, the Banks Media access scale, representing the proportion of those with access to radio sets, TVs, newspapers, and the Internet, is included.

dimension, explaining, in total, 77% of the variance. Given the strong intercorrelation of these indicators, entering all three dimensions separately into regression models can cause serious problems of multicollinearity, where the size and signs of coefficients and standard errors become unreliable. Accordingly, the indicators of media freedom, economic development, and the Globalization Index were first standardized around the mean, with a standard deviation of 1, to give each component equal weighting, and then combined into a single Cosmopolitanism Index. The final index was also standardized around the mean, with a standard deviation of 1.0, as is conventional for multi-level regression analysis, to facilitate interpretation of the coefficients in subsequent models.

TABLE 5.2. *Factor Analysis of the Components of the Cosmopolitanism Index*

	Cosmopolitanism Index
Globalization Index (KOF)	.919
Economic development (GDP in PPP, constant international $) (World Bank)	.922
Media freedom (Freedom House)	.799

Note: All scales were first standardized around the mean. The principal-component factor analysis with varimax rotation generated a single dimension that accounted, in total, for 77% of the variance in the composite index. For the definition and measurement of each item, see Technical Appendix A.

The Cosmopolitanism Index Rankings

On the basis of these considerations, we can operationalize and apply the Cosmopolitanism Index to the classification of 118 countries where data are available (Figure 5.6) and briefly describe some illustrative cases.

Cosmopolitan Societies

The most cosmopolitan societies are classified in this study as those with the lowest external and internal barriers to accessing information, and these include the countries ranked at the top of Figure 5.6. Many of these are affluent postindustrial economies and established democracies, especially small societies such as Luxembourg, Switzerland, Norway, Belgium, and the Netherlands, as well as larger West European countries such as Germany and France. Anglo-American countries, including the United States, the United Kingdom, and Australia, are also well represented. It is striking that a range of relatively new democracies and middle-income emerging economies from different regions around the world are also relatively cosmopolitan; among these are the Czech Republic, Hungary, Slovenia, South Korea, and Chile. These countries have made rapid strides in freedom of the press in recent years, as well as in a broader range of political rights and civil liberties, and they have also become leading nations that are integrated into multilateral networks of trade, communications, and governance.

Switzerland most clearly exemplifies cosmopolitan communications. A small multilinguistic country at the cultural cross-roads of

Europe, with a population of 7.5 million, it borders on Germany, Austria, Lichtenstein, Italy, and France. It is one of the most affluent countries in the world, with a GDP per capita of $41,100, and the prosperous Swiss economy has a large service sector that is closely tied to international finance, insurance, banking, and tourism, as well as a manufacturing sector in chemicals and precision instruments. Although not a member of the European Union, Switzerland is closely tied to multilateral organizations, with many UN agencies and bureaus headquartered in Geneva, including the World Health Organization, World Trade Organization, and International Labor Organization. Switzerland also lays claim to being the world's oldest democracy, where freedom of the press was enshrined in the federal constitution in the mid-19th century. According to Reporters sans Frontières, in 2007 Switzerland ranked 11th highest of 169 nations in freedom of the press, above the United Kingdom, Canada, and Germany. Freedom House ranks it even higher (7th of 195 countries).

Today broadcasting is dominated by the public service Swiss Broadcasting Corporation (SRG/SSR), founded in 1952, which operates 7 TV networks and 18 radio stations.[32] Most of its funding comes from license fee revenues; a smaller proportion comes from TV advertising. Public service broadcasting is organized as a nonprofit company, with a complicated set of regional associations, including audience councils, that are intended to safeguard the public interest. The Swiss Broadcasting Corporation has a mandate to produce programming for domestic consumption, as well as information programs to promote Switzerland's image abroad and to support contact with the Swiss expatriate community. Since 1982, Switzerland has operated a dual system, and multiple private (commercial) radio and TV stations offer programs at the national and regional levels. In addition, television stations from France, Germany, and Italy are widely available, thanks to the high penetration of multichannel cable and satellite TV. By 2002, more than 80% of all households were equipped with either satellite receivers or broadband cable networks. There are about 40 German-language television channels available in Switzerland, such as RTL, ARD and Pro, and some German commercial broadcasters provide tailored versions of their channels for the Swiss market. Similarly, the French-speaking and Italian-speaking regions show a lot of programming imported from outside the country. English-language

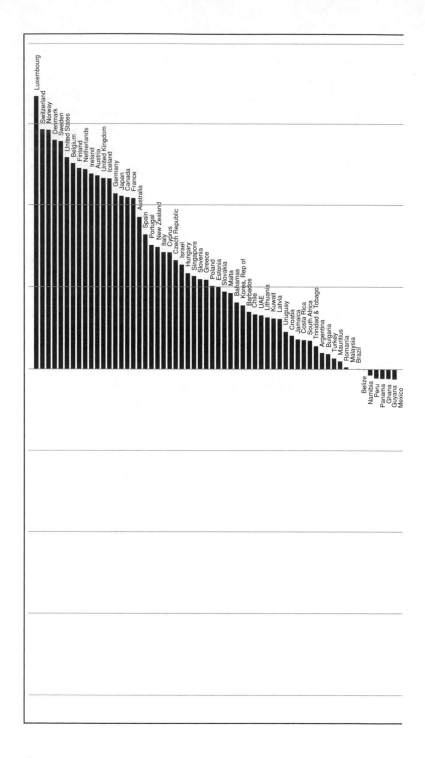

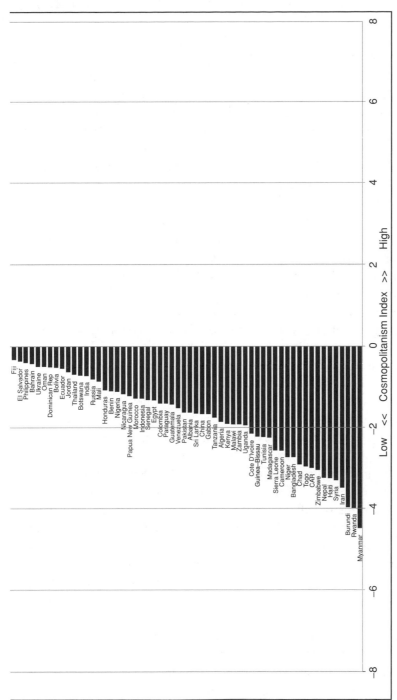

FIGURE 5.6. Cosmopolitanism Index Rankings, 2005. The Cosmopolitanism Index is conceptualized as the permeability of societies to information flows, and it is constructed according to levels of globalization, media freedom, and economic development, with all indices standardized. See the main text for details.

programs are commonly dubbed into other languages in Switzerland, while CNN International, BBC Prime, EuroNews, Sky TV, and CNBC are all available in English, along with World Radio Switzerland. The European Audiovisual Observatory analyzed the daily audience market share for TV viewing and estimated that, in 2002, more than 60% of the Swiss audience was watching foreign channels.[33] With a highly educated and affluent population, the telecommunication infrastructure in Switzerland is also well developed. There is extensive access to computers and to landline and mobile telephones, and Switzerland has one of the highest rates of broadband wireless access to the Internet in Europe; in 2006, just over two-thirds (68%) of the population used the Internet, according to Nielsen Net/Ratings. There are also multiple leading daily newspapers, such as *Blick* and *Tagesanzeiger* published in Zurich, *Le Matin* in Lausanne, and *Corriere del Ticino* in Lugano, as well as general-interest magazines and multiple publishing houses.

But not all cosmopolitan societies are affluent postindustrial societies; some emerging economies such as South Africa are also increasingly cosmopolitan. Since the transitional democratic elections in April 1994, the South African media landscape has experienced the liberalization and deregulation of state control of broadcasting, the diversification of the print sector, constitutional and legal guarantees of freedom of access to state-held information, and growing use of the Internet. Deregulation in 1996 led to a proliferation of radio stations. Listeners in Johannesburg can choose from among 40 radio services, from the national broadcasts of the state-owned South African Broadcasting Corporation (SABC) to community stations targeting local neighborhoods or ethnic groups. SABC operates three national TV networks and two pay-TV channels, while commercial national broadcasters offer free and pay-TV channels, with the usual mix of news and current affairs, sports and entertainment, movies, reality shows, and soaps, which combine locally produced and imported programming. The constitution provides for freedom of the press, and this is generally respected. In 2006, for example, out of 168 nations worldwide, Reporters sans Frontières ranked South Africa 44th from the top in freedom of the press, higher than the United States (53rd) and Japan (51st) and roughly similar to Italy and Spain.[34] Legal regulation and political control of media content are considered moderate. Human Rights Watch, an international watchdog body, praises the progress that South Africa has made in freedom of expression, although it remains critical of the country's human rights record on other issues, including severe rural poverty, the challenges of patriarchy and gender equality, and violations of the rights of asylum seekers and economic migrants.[35] Newspapers and magazines publish reports and comments that are critical of the government, and the state-owned SABC is far more independent now than it was during the apartheid era. As a result, although there remain tensions in the complex relationship between journalists and the African National Congress, during the past decade the news media has emerged as an increasingly autonomous actor, less closely aligned with the interests of the government or political parties.[36] South Africa is one of the leading countries on the continent in terms of integration into the global economy, with the 2008 KOF index ranking the country as the 48th most globalized of 120 nations, roughly comparable to Japan, the Philippines, and South Korea. Countries in the globalized-pluralist category of media environments are most vulnerable to the impact of cross-border information flows, given that there are minimal protectionist barriers to foreign imports and global influences on indigenous national cultures.

Provincial Societies

By contrast, in provincial societies, communication and information networks are more strongly rooted within a particular local community or region, with more rigid barriers to external forces. We expect to find that the beliefs and attitudes of the people living in provincial societies will be less affected by the cultural impact of cross-border information flows. Provincial societies are ranked at the bottom of Figure 5.6. The most extreme outliers, such as Myanmar, Iran, Syria, Haiti, Nepal, Burundi, and Rwanda, are poorly integrated into global markets; they are also relatively isolated from major international and regional communication networks, since they lack investment in their telecommunication infrastructure, and tolerate limited internal freedom of the press for journalists and reporters in civic society. Some of these societies, including Zimbabwe, Iran, Egypt, Syria, and Pakistan, have experienced intermittent periods of media liberalization followed by state clampdowns, with sporadic battles involving the governing authorities, conservative forces, opposition reform movements in civil society, and independent journalists in the struggle over control of the press.[37]

Syria is an example of how the state contributes to isolationism. In this country, the government owns and controls much of the media, including the daily newspapers, *Al-Thawra* (The Revolution), *Tishrin*, and the English-language *Syria Times*, while the Baath party publishes *Al-Baath*. There was a brief flowering of freedom of the press after Bashar al-Assad became president in 2000. The normally staid government newspapers cautiously started to discuss reform and democracy. For the first time in nearly 40 years, private publications were licensed. The new titles included the political party papers *Sawt al-Shaab* and *Al-Wahdawi* and a satirical journal. But within a year, under pressure from the old guard, the president cautioned against overzealous reform, a subsequent press law imposed a new range of restrictions, and publications were subject to suspension for violating content rules. Criticism of President Bashar al-Assad and his family is now banned, and the domestic and foreign press is censored if material is deemed to be threatening or embarrassing. Journalists practice self-censorship and foreign reporters rarely get accreditation. Reporters sans Bordières document common abuses: 'Journalists and political activists risk arrest at any time for any reason and are up against a whimsical and vengeful state apparatus that continually adds to the list of things banned or forbidden to be mentioned. Several journalists were arrested in 2006 for interviewing exiled regime opponents, taking part in conferences abroad or for criticizing government policies. They were subjected to lengthy legal proceedings before the Damascus military court that, under a 1963 law, tries anyone considered to have undermined state security.'[38] Critical journalists outside the country write for the Lebanese or pan-Arab press, such as the Beirut daily *Al-Nahar* and the influential London daily *Al-Hayat*, as well as contribute to Al Jazeera and other regional satellite channels.[39] Syrian TV, operated by the Ministry of Information, operates two terrestrial channels and one satellite channel. It has cautiously begun carrying political programs and debates featuring formerly taboo issues and occasionally airs interviews with opposition figures. Syria launched some privately owned radio stations in 2004, but these were prevented from airing news or anything with political content. With an estimated 1.5 million Internet users in Syria by 2007, the Web has emerged as a vehicle for dissent. In the view of Reporters sans Bordières, however, Syria is one of the worst offenders against

Internet freedom because the state censors opposition bloggers and independent news Web sites. Human Rights Watch notes that the government of Syria regularly restricts the flow of information on the Internet and arrests individuals who post comments that the government deems too critical.[40] Overall, Syria ranks 154th out of 166 countries in the Reporters sans Bordières 2007 Worldwide Press Freedom Index. Similarly, in terms of freedom of the press, Freedom House ranks the country 179th out of 195 states worldwide.[41]

Burma (Myanmar) is even more draconian in its attempts to suppress internal dissent and to exercise total control over the media message flowing across national borders. In September 2007, for example, thousands of monks and civilians took to the streets of Rangoon in a weeklong uprising against the Burmese government. In response, the military junta shut down the Internet, arrested or intimidated Burmese journalists, and severed mobile and landline phone links to the outside world. A Japanese video journalist from AFP news was killed. Cameras and video cell phones were confiscated by soldiers. The official Division for Press Scrutiny and Registration pressured local editors to publish stories claiming that the unrest was organized by 'saboteurs.' In the immediate aftermath of these events, thousands of monks were said to have been arrested, but after the media clampdown no images of these events were published in the domestic and international news.[42] The pattern was repeated after Cyclone Nargis struck, killing tens of thousands in May 2008. Even in less turbulent times, critical coverage of the Burmese junta is severely restricted in domestic news media, and negative stories about the military leadership are silenced. Everything from poetry to films is censored. Foreign short-wave radio is a key source of information about both the outside world and events at home. The BBC World Service, Voice of America, the U.S.-backed Radio Free Asia, and the Norway-based opposition station, Democratic Voice of Burma, drawing on reporters exiled to Thailand, target listeners in Burma. But if caught, citizens can be punished for listening to overseas radio broadcasts. Internet access is tightly controlled by the government. It is further hampered by a poor telephone infrastructure and an unreliable supply of electricity. Nor are these isolated instances of state control of the airwaves. Although Burma is an extreme case, regularly ranking near the bottom of worldwide annual assessments of freedom of the press produced by Reporters sans Frontières and Freedom House, human rights observers report that many other states routinely suppress independent journalism, manipulate and slant news selectively in their favor, and limit critical coverage of the regime.

China and Russia constitute additional, although less isolationist, cases. These countries are highly integrated into global markets economically, with well-developed infrastructures for transnational communications; they are also leading powers in the institutions of multilateral governance. However, they allow only limited internal freedom of the press. China, for example, liberalized its newspaper market during the 1990s by reducing state subsidies, so that publishers need to attract readers, and thus commercial advertising, to remain financially viable. Nevertheless, the Committee to Protect Journalists, a New York nonprofit organization, claims that China is the world's leading jailer of journalists, and there remain serious restrictions on reporting sensitive political topics like ethnic conflict and religion; for example, the state obstructed foreign journalists trying to cover the Tibetan uprisings in March 2008.[43] Strict limits on the airwaves continue through state control of China Central Television (CCTV), the only nationwide broadcaster, which offers 16 major television channels and functions as a subministry within the State Administration of Radio, Film, and Television.[44] The central government and party leadership own and control the Xinhua News Agency, China Radio International, China Central Television, the *Guangming Daily*, and the *People's Daily*. Text messaging is an important and growing source of interpersonal communication, but the government *uses* sophisticated technology and an estimated 30,000 e-mail police to intercept and censor sensitive topics in e-mails and on the Internet (such as Web sites about human rights) by means of proxy firewalls, blocking routers, software filters, and restricted access. Beijing also actively persecutes and imprisons cyber dissidents.[45] While seeking to maintain strict internal control, however, the Communist Party faces several growing challenges. In particular, China wanted to reinforce national pride and its positive world image as an emerging global economy by hosting the 2008 Beijing Olympics, but this event offered activists an opportunity to raise difficult issues of human rights for ethnic minorities in Tibet and elsewhere. In Russia, as well, many observers reported that, even though the old forms of censorship and overt state control are no longer in force, in recent years the country has experienced growing restrictions on independent media, including subtle forms of persecution and intimidation of journalists, as well as pro-government bias on television election news.[46] Russia and China are potentially becoming more open to cross-border information flows, especially through the expansion of opportunities for international trade and travel, but there remain serious internal restrictions on the main media channels (especially broadcasting) that disseminate information about the world.

Isolation from international communication networks is not simply the product of state repression, however; some poor democracies, such as Mali, Ghana, and Benin, have a diverse independent press and few major restrictions on journalism, but they also have little public access to mass communications. In Mali, for example, freedom of expression is guaranteed by the constitution, and observers report that this is generally respected by the democratic government. More than 40 privately owned newspapers and magazines are published in French, Arabic, and local languages. Alongside about 125 commercial and community radio stations, and public service radio and television, there is access to multichannel satellite and cable television stations by subscription. But at the same time Mali remains relatively isolated from global markets and multilateral institutions, so that its communication infrastructure remains underdeveloped.[47] Mali is one of the poorest countries in West Africa, ranking 173rd out of 177 nations, according to UNDP's 2007 Human Development Index, in one of the poorest regions in the world.[48] In 2005, per capita income was $1,003 (in U.S. dollars PPP). Malians have access to an estimated 570,000 radios and 160,000 television sets, and there are 30,000 Internet users in an estimated population of about 12 million. Multimedia campaigns using traditional music and village performing arts and free wind-up radios have been distributed for development projects in order to disseminate, for example, information about family planning and environmental programs. Less than half the adult population is literate, which hampers newspaper readership and circulation. The country has an estimated 100,000 landline and cell telephones, but telecommunications are expensive, geographic coverage is poor, and distances are large. In theory those living in Mali, like those in Benin and Botswana, have a relatively free news media, but in practice public access is severely restricted by a lack

of the basic infrastructure for mass communications and new information technologies. The population has restricted levels of Internet
connectivity, access to satellite and cable broadcasting, and telecommunications.

Discussion and Conclusions

Many communication theorists have attempted to compare media systems systematically; a notable example is the classic Siebert et al.
attempt to distinguish between libertarian and social responsibility
notions of the press.[49] Unfortunately, the Siebert approach is outdated, and it is difficult to operationalize with any degree of reliability
and consistency. More recently, Hallin and Mancini have developed
a typology of media systems found in established democracies, but it
remains too limited for global comparisons, including those related to
the role of the media in nondemocratic regimes.[50]

This chapter has developed an alternative comparative typology of
cosmopolitan communications based on a society's internal and external openness to information flows. The striking contrasts between the
rich and open communication environments found in affluent cities
such as Geneva, Luxembourg, and Oslo and those of the mass public in Port-Au-Prince, Kigali, and Damascus are obvious to any casual
observer, but the implications of these differences for the penetration of
global information into local cultures has been underestimated. Oper-
ationally, the Cosmopolitanism Index combines the Freedom House
indicators of levels of press freedom (for internal openness), the KOF
indicators of levels of globalization (for external openness), and level
of economic development (as a proxy indicator for media access). The
classification was applied to 118 countries worldwide, where data were
available, including the 93 states included in the WVS.

Any classification of media systems should ideally meet the standards of logical and theoretical coherence, and its empirical indicators
must also be valid – that is, they must closely match the underlying
concepts they purport to measure. Moreover, a key test of the utility
of this classification is whether it reflects the distinct effects that are
predicted theoretically. There are strong reasons to believe that the
free flow of information within societies and across previously rigid

national borders will have important consequences by interacting with patterns of media use.[51] The second part of this book goes on to test empirically whether people who pay attention to television, the Internet, and newspapers and who live in cosmopolitan societies are indeed the most open to cultural change, as hypothesized.

PART II

CONSEQUENCES

6

Citizens

National and Cosmopolitan Identities

The second part of this book applies the analytic framework we have developed to test the consequences of the growth of cosmopolitanism communications. Convergence theorists assume that the globalization of the mass media, especially the exposure of traditional developing societies to a barrage of Western entertainment, Hollywood movies, commercial advertising, and international news, has the capacity to transform national identities, social values, and ideas of democracy. One of the most common arguments is that the flow of cross-border information expands awareness about other people and places, so that widespread access to news from abroad may encourage greater understanding, tolerance, and trust of foreigners, while simultaneously weakening national identities and a sense of belonging to local communities. In the social sphere, conservatives fear that images of professional working women depicted in Western media could encourage more egalitarian sex roles in ultratraditional societies, such as Saudi Arabia and Kuwait, challenging conventional views about the appropriate roles of men and women in the home, workforce, and public sphere. Conservatives are also concerned that explicit sexuality in Western advertising, pornographic Web sites, and Hollywood movies could loosen moral standards in traditional societies and bring more tolerant attitudes toward homosexuality, abortion, and divorce. Theorists such as Herbert Schiller, Edward Hermann, and Robert McChesney have long argued that the Western media is the missionary that will spread the values of consumer capitalism around the world.[1]

If this claim is true, then in post-Communist Central and Eastern Europe, exposure to the ideas and images of free market individualism imported by the Western mass media should leave a distinct imprint on attitudes toward the role of markets and the state. In the field of international relations, soft-power theorists claim that the use of the mass media for public diplomacy has the capacity to win hearts and minds, and that the ideas and images conveyed by American or Western media will contribute to the end of the cold war, reinforce public support for reform movements around the world, and thus facilitate the process of democratization.[2] Street battles to control television during the 'color' revolutions also suggest that the mass media has the capacity to play a vital role in regime change.[3] In states such as Zimbabwe, Sudan, and Uzbekistan, people with access to BBC World Service, Voice of America, Radio Free Europe, Deutsche Welle, Radio Liberty, or Radio Monte Carlo have opportunities to learn about democracy in other nations, as well as to listen to reporting that is critical of human rights in their own country.

These sorts of consequences are often assumed to arise from the globalization of mass communications, but the empirical evidence in support of this assumption is scanty. In fact, there are good reasons for being skeptical about the more extravagant claims; socialization theory suggests that we learn about society and the world from multiple sources, and that deep-rooted values and social norms are acquired from interactions with family members and teachers, friends and neighbors, and from firsthand experiences during our formative years.[4] The mass media is only one potential socialization agency – and it is not necessarily more important than interpersonal communications. As noted in earlier chapters, when confronted with ideas that conflict with local cultural norms and beliefs, people may gradually modify their views, but alternatively they may simply choose to reject or ignore these ideas. Subsequent chapters will examine the direct impact of exposure to the media on each of these dimensions of public opinion. In this chapter we start by analyzing evidence concerning one of the most important and influential claims, namely that exposure to global mass communications will not only gradually weaken national identities, but will strengthen understanding, trust, and tolerance of people from other countries. We outline the theoretical debate surrounding these issues, reviewing what has been established in the literature, and then examine the empirical evidence. Descriptive comparisons and multilevel regression models are useful for analyzing the pooled sample containing all nations in the fifth wave of the World Values Survey.

Do Global Communications Encourage Cosmopolitan Orientations?

Some writers offer several plausible theories as to why the globalization of mass communications can be expected to weaken the bonds of nationalism.[5] At the broadest level, many observers argue that globalization has led us toward the 'end of the nation state.' Hence, Ohmae argues that the modern period represents a new historical era dominated by the growth of the agencies of global governance, world market forces, and Western consumerism, a tide that national governments and economies have become powerless to halt.[6] Transformational accounts suggest that the nation-state remains in place, but nevertheless its identity as a political institution and its core capacities are profoundly undermined by globalization, while transcendentalists go even further by suggesting that globalization implies the ultimate dissolution of the nation-state.[7] Anthony Giddens claims that contemporary globalization is historically unprecedented and that it reshapes modern societies, economies, governments, and the world order.[8] Held and his colleagues suggest that this process has been the most extensive in the European Union, where the future of sovereignty and autonomy within nation-states has been most strongly challenged by European integration, but they argue that all of the world's major regions are affected, which results in overlapping 'communities of fate.'[9] The interdependence is evident. When the subprime mortgage market crumbles in the United States, stock markets sink in Tokyo and the Northern Rock Bank goes bankrupt in the United Kingdom.[10] When Brazilian rain forests shrink, the polar ice caps melt in the South Atlantic and wildfires blaze in California. The world clearly *is* becoming more closely interconnected. Media reporting of these events provides information about globalization, and direct experience, such as international travel, tourism, and immigration across national borders, is also expected to broaden people's minds by exposing individuals to other lifestyles, unfamiliar practices, and alternative beliefs.[11] For pro-globalists, the acceleration and deepening of transborder information flows through the spread of ICTs are regarded as providing new opportunities to learn about the world and other places indirectly. Among the consequences, this process is expected to expand cosmopolitan orientations, contributing to a greater understanding of, and respect for, habits and customs found in other cultures, strengthening trust and tolerance of other peoples, weakening parochial feelings of nationalism, and encouraging trust and confidence in the ability of major agencies of multilateral cooperation and global governance to overcome shared world challenges. Most of these consequences are viewed by pro-globalists as positive developments, although in fragile multiethnic states emerging from conflict, the lack of a nationwide TV and radio broadcasting system, or a linguistically segmented newspaper market, may exacerbate existing divisions among communities and thereby limit the capacity of the state to rebuild a sense of common identity and national unity.

Despite these conjectures, it has not been demonstrated whether the process of globalization – and in particular the role of cross-border information flows – actually *has* fostered more cosmopolitan orientations among the general public in most countries. Skeptics doubt whether identification with the nation-state has been seriously weakened among the general public and whether an emerging 'cosmopolitan identity' is sufficiently powerful to replace the visceral tribal appeals of nationalism.[12] In Anthony Smith's view, we are witnessing the growth of regional blocs, where nation-states remain the primary actors, rather than the emergence of a new world order that transcends states. The expanding role of the United Nations in development, peacekeeping, and human rights has occurred, Smith suggests, without fundamentally eroding – indeed, perhaps even strengthening – deep-rooted attitudes about nationalism and the nation-state: 'We are still far from even mapping out the kind of global culture and cosmopolitan ideals that can truly supersede the world of nations.'[13] Supporting the polarization thesis, Mann argues that there are complex patterns involving possible threats to the nation-state rather than clear-cut trends, but a popular backlash against the forces of globalization has probably strengthened, not weakened, national identities.[14] Hooson also perceives a resurgence of nationalism: 'The last half of the twentieth century will go down in history as a new age of rampant and proliferating nationalisms. . . . The urge to express one's identity, and to have it recognized tangibly by others, is increasingly contagious and has to be recognized

as an elemental force even in the shrunken, apparently homogenizing, high tech world of the end of the twentieth century.'[15] Support for this interpretation is suggested by contemporary struggles for
succession, resulting in the birth of new nation-states, such as Timor
Leste and Kosovo, and in persistent unresolved internal conflict over
ethno-nationalist identities, exemplified by demands for autonomous
self-government in the Kurdish region of Iraq, by the Tamil Tigers in
Sri Lanka, and by ETA's violent actions in the Basque region of Spain,
as well as the peaceful divorce in Czechoslovakia, the dissolution of
Yugoslavia, and debates about a split among linguistic communities
in Belgium. Arguing along similar lines, Castells suggests that globalization has encouraged organized resistance as diverse as that of the
Zapatistas in Chiapas, the right-wing militia in the United States, and
Al Qaeda in Afghanistan: 'People all over the world resent the loss of
control over their lives, over their environment, over their jobs, over
their economies, over their governments, over their countries, and, ultimately, over the fate of the Earth.'[16] This view emphasizes burgeon-
ing antiglobalization social movements, exemplified by mass protests
against meetings of the WTO, International Monetary Fund (IMF),
and G8 and by the actions of eco-gastronomy 'slow-food' groups,
which embrace traditional local products and deplore the loss of distinct cultural communities. If these forces reflect a widespread popular
phenomenon rather than the activities of small but noisy minorities,
this could indicate that local and national identities have not faded
away and may even have resurfaced with new vigor in a reaction
against globalization.

Evidence from Previous Studies

What evidence enables us to evaluate the claims underlying this debate?
The bulk of the literature postulating links between globalization, use
of the mass media, and nationalist and cosmopolitan orientations has
been polemical and purely theoretical. Most commentators seek to
account for contemporary developments in international relations,
European integration, or transnational social movements by citing
social observation, selected cases, and historical illustrations, without
examining public opinion data systematically. But recent years have
also seen a growing body of literature analyzing the empirical survey

evidence concerning the strength of national identities, attitudes toward open borders for labor migration and free trade, trust and tolerance of other nations, and confidence in the multilateral agencies of global governance, all of which can throw light on these arguments.[17]

The most systematic time-series analysis has focused on whether a sense of national identity has declined since the early 1970s within the European Union. Renewed interest in understanding the dynamics of public support within the Union has been spurred by the continuing process of European integration despite the results of referenda in which, when people were asked to express their views, the majority rejected the proposed adoption of the euro in Denmark (2000) and Sweden (2003), the proposed constitution for Europe in France (2005) and the Netherlands (2005), and the proposed Treaty of Lisbon in Ireland (2008). Europe provides an appropriate context for testing some of the core claims about the emergence of cosmopolitan orientations, since the process of European integration has been gradually strengthening, deepening, and widening the institutions and powers of the European Union over successive decades. If nationalism has faded anywhere, the experience of economic and political integration within the European Union, with people working, living, studying, and traveling in different member states, can be expected to have dissolved traditional barriers in the most discernible way, particularly among citizens of the countries that have lived under European institutions for a long time, such as Italy, France, and Germany.[18] There are other reasons for making Europe a test case. As we saw in Chapter 3, the European Union has imported a growing proportion of American TV entertainment, with a smaller internal market trading audiovisual goods within Europe. EU member states are relatively affluent postindustrial societies, with well-educated populations and a large professional middle class, characteristics that are typically expected to strengthen cosmopolitan orientations, such as trust and tolerance of other societies. Public opinion about national identities and the organizations of multilateral governance has been closely monitored in the Eurobarometer time-series surveys conducted since the early 1970s.

Far from finding a steady increase in cosmopolitan attitudes, however, successive studies based on Eurobarometer surveys have reported that the public's identification with Europe has fluctuated over time, often in response to specific political events, such as the Maastricht Treaty and the launch of the euro under the European Monetary Union, as well as in reaction to economic performance.[19] For example, a recent study that explored longitudinal support for European integration from 1973 to 2004 in eight long-term member states concluded that support grew following the Maastricht Treaty, peaking around 1991, and subsequently fell.[20] Little evidence suggests that European integration has generated a steadily growing sense of European identity and community among its citizens, even among the public in long-standing member states and in affluent postindustrial societies.[21] In predicting public support for further European integration, Hooghe and Marks argue that national identities remain more influential than economic calculations.[22] Related attitudes, including approval of EU policies, satisfaction with the performance of the Union, and confidence in the European Commission and European Parliament, also display a pattern of trendless fluctuations since the early 1970s rather than growing public support for the European institutions.[23] Persistent cross-national differences are also evident, dividing Europhile states such as Ireland, the Netherlands, and Belgium, where the public is relatively positive across most indicators (despite the rejection of the referenda mentioned earlier), from deep-seated Euroskeptic states, such as Austria, Sweden, and Britain.[24] There has been little convergence in these differences; for example, during the affluent 1990s, British public opinion drifted in an ever more Euroskeptic direction, with almost half the public opting for complete withdrawal by the end of the decade.[25]

Although Eurobarometer trends do not indicate a steadily growing sense of European identity, more specific factors do help to predict support for the European Union. For example, a study based on a recent Germany survey reports more tolerance of foreigners and greater support for the institutions of global governance among Germans with direct personal experience of transnational social relations and border crossing – for example, if they travel to work in another European state or if they have relatives or friends living in another country.[26] Studies comparing 21 countries in the European Social Survey found that Euroskepticism was associated with lower income and education, as well as with distance from Brussels and the duration of the country's EU membership.[27] Attitudes toward EU enlargement have also been

linked to exposure to the mass media, with 'priming' effects shaping
the standards used by the public to evaluate applicant member states.[28]

If there is little systematic comparative evidence of growing cosmopolitan identities based on cross-national time-series trends since
1970 within the European Union, what is the situation elsewhere?
One of the most thorough studies of attitudes toward international
organizations, by Evert, suggests a pattern similar to that already
observed with respect to the European Union. Evert reported that
support for NATO and the United Nations is multidimensional, with
attitudes influenced by responses to specific issues and events rather
than arrayed on a broad continuum stretching from nationalism to
internationalism. Fluctuations over time in the public's approval of
NATO displayed no secular trends, although there were persistent differences in support between member states.[29] Previous analysis by one
of the authors, based on comparisons over time using the WVS data,
provided only limited support for the argument that public opinion has
consistently moved in a more cosmopolitan direction.[30] Instead, the
evidence strongly suggests that, rather than long-term secular trends,
public opinion responds to the impact of specific events arising from
UN interventions in security and defense, such as its peacekeeping role
in the Balkans, Haiti, Somalia, and Angola, the Security Council reso-
lutions after 9/11 authorizing the use of force in the Afghanistan war,
and the role of the international community and the Security Council
in the Iraq war, in Palestine, and in the conflict in the Middle East.
The pattern of trendless fluctuations seems to fit what we know about
public support for the European Union. Moreover, a series of studies
of longitudinal trends in public opinion within the United States suggests that over time there have been waves of support for unilateralism
and internationalism concerning America's role in the world and for
international organizations.[31] These waves have occurred in response
to specific foreign policy events, such as military action in Vietnam,
Somalia, and Iraq, rather than consistently shifting toward a more
secularist internationalist perspective. In the United States, a series of
polls have consistently confirmed that the gut appeal of flag-waving
symbolic patriotism, such as pride in America, remains extremely
strong.[32]

The one important qualification to this argument, however, has to
do with generational change, since young people and the well educated

are usually found to be less nationalistic than older and less-educated groups.[33] Global comparisons of cosmopolitan orientations, indicated by a sense of belonging 'to the world as a whole,' based on the 1981–2001 waves of the WVS, confirmed this pattern.[34] Similar findings were reported in survey-based cross-sectional studies of national identities, national pride, and support for the agencies of multilateral governance in other countries, such as Britain, Australia, and Sweden.[35] If this is a generational pattern, as Tilley and Heath argue, it remains possible that any fundamental transformation of national identities is a lagged process that will become apparent only over successive generations, through the process of demographic turnover.[36] During their formative years, members of the younger generation have been the most exposed to the late-20th-century wave of globalization through their experiences with cross-border information flows in popular culture, via MTV, iPods, and YouTube, as well as their international travel and tourism. In that it provides information and knowledge, education is in many regards similar to the mass media; both potentially expand our understanding and awareness of other places and peoples. On the other hand, if the age-related pattern of cosmopolitan orientations is a life-cycle effect, as Jung argues, there may be no consistent predictions of future trends over time.[37] Jung uses a multilevel model to examine whether a country's integration into the global economy was related to supranational identities and concludes that there is no evidence for this claim. In general, generational and educational patterns are some of the strongest and most consistent predictors of broader dimensions of value change – for example, in terms of adherence to self-expression values and attitudes toward gender equality.[38] These are some of the most important factors to include in any analysis of cosmopolitan orientations, national identities, and support for agencies of global governance.

Therefore, despite plausible theoretical reasons for assuming that globalization and transborder information flows have encouraged growing cosmopolitan orientations in public opinion, on the basis of the existing research literature it seems fair to conclude that most empirical studies lean toward a more skeptical perspective. At least in Europe, national populations vary significantly in their support for the institutions and policies of the European Union, and recent decades have not seen the rise of stronger pan-European identities, although a European identity is stronger among the younger generation and the well educated. Yet the evidence requires further analysis, because studies of cross-national survey results have been limited mainly to postindustrial societies, and given the experience of globalization, different trends may well be occurring in the global South, as well as in particular regions such as the Middle East, Africa, and Central and Eastern Europe. Most importantly, we need to consider evidence relating cosmopolitan orientations directly to the differential impact of transnational information flows and use of the mass media, because the convergence thesis suggests that cosmopolitan orientations should have progressed farther and fastest among those who are most exposed to globalized mass communications. Our research design allows us to do this by contrasting attitudes among users and nonusers of the news media living within different types of media environments. If transborder information flows shape cosmopolitan orientations among media users, the core theory developed in earlier chapters predicts that this effect should be strongest in the open types of information environments. The interpretation of the existing evidence, although leaning toward skepticism, is by no means certain, and it is important to reexamine these issues.

Concepts, Evidence, and Indicators

Before analyzing the empirical data, we need to clarify the underlying concept of 'nationalism,' which is complex to define and operationalize. In this study, the idea of 'national identity' is understood to mean the existence of communities with bonds of 'blood and belonging' that arise from the sharing of a homeland, cultural myths, symbols and historical memories, economic resources, and legal-political rights and duties.[39] Nationalism can take 'civic' forms, meaning ties of soil based on citizenship within a shared territory and boundaries delineated by the nation-state, or it may take 'ethnic' forms, drawing on more diffuse ties based on religious, linguistic, or ethnic communities.[40] National identities are usually implicit and latent, and they may rise to the surface only in response to an 'other,' where we know what we are by virtue of what we are not. In the modern world, national identities underpin the state and its institutions, which exercise political authority within a given territory, although there are many multinational states, such as the United Kingdom, as well as stateless nations, such as those of the Kurds and the Roma. By contrast, cosmopolitan identities are understood to be those outlooks, behaviors, and feelings that transcend local and national boundaries.[41] Typically, cosmopolitans are tolerant of diverse cultural outlooks and practices, valuing human differences rather than similarities, favoring cultural pluralism over convergence, and deemphasizing territorial ties and attachments. Nationalism and cosmopolitanism are usually regarded theoretically as opposites, although it remains to be seen empirically whether these feelings could potentially coexist without contradiction – for example, if people have strong feelings of national pride but also favor multilateral solutions to world problems. We view nationalism and cosmopolitanism as multidimensional phenomena with different forms of expression that manifest, for example, in attitudes toward the institutions of multilateral governance, feelings of belonging and attachment to different communities, or support for policies that facilitate protectionism or globalization, such as attitudes toward free trade or open labor markets.

What survey evidence allows us to examine whether regular use of the news media generates more cosmopolitan orientations within the most globalized and open communication environments? National and cross-national surveys help to illuminate trends in public and elite opinion, the most notable being the occasional studies on world public opinion conducted by the Program on International Attitudes at the University of Maryland, the Pew Global Attitudes Project, the BBC World Service, and the Chicago Council on Foreign Relations.[42] Surveys of American and European public opinion often monitor foreign policy attitudes within specific nations, and studies have compared attitudes among some of the major donor countries.[43] Nevertheless, consistent comparisons are limited when these resources are used, and it is difficult to link attitudes to patterns of media consumption. Previous comparative studies have often relied on the Eurobarometer monitoring of public opinion about these issues since the early 1970s within EU member states. Modules on nationalism have also been included in the annual International Social Survey Programme (ISSP), covering almost two dozen countries.[44] These are invaluable sources, but systematic cross-national time-series surveys of attitudes remain limited, especially systematic studies comparing public opinion and use of the media across a wide range of developing nations, countries with different levels of globalization and different types of media environment. To provide the broadest cross-national analysis, this book utilizes the most comprehensive comparative data available from the WVS and European Values Surveys carried out from 1981 to 2007, covering more than 90 societies worldwide.

The success of attempts to conceptualize and measure the core concepts of nationalism and cosmopolitanism remains in question.[45] Hence, Roudometof suggests a one-dimensional operationalization, with a single scale based on a continuum of territorial identities, ranging from cosmopolitan to local orientations.[46] Others who criticize this measure as too simple have recommended a two-dimensional operationalization that also takes account of attitudes toward transnationalism, ranging from cultural or economic protectionism to openness.[47] Still others have specified a multidimensional perspective; for example, Woodward et al. suggest that Australians respond differently to distinct aspects of this phenomenon, favoring the increased flow of cultural goods and supporting cultural diversity but experiencing greater anxiety over such issues as the impact of globalization on jobs, the environment, and human rights.[48] The present study also adopts a multidimensional approach. The concept of cosmopolitanism can be understood to reflect both values and identities. Cosmopolitans express tolerance and trust of people from other countries, rejecting the politics of fear and xenophobia. Cosmopolitan orientations should lead to a willingness to understand other peoples and places, expressed, for example, by an interest in foreign travel or working abroad and tolerance of immigrants, strangers, and visitors from other nations. Conversely, nationalists are understood in this study to be those who identify strongly with their country of origin (or with regions and local areas within the territorial boundaries of the nation-state), who express strong pride in their country, and who are less trusting of other nationalities and more intolerant of foreigners than average. These core values and identities should also influence attitudes toward specific institutions and public policies; for example, cosmopolitans are expected to support policies favoring open labor markets and free trade, while nationalists are more likely to support economic policies that protect local jobs or industries, an issue explored in more depth in the next chapter.

TABLE 6.1. *Dimensions of Cosmopolitan Orientations*

	Nationalist Identities	Trust in Outsiders
V212 Sees self as a national citizen	.802	
V211 Sees self as part of a local community	.731	
V209 Expresses national pride	.646	
V75 Willingness to fight for country	.450	
V130 Trust in people of another nationality		.930
V146 Trust in people of another religion		.929
Total variance	30.3	28.5

Note: Extraction method: principal-component factor analysis. Rotation method: varimax with Kaiser normalization. Coefficients of .40 or less were dropped from the analysis. See Technical Appendix A for the construction of these scales.
Source: World Values Survey (2005–2007).

Principal-components factor analysis with varimax rotation was used to test whether this conceptual typology reflected the underlying dimensions of public opinion in the selected items contained in the WVS and listed in Table 6.1. Survey items monitored trust in outsiders, or those from other places and societies and those of other faiths. The strength of national identities was gauged by multiple items concerning the strength of national pride, willingness to fight for one's own country, and one's attachment to different territorial areas, all items commonly used in previous studies.[49] The 2005–2007 WVS monitored identities using multiple items, where people could specify several overlapping geographic identities, rather than treating alternative identities as trade-off responses, a practice followed in previous waves of the study.[50] The 2005–2007 measure assumes that one can have multiple nested identities, so that people can maintain their national and local identities while also having a growing sense of supranational attachments; people can be proud of living in local communities in Flanders or Wallonia, for example, while simultaneously seeing themselves as citizens of Belgium and part of the European Union. Accordingly, respondents were asked the following in the WVS:

People have different views about themselves and how they relate to the world. Using this card, would you tell me how strongly you agree or disagree with each of the following statements about how you see yourself? I see myself as a citizen of the [French]* nation. . . . I see myself as a member of my local community. . . . [*substitute nation of the survey].[51]

The results of the factor analysis presented in Table 6.1 show the relationships among the selected variables with the rotated matrix, accounting, in total, for more than half (58%) of the variance in responses. The analysis confirmed the existence of two distinct dimensions of public opinion: trust in outsiders and feelings of nationalist identity. Technical Appendix A provides more details about the questionnaire items selected for analysis and their coding and measurement. The analysis presented in this chapter focuses on data drawn from the fifth wave in 2005–2007, as not all the items selected for analysis were included with identical wording in all previous waves. To construct value scales, the separate items listed in Table 6.1 were summed and converted into two standardized 100-point scales for ease of comparison across each dimension. Any single item may generate specific responses in particular countries and contexts; for example, a question about the willingness to fight for one's country may trigger a specific reaction for Rwandans, Iraqis, or Russians living near conflict zones, whereas value scales across a wider range of items are more likely to generate reliable cross-national comparisons reflecting more general attitudes toward nationalism.

Explaining Trust in Outsiders

To examine the associations of these dimensions of public opinion with the use of news media, as a first step we can look descriptively at the contrasts in mean levels of trust in outsiders (measured on a 100-point scale) by level of news media use among each type of society, without any controls. Trust in foreigners and in people of other religions is an important indicator of broader orientations toward other countries and world regions, with implications for public support for bilateral alliances and for multilateral cooperation in the international community. Taken to an extreme, xenophobia and faith-based hatred can have disastrous consequences for social stability and for international relations, while tolerance of other peoples and faiths is beneficial for harmonious relations. The pattern in Figure 6.1 illustrates the average level of trust in outsiders expressed by low, moderate, and high news media users (categorizing the combined media scale) living within each type of society.

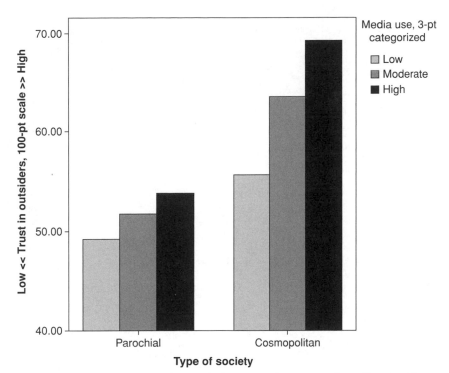

FIGURE 6.1. Trust in Outsiders Scale by Type of Society and Media Use. The question asked (Q130) was as follows: 'I'd like to ask you how much you trust people from various groups... People of another nationality / People of another religion. Could you tell me for each whether you trust people from this group completely (coded 4), somewhat (3), not very much (2), or not at all (1)?' The responses were combined into a 100-point trust in outsiders scale. The chart shows the mean level of trust in outsiders for each type of society and category of media use, without any prior controls. *Source:* World Values Survey (2005–2007).

The figure clearly illustrates the sharp contrasts in trust among those living in cosmopolitan and parochial societies. Moreover, those who are most attentive to the news media are far more tolerant of outsiders than are those who are less attentive, a pattern consistently found in each type of society. The contextual effects are particularly striking: low media users in cosmopolitan societies are more trusting of outsiders than are the most attentive media users in parochial societies. We can speculate about some of the underlying reasons for these patterns.

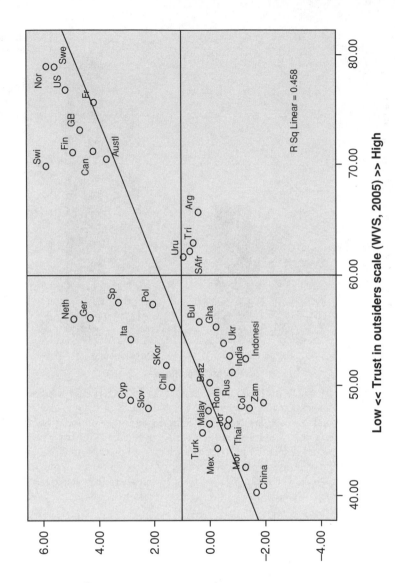

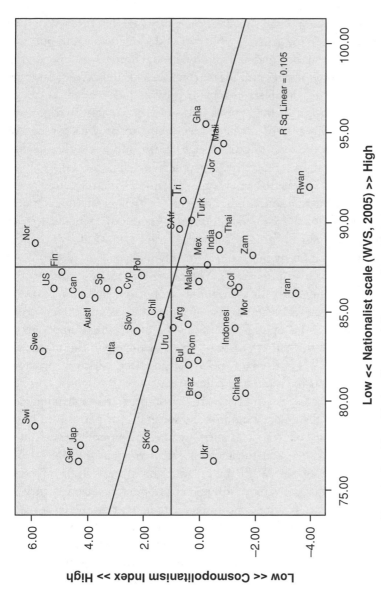

FIGURE 6.2. Trust in Outsiders, Nationalism, and Cosmopolitan Societies.

In the most cosmopolitan societies, such as Switzerland, Norway, and the United States, the general public has widespread access to multiple sources of information and news, and national borders are open to the flow of imported images and ideas from abroad. Reporters and journalists enjoy considerable freedom to provide independent coverage that can be critical of the actions and policies of their own government, and a plurality of media outlets helps to provide a range of perspectives in the reporting of foreign affairs and news about other societies and cultures. By contrast, people living in parochial societies, such as Haiti, Syria and Nepal, often have far less access to a wide range of information sources that provide awareness and understanding of international events and cultures. Where governments restrict freedom of expression, domestic news coverage is more likely to reflect the official position of the state, with less independent reporting or international sources providing coverage critical of the regime. These descriptive findings provide some initial support for the claim that regular use of the news media exposes people to ideas and images from other societies and peoples, encouraging a more cosmopolitan view of the world, and this pattern appears to be strongest in the most cosmopolitan places. Far from any polarization effect, what this provides tentative support for is the convergence thesis.

Because the contrasts by type of environment are so striking, the scattergram in Figure 6.2 examines the societal-level patterns in more detail, showing countries classified by the Cosmopolitanism Index on the vertical axis and the mean level of trust in outsiders from the fifth wave of the WVS on the horizontal axis. It is immediately obvious that a cluster of affluent cosmopolitan societies, such as Norway, the United States, and France, are highest on the trust scale. These are the societies with the densest access to information technologies, as well as a free press and open borders. Moreover, many of the most parochial nations under comparison, including China, Morocco, and Russia, are the *least* trusting of outsiders. At the same time, although generating a moderately strong correlation ($R = .458$, sig. 000), there are also some countries located in the top left quadrant, such as the Netherlands, Germany and Italy, which are relatively cosmopolitan in their social characteristics and media environments, and yet appear to be less trusting of outsiders than might be expected.

Such descriptive results are limited; as we established in the preceding chapter, many factors such as age, education, and income are closely associated with use of the news media, and are often linked with social values and attitudes. Multilevel models using regression analysis are needed to determine whether exposure to the news media remains significantly related to trust in outsiders after the other individual-level social characteristics and attitudes that help to predict use of the media are controlled for and interaction effects between the societal-level media environments and individual use of the media are tested. Table 6.2 presents the results of the multilevel regression models in the pooled sample for all societies in the fifth wave of the WVS. The standardized 100-point trust in outsiders scale (combining trust in people of other nationalities and other faiths) is the dependent variable. These models control for the factors that, as we have already established, are some of the key predictors of media use, including individual-level demographic characteristics (gender and age) and socioeconomic resources (education and income).[52] The models also entered the societal-level Cosmopolitanism Index and tested the cross-level interaction effect. As is common in multilevel models, all variables were standardized to the mean to facilitate interpretation of the coefficients. The multilevel regression models were also double-checked to ensure that they were free of collinearity problems. The core results for the Cosmopolitanism Index are summarized in Model A, but in addition four other models were run to explore the impact of alternative national-level components in more detail, including the separate effects of globalization, economic development, media freedom, and societal-level media access.

The results of all the models presented in Table 6.2 confirm that *individual-level use of the news media is significantly associated with greater trust in outsiders*, even after the other individual-level characteristics that we have already established contribute to news media use are controlled for. Since the scale for trust in outsiders is measured using standardized 100-point scales, the models suggest that those who use the news media heavily are, on average, approximately 15% more likely to trust outsiders than are others. Overall education remains the strongest individual-level predictor in the model. This result confirms numerous previous studies that have established that the cognitive skills, knowledge, and information associated with schooling are

TABLE 6.2. *Multilevel Regression Models Explaining Trust in Outsiders*

	A Cosmopolitanism Index	B Globalization Index	C Economic Development	D Media Freedom	E Media Access
INDIVIDUAL LEVEL					
Demographic characteristics					
Age (years)	1.45***	1.46***	1.46***	1.46***	1.46***
	(.099)	(.099)	(.099)	(.099)	(.102)
Gender (male = 1)	−.099	−.099	−.099	−.099	−.099
	(.090)	(.090)	(.091)	(.091)	(.091)
Socioeconomic resources					
Household income, 10-pt scale	.628***	.627***	.628***	.628***	.627***
	(.101)	(.101)	(.101)	(.101)	(.101)
Education, 9-pt scale	2.177***	2.180***	2.177***	2.180***	2.180***
	(.119)	(.118)	(.118)	(.118)	(.118)
Media use					
News media use scale	1.53***	.1.54***	1.53***	1.53***	1.54***
	(.112)	(.112)	(.106)	(.106)	(.112)
NATIONAL LEVEL					
Cosmopolitanism Index	5.489***				
(Globalization + development + freedom)	(1.221)				
Globalization Index		2.870*			
		(1.382)			

Economic development			5.621***		
			(1.166)		
Media freedom				6.103***	
				(1.213)	
Societal-level media access					3.186**
					(1.284)
CROSS-LEVEL INTERACTIONS					
Cosmopolitanism × media use scale	.793***	.793***	.790***	.797***	.794***
	(.100)	(.101)	(.101)	(.101)	(.101)
Constant (intercept)	56.3	56.7	56.6	56.1	57.6
Schwartz BIC	493,505	493,518	493,503	493,554	493,567
No. of respondents	55,108	55,073	55,112	55,113	55,113
No. of nations	44	44	44	44	44

Note: All independent variables were standardized using mean centering (*z*-scores). Models present the results of the REML multilevel regression models (for details, see Technical Appendix C). The 100-point trust in outsiders scale, from the items listed in Table 6.1, is the dependent variable. The 100-point media use scale combined use of newspapers, radio/TV, Internet, books, and magazines. Models report the beta coefficient slopes (*b*), standard errors (in parentheses), and their significance (*p* = .05; ** *p* = .01; *** *p* = .001). See Technical Appendix A for details about the measurement, coding, and construction of all variables. Significant coefficients are indicated by asterisks.

Source: World Values Survey (2005–2007).

closely associated with more tolerant and trusting attitudes.[53] Greater
trust in outsiders was also found among the more affluent households,
and there was no significant effect of gender, although somewhat unexpectedly, greater trust was evident among the older population, a pattern that persisted in the data regardless of whether or not the age
variable was logged.

At the national level, *living in a cosmopolitan society makes people
more trusting of outsiders*. This suggests that exposure to information
flows from outside national borders does not generate a negative backlash; instead, people who live in isolated and parochial societies with
minimal information about the outside world tend to be more fearful
of strangers and foreigners. Those who are bound to other countries
by communication networks, ties of trade, and news about the world
are generally more trusting. But how do we know which aspect of the
Cosmopolitanism Index was most important for this relationship – in
particular, how do we know whether it was simply the product of living in a more affluent postindustrial society or whether globalization,
media freedom, and media access played a role? These factors cannot
be entered simultaneously, due to their strong intercorrelation (rich
economies also tend to have well-developed media access, freedom of
expression, etc.). But we can enter each of these national-level variables
in successive models to test their effects. The results of the alternative
models in Table 6.2 indicate that, as theorized, each of these societal characteristics at the national level can be regarded as strong and
significant drivers in this relationship. In particular, economic development does have a strong effect on trust in outsiders; as previous
studies have found, the people of more affluent countries are more
likely to trust people from other countries and religions than are those
of less affluent countries. But it is striking that media freedom has a
stronger effect on trust in outsiders than does economic development
alone; this suggests that countries with a pluralistic range of media
outlets and minimum internal restrictions on freedom of expression
are the most likely to trust foreigners and people of other faiths. The
separate impacts of media access and the KOF Globalization Index
were statistically significant but weaker than the predictive capacity of
the composite Cosmopolitanism Index.

Finally, the models also enter the cross-level interaction effect, and
the results confirm the positive impact on trust of use of the media

within more cosmopolitan societies. The coefficients are significant and moderately strong; on the 100-point scale, for example, after all the other controls are applied, heavy users of the news in cosmopolitan societies are about 8% more trusting of outsiders than are others. The multilevel model provides support for the argument that people's openness to foreigners and people of different faiths is affected by use of the news media and by the permeability of the society in which they live.

Feelings of National Identity

To establish whether these findings are robust, we will use similar models to explore the factors associated with nationalist identities. The composite nationalist scale was constructed by summing responses on the extent to which respondents expressed a sense of national pride and the extent to which they were willing to fight for their country, as well as the extent to which people saw themselves as national citizens and members of a local community. The scatter plot in Figure 6.2 shows the modestly negative relationship between the societal level of cosmopolitanism and the nationalist scale; some of the most cosmopolitan societies, such as Switzerland, Germany, Sweden, and Japan, are also the least nationalistic. At the same time, some of the most provincial societies, such as Mali, Ghana, and Jordan, are the most nationalistic. But there is quite a wide distribution of countries, including parochial societies such as Indonesia, China, and Ukraine, that are not very nationalistic and only a weak correlation between these two dimensions ($R = .105$).

Again many factors could be contributing to these patterns, and multilevel regression may help us to interpret the data. The results of the models presented in Table 6.3 show that after all individual-level controls are included, in general, *nationalist identities were usually positively and significantly associated with individual-level use of the news media*. In addition, feelings of nationalism were diminished by education, but they were stronger among more affluent households, among the older generations, and among men.

At the national level, *living in a cosmopolitan society was strongly related to less nationalistic orientations*. The results of the alternative models suggest that overall the degree of globalization was

TABLE 6.3. *Multilevel Regression Models Explaining Nationalism*

	A Cosmopolitanism Index	B Globalization Index	C Economic Development	D Media Freedom	E Media Access
INDIVIDUAL LEVEL					
Demographic characteristics					
Age (years)	1.11***	1.11***	1.11***	1.11***	1.11***
	(.060)	(.060)	(.060)	(.060)	(.060)
Gender (male = 1)	.505***	.505***	.505***	.505***	.505***
	(.054)	(.054)	(.054)	(.054)	(.054)
Socioeconomic resources					
Household income, 10-pt scale	.189***	.189***	.189***	.189***	.189***
	(.060)	(.060)	(.060)	(.060)	(.060)
Education, 9-pt scale	-.289***	-.289***	-.289***	-.289***	-.289***
	(.071)	(.071)	(.071)	(.071)	(.071)
Media use					
News media use scale	.382***	.382***	.382***	.382***	.382***
	(.066)	(.066)	(.066)	(.066)	(.066)
NATIONAL LEVEL					
Cosmopolitanism Index	-2.822***				
(Globalization + development + freedom)	(.818)				
Globalization Index		-2.986***			
		(.805)			

	Model 1	Model 2	Model 3	Model 4	Model 5
Economic development			−2.555** (.766)		
Media freedom				−1.664 (.928)	
Societal-level media access					−2.857** (.720)
CROSS-LEVEL INTERACTIONS					
Cosmopolitanism × media use scale	−.180** (.062)	−.182** (.061)	−.182** (.061)	−.182** (.061)	−.181 (.061)
Constant (intercept)	84.8	84.7	84.7	84.7	84.7
Schwartz BIC	332,921	332,920	332,922	332,922	332,922
No. of respondents	43,883	43,407	43,407	43,407	43,407
No. of nations	39	39	39	39	39

Note: All independent variables were standardized using mean centering (z-scores). Models present the results of the REML multilevel regression models (for details, see Technical Appendix C). The 100-point trust in outsiders scale, from the items listed in Table 6.1, is the dependent variable. The 100-point media use scale combined use of newspapers, radio/TV, Internet, books, and magazines. Models report the beta coefficient slopes (b), standard errors (in parentheses), and their significance (*p = .05; **p = .01; ***p = .001). See Technical Appendix A for details about the measurement, coding, and construction of all variables. Significant coefficients are highlighted in bold.
Source: World Values Survey (2005–2007).

the strongest national-level predictor of less nationalistic attitudes, although the effects of globalization, economic development, and societal-level media access were very similar. Many factors closely associated with economic development are expected to contribute to the erosion of nationalism, including, in particular, greater access to education, the growth of the professional middle classes, and the affluence generated by economic growth. But the results also suggest that the expansion of access to the mass media and the direct experience of living in a more permeable society open to outside influences also play important roles in this process. Finally, the interaction effect of use of the news media in cosmopolitan societies was significantly negative. News media use was usually associated with slightly stronger nationalist identities. Nationwide broadcasting systems and national newspapers can reinforce a sense of belonging to a single community and allegiance to the nation-state, such as feelings of national pride or willingness to serve and defend one's country militarily. But this effect is contingent on the context: nationalist identities are *weaker* in the most globalized societies, such as the Netherlands, Switzerland, and Sweden, which are characterized by dense networks of cosmopolitan communications with easy access to foreign television channels, as well as international communication networks. Moreover, national identities are *especially weak among news users in these cosmopolitan societies*. As some hope and others fear, denser and faster interconnections across territorial borders *do* seem to gradually erode older allegiances and promote a more multicultural ethos. Media use is not the strongest factor in this process, but it is a significant one, interacting with the direct experience of living in an increasingly globalized world.

Conclusions and Discussion

The growth of broadcasting systems within each country has traditionally been regarded as an important factor in the strengthening of national communities and feelings of national identity, especially in multicultural societies with contested national boundaries. Public service broadcasters, in particular, often regard their role as bringing together diverse sectors, subregions, and communities, as well as representing the nation to the outside world. These are key components of the mandate for the BBC, set forth in its royal charter.[54] This role has come under increasing challenge from deregulation and the new competitive multichannel environment, leaving public service broadcasters to reinvent their distinct mandates and missions.[55] The globalization of the news media and the expansion of cross-national information flows may potentially disrupt these processes of nation building if this gradually generates broader identities and allegiances. Cosmopolitan communications can be regarded as having potentially beneficial consequences – for example, if ideas about universal human rights and democratic governance are disseminated around the world. But this process is also often regarded as threatening – for example, when foreign ideas and imported programs limit the ability of fragile multicultural states and post-conflict societies to develop stronger bonds and allegiances across diverse social sectors and ethnicities. Although theorists have often speculated about the impact of cross-national information flows on nationalist and cosmopolitan orientations, systematic empirical evidence regarding public opinion that spans many types of societies and media systems has generally been lacking.

The findings presented here suggest that exposure to the news media does indeed have the effect of strengthening trust and tolerance of outsiders, including people of different nationalities and faiths. But far from automatically eviscerating national identities, as some fear, the impact of the news media is conditional on the societal environment. General use of the news media is usually linked to stronger national identities, but this effect is less marked in cosmopolitan societies, especially among news users. These relationships remain significant after the application of multiple prior controls for education, income, age, and gender, factors that help to predict both use of the news media and social values.

At the same time, the interpretation of the empirical results must be qualified in certain important respects. Media use and demographic characteristics represent only some of the factors underlying trust in outsiders and broader nationalistic orientations. We do not endorse a monocausal theory. If xenophobia or trust in other religious communities is a social psychological trait that is deeply rooted in early socialization experiences, in social networks, or in structural conditions in society, these feelings could be explained by many other factors not included in these analytical models.[56] Hence, social capital theories, explaining the related concepts of generalized trust and tolerance within society, emphasize the importance of personal bonds and networks formed during face-to-face interactions; the degree of ethnic, linguistic, or racial heterogeneity or homogeneity in a given society; and the role of associations in bridging social divisions.[57] And classic accounts of the 'authoritarian personality' regard trust in others as a psychological trait closely associated with feelings of powerlessness, frustration, and resentment.[58] Spatial explanations suggest that attitudes toward foreigners could be related to a society's geocultural location, including its proximity to neighboring states that share certain linguistic, religious, or ethnic characteristics and historical traditions. If so, the geographic location of respondents living in particular regions and of national communities within multicultural states, such as Belgium, Canada, and the United Kingdom, could also prove important.[59] Theories based on party competition emphasize that a sense of nationalism can be exacerbated by the rhetorical appeals of political elites and party leaders (especially on the radical right) when they emphasize the salience of immigration and asylum seekers as political issues.[60] Within international relations, explanations often stress that public opinion reflects the international power of the state, elite cues from the domestic political leadership, and foreign relations with other countries.[61] Openness to people from other countries and tolerance of outsiders of different faiths may also be affected by interpersonal experience with transborder social relations arising from immigration, travel, and job mobility.[62]

In short, feelings of nationalism and trust in outsiders are complex and cannot be explained by a single factor; the role of the media in this process is only one part of the story, but it does seem to have an impact on cosmopolitan orientations and generalized trust. It remains to be seen whether similar patterns will be evident when we examine other dimensions of public opinion. Subsequent chapters will explore whether exposure to cosmopolitan communications has the capacity to expand neoliberal support for free markets and to reduce faith in the role of the state in the economy, to alter traditional moralities, or to expand support for democratic values. If we find patterns similar to those presented in this chapter, this will increase our confidence in the reliability and robustness of the results.

7

Consumers

Economic Values

A central feature of globalization has been the integration of world markets, binding together the fortunes of Wall Street, the City of London, and the Deutsche Börse; linking call centers in Bangalore with customers in Toronto; and shipping Asian-made goods to American shelves. Indeed, contemporary commentators such as Martin Wolf regard the economics of globalization as the driving force for almost all other aspects of globalization.[1] Improvements in transport and communications have opened new opportunities for commerce; the railway, steamship, and transatlantic telegraph bound economies together in the 19th century, just as container ships, satellite, and the Internet led to faster trade in the 20th. Debate continues about how to interpret economic globalization, including whether what is happening amounts to growing segmentation into major regional trading blocs (principally the European Union, APEC, and NAFTA) rather than growing integration of the entire world. It is also questioned whether contemporary patterns of economic integration are unprecedented or whether earlier historical eras experienced cycles of internationalization that were longer than those of the current period.[2] We have examined rising levels of economic globalization during recent decades: trends in the KOF index illustrated in Figure 4.3 suggest relatively slow growth in economic integration during the 1970s and 1980s, followed by a spurt since the early 1990s. Chapter 4 also showed the persistent globalization gap between rich and poor nations, with the major OECD economies bound together most strongly by intensified flows of capital and trade across national borders, a process also affecting the leading emerging market economies in Europe, Latin America, and East Asia. Yet many of the poorest economies, containing the bottom billion of the world's population, remain largely excluded from global markets of trade and capital flows, while experiencing the loss of their most skilled workforce through migration.[3] Collier and Stigletz emphasize that many of the world's least developed countries have failed to benefit substantially from trade liberalization and export-led growth.[4] The breakdown of the Doha negotiations over agricultural subsidies in July 2008 illustrates the limits of further economic integration, constituting an important reversal.

How have economic globalization and the globalization of mass communications transformed economic values? This chapter outlines the theoretical debate over this issue, including claims that globalization has encouraged the triumph of the Washington consensus emphasizing free market economics and the counterargument that a backlash has occurred against neoliberal ideas, led by oil-rich states such as Russia and Venezuela. Most of the political economy literature on this topic has adopted an instrumental approach. Studies have examined the extent to which rational calculations of self-interest have influenced policy attitudes toward trade and economic integration, without considering the role of mass communications. If the cultural convergence thesis is correct, exposure to globalized mass communications should gradually expand support for the neoliberal free market values at the heart of capitalism: we should find increasing emphasis on achieving individual success and getting rich, as well as changing mass attitudes toward the role of the state, the creation of wealth, and economic incentives. This process should also gradually erode support for the collective values crucial to socialism, such as those of solidarity and community, social protection, and economic equality. On the other hand, if the polarization argument is right, greater exposure to news media in developing societies should be expected to generate a backlash against the neoliberal economic ideas central to the Washington consensus, leading to a rejection of capitalist values.

As in the preceding chapter, to test these questions using the World Values Survey data, we first select a wide range of multidimensional indicators of economic values and employ factor analysis to identify and construct standardized scales. Focusing on any single attitudinal item can produce idiosyncratic results, reflecting contextual factors such as the debate about NAFTA in Mexico, specific trade agreements in Ireland, or Muslim migrant workers in Denmark. Scales based on a broader range of items enable us to generate more reliable and consistent measures for comparison. The images and messages of neoliberalism are expected to penetrate cosmopolitan societies to the greatest extent, with their minimal barriers to foreign cultural imports, relative freedom of the press, and widespread access to mass communications. Countries that meet these conditions, such as South Africa, Chile, Taiwan, and Latvia, would be expected to be more strongly influenced by transborder information flows than are provincial societies, such as Ethiopia and Malawi. We analyze whether economic values are related directly to individual use of the mass media, controlling for many other social characteristics, including age, education, and income, that we know to be important in predicting news media use. These multilevel regression models clarify whether use of the media has an especially strong impact in the most open societies, where information from abroad is the most widely available.

The Debate over Economic Globalization

The convergence thesis holds that the expansion of multinational corporations into world markets, with their iconic brand images, mass advertising, and high-status products, has encouraged the spread of American or Western economic values. The cultural imperialism thesis proposed by Herbert Schiller during the early 1970s claimed that capitalist values conveyed in American news, advertising, and entertainment have spread to developing societies, a process designed to reinforce the market share of corporate capitalism.[5] For Schiller, the 'tidal flow' of American TV programs, films, music, and other cultural products conveys the predominant transnational images and messages that have the capacity to shape the values and behavior of audiences everywhere, potentially 'turning the world into one vast shopping mall' and opening new markets for American business.[6] Schiller's work was originally developed at the height of the decolonization era, when many newly independent developing countries, with left-wing governments, were highly critical of the legacy of colonialism. So much has changed since then that it might be thought that this perspective has lost credibility and now represents something of a straw man. Never-theless, during the early 1990s Schiller argued that his interpretation was more relevant than ever, as the capacity of the United States to reach previously closed markets expanded after the collapse of the Soviet Union as a rival superpower, the removal of trade barriers, and the deregulation of state and public service broadcasting in many parts of the world.[7]

Other theorists have echoed similar themes. One of the strongest contemporary arguments has been advanced by Herman and Mc-Chesney, who suggest that the problem with the growth of transna-tional media corporations is not that their products reflect U.S. culture per se, since they often diversify goods and services to meet the needs in local markets, but rather that they reflect the commercial interests of investors, advertisers, and affluent elites.[8] As a result, they argue, the values of consumerism and individualism have pervaded popular culture, television news and entertainment, recorded music, and books and newspapers, as well as explicit advertising messages. Corporations marketing Levis, Marlboro, and Nike encourage popular consumerism from Beirut to Mumbai; along with brand-name products, they are also thought to sell dreams of personal success, affluence, and mate-rial gratification. Andersen argues that consumer culture is not simply confined to mass advertising; it is an integral part of Western enter-tainment and information.[9] Business and financial news, in particular, is far from neutral; the streaming banners and headlines of CNN Inter-national, MSNBC, and Sky News can be seen as cheerleaders for Wall Street.[10] Commentators such as Joseph Nye celebrate the soft power and cultural predominance of the United States as a way to spread the Washington consensus about the virtues of free market competi-tion, privatization, and deregulation, without resorting to American military force.[11] Many others, referring to the 'Coca-colonization,' 'McDisneyization,' or 'McDonaldization' of the world, fear the cul-tural consequences of the global market economy led by American- or Western-based multinational corporations.[12]

An alternative interpretation of contemporary developments is set forth by the theory of polarization, which emphasizes the limits of the Washington consensus and a strong backlash against economic glob-alization. Perhaps the best known argument has been developed by the economist Joseph Stigletz, who suggests that public discontent has been encouraged by persistent or growing inequalities between rich and poor societies, the loss of blue-collar jobs abroad, European worries about cuts in social protection programs and the shrinking welfare state, and concern about the hegemonic power of American-based corporations.[13] The global rise in oil and gas prices, expanding the economic fortunes and political power of autocratic regimes in Venezuela, Russia, Uzbekistan, Iran, and Saudi Arabia, has also encouraged a pushback against Washington's economic and political agenda, as has the rapidly growing economic power of China and India. Under Chavez, Venezuela is in the process of renationalizing industries, while under Putin's leadership, Russia is showing a resurgent willingness to use military force in neighboring countries. The breakdown of the Doha trade negotiations in July 2008 over agricultural protectionism, after seven years of talks, also indicates the growing chasm concerning trade between the major developing countries, represented by the G20, and the European Union and the United States. Backlash is not limited to political elites, as is evident from the mass antiglobalization demonstrations linked with meetings of the WTO, IMF, and related global agencies, and the active resistance of environmental and labor movements against the forces of economic integration and free trade.[14] Global warming and concerns about food safety have also encouraged public awareness of the importance of local sustainability in food production and a public reaction against the ethos of conspicuous material consumption. The 2008 banking crisis, which rapidly spread from American subprime mortgages to destabilize credit throughout the financial world, also underlined the dangers of growing economic interdependence. Of course, rather than there being a simple either/or interpretation, it could be that complex developments are interacting simultaneously in different parts of the world, providing support for both the convergence and polarization interpretations; as we saw in comparing patterns of economic globalization in Figure 5.4, Estonia, Poland, and Malaysia have followed export-led strategies to growth and have become more open to global markets, while others, such as North Korea and Burma, maintain rigid protectionist economic policies and isolationist foreign policies.

Beyond speculation about historical and contemporary political developments, what systematic empirical evidence about public opinion is available for evaluating mass attitudes toward economic globalization? Understanding these issues is particularly important in monitoring the dynamics of public opinion and support for protectionist policies and market reforms in new democracies, particularly the former Communist states and the Latin American economies that have followed the policies of the Washington consensus most aggressively by deregulating and privatizing the public sector, liberalizing trade, and shrinking the role of the state. A growing body of research has started to explore the factors associated with public support for free trade and economic integration. The most extensive literature in political economy has adopted a rational actor model and examined the instrumental factors leading to policy attitudes most directly related to economic globalization.[15] Political economists have argued that professional workers with high-level skills are more likely to benefit from free trade than are less skilled blue-collar workers, who face greater risks from imported goods. As a result, skill levels (measured by educational attainment) are expected to predict individual trade preferences.[16] On the basis of a similar logic of rational self-interest, others theorize that those employed in export-led sectors are more likely than others to favor free trade policies.[17] Those who are risk averse are also expected to be more likely to prefer protectionist trade policies, although fears of these risks may be mitigated in strong welfare states.[18] Empirical studies have examined attitudes toward free trade and NAFTA in the United States, where direct experience with economic globalization has been found to encourage support for neoliberal attitudes toward free trade, open labor markets, and economic integration, especially in sectors that have most clearly benefited from export-led growth and capital flows.[19] Comparative studies have examined public reactions to economic reform in selected Eastern European and East Asian countries.[20] Using longitudinal data, others have analyzed the dynamics of trends in the approval of the single-market European Monetary Union and labor mobility within the European Union, reporting trendless fluctuations in public opinion and marked contrasts among member states rather than steadily growing public support for economic integration.[21]

Evidence based on public opinion also provides some support for the polarization argument that a backlash against the neoliberal Washington consensus has occurred in many parts of the world. For example, a comparative survey conducted in 2007 in 18 developed and developing countries by GlobeScan, on behalf of World Public Opinion, found that majorities in most countries continue to support the free market system, but in recent years support has eroded in 10 countries, and in several cases this drop has been quite sharp.[22] Moreover, a BBC World Service poll of 34 countries around the world, conducted by GlobeScan in November 2007, found widespread public concern that the pace of economic globalization, including trade and investment, was growing too fast.[23] Interestingly, the strongest agreement with this sentiment was expressed in some of the most affluent postindustrial societies, such as Australia (73%), Spain (68%), and France (64%). There was far less agreement with this view among people living in middle-income countries such as Russia (23%), the Philippines (24%), Turkey (15%), and Mexico (23%). Australian survey evidence suggests that the public endorses the way that economic globalization expands opportunities to consume products and to gain access to goods from around the world.[24] But it also shows that the Australian public feels widespread concern about the possible loss of jobs that could arise from open labor markets. Surveys among countries in the southern cone of Africa have found complex attitudes toward different types of economic reform, rather than simple reactions for or against them.[25] Overall, therefore, the growing body of empirical evidence concerning trends in public opinion about economic globalization and the drivers of support for such globalization provides a complex picture of developments, depending on the particular survey, the issues examined, and the comparative framework analyzed by different studies, but it tends to suggest a skeptical interpretation rather than ever-rising levels of public support for economic integration.

Evidence for Economic Values

Previous political economy and public opinion research has not examined the role of cosmopolitan communications in shaping economic attitudes. Arguably, however, our perceptions of the possible benefits of and threats to self-interest arising from economic globalization are derived largely from the news media rather than from firsthand experience. Some Americans, for example, have directly experienced unemployment as a result of jobs moving to low-income countries or the loss of their homes through mortgage foreclosure, but millions more have read news stories about rust-belt factory closures, recalls of dangerous imported Chinese toys, the credit crunch, or reports about salmonella contamination of Mexican-grown produce, all of which may help shape American perceptions about the risks and benefits of more open economic borders.

Moreover, previous studies have focused primarily on analyzing policy *attitudes* – for example, toward free trade, open labor markets, economic integration, and economic globalization in developed and developing nations. Public opinion polls commissioned by the media or policymakers are typically concerned with mass orientations toward specific policies or recent events, such as whether Europeans approve of the Maastricht agreement and whether Americans favor the outcome of the Doha trade negotiations. But this approach has limited utility for understanding the more subtle ways that global communications may shape broader and more enduring economic *values* – for example, by emphasizing the desirability of consumerism, individualism, and competition. Unlike policy attitudes, economic values transcend specific actions and particular situations; for example, the values of competition, cooperation, hard work, and individual success can be applied to work or school, business or politics.[26] Values reflect desirable goals – for the individual, household, society, and indeed the world. People have a variety of goals and the relative importance of those goals determines value priorities. As such, values are understood to tap into relatively durable aspects of social psychology that orientate us toward specific attitudes and cognitive beliefs. Americans who place a high value on both competition and consumption, for example, are expected to approve of free trade agreements such as NAFTA, believing that such policies will benefit economic growth. On the other hand, Americans who give great importance to the values of nationalism and patriotism, and who regard NAFTA as threatening American-owned businesses and U.S. jobs, would be expected to oppose this policy. Hence, Rankin argues that nationalist values often provide important cues about highly technical issues, such as trade preferences, where the public lacks detailed information, so that highly patriotic people are consistently found to prefer trade protectionism.[27]

The diffuse nature of values also facilitates wide-ranging comparisons across diverse countries and cultures; it makes little sense to ask people around the world whether they support the Doha round of trade agreements, the bailout of banks, or even the role and activities of the WTO, NAFTA, or the European Commission, when people have little or no detailed knowledge or awareness of these topics. 'Manufactured,' 'off the top of the head,' and 'nonattitudes' can always be offered by survey respondents and recorded by polls, but such responses are unlikely to prove stable, deeply rooted, well-structured, or reliable indicators of public opinion.[28] Converse first noted that people often try to give some response to survey questions, even if they have no prior attitudes toward the issues at hand.[29] And Zaller points out that people often try to generate opinions from the cues provided by the questions asked during the interview, especially when they lack relevant information or prior experience. These responses are meaningful, but they should not be regarded as reflecting attitudes that existed before the start of the survey.[30] For example, if the survey question asks whether Britain should adopt the euro, without detailed knowledge of the consequences for fiscal and monetary policy people may offer a response based on their broader feelings about British national identities and the European Union or based on partisan cues furnished by party elites. Relatively technical and abstract foreign and economic policy issues, about which the public has little knowledge or direct experience, are particularly vulnerable to these processes.

In these circumstances, a more effective strategy for tapping public opinion about economic globalization is to monitor values rather than attitudes. For example, it makes sense to ask people in Nigeria, Peru, and Sweden whether they emphasize individual success and economic competition, the key ideas of capitalism, or whether they favor solidarity, community, and economic equality. Unlike attitudes, values are applicable to multiple social contexts and life experiences. If mass communications instill an ideology of economic globalization, then support for such values as individualism, the pursuit of material affluence, and economic freedom should be stronger among media users than among nonusers within each society. Studies suggest that the news media often reflects the ethos of consumer capitalism; for example, a longitudinal discourse analysis of the language used in the Norwegian news media since the mid-1980s demonstrated that globalized capitalist market ideology has increasingly permeated this long-established Scandinavian welfare state, with language increasingly reflecting individualism at the cost of communal values.[31] If this language gradually diffuses to many societies, exposure to the news media should help to spread these ideas and messages at the expense of traditional egalitarian values, such as feelings of solidarity and community, and support for the welfare state.

To start examining the WVS survey evidence, let us first ask whether economic values fall on a single dimension arrayed on the conventional left–right spectrum – ranging from those favoring the neoliberal principles that support free markets with a minimal role of the state, to others that favor a more active role for government in the economy – or whether public opinion is more complex and multidimensional. In order to assess this issue, we used factor analysis to examine the correlations among a battery of items included in the fifth wave of the WVS. Six items monitoring economic attitudes were each designed as 10-point scales, where respondents could place themselves anywhere on the left–right spectrum using a series of oppositional statements as pole anchor points.

Now I'd like you to tell me your views on various issues. How would you place your views on this scale? 1 means you agree completely with the statement on the left; 10 means you agree completely with the statement on the right; and if your views fall somewhere in between, you can choose any number in between. (Code one number for each issue):

> Incomes should be made more equal *or* we need larger income differences as incentives for individual effort.
> Private ownership of business and industry should be increased *or* government ownership of business and industry should be increased.
> The government should take more responsibility to ensure that everyone is provided for *or* people should take more responsibility to provide for themselves.
> Competition is good. It stimulates people to work hard and develop new ideas *or* competition is harmful. It brings out the worst in people.
> In the long run, hard work usually brings a better life *or* hard work doesn't generally bring success – it is more a matter of luck and connections.
> People can only get rich at the expense of others *or* wealth can grow so there's enough for everyone.

These were recoded so that a higher score consistently reflects relatively conservative pro–free market orientations. To supplement this approach, we commonly monitor left–right ideological responses by

TABLE 7.1. *Factor Analysis of Economic Values and Attitudes*

	Individual Success Values	Conservative Economic Attitudes
V85 Importance of being very successful; to have people recognize personal achievements	.718	
V86 Importance of adventure and taking risks; to have an exciting life	.698	
V81 Importance of being rich; to have a lot of money and expensive things	.697	
V83 Importance of having a good time; to spoil oneself	.577	
V80 Importance of thinking up new ideas and being creative; to do things one's own way	.603	
V118 People should take responsibility to provide for themselves		.679
V121 Wealth can grow so there's enough for everyone		.500
V116 We need larger income differences as incentives for individual effort		.648
V114 Left–right ideological self-placement scale		.523
Proportion of variance	24.5	15.7

Note: The coefficients are the result of principal-component factor analysis with varimax rotation and Kaiser normalization, with pairwise substitution for missing values. Coefficients below .450 are excluded.
Source: World Values Survey (2005–2007).

asking where people place themselves on a left–right scale. Accordingly, the following scale was used from the WVS:

- V114 In political matters, people talk of the left and the right. How would you place your views on this scale, generally speaking? (Left) 1 2 3 4 5 6 7 8 9 10 (Right)

In addition, five of the value orientation scales developed by Shalom Schwartz were included in the survey, as listed in Table 7.1. These are designed to monitor the desirable goals that motivate people to take action and serve as guiding principles in people's lives.[32] The questions briefly describe the characteristics of certain people and ask respondents to identify the extent to which they resemble each person, using 6-point scales ranging from 'Not at all like me' to 'Very much like me.' These items describe characteristics closely associated with the economic goals and motivations of consumer capitalism – for example, concerning the value of material acquisition (getting rich, having a lot of money and expensive things), individualism (being very successful and having one's achievements recognized), and entrepreneurship (being willing to take risks and having an exciting life).

The results of the rotated factor analysis presented in Table 7.1 show that these items fell into two clusters or dimensions. These are interpreted as representing the overall values of individual success (reflecting the Schwartz value scales) and of conservative economic values. The Schwartz items fell into the expected dimensions, so that those who preferred individual success emphasized excitement and risk, material affluence and individual success, creativity and hedonism. A second value scale tapped attitudes toward the role of government protection versus personal responsibility, income and wealth inequality, economic opportunities, and the 10-point left–right ideological self-placement. Responses to these two separate dimensions were summed and converted into standardized 100-point scales, where higher scores reflect more conservative economic orientations on both dimensions. As with the previous analysis, we will examine the direct association between these values and use of the news media in the pooled sample, including all societies using multilevel regression models with the controls identified earlier. If the convergence thesis is correct, we would expect that individual success and conservative economic values would be positively and significantly associated with exposure to the news media. Moreover, especially strong and consistent relationships would be expected to be evident among news users living in cosmopolitan societies, who are most exposed to globalized mass communications. By contrast, if the polarization thesis is correct, we would expect that the direction of these relationships would be reversed, so that people who are most exposed to the news media would reject the economic values conveyed by mass communications.

As an initial overview of the data, Figure 7.1 illustrates support for individual success values, by category of media user and type of society (cosmopolitan or parochial). The chart shows clear and consistent contrasts; the heaviest users of the news media are the most individualistic in their values, giving higher priority to such goals as being rich and having an exciting life. This suggests that those who are most attentive to the news media are indeed more individualistic in their social values. But it is the parochial societies that are most individualistic, not the

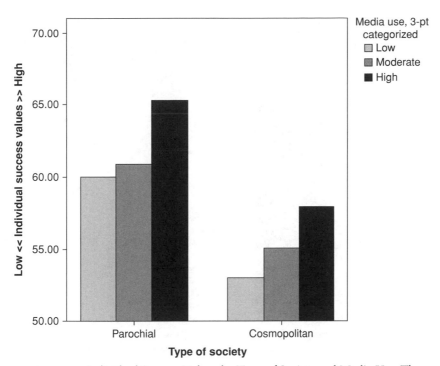

FIGURE 7.1. Individual Success Values by Type of Society and Media Use. The items included in the 100-point individual success value scale are listed in Table 7.1. *Source:* World Values Survey (2005–2007).

cosmopolitan societies. This pattern is consistent with previous re-search, which has found that the values of people in developing societies tend to be more materialistic; their emphasis on individual success, financial affluence, and self-gratification is part of this broader ethos. By contrast, postindustrial societies, which have achieved a minimal standard of economic security, have been found to have an increasingly postmaterialistic culture, placing growing emphasis on self-actualization and aesthetic values. To check the robustness of these results, we compare support for conservative economic attitudes, con-structed from the items listed in Table 7.1 concerning the need for self-reliance, belief in the non-zero-sum view of wealth, approval of income differences, and the left–right ideology scale. Support for these attitudes, illustrated in Figure 7.2, shows a pattern very similar to that found with economic values. Again, conservative economic attitudes are far stronger in parochial than in cosmopolitan societies; and again,

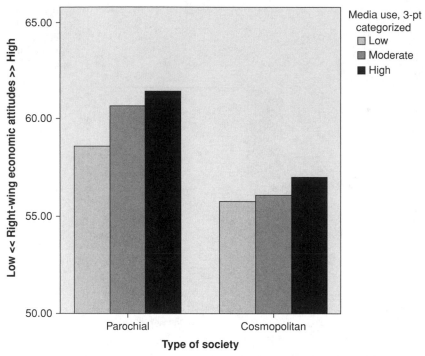

FIGURE 7.2. Conservative Economic Attitudes by Type of Society and Media Use. The items included in the 100-point conservative economic attitudes scale are listed in Table 7.1. *Source:* World Values Survey (2005–2007).

within each type of society, support is strongest among those who are the most attentive to the news media.

So that the societal-level comparisons can be examined in more detail, Figure 7.3 shows the patterns by country and level of cosmopolitanism. The results confirm the negative relationship already observed: the poorest and most isolated countries such as Mali and Ghana, with endemic poverty and hardship, place the heaviest emphasis on the material values of individual economic success. By contrast, the people of more affluent and cosmopolitan societies, such as Sweden, Japan, and the United States, place far less emphasis on these values.

Nevertheless, these initial findings could be spurious – for example, if the social characteristics of those who favor material success values, such as income and education, also predict access to the news

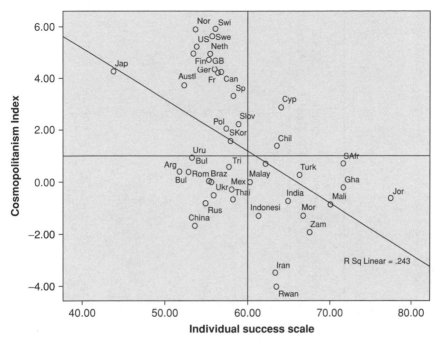

FIGURE 7.3. Individualistic Values by Type of Society. The items included in the 100-point individual success value scale are listed in Table 7.1. *Source:* World Values Survey (2005–2007).

media. We have already noted the substantial socioeconomic and cognitive bias in the identification of those who typically have regular access to the news, with an especially strong bias toward the affluent and well-educated groups in developing societies. Accordingly, multilevel analysis is essential; utilizing the social and attitudinal controls established in Chapter 5 helped to predict access to the news media. These include individual-level demographic characteristics and socioeconomic resources, as well as the contextual variable of the Cosmopolitanism Index, and the interaction effect between the type of society and media use. As before, alternative models were run with the range of contextual variables in order to test these separate effects. Table 7.2 presents the multilevel models, where individual success values are the dependent variable. The individual-level results of Model A show that, as predicted, a statistically significant and positive association exists between regular use of the news media and success values. In general, news media users are more likely than nonusers to favor

TABLE 7.2. *Multilevel Regression Models Explaining Individual Success Values*

	A Cosmopolitanism Index	B Globalization Index	C Economic Development	D Media Freedom	E Media Access
INDIVIDUAL LEVEL					
Demographic characteristics					
Age (years)	−3.336***	−3.336***	−3.336***	−3.336***	−3.336***
	(.066)	(.066)	(.066)	(.066)	(.066)
Gender (male = 1)	1.489***	1.489***	1.489***	1.489***	1.489***
	(.060)	(.060)	(.060)	(.060)	(.060)
Socioeconomic resources					
Household income, 10-pt scale	1.021***	1.021***	1.021***	1.021***	1.021***
	(.067)	(.067)	(.067)	(.067)	(.067)
Education, 9-pt scale	.105	.105	.105	.105	.105
	(.079)	(.079)	(.079)	(.079)	(.079)
Media use					
News media use scale	1.904***	1.904***	1.904***	1.902***	1.906***
	(.074)	(.074)	(.074)	(.074)	(.074)
NATIONAL LEVEL					
Cosmopolitanism Index (Globalization + development + freedom)	−2.987*** (.813)				

	(1)	(2)	(3)	(4)	(5)
Globalization Index		−2.653** (.833)			
Economic development			−3.137*** (.728)		
Media freedom				−1.787 (.927)	
Societal-level media access					−3.279*** (.709)
CROSS-LEVEL INTERACTIONS					
Cosmopolitanism × media use scale	−.203** (.066)	−.204** (.066)	−.203** (.066)	−.205** (.066)	−.203** (.066)
Constant (intercept)	59.6	59.4	59.5	59.3	58.6
Schwartz BIC	441,747	441,749	441,743	441,755	441,741
No. of respondents	54,402	54,402	54,402	54,402	54,402
No. of nations	43	43	43	43	43

Note: All independent variables were standardized using mean centering (z-scores). Models present the results of the REML multilevel regression models (for details, see Technical Appendix C). The 100-point trust in outsiders scale, from the items listed in Table 7.1, is the dependent variable. The 100-point media use scale combined the use of newspapers, radio/TV, Internet, books, and magazines. Models report the beta coefficient slopes (b), standard errors (in parentheses), and their significance. *$p = .05$; **$p = .01$; ***$p = .001$. See Technical Appendix A for details about the measurement, coding, and construction of all variables. Significant coefficients are highlighted in bold.

Source: World Values Survey (2005–2007).

the values of individual success. This pattern suggests that use of the news media does encourage the development of individualistic values associated with a capitalist consumer culture. Moreover, a comparison of the standardized coefficients, summarizing the strength of the relationships, shows that, after age, the news media are the second most important individual-level factor associated with the values of individual economic success, having a stronger impact than education, income, or gender. The age gap is also particularly marked, with the young placing far less emphasis on the values of individual success. Nevertheless, the national-level analysis confirms the initial descriptive findings: individualistic values are significantly weaker in cosmopolitan societies, not stronger. And the cross-level interaction between the type of society and use of the media proved significantly negative. This suggests that use of the news media is generally associated with individualism, but this relationship is reversed with use of the news media in the more cosmopolitan societies. The alternative Models B through E replicate the findings with the separate national-level indicators, including the Globalization Index, economic development, and societal-level media access (with the exception of media freedom, which has a coefficient that just fails [$p = .06$] to reach a conventional level of significance).

To determine whether these results are the product of the specific items included in the individual success values scale or whether they are robust, we replicated the same analyses using the conservative economic attitudes scale as the dependent variable. This measure incorporates attitudes toward government protection versus personal responsibility, income and wealth inequality, economic opportunities, and the 10-point left–right ideological self-placement. The results in Table 7.3 provide strikingly similar results concerning the national-level and cross-level interactive effects. Overall in Model A, individual-level media use again emerges as a strong factor associated with conservative attitudes, but these effects are reversed in more cosmopolitan societies. The replication generates confidence that the findings are not simply due to specific items contained in either scale or to the construction of the Cosmopolitanism Index, but are robust against successive tests. Though many commentators, such as Herman and McChesney, have speculated that the globalization of mass communications encourages the spread of capitalist consumer culture, in fact

TABLE 7.3. *Multilevel Regression Models Explaining Support for Right-Wing Economic Attitudes*

	A Cosmopolitanism Index	B Globalization Index	C Economic Development	D Media Freedom	E Media Access
INDIVIDUAL LEVEL					
Demographic characteristics					
Age (years)	.797***	.797***	.797***	.797***	.797***
	(.080)	(.080)	(.080)	(.080)	(.080)
Gender (male = 1)	.237***	.237***	.237***	.237***	.237***
	(.001)	(.001)	(.001)	(.001)	(.001)
Socioeconomic resources					
Household income, 10-pt scale	1.885***	1.885***	1.885***	1.885***	1.885***
	(.079)	(.079)	(.079)	(.079)	(.079)
Education, 9-pt scale	.324***	.324***	.324***	.324***	.324***
	(.096)	(.096)	(.096)	(.096)	(.096)
Media use					
News media use scale	.596***	.596***	.596***	.596***	.596***
	(.089)	(.089)	(.089)	(.089)	(.089)
NATIONAL LEVEL					
Cosmopolitanism Index	−2.113**				
(Globalization + development + freedom)	(.660)				
Globalization Index		−2.217***			
		(.632)			

(continued)

TABLE 7.3 (continued)

	A Cosmopolitanism Index	B Globalization Index	C Economic Development	D Media Freedom	E Media Access
Economic development			−1.311* (.659)		
Media freedom				−2.284** (.750)	
Societal-level media access					−.937 (.678)
CROSS-LEVEL INTERACTIONS					
Cosmopolitanism × media use scale	−.259*** (.077)	−.260*** (.077)	−.261*** (.077)	−.262*** (.077)	−.263*** (.077)
Constant (intercept)	57.7	57.5	57.5	57.9	57.2
Schwartz BIC	342,190		342,195		
No. of respondents	41,586	41,586	41,586	41,586	41,586
No. of nations	42	42	42	42	42

Note: All independent variables were standardized using mean centering (z-scores). Models present the results of the REML multilevel regression models (for details, see Technical Appendix C). The 100-point trust in outsiders scale, from the items listed in Table 7.1, is the dependent variable. The 100-point media use scale combined the use of newspapers, radio/TV, Internet, books, and magazines. Models report the beta coefficient slopes (b), standard errors (in parentheses), and their significance. *p = .05; **p = .01; ***p = .001. See Technical Appendix A for details about the measurement, coding, and construction of all variables. Significant coefficients are highlighted in bold.

Source: World Values Survey (2005–2007).

the picture that emerges is more complex. In general, users of the news media are more supportive of individualistic values and conservative economic attitudes; nevertheless, as illustrated in Figures 7.1 and 7.2, support is far stronger in parochial than in cosmopolitan societies.

Conclusions and Discussion

Has the denser exchange of goods, services, capital, and labor flowing across national borders shaped public opinion directly, and has the globalization of mass communications also played a major role in encouraging either support for the values of consumer capitalism or a popular backlash against these ideas? Previous literature concerning these issues focused mainly on trends in public opinion about economic integration, as well as the impact of instrumental factors on policy attitudes within particular societies. By contrast, the analysis presented in this chapter focused on the impact of news media exposure on a broader range of economic values and attitudes within various types of societies. The initial descriptive statistics suggested that the type of society and use of the news media were associated with individualistic values and conservative attitudes. When analyzed with the multilevel models, including a battery of controls, the data suggest that the impact of the news media is conditioned by the type of society. News users are more individualistic than average in more parochial societies, in poorer countries, and in countries with media systems that are relatively restricted. News users are *less* individualistic than average in the more cosmopolitan societies and in postindustrial economies. By focusing on the news media, we have failed to directly examine evidence concerning the impact of popular culture, such as movies, music, and entertainment, and these could conceivably generate stronger effects than attention to the news media, an issue that is examined in Chapter 10. But the extensive range of data that we have analyzed concerning news users in multiple countries and contexts provides good reason to be highly skeptical of the argument that the globalization of mass communications is converting people to capitalist values, at least in the economic sphere. We will next examine social mores, including traditional standards of sexuality, morality, and religiosity, in order to explore the impact of the media in this realm.

8

Morality

Traditional Values, Sexuality, Gender Equality, and Religiosity

Theories of powerful media effects assume that a wide range of social values and behavioral practices are learned from the ideas and images conveyed by popular television entertainment, glossy magazines, Internet Web sites, music videos, consumer advertising, feature films, and news reports. Cultivation theory, developed by Gerbner and his colleagues, treats the mass media as one of the standard agencies of socialization, rivaling parents and the family, peer groups, teachers and religious authorities, and social norms operating within the local community and national culture.[1] Socialization is a multidimensional process involving the acquisition of knowledge, attitudes, and values. In particular, cultivation theory suggests that frequent exposure to the mass media, especially television, leads to the internalization of its messages. Through this process, the media is thought to be capable of influencing moral standards, including attitudes toward the family, marriage, and divorce, orientations toward sex roles, support for gender equality, and tolerance of sexual diversity, and beliefs about appropriate ethical standards in public life, as well as of shaping broader religious values, beliefs, and practices. Regular exposure to messages conveyed by mass communications is believed to have a cumulative effect on moral values and behavior, particularly on impressionable young children and adolescents during their formative years as they transition to adulthood.[2]

There are several reasons for thinking that sexual socialization, in particular, might be influenced by mass communications. Media coverage can affect everything one learns about sexuality, from the biology of reproduction and the risks of sexual behavior to attitudes toward love, romantic relationships, and marriage. To begin with, sexuality is pervasive throughout the Western media.[3] From prime-time TV sitcoms and dramas to feature films and magazines, the media presents countless verbal and visual examples of how dating, intimacy, sex, love, marriage, divorce, and romantic relationships are handled. Content analysis studies have shown that the explicit depiction of sexuality has become more common in popular American television entertainment over the years. For example, a longitudinal analysis of American broadcast and cable channels from 1997 to 2002 revealed that talk about sex was shown more often than sexual behavior, though both types of contents increased significantly during the period under review; for example, the percentage of shows portraying sexual intercourse doubled, from 7 to 14%.[4] Content analysis of mainstream magazines has also documented increasingly graphic sexual images and messages; for example, intimate relationships constitute the largest category of topics covered in women's magazines, and references to sexual issues have increased in recent decades.[5] Hollywood feature films are often sexualized; a study of the 50 top-grossing films of 1996 indicated that almost two-thirds contained at least one sex scene.[6] Images in music videos also reflect these patterns; up to three-quarters of all music videos are estimated to contain implicit sexual imagery.[7] Sexuality is pervasive in mass advertising, whether conveyed by images of beauty products or used as a way to sell everything from cars to consumer durables, and this type of content has also been found to have grown over time.[8] But the proportion and explicitness of sexually graphic contents in the traditional mainstream media pale in comparison with the contents of online pornography on adult Web sites, which studies suggest are widely accessed by young people in America.[9] It is difficult to determine the amount of sex on the Internet with any degree of reliability, but it is estimated that the pornography industry generated worldwide revenues of $97 billion in 2006, with an estimated 4.2 million pornographic Web sites (representing 12% of all Web sites), attracting on average 75 million unique visitors per month.[10] Sexual content in popular entertainment is clearly pervasive in the contemporary mass media. This material is also widely consumed, especially among the adolescent population; surveys suggest that young people in America spend more time engaged with the mass media than they typically spend either in school or interacting with their parents.[11]

In addition to sexual socialization, mass communications may affect the acquisition of many other broader moral, ethical, and religious values. In their watchdog role, investigative journalists report extensively about financial and sexual scandals, such as stories of corruption and bribery in public life.[12] This coverage may shape public perceptions about standards in public life, such as attitudes toward transparency and probity, as well as trust in political institutions and leaders. News reports focus on many contemporary issues surrounding the politics of sex and gender – abortion and contraception, euthanasia, stem cell research, sexually transmitted diseases and HIV-AIDS, women's equality and the women's movement, homosexual rights, gay marriage, and the role of gays in the military.[13] Again, this coverage can be expected to influence public opinion, for example, tolerance of homosexuality, abortion, and divorce, as well as attitudes toward the appropriate division of sex roles for women and men in the home, workplace, and public sphere and attitudes toward gender equality.[14] A growing body of literature has also documented how the mass media often touches on broader aspects of religiosity, in the United States and elsewhere.[15] Religious groups and authorities make explicit use of mass communications: proselytizing radio and TV broadcasts, printed publications, cassette tapes, television talk shows, Internet social networking Web sites, soap operas, and documentary films. In addition, the mainstream media frames wider issues of religion and spirituality in an implicit way – for example, in the values conveyed by routine news reports about science and technology, the depiction of religious minorities, or coverage of international affairs.[16] Mass communications can thereby potentially affect the strength of religious values, identities, and beliefs in society.

The belief that moral values and social norms are shaped by media messages is not just academic; these assumptions underpin many of the fears about the impact of Western or American television on developing societies, encouraging government agencies to implement policies of cultural protectionism, as in Bhutan. Societies often limit the import of cultural products that are considered offensive to public decency; for example, they pass laws against trafficking in child pornography.[17] Many countries have official rating systems that classify the contents of movies and are designed to inform parents and to protect young people. Even in relatively liberal countries with a strong tradition of free speech, such as the United Kingdom and the United States, broadcaster self-censorship, government regulation, viewer councils, and sometimes pressures from commercial sponsors prevent certain types of television programming from being shown if they are deemed to offend standards of 'decency' and 'good taste' – for example, in terms of language and offensive speech, violence, or obscenity.[18] Many nations, including Iran, Syria, Bahrain, Egypt, the United Arab Emirates, Kuwait, Malaysia, Indonesia, Singapore, Kenya, India, Cuba, and China, attempt to ban pornography. The most conservative countries exercise the strictest limits on foreign imports; for example, the Saudi state uses filters to block Internet content 'which breaches public decency' or 'which infringes the sanctity of Islam,' and breaches of these standards are subject to criminal law.[19]

Despite the pervasiveness of moral and social values in the media, systematic evidence concerning the relative impact of these messages on public opinion is far from conclusive. For example, much social psychological research about the acquisition of sexual attitudes and values has been based on experimental studies conducted among the American student population, although it is not clear to what extent it is possible to generalize from this group to other peoples and places. A comprehensive meta-analysis of the empirical literature on this topic in the United States suggests that far less is known about the impact of mass communications on sexual socialization and the acquisition of broader moral values than is known about the influence of violence in the media, which has been the focus of thousands of studies.[20] This literature review concluded that social science has failed to establish a direct connection between the total amount of TV viewing and subsequent patterns of sexual behavior and experiences. Studies of the use of more specific programming genres, such as music videos or soaps, have demonstrated slightly stronger but still limited effects on sexual attitudes, expectations, and behaviors. A direct link between the use of the media and subsequent moral attitudes is difficult to establish with experimental or correlational research techniques, and it is even more problematic to trace the indirect consequences for behavior. Cultivation theories suppose a simple 'hypodermic needle' effect, in which frequent viewing is assumed to result in the absorption of messages. More recent studies acknowledge that research must take account of two-way interaction effects that arise from the selection of what to consume (soap operas or documentaries? reality TV or news?), as well as the ways that media messages interact with existing predispositions, cultural standards, and direct personal experiences.[21] Religious predispositions and moral values affect media choices; for example, some people may be inclined to listen to conservative radio talk shows or tune in to religious TV broadcasts, and their values may be reinforced by this exposure.[22] Most mass communication and social psychological research has focused on examining the media content and the audience effects of the media in the United States and Europe, and cross-national evidence about developing societies remains very scarce. If social, sexual, and moral values are indeed shaped by mass communications, these effects should be most clearly evident where Western media, reflecting relatively liberal orientations, penetrates the most traditional conservative cultures. This chapter therefore examines the effects of media use on a wide range of social values; particular attention is paid to whether any of the effects of this process are especially powerful in societies that are most open to cosmopolitan information flows.

Social and Moral Values

To estimate the effects of media exposure on a wide range of social and moral values, we first need to establish suitable measures. Principal-component factor analysis with varimax rotation was used to examine the underlying attitudinal dimensions of 21 items included in the fifth wave of the World Values Survey. The items are listed in Table 8.1, which also shows the five attitudinal dimensions that emerged. The first dimension concerns sexual and moral values, based on where respondents placed themselves on 10-point scales ranging from 'never justified' to 'always justifiable' concerning abortion, divorce, homosexuality, prostitution, euthanasia, and suicide. The second dimension involves attitudes toward ethical standards in public life, including the justifiability of cheating on taxes, avoiding paying a fare on public transport, falsely claiming government benefits, and accepting a bribe. The third dimension concerns religious values (the importance of God, the importance of religion), religious practices (including whether the respondent prayed or meditated and the frequency of attendance at religious services), and whether people identified themselves as religious. In previous research, these items emerged as some of the most

TABLE 8.1. *Dimensions of Social and Moral Values*

	Liberal Sexual and Moral Values	Tolerance of Low Ethical Standards in Public Life	Religious Values and Practices	Egalitarian Gender Values	Liberal Family Values
Justifiable: abortion	.806				
Justifiable: divorce	.782				
Justifiable: homosexuality	.767				
Justifiable: prostitution	.735				
Justifiable: euthanasia	.704				
Justifiable: suicide	.625				
Justifiable: cheating on taxes		.818			
Justifiable: avoiding a fare on public transport		.803			
Justifiable: claiming government benefits		.783			
Justifiable: someone accepting a bribe		.769			
Importance of God			.819		
Religious identity			.782		
Takes moments of prayer, meditation, etc.			.770		
Religion important in life			.752		
Often attends religious services			.682		
Men make better business executives than women do (disagree)				.865	
Men make better political leaders than women do (disagree)				.828	
University more important for a boy than a girl (disagree)				.779	
Woman as a single parent (approve)					.741
Family important in life (disagree)					.588
Marriage is an outdated institution (agree)					.488
Proportion of variance	17.8	13.2	14.9	10.7	5.8

Note: Factor analysis extraction method: principal-component analysis. Rotation method: varimax with Kaiser normalization. Coefficients of .40 or less were dropped from the analysis. See Technical Appendix A for the specific items and the construction of the scales.

Source: World Values Survey (2005–2007).

TABLE 8.2. *Values by Type of Society and Media Use*

Type of Society	Media Use, 3-pt Categorized	Liberal Sexual and Moral Values	Tolerance of Low Ethical Standards in Public Life	Religious Values and Practices	Egalitarian Gender Values	Liberal Family Values
Parochial	Low	27	25	86	66	67
	Moderate	33	28	81	70	70
	High	34	26	80	70	70
	TOTAL	31	27	83	68	69
Cosmopolitan	Low	32	25	79	64	63
	Moderate	43	22	65	73	69
	High	49	21	60	78	72
	TOTAL	43	22	66	73	69
Total	Low	29	25	84	65	66
	Moderate	38	25	75	71	69
	High	43	23	69	75	71
	TOTAL	37	25	76	70	69
Strength of association		.269***	.116***	.327***	.110***	.003

Note: The mean position of categories of media users on the 100-point value scales by type of society, no controls. See Table 8.1 for the items used in the construction of the scales. Anova was used to assess the strength of association (eta) and the statistical significance of the difference between types of society (***$p = .001$).

Source: World Values Survey (2005–2007).

important aspects of religiosity that are applicable to many types of societies and faiths, and they have been widely used as standard measures in the literature on the sociology of religion.[23] The fourth dimension concerns attitudes toward gender equality at work, in politics, and in education. These items have also been used to tap the orientations toward sex roles of women and men in many different cultures.[24] The final dimension comprises three items concerned with attitudes toward family and marriage. Since the responses in each of these dimensions were highly intercorrelated, the items were combined and the resulting scales were standardized to 100-point scales for ease of comparison.

We can start by comparing the mean distribution of responses on these scales for low, moderate, and high news media users living in both parochial and cosmopolitan societies. Analysis of variance (Anova) was used to assess the significance and strength of the difference among groups. As shown in Table 8.2, moderately strong and significant

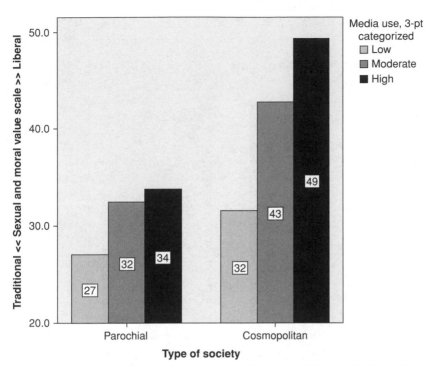

FIGURE 8.1. Social and Moral Values by Media Use and Type of Society. The mean position of categories of media users on the 100-point value scales by type of society, no controls. See Table 8.1 for the items used in the construction of the scales. *Source:* World Values Survey (2005–2007).

differences were found for those living in parochial and cosmopolitan societies for all the value scales except those concerning family values. These values also varied among types of media users. As shown in Figure 8.1, the heaviest news media users proved the most liberal toward homosexuality, abortion, divorce, and so on in both types of society, but the gap by media use was largest (17 percentage points) in cosmopolitan nations. This mirrors the pattern found in terms of religiosity, as illustrated in Figure 8.2, where media users were generally the most secular, and again the largest gap (19 points) was in cosmopolitan societies. Similar results can be seen for responses regarding gender equality in Figure 8.3; media users in cosmopolitan societies were the most egalitarian in their perceptions of the appropriate roles for men and women and also expressed more liberal family values. Similar patterns are evident in attitudes toward cheating on taxes, falsely

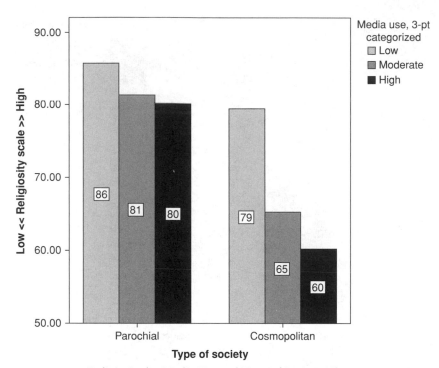

FIGURE 8.2. Religiosity by Media Use and Type of Society. The mean position of categories of media users on the 100-point value scales by type of society, no controls. See Table 8.1 for the items used in the construction of the scales. *Source:* World Values Survey (2005–2007).

claiming government benefits, or accepting bribes, although heavier media users in cosmopolitan societies reject these practices by only a modest margin over lower media users.

Let us apply multilevel regression analysis to see whether these findings are confirmed after we control for the social characteristics of media users. Table 8.3 presents the results of separate models run for each value scale, including the individual-level demographic characteristics and socioeconomic resources plus news media use, as well as the national-level Cosmopolitanism Index and the cross-level interaction effect combining media use with residence in a cosmopolitan society. The individual-level results largely confirm the findings from the descriptive means; even after education, age, and income are controlled for, individual use of the news media was significantly linked to more tolerant and liberal orientations toward sexual and moral values,

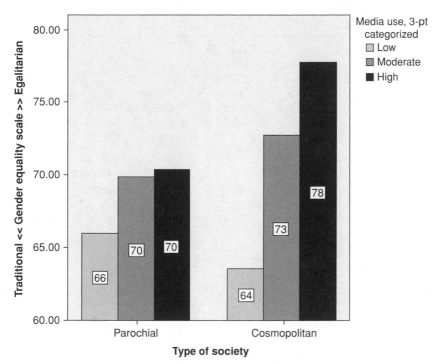

FIGURE 8.3. Support for Gender Equality by Media Use and Type of Society. The mean position of categories of media users on the 100-point value scales by type of society, no controls. See Table 8.1 for the items used in the construction of the scales. *Source:* World Values Survey (2005–2007).

to disapproval of unethical standards in public life, to more secular orientations, to supporting gender equality, and to liberal family values. The strength of the coefficients for media use varied across the different value scales, but in all cases the results were statistically significant. As previous studies have found, younger people and the well educated proved consistently more liberal toward sexual and moral values, family values, and gender equality, less tolerant of low ethical standards in public life, and more secular in their values and practices.

At the national level, living in a more cosmopolitan society was significantly linked to more liberal sexual and moral values, support for gender equality, and more secular values and practices. Previous studies have reported that the people of affluent postindustrial societies tend to be both more egalitarian in their beliefs about appropriate roles for women and men and less religious than those of developing societies,

TABLE 8.3. *Multilevel Regression Models Explaining Social Values*

	Liberal Sexual and Moral Values	Tolerance of Low Ethical Standards in Public Life	Religious Values and Practices	Egalitarian Gender Values	Liberal Family Values
INDIVIDUAL LEVEL					
Demographic characteristics					
Age (years)	**−2.17*****	**−2.34*****	**3.46*****	**−.951*****	**−1.52*****
	(.099)	(.083)	(.113)	(.081)	(.075)
Gender (male = 1)	.064	**.725*****	**−3.05*****	**−3.60*****	**−.679*****
	(.090)	(.075)	(.103)	(.074)	(.068)
Socioeconomic resources					
Household	**1.25*****	**.481*****	**−.507*****	**.351*****	**.721*****
income, 10-pt	(.107)	(.090)	(.124)	(.088)	(.082)
scale					
Education,	**1.66*****	**−.850*****	**−.495*****	**2.283*****	**.291*****
9-pt scale	(.115)	(.097)	(.134)	(.094)	(.088)
Media use					
News media	**.936*****	**−.443*****	**−.277***	**.867*****	**.780*****
use scale	(.112)	(.094)	(.131)	(.092)	(.086)
NATIONAL LEVEL					
Cosmopolitanism	**8.84*****	−1.40	**−9.39****	**4.64*****	1.70
Index					
(Globalization +	(1.47)	(1.77)	(2.42)	(1.14)	(1.18)
development +					
freedom)					
CROSS-LEVEL INTERACTIONS					
Cosmopolitanism ×	**.569*****	−.055	.158	**−.190***	.021
media use scale	(.109)	(.092)	(.123)	(.090)	(.085)
Constant (intercept)	38.5	25.4	72.8	71.0	69.4
Schwartz BIC	380,457	379,100	319,932	387,905	328,937
No. of respondents	43,088	44,565	35,826	45,755	40,198
No. of nations	37	37	30	38	33

Note: All independent variables were standardized using mean centering (z-scores). Models present the results of the REML multilevel regression models (for details, see Technical Appendix C), including the beta coefficient (standard error in parentheses) and the significance. The 100-point scales are constructed from the items listed in Table 8.1. The 100-point media use scale combined use of newspapers, radio/TV news, Internet, books, and magazines. $^*p = .05$; $^{**}p = .01$; $^{***}p = .001$. See Technical Appendix A for details about the measurement, coding, and construction of all variables. Significant coefficients are highlighted in bold.

Source: World Values Survey (2005–2007).

with a few notable exceptions.[25] In terms of cross-level interaction effects, use of the media in cosmopolitan societies was significantly linked to more liberal sexual and moral values, but unexpectedly, the interactive relationship also proved less egalitarian, not more, toward the roles of women and men.

To explore whether the national-level relationships were driven mainly by levels of economic development or by broader characteristics of more open media systems, models were re-run for the sexual and moral value scale specifying, alternatively, national levels of globalization, economic development, media freedom, and societal-level media use. The results in Table 8.4 show that each of these national-level contextual variables proved strong and significant. The results could not simply be reduced to levels of per capita GDP, however, since both the Globalization Index and the Media Freedom Index were slightly stronger predictors of social values than was per capita GDP. The strong correlations that exist among these societal-level variables make it difficult to disentangle this, as economic development is closely linked to patterns of media access, levels of integration into global markets, and levels of media freedom. But the analysis suggests that any comprehensive explanation should take account of more than the impact of economic development.

Conclusions and Discussion

Accounts of strong media effects, including the cultivation theory developed by Gerbner and colleagues, claim that frequent exposure to the mass media, especially habitual television viewing, leads to the gradual internalization of the messages communicated by the media.[26] Through lifetime socialization, the media is thought to be capable of influencing moral standards, especially by presenting powerful images of sexuality, love, the family and marriage, women's and men's roles, and religion and spirituality. Concern about the potential threat to traditional cultures arising from the values contained in Western media, such as the explicit sexuality of movies and entertainment TV, has led regulatory agencies to adopt protectionist measures. In extreme cases, this concern has led some states to ban or censor media contents, and even in democracies with a long tradition of protecting freedom of expression it has encouraged policies that restrict access to certain

TABLE 8.4. *Multilevel Regression Models Explaining Liberal Sexual and Moral Values*

	Cosmopolitanism Index	Globalization Index	Economic Development	Media Freedom	Media Access
INDIVIDUAL LEVEL					
Demographic characteristics					
Age (years)	−2.17***	−2.17***	−2.17***	−2.17***	−2.17***
	(.099)	(.099)	(.099)	(.099)	(.099)
Gender (male = 1)	.064	.064	.064	.064	.064
	(.090)	(.090)	(.090)	(.090)	(.090)
Socioeconomic resources					
Household income, 10-pt scale	1.25***	1.25***	1.25***	1.25***	1.25***
	(.107)	(.107)	(.107)	(.107)	(.107)
Education, 9-pt scale	1.66***	1.66***	1.66***	1.66***	1.66***
	(.115)	(.115)	(.115)	(.115)	(.115)
Media use					
News media use scale	.936***	.936***	.936***	.936***	.936***
	(.112)	(.112)	(.112)	(.112)	(.112)
NATIONAL LEVEL					
Cosmopolitanism Index (Globalization + development + freedom)	8.84***				
	(1.47)				

Globalization Index		**10.01***** (1.61)			
Economic development			**9.14***** (1.52)		
Media freedom				**10.64***** (1.60)	
Societal-level media access					**6.65***** (1.64)
CROSS-LEVEL INTERACTIONS					
Cosmopolitanism × media use	**.569***** (.109)	**.579***** (.109)	**.547***** (.123)	**.583***** (.109)	**.649***** (.085)
Constant (intercept)	38.5	33.4	38.0	37.0	
Schwartz BIC	380,457	380,455	380,457	380,453	380,457
No. of respondents	43,088	43,088	43,088	43,088	43,088
No. of nations	37	37	37	37	37

Note: All independent variables were standardized using mean centering (z-scores). Models present the results of the REML multilevel regression models (for details, see Technical Appendix C), including the beta coefficient (standard error in parentheses) and the significance. The 100-point scales are constructed from the items listed in Table 8.1. The 100-point media use scale combined use of newspapers, radio/TV news, Internet, books, and magazines. *p = .05; **p = .01; ***p = .001. See Technical Appendix A for details about the measurement, coding, and construction of all variables. Significant coefficients are highlighted in bold.

Source: World Values Survey (2005–2007).

types of media contents in order to protect children and adolescents. But the media is only one agency of socialization, and deep-rooted moral values and behavioral norms are acquired from many other sources, such as parents and the family, as well as other role models and experiences of growing up in the local community. In highly conservative societies, these agencies may outweigh the images and ideas conveyed by imported cultural products, so that the meaning of liberal or secular messages can be reinterpreted, or simply rejected, by the audience.

The survey evidence presented in this chapter suggests a consistent linking of media use with moral values; even after controls are introduced, the heaviest users of the mass media are generally more liberal toward sexual and moral values, less tolerant of unethical standards of public life, less religious, more liberal in family values, and more egalitarian toward the roles of women and men than are other users. Moreover, these relationships are strongest in cosmopolitan societies, which are most open to information flows across national borders, while having only a limited impact in parochial societies. The strongest interaction concerns sexual and moral values, where greater media use within cosmopolitan societies was associated with more liberal and tolerant orientations toward such issues as homosexuality, divorce, and abortion.

Though derived from a comparison of a comprehensive range of social values using multilevel models in many more societies than in any previous research, the data we have examined remain limited in certain regards. Most importantly, the cross-national comparisons cannot conclusively establish the direction of causality implied in this relationship; it may be that exposure to the mass media generates more liberal and less traditional value orientations, but self-selection bias is also likely to operate in what people are predisposed to watch or read. As the 'uses and gratification' theory suggests, people actively choose how to spend their leisure time and how the media can best meet their interests and needs, such as for information, entertainment, escape, or social interaction.[27] In fact, we believe that a two-way reciprocal interactive process is probably at work here, where prior motivation determines information exposure and, in turn, media use reinforces cultural values. Without experimental studies or panel survey data derived from interviews of the same respondents over time, it is impossible to determine how this process works. In addition, establishing more conclusive findings will require more specific information about particular genres and contents of the mass media that people in the survey regularly accessed; this would include analysis of cross-cultural variations in the moral and social values reflected in television, newspapers, Web sites, and magazines in different countries. We need to know what people are typically watching or reading in far more detail – and over a long period – to establish cumulative effects. These challenges remain for future research.

Nevertheless, the survey evidence analyzed here establishes the general pattern of use of a wide range of media sources in a diverse range of societies. In keeping with our overall argument, exposure to the news media is consistently linked with liberal and egalitarian moral and social values. In this regard, the use of mass communications seems to have an impact similar to that of education and age, reinforcing modern values and more tolerant attitudes. These patterns are also found in more parochial societies, but the strength of the correlations remains more limited. In these places, the combined effects of lack of economic development, lack of integration into global communication markets and networks, lack of media freedom, and lack of media access limit the degree of cultural change linked with cross-border information flows.

9

Activists

Civic Engagement

The logic of the cultural convergence thesis is that, in open societies, the flow of mass communication will gradually result in the spread of Western ideas about democratic practices and principles around the world. Information conveyed by international news agencies and transnational broadcasters – such as coverage of the American presidential election, images of monks protesting on the streets of Rangoon, or reports highlighting human rights abuses in Zimbabwe or the Democratic Republic of Congo – will thereby strengthen reform movements, grassroots activism, and public support for democratic values. At the same time, in closed societies where the news media are controlled by powerful governing elites, whether through state ownership of broadcasting, overt censorship, intimidation of independent journalists, or other mechanisms and where information from abroad is heavily filtered or restricted, mass communications can be expected to function as a mechanism of state control and propaganda. The impact of the news media on the process of democratization has attracted a great deal of research, but nevertheless many key questions remain unresolved. To examine these issues, in this chapter we first consider theoretical debates about the role of the news media in democracy and review the literature based on societal-level econometric studies and individual-level behavioral survey analysis of media users. Building on this foundation, we then examine evidence derived from the fifth wave of the World Values Survey concerning multiple dimensions of civic engagement, including institutional confidence, membership in voluntary associations, involvement in protest politics, citizen interest, support for democratic values, and evaluations of democratic performance. The data generated by the multilevel regression models indicate two main findings. First, individual use of the news media is consistently related to stronger patterns of civic engagement, even with a battery of prior controls for the typical characteristics of the media audience. There is no support here for the 'media malaise' thesis; instead, democratic participation is likely to be strengthened by exposure to the press. Second, exploration at the national level suggests that this pattern is usually reinforced by media use in cosmopolitan societies. The conclusion reflects the implications of these findings.

Theories and Evidence Linking Wealth, Media Access, and Democracy at the Societal Level

The start of the third wave of democracy during the early 1970s renewed interest in the factors that contribute to processes of regime transition and consolidation. Most attention has been focused on the role of economic development, state institutions, and political culture.[1] The proposition that wealthy societies are usually more democratic than poor societies has a long lineage, and the mass media has often been regarded as one of the central drivers of this relationship. The political sociologist Seymour Martin Lipset laid the groundwork for this thesis in 1959, claiming, 'The more well-to-do a nation, the greater the chances that it will sustain democracy.'[2] This process operates, Lipset theorized, where development raises levels of literacy, schooling, and media access, which he considered essential for mass participation. Economic growth also broadened the middle classes, reduced extreme poverty, facilitated the action of intermediary organizations in civic society, and promoted democratic values. During the early 1970s, Dankwart Rustow reinforced the argument that the transition to democracy could be attributed to economic development and societal modernization, as predicted by such measures as newspaper circulation, radio and television ownership, per capita energy consumption, literacy, school enrollment, urbanization, life expectancy, infant mortality, and the size of the industrial workforce.[3]

Subsequently, the societal-level relationship between wealth and democracy has been subjected to rigorous empirical inquiry. For more than half a century, the association has withstood empirical tests under a variety of conditions. Cross-sectional and time-series data for a large sample of countries and years have been used, as have increasingly sophisticated statistical tests and historical case studies of regime transitions within particular nations. Studies have repeatedly confirmed that a nation's wealth is associated with the standard indicators of democratization, although the accuracy of estimates is sensitive to the choice of time period, the selection of control variables specified in causal models, and the basic measurement of both democracy and economic growth.[4] The Lipset hypothesis has been replicated in a series of research studies.[5] Recently, Norris also confirmed this relationship, using cross-sectional time-series analysis that established that between one-half and two-thirds of the variance in democratization found worldwide during the third-wave era could be attributed to a range of structural conditions, including per capita level of GDP (in PPP), controlling for colonial legacies, regional diffusion, ethnic heterogeneity, and population size.[6]

At the same time, although the results are often replicated, certain issues remain unresolved in the research literature. In particular, the relationship between wealth and democracy is probabilistic, and even a casual glance at the standard indicators reveals many important contemporary outliers. Affluent autocracies are exemplified by Singapore, Saudi Arabia, and Kuwait, with high per capita GDP, and today there are also many poor democracies, such as Benin, Ghana, Mali, Costa Rica, and Nepal, as well as the classic case of India. These outliers suggest that economic development is neither necessary nor sufficient for democratization.

Econometric models also commonly fail to incorporate evidence about the role of the mass media as an intermediary condition in democratization. Lipset and Rustow theorized that one of the direct effects of economic development was to expand access to mass communications. This pattern was examined in Chapter 5, and a strong correlation (.742) was found between levels of media access and economic development. Lipset and Rustow argued that, in turn, wider access to the mass media strengthened the process of democratization, primarily by enabling civic engagement and political participation.

A growing series of selected case studies have described the roles of the news media in relatively new democracies, but this indirect link between economic development and democratization has attracted less systematic attention in the research literature.[7] The societal-level evidence lends partial support to the Lipset and Rustow thesis, however; cross-national time-series regression analysis confirms that freedom of the press was significantly related to national-level patterns of democratization during the third-wave era.[8] This relationship proved robust when replicated by the use of two independent indicators of democracy, even after a battery of controls was employed for related factors predicting democracy, including colonial legacies, regional diffusion, ethnic heterogeneity, and population size.

Equally important, previous econometric models are commonly underspecified because of a failure to take account of the role of political institutions and political culture. For example, Przeworski et al. provide the standard contemporary account of the relationship between wealth and democracy, but they do not control for the effects of the type of power-sharing arrangements in the electoral system or federalism.[9] In addition, Inglehart and Welzel have shown that political culture has a significant impact on the consolidation of democracy; in particular, self-expression values, a syndrome of mass attitudes that tap a common underlying dimension reflecting an emphasis on freedom, tolerance of diversity, and participation, are strongly related at the aggregate level to patterns of liberal democracy, as measured by Freedom House.[10] Self-expression values, reflecting human choices, tap a broader set of cultural attitudes and orientations than support for democratic values per se. Inglehart and Welzel also show that self-expression values measured in the early 1990s had a strong effect on subsequent levels of liberal democracy. By contrast, prior levels of liberal democracy had only a weak and statistically insignificant effect on the strength of subsequent self-expression values. Inglehart and Welzel demonstrate that culture (self-expression values) affect the performance of a country's democratic institutions.

Questions also remain about the most appropriate interpretation of the direction of causality in the complex relationship linking democracy with wealth, political institutions, and cultural attitudes. According to the standard view, economic factors are usually regarded as endogenous, the foundation on which democratic regimes and political culture arise as superstructure. But it is equally plausible to assume, as Perrson and Tabellini argue, that constitutional arrangements, such as electoral systems and coalition governments, have the capacity to influence economic policies and economic performance – for example, patterns of government spending, budget deficits, and labor productivity, and thus patterns of socioeconomic development.[11] These arguments reverse the assumed direction of causality; Perrson and Tabellini suggest that democratic institutions may affect a country's stock of wealth.

Theories and Evidence Linking Individual-Level Media Use and Civic Engagement

What are the individual-level links between media use and civic engagement? An extensive literature has explored this issue, but interpretations remain divided between the 'media malaise' and the 'virtuous circle' perspectives.

Far from strengthening democracy, mass communications in the United States and Western Europe are blamed by proponents of the media malaise thesis for growing public disengagement, ignorance of civic affairs, and mistrust of government. According to this viewpoint, common journalistic practices hinder civic engagement, including what the public learns about public affairs, whether they trust government, and the extent to which they become involved in political activism.[12] The modern idea of 'media malaise' emerged in the political science literature in the 1960s; Kurt and Gladys Lang were the first to make the connection between the rise of network news and broader feelings of disenchantment with American politics. TV news broadcasts, they argued, fueled public cynicism by overemphasizing political conflict and downplaying routine policymaking.[13] The idea gained currency in the mid-1970s, since media malaise seemed to provide a plausible reason for growing public alienation in America during the post-Vietnam and post-Watergate eras. Michael Robinson popularized the term 'videomalaise' to describe the link between reliance on American television journalism and political cynicism, social mistrust, and lack of political efficacy. Greater exposure to television news, he argued, with its high 'negativism,' conflictual frames, and anti-institutional themes, generated political disaffection, frustration, cynicism, self-doubt, and malaise.[14]

Many other commentators have echoed these claims over the years in the United States.[15] Hence, Neil Postman argued that the major American TV networks, driven by viewers' preference for cable, substituted entertainment-oriented and crime-, celebrity- and consumer-obsessed tabloid television for serious political coverage of national and world affairs.[16] The result, he suggests, is endless coverage of Hollywood, the 'health beat,' and sports rather than the serious problems facing society, so that Americans are 'entertaining [them]selves to death.' For Roderick Hart, television news charms the modern voter into an illusion of political participation and information, while encouraging couch potato passivity.[17] Others suggest that the problem of civic disengagement is rooted primarily in mainstream TV popular entertainment rather than TV journalism. Hence, cultivation theorists argue that TV drama, with its focus on violent crime, threats, and urban conflict, cultivates fear, alienation, and interpersonal mistrust among the audience.[18] According to the theory of social capital developed by Robert Putnam, the tremendous amount of time that Americans devote to watching TV entertainment has been responsible for the substantial erosion of civic engagement among the younger generation during the postwar era, as people have increasingly turned away from traditional forms of social and political activism in voluntary associations and community affairs.[19]

Similar arguments about media malaise have been made in many other countries; according to a widely influential report for the Trilateral Commission published in the mid-1970s, *The Crisis of Democracy*, for example, the news media were to blame for eroding respect for government authority in many postindustrial societies.[20] Along related lines, two decades later Jay Blumler identified a 'crisis of civic communication' afflicting Western Europe.[21] In increasingly complex societies, Blumler argues, governing has become more difficult, popular support more contingent, and mass communications more vital. Yet at the same time, structural failures in the news media have reduced the capacity of journalists to function in a way that promotes civic communications and the public sphere. The core problem, for Blumler, lies in the adversarial relationship between politicians and journalists.

Despite the popularity of the media malaise thesis, a growing number of skeptics have questioned the empirical evidence for these claims. The 'virtuous circle' interpretation provides an alternative view of developments. If Lipset and Rustow are right, then expanding access to mass communications should have a positive, not a negative, impact on attitudes at the heart of civic engagement, exemplified by social tolerance and trust, confidence in political institutions, and political interest and knowledge, as well as involvement in things like voting turnout, political activism, and protest politics. Support for these claims, based on cross-sectional surveys and experimental methods, has been found in many postindustrial nations, including America. In Britain, for example, reading a broadsheet newspaper and watching a lot of television news are found to be associated with greater political knowledge, as well as an interest in and understanding of politics.[22] Similar patterns are associated with attention to the news media in Germany and the Netherlands.[23] In the United States, research has shown that trust in politics and trust in the news media go hand in hand, with no evidence that use of the news media encourages political cynicism.[24] Comparison of a range of postindustrial societies, including the United States, revealed that, contrary to the media malaise thesis, although the total hours of watching television was indeed related to some signs of apathy, attention to the news media and current affairs programs was associated with positive indicators of civic engagement, including political knowledge, trust, and mobilization.[25] The growing body of individual-level research conducted in established democracies strongly indicates that media use is consistently linked with political activism. In interpreting this relationship, the virtuous circle thesis suggests that prior interest in public affairs habitually motivates people to seek out news sources such as political commentary in newspapers, to watch the evening news, and to surf the Internet for political Web sites and blogs. The thesis suggests that habitual use of the news media, in turn, contributes to greater awareness about current events and knowledge about public affairs, which in turn reduces the cognitive and informational barriers to political participation. During elections, for example, people who read about the campaign or watch the debates learn about the candidates, parties, and issues, facilitating their ability to make an informed choice. News use and civic engagement are therefore regarded as complementary processes in an interactive cycle.

Several limitations of the existing research, however, make it difficult to resolve the dispute between the media malaise and virtuous circle theories. First, most of the media malaise literature is based on structural developments in journalism and the news media industry, such as growing commercial pressures on TV ratings and newspaper sales, but does examine direct survey evidence for the impact of these processes on public opinion. Analysis of individual-level survey data is more appropriate for understanding the impact of media use on attitudes, values, and behaviors, but cross-sectional surveys (taken as a snapshot at one point in time) cannot conclusively establish the direction of causality underlying the relationship. Correlation analysis suggests a consistent linkage between media use and political activism, a pattern now reported in many postindustrial societies, but extended longitudinal time-series panel surveys and experimental designs are required to disentangle the causality.

In addition, further research is needed to broaden the comparative framework. A series of studies have examined these relationships within established democracies, such as America, Britain, and the Netherlands, but it has still not been established whether use of the news media has positive or negative effects on civic engagement in a wider range of countries and contexts, and under different types of regimes, as well as in many poor developing societies. Arguably, significant contrasts in journalistic cultures, such as more partisan reporting and closer state–media relations, could affect the public's civic engagement. In rigid autocracies such as Syria, for example, state control of the primary channels of broadcasting and lack of freedom of expression could plausibly mean that the public will mistrust the news media as a source of independent information. Practices of official censorship and state control in places such as Burma, Zimbabwe, and North Korea are designed to suppress opposition movements and dissident organizations, potentially dampening political activism. In addition, it is not clear whether any positive effects of media use on civic engagement are reinforced by societies with more open borders and greater freedom of expression. This is a plausible proposition, for example, if the ideas and images about democracy diffuse most widely within the most cosmopolitan societies. Where people have access to mass communications, greater familiarity with democratic practices and human rights derived from the Western news media may gradually cause these ideas to spread across national borders, thereby encouraging reform movements and human rights activism in previously closed societies and autocratic regimes. For example, in Africa, news about free and fair elections held in Ghana, Benin, and South Africa may encourage opposition forces to demand similar rights in Zimbabwe. By contrast, autocracies that restrict freedom of expression and cross-border information flows, such as China and Saudi Arabia, are most likely to suppress news and information flowing from abroad about democracy and human rights around the world. For all these reasons, we need to use multilevel modeling, as described in previous chapters, to disentangle the complex relationships linking habitual media use with democratic values and practices in a wide range of societies.

Measuring Civic Engagement

As in previous chapters, principal-component factor analysis with varimax rotation can be used to establish the underlying dimensions in civic engagement. The results in Table 9.1 show the 33 items related to civic engagement that were selected from the fifth wave of the WVS, and these fell into six dimensions. The first reflected confidence in political institutions, including parliaments, the judiciary, and the executive. This dimension represents the core institutions of state, as well as confidence in newspapers and television. Institutional confidence is an important indicator of public perception of the legitimacy of the state, representing the middle level of David Easton's concept of systems support.[26] Comparative studies have documented the erosion of confidence in these institutions that has occurred in recent decades in many postindustrial societies, as well as the low levels of trust that exist in many new democracies in Central Europe and Latin America.[27] This trend has been attributed, on the supply side, to problems of performance, if the erosion of national sovereignty in a globalized world means that traditional democratic institutions can no longer function effectively to connect citizens and the state.[28] Alternatively, explanations based on the growth of more critical citizens, on the demand side, emphasize that growing cognitive skills, knowledge, and education among the mass public has generated an erosion of deferential loyalties and rising public expectations about democracy and government.[29]

The second dimension reflects involvement in civic organizations and voluntary associations, one aspect of the concept of social capital

TABLE 9.1. *Dimensions of Civic Engagement*

	Confidence in Institutions	Civic Membership	Protest Politics	Citizen Interest	Democratic Values	Democratic Performance
V140 Confidence: parliaments	.782					
V138 Confidence: the government	.770					
V137 Confidence: the justice system	.765					
V136 Confidence: the police	.744					
V141 Confidence: the civil services	.736					
V139 Confidence: political parties	.709					
V132 Confidence: the armed forces	.605					
V142 Confidence: major companies	.604					
V135 Confidence: labor unions	.597					
V134 Confidence: television	.571					
V133 Confidence: the press	.557					
V29 Member of environmental group		.729				
V32 Member of consumer organization		.694				
V31 Member of charitable organization		.686				
V30 Member of professional organization		.674				
V26 Member of art, music, or educational organization		.645				
V28 Member of political party		.568				
V27 Member of labor union		.547				
V25 Member of sports/recreational group		.522				

(continued)

TABLE 9.1 *(continued)*

	Confidence in Institutions	Civic Membership	Protest Politics	Citizen Interest	Democratic Values	Democratic Performance
V98 Attended demonstrations			.793			
V97 Joined boycotts			.784			
V102 Recently attended demonstrations			.673			
V101 Recently joined boycotts			.673			
V96 Signed a petition			.667			
V100 Recently signed a petition			.603			
V95 Interest in politics				.789		
V7 Politics important in life				.787		
V234 Voted in recent parliamentary elections				.457		
V148 Approve having a strong leader					.787	
V149 Approve having experts decide					.772	
V150 Approve having the army rule					.610	
V162 Importance of democracy						.854
V163 Democratic performance of country						.823

Note: Principal-component factor analysis. Rotation method: varimax with Kaiser normalization.

Source: World Values Survey (2005–2007).

that has received a lot of attention in recent years.[30] Theorists from de Tocqueville and John Stuart Mill to Durkheim, Simmel, and Kornhauser have emphasized the importance of civic society and voluntary associations to the lifeblood of democracy. The face-to-face interactions promoted through dense networks of voluntary associations in the local community are theorized by Putnam to promote social trust among members, especially 'bridging' groups attracting diverse participants and sectors, with beneficial spillover effects for solving collective action problems and making democracy work.[31] The eight groups included in this study range from the traditional, such as labor unions, professional organizations, and political parties, to active social movements concerned with the environment and consumers' rights. The third dimension monitors protest politics, measured by engagement in consumer boycotts, attendance at demonstrations, and the signing of petitions. These are all part of 'protest politics,' which Barnes and Kasse used in the late 1970s as a measure of the potential willingness or actual experience of citizen dissent.[32] The fourth dimension reflects citizen interest, including interest in politics, the importance of politics, and reported voting turnout in national elections. The fact that voting participation is closely related to interest rather than other types of activism, such as party membership or protest politics, suggests that, although widespread, this is one of the least demanding forms of civic engagement. The fifth dimension concerns support for democratic values and rejection of autocratic alternatives, including military rule, having experts decide, or simply having a strong leader. Two items were included in the final dimension: a 10-point scale measuring how respondents rated the importance of democracy and a 10-point scale indicating how respondents rated the performance of democracy in their own country. As in previous chapters, for comparison across these dimensions, a series of standardized 100-point scales were constructed by combining the items listed for each dimension in Table 9.1, with the exception of the assessment of democratic performance and the importance of democracy, which were kept as separate items for analysis.

The Link Between Individual Media Use and Indicators of Civic Engagement

For an initial description of the contrasts in political values and practices, we can compare the distribution of the mean scales by type of media user and by type of society, without any controls. The strength and significance of the differences between groups are summarized by Anova. As Table 9.2 shows, the strongest contrasts emerged in the protest politics and the democratic values scales, although there were significant differences between types of societies across all the scales, except that for citizen interest. In addition, media use made no significant difference for evaluations of the performance of democracy or for the importance of democracy, which were both omitted from further analysis.

Figure 9.1 shows the main contrasts in levels of protest politics, including activism through boycott, demonstrations, and petitions. In both types of societies, there are marked media effects, with more than twice as many people reporting protest activism among the heavier users of the news media than among the low users. But both the levels of protest politics and the contrasts between high and low media users are far greater in cosmopolitan societies than in parochial societies. The pattern concerning support for democratic values, illustrated in Figure 9.2, shows a similar but more modest media gap in cosmopolitan societies, although media use did not distinguish support for democratic ideals in parochial nations.

To explore these general patterns in more detail, we can again use multilevel regression models across all the scales of political values and practices, as in previous chapters, controlling for individual-level demographic characteristics, socioeconomic resources, and media use. The results show a familiar pattern for the age profile of activists; across all dimensions of civic engagement, the older generation was significantly more engaged than the younger. Even by the measures of protest politics, which was once thought to be the province of young student radicals, it now appears that the typical activist is middle-aged or older, with a 'normalization' of participation.[33] The gender profile is more mixed, with voluntary membership in civic associations skewed toward women, a pattern that has been reported elsewhere, although this depends in part on the particular mix of organizations that are included in the comparison.[34] By contrast, protest politics and interest in politics are skewed toward men, again a long-standing finding in the literature.[35] The socioeconomic bias in political participation, highlighted in the early 1970s by Verba, Nie, and Kim, has proved a persistent pattern in civic engagement in many countries.[36] Our results confirm that the more affluent are more likely than others to express confidence

TABLE 9.2. *Political Values and Practices by Type of Society and Media Use*

Type of Society	Media Use	Confidence in Institutions	Membership in Voluntary Organizations	Protest Politics	Citizen Interest	Democratic Values	Democratic Performance of Own Country	Importance of Democracy
Parochial	Low	62	6	13	59	65	60	80
	Moderate	61	9	19	62	65	60	80
	High	62	12	24	67	64	60	90
	TOTAL	62	8	17	62	65	60	80
Cosmopolitan	Low	56	5	19	50	72	70	80
	Moderate	59	8	34	61	76	70	90
	High	61	12	45	67	79	70	90
	TOTAL	59	10	37	62	76	70	90
Total	Low	61	6	14	57	66	60	80
	Moderate	60	9	27	61	70	60	90
	High	61	12	38	67	73	70	90
	TOTAL	61	9	27	62	70	60	90
Strength of association		.086***	.059***	.356***	.006	.330***	.121***	.112***

Note: The mean position of categories of media users on the 100-point value scales by type of society, no controls. See Table 9.1 for the items used in the construction of the scales. Anova was used to assess the strength of association (eta) and the statistical significance of the difference between types of society. ***$p = .001$.

Source: World Values Survey (2005–2007).

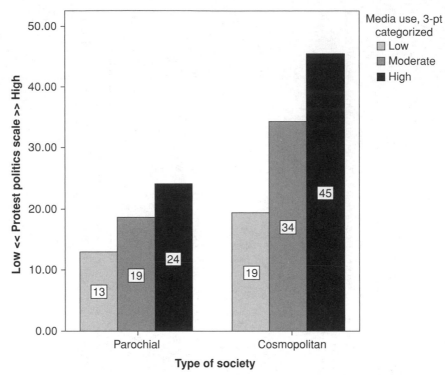

FIGURE 9.1. Protest Politics by Media Use and Type of Society. The mean position of categories of media users on the 100-point value scales by type of society, no controls. Protest politics was measured by willingness to join or recent experience of joining boycotts or demonstrations or signing a petition. See Table 9.1 for the items used in the construction of the scales. Anova was used to assess the strength of association (eta) and the statistical significance of the difference between types of society. ***$p = .001$. *Source:* World Values Survey (2005–2007).

and trust in political institutions, to be more active in voluntary associations and protest politics, and to report more interest in politics, although it is striking that there is no socioeconomic skew in adherence to democratic values. Education provides cognitive skills and knowledge that help people to circumnavigate public affairs and usually represents one of the most reliable indicators of civic engagement. It proved to be so here for membership in voluntary organizations, involvement in protest politics, and interest and support for democratic values, but the more educated also proved to have less confidence than others in political institutions, not more. The phenomenon

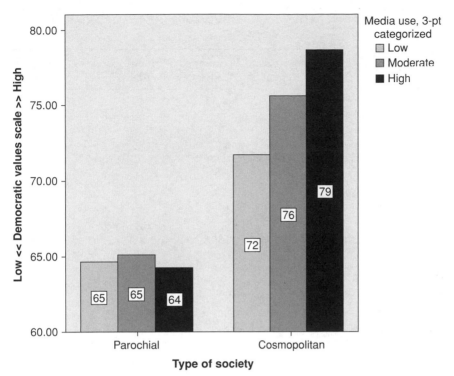

FIGURE 9.2. Democratic Values by Media Use and Type of Society. The mean position of categories of media users on the 100-point value scales by type of society, no controls. Democratic values were measured by rejection of rule by the army, experts, or strong leaders. See Table 9.1 for the items used in the construction of the scales. Anova was used to assess the strength of association (eta) and the statistical significance of the difference between types of society. ***$p = .001$. *Source:* World Values Survey (2005–2007).

of the critical citizen has been widely noted, whereby the cognitive skills and awareness derived from education raise expectations about democratic governance, reducing deferential loyalties to traditional institutions and encouraging challenges to forms of authority represented by parliaments, the police, and the judiciary.[37]

Most importantly for this study, after all these controls were included, as shown in Table 9.3 use of the news media was significantly and positively related to confidence in institutions, membership in volunteer organizations, involvement in protest politics, and citizen interest, although not to support for democratic values. Although the media malaise thesis suggests many reasons for citizens' aversion to

TABLE 9.3. *Multilevel Regression Models Explaining Political Values and Practices*

	Confidence in Institutions	Voluntary Membership	Protest Politics	Citizen Interest	Democratic Values
INDIVIDUAL LEVEL					
Demographic characteristics					
Age (years)	.439***	.418***	.351***	3.59***	.855***
	(.065)	(.042)	(.118)	(.089)	(.077)
Gender (male = 1)	−.106	−.211***	1.41***	1.91***	.058
	(.059)	(.038)	(.107)	(.081)	(.070)
Socioeconomic resources					
Household income, 10-pt scale	.530***	.521***	.537***	.536***	−.086
	(.065)	(.042)	(.119)	(.089)	(.078)
Education, 9-pt scale	−.661***	1.26***	4.89***	2.81***	2.23***
	(.077)	(.050)	(.141)	(.108)	(.092)
Media use					
News media use scale	.522***	1.68***	3.60***	2.78***	−.046
	(.183)	(.171)	(.406)	(.317)	(.154)
NATIONAL LEVEL					
Cosmopolitanism Index	−2.18	−854	6.42*	−3.38**	4.54***
(Globalization + development + freedom)	(1.17)	(.771)	(2.93)	(1.13)	(.934)
CROSS-LEVEL INTERACTIONS					
Cosmopolitanism × media use scale	.116	−.064	1.20**	1.12***	.894***
	(.189)	(.171)	(.395)	(.317)	(.154)
Constant (intercept)	61.3	8.75	29.4	61.3	68.8
Schwartz BIC	395,597	445,475	406,244	441,188	428,499
No. of respondents	49,484	60,759	44,583	50,907	51,171
No. of nations	49	48	41	41	49

Note: All independent variables were standardized using mean centering (*z*-scores). Models present the results of the REML multilevel regression models (for details, see Technical Appendix C), including the beta coefficient (standard error in parentheses) and the significance. The 100-point scales are constructed from the items listed in Table 9.1. The 100-point media use scale combined use of newspapers, radio/TV news, Internet, books, and magazines. *$p = .05$; **$p = .01$; ***$p = .001$. See Technical Appendix A for details about the measurement, coding, and construction of all variables. Significant coefficients are highlighted in bold.

Source: World Values Survey (2005–2007).

journalism – for example, negative campaign coverage or a focus on celebrities rather than serious reporting about current affairs, parliamentary debates, and public policy issues – in fact exposure to the news media is linked to more civic engagement, not less. The results extend this pattern, which has been widely reported in established democracies, by confirming that these generalizations also hold in a wide range of developing societies around the world. Admittedly, this evidence does not allow us to claim that there is a one-way direction of causality from media use to civic engagement, as a reciprocal relationship could also be at work (since interest in politics could plausibly cause people to pay attention to reporting about current events in newspapers and TV). Other types of longitudinal panel surveys or experimental evidence, which are unavailable on a cross-national basis, are required to establish this more conclusively. Nevertheless, we can certainly rule out the media malaise thesis with more confidence: across all the dimensions, there is no evidence here for any negative process linking media use with significantly greater civic disengagement. No matter how many commentators blame the messenger for political apathy, disenchantment, and cynicism, there is no support for these claims in the data.

What of the national-level effects of living in a more cosmopolitan society? Here the results are more mixed; protest politics and support for democratic values are significantly higher in cosmopolitan societies, but interest in politics appears to be depressed, and there is no significant difference in the other indicators. The analysis of cross-level interactions shows that, where there is a significant effect, media use in cosmopolitan societies had a positive impact on democracy by reinforcing protest activism, interest in politics, and democratic values. To test which national-level component of the Cosmopolitanism Index was most clearly linked to patterns of civic engagement, whether economic wealth, the Globalization Index, media freedom, or media access, alternative models were run in which the democratic values 100-point scale was the dependent variable (Table 9.4). The national-level coefficients all proved significant, with the composite Cosmopolitanism Index the strongest predictor of democratic values, closely followed by economic development and media freedom. By contrast, media access, emphasized in the original Lipset hypothesis, although significant, proved a slightly weaker predictor of democratic values. The results confirm

TABLE 9.4. *Multilevel Regression Models Explaining Support for Democratic Values*

	Cosmopolitanism Index	Globalization Index	Economic Development	Media Freedom	Media Access
INDIVIDUAL LEVEL					
Demographic characteristics					
Age (years)	.855***	.855***	.855***	.855***	.855***
	(.077)	(.077)	(.077)	(.077)	(.077)
Gender (male = 1)	.058	.058	.058	.058	.058
	(.070)	(.070)	(.070)	(.070)	(.070)
Socioeconomic resources					
Household income, 10-pt scale	−.086	−.086	−.086	−.086	−.086
	(.078)	(.078)	(.078)	(.078)	(.078)
Education, 9-pt scale	2.23***	2.23***	2.23***	2.23***	2.23***
	(.092)	(.092)	(.092)	(.092)	(.092)
Media use					
News media use scale	−.046	−.046	−.046	−.046	−.046
	(.154)	(.154)	(.154)	(.154)	(.154)
NATIONAL LEVEL					
Cosmopolitanism Index (Globalization + development + freedom)	4.54***				
	(.934)				
Globalization Index		2.91**			
		(1.08)			

	Model 1	Model 2	Model 3	Model 4	Model 5
Economic development			**4.40*** (.804)		
Media freedom				**4.06*** (1.03)	
Societal-level media access					**3.29*** (.934)
CROSS-LEVEL INTERACTIONS					
Cosmopolitanism × media use	**.894*** (.154)	**.860*** (.155)	**.889*** (.154)	**.869*** (.154)	**.858*** (.156)
Constant (intercept)	68.8	69.2	69.1	69.1	70.2
Schwartz BIC	428,499	428,511	428,495	428,495	41,703
No. of respondents	51,171	50,374	50,966	50,966	49,378
No. of nations	49	49	49	49	47

Note: All independent variables were standardized using mean centering (z-scores). Models present the results of the REML multilevel regression models (for details, see Technical Appendix C), including the beta coefficient (standard error in parentheses) and the significance. The 100-point scales are constructed from the items listed in Table 9.1. The 100-point media use scale combined use of newspapers, radio/TV news, Internet, books, and magazines. $*p = .05$; $**p = .01$; $***p = .001$. See Technical Appendix A for details about the measurement, coding, and construction of all variables. Significant coefficients are highlighted in bold.

Source: World Values Survey (2005–2007).

that democratic values flourish in affluent postindustrial nations, as many previous studies have reported, but economic development is not the only driver at work here. Democratic cultures are strongest in open societies that combine affluence with media freedom and borders open to information flows from abroad.

Conclusions and Discussion

The earliest sociological theories of Lipset argued that democracy is strengthened by economic development, particularly where rising affluence has increased public access to the mass media within each country. According to Lipset, by obtaining news about government and current affairs from the radio, television, and newspapers, citizens can participate more effectively in democratic processes, thereby sustaining and strengthening democratic consolidation. There are many reasons why, if journalism works well, democracy should benefit.[38] As a result of independent scrutiny by media watchdogs, the public policymaking process can become more transparent, which encourages government accountability. By strengthening the public sphere, journalism can enrich civic society and encourage public deliberation. Through inclusive and impartial reporting of major challenges facing society, multiple voices can be heard in public discussions. Balanced campaign coverage enlightens the public about electoral choices and allows citizens to cast informed votes. Moreover, governing elites can be more responsive to social needs when the news media highlight social concerns and public preferences, with reporters acting as a channel between citizens and the state. Serious questions are raised about how well journalism lives up to these ideals in practice, particularly in societies with severe limits on freedom of expression and publication. Moreover, media malaise theories cast serious doubts on the capacity of the mass media to achieve these objectives, suggesting that reporting commonly erodes trust in government institutions and generates civic apathy rather than activism.

The survey evidence we have analyzed here extends previous empirical studies about the relationship between use of the news media and political orientations in established democracies and affluent societies. The results of the analysis demonstrate that use of the news media is positively associated with many types of civic engagement: it strengthens confidence in institutions such as parliaments and parties, membership in voluntary organizations and civic associations such as charitable groups, unions, and parties, interest in politics, and support for democratic values. Although we cannot establish conclusive proof, these results are certainly consistent with the virtuous circle thesis, in which media use and civic engagement are considered to be complementary.[39]

In addition to internal processes, we theorized that in open societies the flow of mass communications from the global North to South will also gradually encourage the adoption of ideas about democratic practices and principles around the world. The results here are not as clear-cut, but nevertheless we established an important national-level effect; living in a more cosmopolitan society was positively associated with engagement in protest politics and support for democratic values, and use of the news media within cosmopolitan societies reinforced these effects. Cosmopolitan societies are more affluent than parochial societies, but they also have more freedom of the press and more open borders, and each of these factors can be understood to play a role in this relationship. The results lend some support to the theory of cultural convergence around the values and practices of democracy, but with the important proviso that the type of society also conditions or moderates the link between the media and democracy.

CONCLUSIONS

10

Cultural Convergence over Time?

We have argued throughout this book that the various versions of the cultural convergence thesis are deeply flawed, whether one has in mind the 'media imperialism' argument that was fashionable during the 1970s, the 'Coca-colonization' claim that was popular during the 1990s, or contemporary approaches advocating 'cultural protectionism.'[1] The convergence thesis rests on the premise that repeated exposure to the ideas and images transmitted by CNN International, MTV, and Hollywood will gradually undermine indigenous values and norms. Consequently, many deeply conservative cultures fear that opening the floodgates to the American or Western media will erode faith in religion, respect for marriage and the family, and deference toward traditional sources of authority. But earlier chapters demonstrated how lack of access to globalized mass communications persists in many poor nations, limiting the diffusion of Western ideas and images. This book has documented the existence of multiple firewalls that prevent the mass media from penetrating parochial societies and thus influencing the culture in these places.

In this chapter let us loosen this premise, however, on the grounds that cosmopolitan communications continue to expand worldwide. Even if they have not yet reached all peoples and places, channels of mass communications and new information technologies have become widely accessible to the public in many middle-income emerging economies, such as South Africa, Mexico, and Argentina. Barriers to information have also fallen since the third wave of democracy

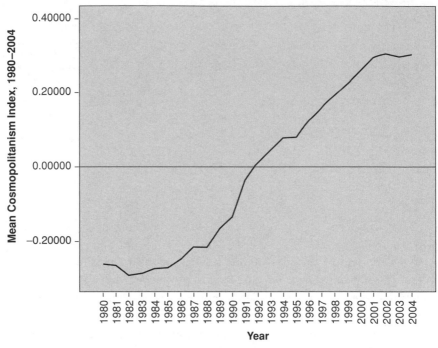

FIGURE 10.1. The Rise in Cosmopolitanism Worldwide, 1980–2004. The Cosmopolitanism Index is constructed according to levels of globalization, media freedom, and economic development, with all indices standardized around the mean (z-scores). See the main text for details.

began in the early 1970s; we have witnessed the expansion of independent journalism, freedom of expression, and rights to information, as well as the rise of a variety of media channels and outlets available to the public. Protectionist barriers to free trade in cultural goods and services have been lifted, following deregulation and the integration of economies into global markets. Figure 10.1 illustrates the dramatic sustained growth in cosmopolitanism worldwide, an especially steep rise having taken place during the past fifteen years. As a result of these developments, the networks within many cosmopolitan societies are now denser and faster, and multilateral media conglomerates have a far greater capacity to reach, and thus alter, cultural values in these nations.

These changes may have important potential in the future. But this chapter will examine the extent to which a process of cultural convergence has *actually* occurred among contemporary societies around the world. The chapter is divided into three parts. Previous chapters relied on data drawn from the most recent wave of the World Values Survey conducted in 2005–2007, which contains the richest battery of items monitoring individual-level use of the news media in a wide range of societies. Part I of this chapter utilizes all of the time-series data contained in this survey, aggregated at the national level, to see if there is any systematic evidence that cultural convergence has occurred during the past quarter of a century among cosmopolitan societies. The WVS contains time-series survey data spanning 25 years, since the early 1980s, for 11 nations. By examining trends over time in these societies, we can explore whether the rise in cosmopolitan communications has reduced divergence among national cultures. Part II uses more systematic cross-sectional time-series models, with panel-corrected standard errors, to analyze these issues. Part III compares the use of television or radio news, the use of newspapers, and access to the Internet in order to explore the question of whether the effects vary significantly by the type of media.

Comparing Trends in Mass Attitudes from 1981 to 2005

The 11 countries included in each of the five successive waves of the WVS since the early 1980s clearly are not a representative sample of all nations in the world. Nevertheless, these surveys cover countries on five different continents and reflect a variety of religious traditions, levels of democracy, and linguistic cultures; some of the countries, such as Sweden and Japan, are at the forefront of cosmopolitanism, whereas others, such as Mexico and South Africa, have lagged behind in this process, and others, such as South Korea, have sharply accelerated their integration into global communication networks during the past quarter of a century. Also included are some of the leading producer nations that dominate the sale of cultural products exchanged in global markets, including the United States, Britain, and Germany, as well as some affluent societies with open borders that are net importers of audiovisual programs and are at the forefront of Internet access, such as Sweden and Finland. The cross-national comparison also includes three emerging market economies with moderate levels of human development: Mexico, Argentina, and South Africa. During the late

20th century, economic growth remained relatively flat in Mexico, Argentina, and South Africa, although democracy made rapid strides after the restoration of constitutional rule in 1983 in Argentina, the end of apartheid in South Africa in 1994, and the demise of the Institutional Revolutionary Party (PRI) after its long period of predominance in Mexico, following the victory of President Vincente Fox in 2000. Today these three economies are classified as middle income, with an average per capita GDP of around $9,000–10,000 in 2005, about one-third of the level of the United States. The comparison also includes one transitional case – South Korea – which has been transformed by rapid social, economic, and political change in recent decades. During the late 20th century, the country shifted from an agrarian/industrial to a postindustrial service sector economy, and politically from autocracy to democracy. Today the population enjoys an affluent and secure lifestyle; for example, the average income for South Koreans roughly quadrupled during the past quarter of a century (measured by per capita GDP in constant international dollars PPP). Using each wave of the WVS for the 11 countries, with the results aggregated at the societal level, generated a total of 55 nation-wave observations as the units of analysis.

Most importantly for our purposes, while this database does not include the most isolated and remote developing societies, the comparison includes countries that differ substantially in their levels of cosmopolitanism. In Chapter 5 we constructed the Cosmopolitanism Index to reflect the permeability of societies to information flows, reflecting three subfactors: level of globalization, level of media freedom, and level of economic development. We operationalized the concept by combining standardized annual measures for the KOF Globalization Index, the level of economic development (measured in constant international dollars PPP, from the World Bank), and the Freedom House Press Freedom Index. One minor amendment had to be introduced to the version of the Cosmopolitanism Index used in previous chapters. The Freedom House 100-point scale of media freedom is available only from 1994 onward, so this could not be used to analyze the 1981 and 1990 waves of the WVS. In this chapter, therefore, when constructing the composite index we changed the Freedom House categories of media freedom in each nation-state to 'free,' 'partly free,' and 'not free' – based on information that has been available annually since

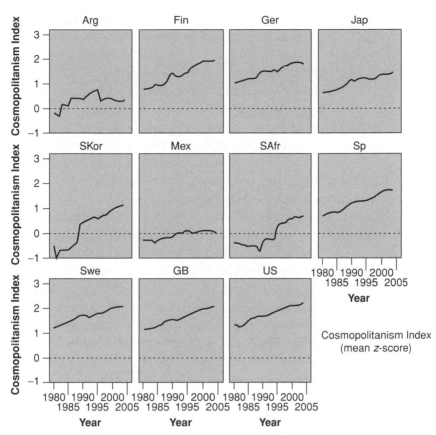

FIGURE 10.2. The Rise in Cosmopolitanism, Selected Nations. For the construction of the 100-point Cosmopolitanism Index scale, see Chapter 5 and Technical Appendix A. The graphs illustrate the standardized (*z*-score) national means for each year, from 1980 to 2005.

1980. Fortunately, the Freedom House categorization of media freedom was closely correlated ($R = .893^{***}$) with the 100-point Freedom House index, so this procedure should not greatly affect the results.

As illustrated in Figure 10.2, the 11 nations with data based on the longest time series vary substantially in their intercepts (starting point) and slopes (degree of change), as gauged by the annual Cosmopolitanism Index from 1981 to 2005. Seven countries show high and steadily rising levels of cosmopolitanism, including Finland, Germany, Spain, Sweden, Britain, Japan, and the United States. South Korea shows the strongest transformation over these decades, becoming

far more closely connected to global markets and networks than it used
to be. Finally, Mexico, South Africa, and Argentina lag behind on the
Cosmopolitanism Index and can be classified as relatively parochial
societies. The logic of the convergence thesis suggests that globalized
mass communications should exert the strongest impact on social values in the most open societies. If this argument is indeed correct, then
cosmopolitan societies should display considerable similarities in cultures today and growing convergence over time, as these nations have
the weakest barriers to information exchanges. The existence of permeable cultural boundaries, integration into cultural trade on world
markets, and the expanded volume and pace of news information and
audiovisual entertainment exchanged across national borders imply
that countries like Britain, the United States, Japan, Germany, and
Sweden, which have different historical traditions, social structures,
and religious legacies, will gradually come to share increasingly similar values and attitudes. Indeed, this fear is at the root of French
concerns about 'Americanization,' which assumes that the combined
forces of *CSI*, McDonald's, and Hollywood will undermine the culture of Molière, Sartre, and haute cuisine, unless they are offset by new
measures to protect European television within the European Union.[2]
It follows that more diverse values and attitudes should persist in
more parochial societies, such as South Africa, Argentina, and Mexico,
which are not as tightly integrated into international information flows,
global cultural trade, or multilateral communication networks across
national borders.

Measuring Value Change, 1981–2005

What measures are available from the WVS to tap enduring aspects
of value change over the past twenty-five years? The survey contains
hundreds of items, but our selection is restricted because not all of
these are closely or consistently related to each other, nor are they
all carried over successive waves. To identify consistent trends since
1981, we must analyze identical items to ensure that any significant
changes over time reflect genuine shifts in public opinion, rather than
measurement errors arising from differences in question wording or
coding. Building on previous chapters, we selected a subset of items for
time-series analysis since 1981, covering five dimensions reflecting the
values of religiosity, sexual morality, free market economics, political

TABLE 10.1. *Dimensions of Cultural Values*

	Religiosity	Liberal Sexual Morality	Free Market Economics	Political Engagement	Nationalism
Religious identity	.829				
Importance of God	.827				
Frequency of attendance at religious services	.749				
Approval of divorce		.840			
Approval of abortion		.786			
Approval of homosexuality		.780			
Approval of income differences as incentives			.720		
People should take responsibility to provide for themselves			.694		
Left–right self-placement scale			.504		
Participated in a demonstration				.778	
Participated in a boycott				.774	
Political interest				.606	
Willingness to fight for country					.783
National pride					.682

Note: Individual-level principal-component factor analysis. Rotation method: varimax with Kaiser normalization.
Source: World Values Survey (1981–2005).

engagement, and nationalism. The factor analysis in Table 10.1 lists the items in each scale and the factor loadings, indicating the strength of the correlations among the values.

Trends in Religiosity
To what extent has a change in values accompanied the accelerated information flows across national borders, especially in the most open

societies? We can first describe trends in value change and then use time-series regression models to analyze these patterns more systematically. Elsewhere we have presented extensive evidence for long-term processes of secularization that have eroded religious values and practices in most affluent nations during the 20th century, although the historical imprints of religious traditions such as Protestantism and Catholicism remain evident even in contemporary societies.[3] Predominant religious cultures seem to be path dependent, adapting and evolving in response to developments in the contemporary world, and yet also strongly reflecting the legacy of past centuries.[4] We have demonstrated elsewhere that religiosity persists most strongly among vulnerable populations, especially those of poor nations, that are facing personal threats to survival. We argue that feelings of vulnerability to physical, societal, and personal risks are a key factor driving religiosity, and we show that the process of secularization – a systematic erosion of religious practices, values, and beliefs – has occurred most discernibly among the most prosperous social sectors in affluent and secure postindustrial nations.[5]

Our previous analysis was based on the first four waves of the WVS, from 1981 to 2001. Figure 10.3 updates this analysis to include the fifth wave, in 2005–2007. The 11 nations for which we have consistent time-series data include predominantly Protestant and Catholic societies, as well as countries in which the religious tradition is Buddhist (South Korean) or Shinto (Japan). The graph presents trends in the standardized religiosity scale, reflecting whether people expressed a religious identity, the degree to which they value religion, as measured by their belief in the importance of God, and the frequency of their attendance at religious services. The religiosity scale was standardized around the mean. In the predominantly Protestant European countries under comparison, the level of religiosity across the five waves of the WVS proved relatively steady and persistently lower than average; in secular Sweden, for example, only one-third of the public expressed a religious identity and church attendance was consistently low. Similar patterns were found in Britain and Germany. By contrast, from 1995 to 2005 Catholic Spain registered a sharp decline in religiosity, across all indicators that were included in the composite scale; thus, the proportion of Spaniards expressing a religious identity fell from two-thirds to less than one-half. The distinction observed here reflects

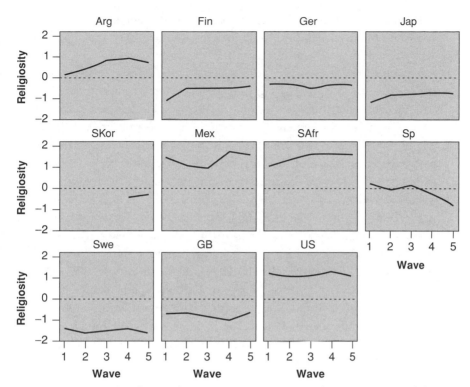

FIGURE 10.3. Trends in Religiosity, 1981–2005. For the construction of the 100-point religiosity scale, see Table 10.1. The graphs illustrate the standardized (*z*-score) national means for each wave of the WVS, from Wave 1 (1981–1983) to Wave 5 (2005–2007). *Source:* World Values Survey (1981–2005).

trends in attendance at religious services documented in the series of Eurobarometer surveys since the early 1970s, where active religious practices appear to have fallen farther and earlier in Protestant than in Catholic European societies.[6] The time-series evidence for South Korea is limited, but the available data indicate that the two Asian nations in the comparison are also relatively secular; for example, only one-quarter of the Japanese public expressed a religious identity.

Yet there are also some persistent contrasts, particularly the high level of religiosity found in the United States, which remains a special case among affluent societies and cosmopolitan nations, as many others have observed, and where all the indicators remain relatively high.[7] Many factors contribute to American exceptionalism. As we have argued elsewhere, rising levels of existential security tend to bring a diminishing emphasis on religion; but despite its high level of wealth, the United States lacks the cradle-to-grave welfare state and the universal health care system found in other postindustrial societies. Most strikingly, religiosity is well above average in the three middle-income societies, and Argentina and South Africa have registered a modest rise in religiosity over time, while Mexico shows some trendless fluctuations. On this specific dimension of social values, we can conclude from examining the descriptive trends that clear and persistent contrasts are evident between most of the cosmopolitan societies (with the exception of the United States) and most of the parochial societies, with no apparent evidence of any convergence among societies during the past quarter of a century. The parochial societies were consistently above average in religiosity at the start of this period, and they remain so – indeed, they became slightly more religious over time. Most of the cosmopolitan societies (except the United States) are more secular in their values, with an erosion of religiosity in Catholic Spain. The comparative framework is limited, but it confirms previous findings covering a wider range of societies. During the period since 1981, though globalization rose sharply, there is no clear indication of convergence over time in the religious values of these societies.

Trends in Sexual Morality, 1981–2005

Elsewhere we have documented how perceptions of sexual morality, issues such as tolerance of homosexuality and support for gay rights, attitudes toward marriage and divorce, and ideas about the appropriate division of sex roles in the home and family, paid employment, and the political sphere, are shaped by the predominant culture – the social norms, beliefs, and values existing in any society – which in turn rest on levels of societal modernization and religious traditions.[8] Relatively liberal social values are found in most affluent postindustrial societies – in particular, high levels of tolerance toward homosexuality and egalitarian roles for women – while more conservative values are characteristic of most developing nations.[9] Social values are monitored in this chapter by the liberal sexual morality scale, which compares attitudes toward divorce, abortion, and homosexuality.

Figure 10.4 illustrates the descriptive trends, revealing a complex pattern. If we compare the positions of countries at the start and end of the time series, it is apparent that most of the cosmopolitan societies

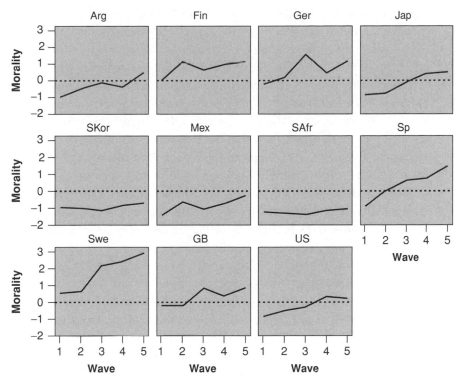

FIGURE 10.4. Trends in Liberal Sexual Morality, 1981–2005. For the construction of the 100-point liberal sexual morality scale, see Table 10.1. The graphs illustrate the standardized (z-score) national means for each wave of the WVS, from Wave 1 (1981–1983) to Wave 5 (2005–2007). *Source:* World Values Survey (1981–2005).

have become more liberal and tolerant in their values during the past quarter of a century. This shift is strongest (despite different religious traditions) in Sweden, Spain, Japan, and the United States. By contrast, South Africa remains the most conservative society in its moral values in the modern era. Argentina and Mexico are also relatively conservative, but they register a more liberal trend. South Korea is an interesting case, remaining fairly conservative in moral values according to the composite scale, but Korean attitudes have become more liberal toward homosexuality and divorce, while becoming less permissive toward abortion rights. Fluctuations in public opinion are also notable in certain waves of the survey in Germany (1995), Finland (1990), and the United Kingdom (1995), which may reflect contemporary policy debates and legislation about these issues, elite opinion and rhetoric, and the strength of conservative and liberal social movements in each of these countries.[10] Overall the descriptive trends suggest that societies continue to differ sharply in their attitudes toward sexual morality issues, as evidenced by the contrasts between contemporary Sweden and South Africa, or between contemporary Spain and Mexico. South Africa is the clearest example of a parochial society with conservative social values that have not changed during the past quarter of a century, in contrast to the dramatic transformation that has occurred during this period in Spain. The pattern is complex, but it does not support the claim that these societies are converging in their social and moral values. In fact, we find divergent trends. Most of these societies have become more liberal, but they have done so without their values converging.

Trends in Nationalism, 1981–2005

The claim that, as a result of globalization, the world's societies are abandoning the visceral appeals of nationalism and moving steadily toward cosmopolitanism was not established in previous chapters, and this claim receives little or no support from the time-series data. Trends in the strength of nationalism over successive waves of the WVS are monitored with two items, which measure the strength of national pride and the willingness to fight for one's country. Figure 10.5 illustrates the contrasts in the starting and end points of this series among contemporary societies and the trends over time.

The citizens of Germany and Japan express the lowest support for nationalism – a persistent pattern that seems attributable to the enduring legacy of their defeat in World War II and the backlash that this experience generated against the use of military force by these countries. This outlook is also reflected in current debates in each country about the deployment of their armed forces overseas in a peacekeeping role. There has also been a sharp erosion of nationalism in South Korea during this era, especially in willingness to fight for the country. On the other hand, the United States displays relatively high levels of nationalism, although there has been a decline on both indicators during the past decade (thus predating contemporary controversies over the Bush administration's use of force after 9/11 in Afghanistan and Iraq). Public opinion is also relatively nationalistic in two parochial societies, Mexico and South Africa, while rising over time in Argentina. The

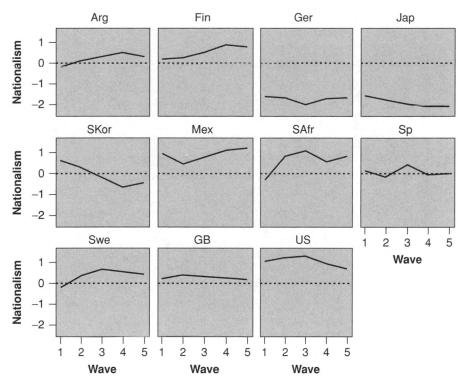

FIGURE 10.5. Trends in Nationalism, 1981–2005. For the construction of the 100-point liberal nationalism scale, see Table 10.1. The graphs illustrate the standardized (*z*-score) national means for each wave of the WVS, from Wave 1 (1981–1983) to Wave 5 (2005–2007). *Source:* World Values Survey (1981–2005).

trends in nationalist feelings vary considerably across the 11 nations under comparison, with the United States again something of an outlier among postindustrial societies. Overall at least two of the three parochial societies are more nationalistic than average, and there is no evidence that the appeal of nationalism has been eroded; there is no indication that these attitudes have been converging toward the low levels of nationalism found in Spain, Britain or Germany.

Trends in Political Engagement, 1981–2005

Trends in civic activism are monitored by political interest and by the propensity to demonstrate and engage in consumer boycotts (see Figure 10.6). Sweden consistently ranks highest on civic activism, among the countries examined here. This confirms previous findings

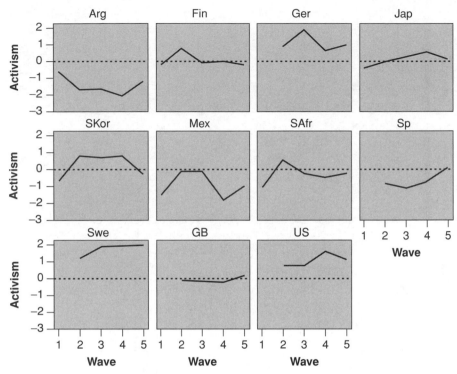

FIGURE 10.6. Trends in Political Engagement, 1981–2005. For the construction of the 100-point political engagement scale, see Table 10.1. The graph illustrates the standardized (z-score) national means for each wave of the WVS, from Wave 1 (1981–1983) to Wave 5 (2005–2007). *Source:* World Values Survey (1981–2005).

that the publics of the Scandinavian countries rank high on democratic engagement, including voting turnout and campaign activism, membership in voluntary associations, and generalized social trust, as well as involvement in protest politics.[11] After Sweden, the United States and Germany show relatively high levels of political engagement, although with greater volatility. Certain fluctuations can probably be attributed to specific events, such as the reunification of Germany during the early 1990s, or to particular elections that mobilized and activated the public, such as the 2000 U.S. presidential election, the exceptionally close outcome of which generated so much controversy. Similarly, the end of apartheid and the rise of majority rule in South Africa gave rise to an outpouring of political activism and interest during the early 1990s. Despite the fluctuations over time, we again find no indications that all of these countries (or even the most cosmopolitan ones) have been converging toward the mean or toward the level of the dominant media sources. On the contrary, persistent cross-national differences remain evident, even among relatively similar nations, such as those found between active Sweden and relatively apathetic Britain, or between Argentina and Mexico.

Trends in Economic Values, 1990–2006

We lack sufficient time-series data to monitor support for capitalist economic values over the full time series, but we do have time-series data from 1990 to 2006 that enable us to compare ideological left–right orientations, support for greater income equality, and attitudes toward the role of the state and markets. If the spread of cosmopolitan communications, especially the consumer values reflected in commercial advertising and popular entertainment, has encouraged the diffusion of support for global capitalism in recent decades, as McChesney claims, then this should be evident from trends in public opinion.[12] Figure 10.7 shows the relevant evidence. On economic values, public opinion across the 11 countries under comparison indeed displays a greater cross-national consensus than is found with the other dimensions of public opinion examined so far. Despite the diverse roles played by the state in these countries and despite the diverse political ideologies of the regimes in power, we find broadly similar and relatively steady levels of support for liberal economic values. Indeed, the overall trends in the relatively small welfare state of Sweden and in the pro–free market and neoliberal United States appear to be remarkably similar. Although free trade agreements and the reduction of protectionism have gradually opened economic borders throughout this period, especially within the European Union, we actually find a gradual trend in economic values toward more *collectivist* or leftist values, as shown most clearly in Germany, Argentina, and even the United States. The shift is modest, but it is in exactly the opposite direction from that predicted by the thesis that globalization is converting people to capitalist values.

To summarize and compare change across each of these scales, the countries included in all waves of the WVS were classified into types of society. An examination of the mean annual ratings of nations on the Cosmopolitanism Index during this 25-year period indicated that three countries – Mexico, Argentina, and South Africa – could be classified as clearly more parochial than average. Seven other

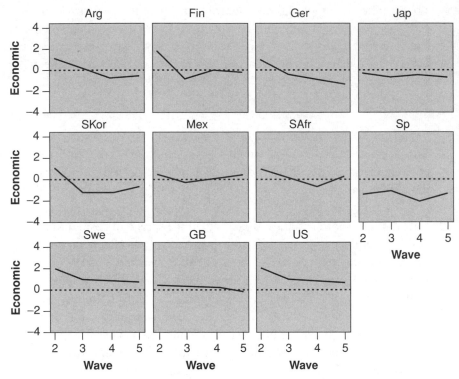

FIGURE 10.7. Trends in Support for Free Market Economic Values, 1990–2005. For the construction of the 100-point economic values scale, see Table 10.1. The graphs illustrate the standardized (*z*-score) national means for each wave of the WVS from Wave 2 (1990–1991) to Wave 5 (2005–2007). *Source:* World Values Survey (1981–2005).

nations – Sweden, Finland, Germany, Britain, the United States, Japan, and Spain – could be classified as consistently more cosmopolitan than average in every year. South Korea didn't fit into this comparison, since it moved from being a relatively parochial to a relatively cosmopolitan society during this era. Figure 10.8 examines trends in

FIGURE 10.8. Persistent Divergence Between Parochial and Cosmopolitan Societies, 1981–2005. Trends from 1981 to 2005 in mean value scales in successive waves of the WVS in 10 nations, including 3 persistently parochial societies (Mexico, Argentina, and South Africa) and 7 persistently cosmopolitan societies (Sweden, Finland, Germany, Britain, the United States, Japan, and Spain). For the construction of the 100-point value scales, see Table 10.1. *Source:* World Values Survey (1981–2005).

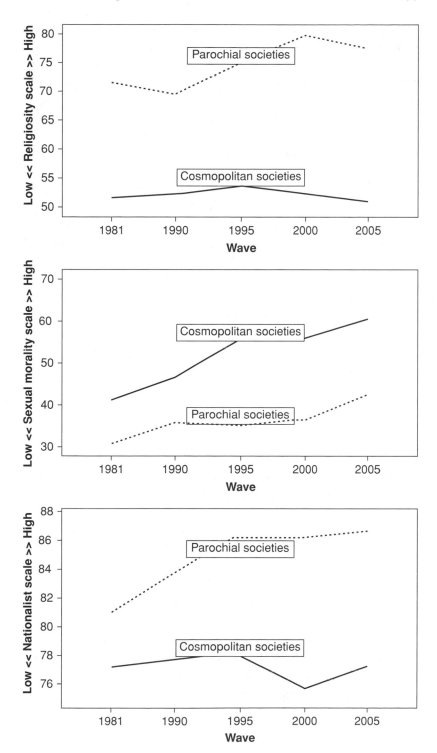

three of the value scales for each wave of the survey and for each type of society. This summary demonstrates that, during the past 25 years, the gap in values between parochial and cosmopolitan societies either persisted (on the liberal sexual morality scale) or even widened (with respect to nationalism and religiosity). There is no evidence here, or with the other value scales, of convergence between the two types of society. This confirms the evidence presented in earlier chapters for the persistence of cultural differences between nations – even between societies that are most interconnected and tied together by deep cultural bonds and communication networks, such as Britain and the United States in the Anglophone world, Sweden and Finland in Europe, Argentina and Mexico in Latin America, and Japan and South Korea in Asia. The slopes may be similar (the degree of change over time, such as the shift toward more liberal and tolerant views on sexual morality in cosmopolitan and parochial societies), but the intercept (the starting point for the series for each nation and type of society) continues to be distinct. Increasingly dense communication flows have been claimed to produce convergence over time, but the empirical evidence reveals the enduring imprint of distinctive historical traditions that continue to be apparent today.

Cross-Sectional Time-Series Models

Does the growth of cosmopolitan communications actually drive changes in values? So far we have relied on descriptive statistics and visual graphics based on national means, but multivariate analysis is necessary to determine the significance of any changes over time. To carry out more rigorous tests, we will analyze cross-sectional time-series data from the pooled WVS, including all five waves, which will facilitate comparison over space and time. This sort of panel dataset consists of repeated observations (by wave) on a series of fixed (non-sampled) units (the nations included in the WVS). The survey, conducted in five waves since 1981, covers a total of 95 contemporary nation-states (excluding dependent territories and subregions, such as Northern Ireland and Puerto Rico). The nation-wave is thus the basic unit of analysis, generating a maximum of 239 observations across the whole survey, although the number can be lower where data are missing for specific items in particular countries.

The analysis of cross-sectional longitudinal data faces certain challenges similar to those encountered with multilevel analysis.[13] Ordinary least squares (OLS) regression estimates are based on the assumption that errors are independent, are normally distributed, and have constant variance. Survey data of the same nations measured in successive waves over time violate these assumptions and raise potential statistical problems. In particular, autocorrelations are generated because, with time-series data, the same countries are being measured repeatedly and the additional observations do not provide substantially new information. The danger of using OLS is that the study will fail to identify the lack of independence between cases and will subsequently reach false conclusions. The beta coefficients in any regression analysis will remain unbiased, but the disturbance terms from the errors (i.e., omitted variables) are likely to be correlated. In these circumstances, OLS regression models would tend to underestimate standard errors, suggesting that significant relationships exist when in fact they do not.

Various options are available to overcome the problem of both autocorrelated and heteroscedastic disturbances found in cross-sectional time-series datasets, such as generalized least squares models, as used in earlier chapters for the multilevel regression analysis. Following the advice of Betz and Katz, however, when comparing relationships across countries and across time in this chapter, we used OLS linear regression with panel-corrected standard errors to measure the impact of the independent variables (societal levels of cosmopolitanism, time, and media access) on the value scales across each nation and wave of the survey.[14] This approach is particularly well suited to the dataset, as the number of countries under comparison (95) is considerably greater than the number of waves (5). Nevertheless, the robustness of the results must be checked, given the potential problem of missing data where the same countries are not observed in successive waves.[15] The use of panel-corrected standard errors with fixed effects is also an appropriate approach in which the data contain a convenience sample of nations. Estimating random effects would be more suitable if the survey were based on a random sample of all countries worldwide.[16] The use of fixed effects has its costs, however, because this makes it harder for any slowly changing variables to appear substantively or statistically significant.[17]

TABLE 10.2. *Cross-Sectional Time-Series Regression Models Explaining Societal-Level Mean Value Scales*

	Religiosity	Liberal Sexual Morality	Free Market Economics	Political Engagement	Nationalism
Cosmopolitanism Index	**−9.37*****	**10.25*****	.295	**3.87****	**−3.02*****
(Globalization + development + freedom)	(1.04)	(1.06)	(.415)	(.497)	(.250)
Survey year	**−2.44*****	.495	−1.11	**−.571****	.938
	(.402)	(.549)	(.609)	(.223)	(.066)
Constant	61.6	32.6	59.3	38.1	81.2
R^2	.32	.54	.05	.29	.15
No. of observations	195	199	161	170	176
No. of nations	75	76	72	74	72
Max no. of waves	5	5	4	5	5

Note: The independent variables were standardized using mean centering (z-scores). Models present the results of the cross-sectional time-series linear regression models with panel-corrected standard errors, using Stata/SE.xtpcse (for details, see Technical Appendix C). Missing data were treated on a pairwise basis. The table presents the beta coefficient (panel-corrected standard error in parentheses) and the significance. $*p = .05; **p = .01; ***p = .001$. See Technical Appendix A for details about the measurement, coding, and construction of all variables. Significant coefficients are highlighted in bold.
Source: World Values Survey (2005–2007).

The analysis tests the effects on the cultural value scales of the national-level Cosmopolitanism Index, which represents the permeability of societies to information flows, and the particular wave of the survey, which represents change over time. Table 10.2 presents the results of the analysis, including the beta coefficient (the slope), the panel-corrected standard error, and the intercept (constant), along with the number of observations (nation-waves) and the number of nations and waves used for each model.

The results confirm that the Cosmopolitanism Index is significantly related to each of these value scales and in the expected direction, a conclusion that was already derived from the descriptive evidence. In comparison with relatively parochial societies, the more cosmopolitan societies were consistently less religious and nationalistic in their cultural values, and displayed more liberal sexual morality and greater political engagement. They were also *less* supportive of neoliberal free market economics. Although often assumed to be the bastion of capitalist values, in fact affluent societies tend to believe that the state must continue to play an important role in the economy.

The degree to which societies are open to cosmopolitan communications is linked with the presence of modern social values, but this does not mean that the rest of the world is converging toward common values. As discussed further in the last chapter, culture is not static. We do not find that parochial societies are converging to become similar to cosmopolitan ones. Instead, most societies are gradually shifting toward more modern values, but the pace of change is such that the relatively affluent postindustrial nations and open societies around the world are moving farther and faster in this process, and are thus experiencing a growing gap between their values and those found in developing societies.

Does the Type of Media Matter?

One important issue has not yet been addressed in this study; it concerns whether different effects arise from the use of television or radio news, newspaper readership, and Internet use. As the most international information resource, the Internet might well be expected to encourage more cultural change than either TV news or newspapers, which are typically far more localized and nationalized in their structure and contents. Obviously there is no watertight contrast; people often use multiple, overlapping sources of information, such as a morning newspaper, radio news on the commute to work, the Internet for breaking stories during the day, and the radio or TV news in the evening. As a result, we would not expect very strong effects to arise from any single type of news medium. In addition, many use the Internet to find out about community events and local news, just as they seek out international coverage of foreign affairs on channels like CNN International or in world news reports in newspapers. We would need more detailed data monitoring patterns of media use to try to tease out such contrasts. Nevertheless, it seems safe to assume that the Internet has the greatest capacity to connect us to events happening around the world, because it is genuinely global in its input and now penetrates almost all of the world's countries, apart from a few that have governments with very strict censorship and high levels of information

technology capability, such as China. By contrast, the use of newspapers, radio, and/or TV is more local and more readily controlled
by governments, and could be expected, on balance, to provide more
local and national information.

To test for the effects of using these different news media, we will
run multilevel models similar to those already used for monitoring
the effects of the media use scale. These control for the social and
demographic characteristics of individuals, compare the effects of use
of TV or radio, newspapers, and the Internet, and the societal-level
effect of living in a relatively cosmopolitan society. For comparison
across different cultural values, we will use the five value scales already
developed in this chapter, comparing all the societies included in the
fifth wave of the WVS, which monitored patterns of news media use.
The results, summarized in Table 10.3, show that use of the Internet is indeed strongly and significantly related to a lower level of
support for religious values and nationalism, but positively associated with liberal sexual moral values and political engagement. In
this regard, use of the Internet reflects the typical pattern linked with
higher levels of education, which goes with more secular, liberal, and
tolerant modern values. Use of newspapers is also negatively related
to religiosity and positively associated with liberal sexual morality,
free market economic values, political engagement, and, by contrast
to use of the Internet, more nationalistic feelings. The pattern for TV
and radio use was mixed, contrary to the claim that the electronic
audiovisual media inherently leads to more modern values. Habitual
use of radio or TV news is linked to stronger religious values and
practices and more nationalistic feelings, as well as to greater political engagement and support for free market values, while having no
significant impact on liberal sexual morality values. Obviously, these
tests are limited in certain important regards, as we would need more
information about the frequency of use and attention, and the typical
local, national, and international contents that people were exposed
to through these media, in order to carry out a detailed analysis of
media effects. Still, the results found so far lead us to question the
sweeping assumptions about the effects of the globalization of electronic media. The analysis suggests that the impact of this process
varies by type of media, as well as by type of society and type of social
sector.

TABLE 10.3. *Multilevel Regression Models Explaining Social Values by Type of Media*

	Religiosity	Liberal Sexual Morality	Free Market Economics	Political Engagement	Nationalism
INDIVIDUAL LEVEL					
Demographic characteristics					
Age (years)	2.96***	−2.28***	.681***	1.00***	.625***
	(.093)	(.101)	(.093)	(.093)	(.083)
Gender (male = 1)	−3.09***	−.887***	.566***	2.16***	1.18***
	(.083)	(.090)	(.082)	(.083)	(.074)
Socioeconomic resources					
Household income, 10-pt scale	−.155	1.15***	2.12***	.446***	.538***
	(.093)	(.100)	(.090)	(.092)	(.082)
Education, 9-pt scale	−.224*	2.44***	.278**	4.08***	−.928***
	(.109)	(.118)	(.108)	(.109)	(.097)
Media use					
Newspaper use scale	−.597***	.339**	.265*	1.15***	.701***
	(.123)	(.136)	(.117)	(.127)	(.101)
TV/radio use	.655***	−.130	.211*	1.09***	1.22***
	(.091)	(.100)	(.096)	(.094)	(.081)
Internet use	−1.31***	1.271***	−.099	.770***	−.784***
	(.121)	(.132)	(.112)	(.124)	(.100)
NATIONAL LEVEL					
Cosmopolitanism Index	−10.7***	12.9***	−2.41	−1.12	−4.55***
(Globalization + development + freedom)	(2.32)	(1.39)	(.690)	(1.00)	(1.13)
Constant (intercept)	65.30	39.56	55.25	35.46	84.33
Schwartz BIC	518,830	498,975	359,445	482,119	427,223
No. of respondents	58,641	55,787	42,283	54,928	49,837
No. of nations	45	44	42	45	43

Note: All independent variables were standardized using mean centering (z-scores). Models present the results of the REML multilevel regression models (for details, see Technical Appendix C) including the beta coefficient (standard error in parentheses) and the significance. The 100-point scales are constructed from the items listed in Table 10.1. The media use variables monitored regular use of newspapers, radio or TV news, and the Internet as binary (o/1) dichotomies. $*p = .05$; $**p = .01$; $***p = .001$. See Technical Appendix A for details about the measurement, coding, and construction of all variables. Significant coefficients are highlighted in bold.

Source: World Values Survey (2005–2007).

Conclusions and Discussion

The cumulative findings from the WVS data suggest that the polarization thesis is a more accurate depiction of cultural change than is the convergence thesis. But any growing divergence that has occurred is the result of value change in affluent societies, not the product of a supposed backlash against the West in traditional cultures. In an earlier study, based on the first four waves of the WVS, Inglehart and Welzel concluded:

In recent decades, a simplistic version of globalization theory gained widespread currency, holding that the globalization of the mass media and communication networks was producing cultural convergence; we were heading towards a 'global village' in which everyone was on the same wavelength. The evidence presented here demonstrates that this view is false – in fact global trends are moving in the opposite direction. The values of the publics in rich countries are changing rapidly, while those of low-income societies are changing much more slowly or not at all. As a result, a growing gap is opening up between the basic values of the publics of rich versus poor countries.[18]

Elsewhere we have documented the growing divergence around the world of religiosity, with rich societies usually becoming far more secular in their values and practices than poor ones.[19] We have also shown the expanding gap in attitudes toward gender equality; egalitarian attitudes are spreading throughout postindustrial societies, whereas views of women's and men's roles are far more traditional in developing nations.[20] These studies conclude that the imprint of historical cultural traditions, such as the distinct values and beliefs found in predominantly Protestant, Catholic, and Muslim societies, persists in the face of societal modernization, even when religious practice has declined.

Building on this foundation, we can now update this evidence in order to examine whether cosmopolitan societies are similar in their value orientations and whether they have experienced a gradual convergence over time. Comparison of societies classified in accordance with the Cosmopolitanism Index enables us to go farther than previous studies by testing whether cultural values in cosmopolitan societies have indeed changed faster and to a greater extent than those in parochial nations.

The results of the analysis presented in this chapter suggest some important points that the convergence thesis overlooks or underestimates. The evidence indicates that culture in postindustrial nations is far from static or uniform. Convergence implicitly assumes that unchanging cultural values exist in rich nations and exaggerates the degree of consensus between the core values of Americans and Europeans. The convergence thesis then goes on to assume that developing societies assimilate this monolithic American or Western culture. But postindustrial societies themselves are experiencing profound long-term processes of value change – and they also differ significantly among themselves. There is a wealth of research demonstrating that the young people in rich nations differ significantly from their parents and grandparents in terms of self-expression values, such as tolerance of homosexuality, support for gender equality, concern about environmental protection, and willingness to take part in direct political action.[21] The process of value change creates a moving target that affects all countries in the world. As we will demonstrate, countries such as Sweden, Britain, and Germany have all experienced important changes in their core values during the past quarter of a century. In this respect, the process of cultural change is similar to the increase in living standards in OECD nations; living standards have improved in many emerging market economies, such as India, Brazil, and China, fueled by surging growth rates, but average incomes in these countries have not converged with those of postindustrial societies, which have also been growing. Moreover, important cultural differences exist between Protestant and Catholic Europe, and between Western and orthodox Europe, as well as between Europe and the United States. The persistent imprint of deep-rooted cultural traditions, left by each society's religious heritage as well as its distinctive historical experiences, ethnic cleavages, and social structures, means that the values found in contemporary postindustrial societies differ in important ways. The evidence we have considered throughout this book provides strong grounds for skepticism about exaggerated claims concerning the threats to cultural diversity among the world's countries. Their values are indeed changing, as they have been for the past two centuries. The media does indeed matter, but only under certain conditions and to a limited degree. Parochial societies continue to display distinctive cultural values in comparison with those found in more cosmopolitan nations, which also diverge sharply among themselves. To emphasize some of the outliers among the countries we have compared, America is far more religious and nationalistic than most postindustrial societies, and Sweden remains the most liberal in terms of sexual morality and the most politically engaged. Even when countries move in a similar trajectory as they evolve over time, there is little evidence that these national differences have been gradually merging in the past quarter of a century; despite being one of the most open and globalized societies in the world, Sweden is not in the process of becoming America, nor is the United States becoming Sweden.

In the final chapter of this book, we will consider the policy debates surrounding these issues that are taking place in multilateral forums, such as the European Union and UNESCO, and that reflect the broader implications of changing cultural values for protectionist or free market communication policies.

The Implications for Cultural Policies

A massive body of evidence has documented the growth of cosmopolitan communications. The international market for cultural goods and services expanded rapidly during the late 20th century, and these changes contributed to faster and denser flows of information across national borders. Until the early 1980s, the contents of mass communications in most countries were still mostly domestically generated, conveyed by local, regional, or national newspapers, magazines, television stations, and radio networks. The globalization of mass communications was driven by the spread of satellite and cable TV, cellular mobile telephones, the Internet, and multimedia convergence. Privatization, deregulation, and liberalization of the broadcasting and telecommunication sectors, and a relaxation of the rules limiting foreign media ownership, also played major roles, causing a decline in the number of people tuning in to state or public service broadcasting, a proliferation of commercial, privately owned radio and television stations, and cross-media ownership of newspapers and magazines. These developments encouraged the growth of international advertising companies and the market research sector, producing revenue for commercial media outlets. New TV channels fueled a growing demand for entertainment content, much of which was imported from a few core Western producer countries. As Chapter 3 demonstrated, far from decreasing, America's market share of the global cultural trade in audiovisual goods and information services has expanded in recent decades. Moreover, within the core producer countries, exports of cultural goods and services in world markets are highly concentrated in a handful of multinational conglomerates, such as Time Warner, Viacom, and Disney, which distribute multiple products across media platforms, including transnational news shown on satellite and cable TV stations, news wire services, movies, recorded music, book publishing, and online Web sites.

These major developments are not in question. But there is no consensus about their consequences. There has been a good deal of speculation, but few systematic studies have analyzed the empirical evidence of the impact of these developments on social values and attitudes.[1] The cultural implications of cosmopolitan communications have been debated from the perspective of three main scenarios: those predicting convergence, polarization, and fusion. Each scenario takes a very different view of contemporary developments and future trends.[2] We have tried to offer a more balanced interpretation, emphasizing the importance of a progressive series of firewalls that condition the impact of cosmopolitan communications and, even in the most open global markets, limit the degree of convergence among diverse national cultures. To conclude, this chapter reviews the debates, considers the limits of what we know about media effects, and summarizes the key findings of this study.

Scenarios About the Consequences of Cosmopolitan Communications

Convergence Toward American or Western Values?
In the first scenario, the expansion of global communications is seen to be homogenizing the world's cultures. The convergence thesis holds that these denser interconnections do not simply bring about a mixture of many national cultures, analogous to the UN General Assembly. Instead, it emphasizes an asymmetrical flow of cultural products and services, in which entertainment, news, and advertising are exported disproportionately from the global North to the South. Consequently, in this scenario, developing societies are viewed as absorbing American or Western values, attitudes, and beliefs.

The normative implications of these developments are fiercely debated. For many observers, this process represents a threat to national diversity, wiping out minority languages, historical traditions, and indigenous belief systems, just as uncontrolled tourism destroys fragile environments. The cultural imperialism school, in particular, argues that the expansion of global communications is exposing indigenous cultures to a flood of commercialism, advertising, and corporate capitalism, as well as popular American entertainment dominated by graphic violence and explicit sexuality. According to this view, globalization threatens cultural diversity.[3] Some other observers, however, such as American proponents of 'soft power,' see this process in a more positive light, arguing that it encourages public support for universal principles accepted by the international community, such as the values embodied in the 2005 World Summit Declaration, in which all governments pledged to uphold and respect the principles of freedom, equality, solidarity, tolerance, and human rights.[4]

Or Global Polarization?

Claims that the world is converging toward a common culture have been challenged, however, by the polarization thesis. From this perspective, the loss of national autonomy associated with globalization is generating local resistance and countermovements, and catalyzing new culture wars between and within societies. The rise and dissemination of a global culture is often perceived as a potent threat to traditional societies, engendering stronger tribal loyalties and ethnic identities.[5] Benjamin Barber articulated this argument when he suggested that the global spread of new technologies, mass popular entertainment, and consumerism might lead to 'McWorld,' where Disney, CNN, and Coke create a uniform culture around the world, but that it also tends to generate a reaction against globalization, mobilizing the forces of Jihad and catalyzing a resurgence of tribal and local identities.[6] The events of 9/11 seemed to support this interpretation. It appeared that hatred of American consumerism, sexual liberalization, and lack of respect for historical traditions and family values had fueled the anger of Al Qaeda sympathizers in the Middle East and triggered a groundswell of public support for Islamic fundamentalism.[7] Digital technologies break down physical barriers among societies and peoples, but they also expand opportunities for communication among dispersed terrorist cells and provide mechanisms for distributing propaganda. Moderate social movements also seem to represent reactions against cultural globalization, as manifested by the growing market for Mecca Cola in the Middle East, the slow-food movement that promotes artisanal cuisines, and street protests against meetings of the G8 and the World Trade Organization.[8]

The polarization thesis argues that exposure to the Western culture reflected in the global media does not necessarily encourage emulation; instead, it can lead to rejection or backlash in traditional societies that are offended by the ideas and images of explicit sexuality and violence, consumerism, and the permissive morality conveyed by much imported news, entertainment, and advertising. The picture is further complicated by the fact that both convergence and polarization may be occurring simultaneously among different social sectors; for example, the affluent governing elites and intellectuals in Karachi, Rio, and Manila may come to share a similar worldview with their counterparts in Europe or North America, while a growing rift emerges between cosmopolitan elites and more conservative groups in poor rural communities within each society.

Or Multicultural Fusion?

Finally, the fusion or hybridization thesis argues that globalization encourages a blending of diverse cultural traditions through cross-border fertilization and borrowing. Mutual exchanges may result in a mixture of music, art, foods, and languages, where locally sensitive marketing leads to variations in packaging and products and where, for example, American planes fly in eco-tourists and bring back Colombian roses, Kenyan snow peas, and Turkish rugs. Rather than a one-way flow, this perspective suggests multiple complex countercurrents represented by the cosmopolitan mix of immigrant communities, foods, music, and lifestyles found in contemporary urban neighborhoods in London, Paris, New York, and Los Angeles.[9] America itself is being transformed profoundly by these two-way flows. Indeed, President Barack Hussein Obama, born in Honolulu to a Kenyan father and a Kansas-born mother, educated in Jakarta, Los Angeles, New York, and Cambridge, Massachusetts, is a striking symbol of this process. The blending of alternative cultures into a new cosmopolitan amalgam is believed to generate values, attitudes, and lifestyles that are neither traditional nor modern, but a new synthesis of both. The fusion thesis suggests that this process not only transforms cultures in postindustrial societies, heightening domestic nationalistic sensitivities with, for example, conflict over the publication of religious cartoons in Denmark and bans on the use of head scarves in French schools, but also changes cultures in developing nations, as manifested in the growth of economic development and tourism, which has transformed Mexican border towns.

Pro-Globalization Arguments Favoring the Free Marketplace of Ideas

Debate continues in academic circles and within the international community about the policy implications of the growth of cosmopolitan communications.[10] On one hand, pro-globalists regard competition in the free marketplace of ideas and the unrestricted flow of information and communications across national borders as desirable for many reasons.[11] A greater connectedness among the countries of the world can be conducive to economic, political, and social development.[12] The potential economic advantages include generating growth and reducing poverty by linking remote populations and workforces with global markets, and facilitating the greater efficiencies and productivity generated by the knowledge economy.[13] Stronger connections between countries and continents can lead to the spread of new ideas in previously isolated developing societies, spurring innovations in science and technology, health care, agriculture, and education. Politically, the use of the Internet and computers for e-governance can improve the ability of the state to deliver services to remote areas; this can also make it possible for ordinary citizens to become better informed and more effective in organizing themselves in order to make their governments more responsive.[14] The scrutiny of government by investigative news journalists can increase the accountability of public officials; the disinfectant of transparency can reduce corruption and abuses of power by the state.[15] Access to information can also strengthen transitions to democratic governance by spreading ideas about and awareness of the internationally agreed-upon principles of human rights. For people living under repressive regimes with poor human rights records, access to political information from abroad can help bolster opposition movements and demands for political reform at home. Transnational social movements can link environmental activists based in Brussels and Berlin with grassroots rural communities in Brazil and Bolivia. Greater access to information provides an important learning resource for rural schools and health clinics, connecting isolated areas to doctors, libraries, and markets. Better information also makes states, publics, and world leaders more aware of international disasters and humanitarian emergencies, which can potentially influence the distribution of development aid and timely relief efforts.[16]

For all of these reasons, the international development community has sought to maximize access to information and communications in low- and middle-income societies. For pro-globalists, more cosmopolitan communications are therefore regarded as a positive opportunity for societal development, with the potential to strengthen international understanding among peoples, to expand economic growth in stagnant regions, and to diffuse ideas about democracy and human rights among societies, peoples, and governments. According to this view, it follows that decision makers should encourage policies designed to promote the exchange of cultural goods and services and the free flow of information across territorial borders, by lifting remaining trade barriers and tariffs, encouraging investment in digital technologies, communication infrastructure, and human capacity in developing societies, shrinking societal disparities in Internet access, expanding freedom of expression and rights to information, and further deregulating the broadcasting and telecommunication sectors.[17]

Antiglobalization Arguments for Protectionist Cultural Policies

Anti-globalists harbor darker visions and anticipate more negative consequences from these developments, arguing that convergence toward Western or American values means the loss of traditional indigenous cultures and a reduction in the diversity of minority languages, customs, and local traditions found around the globe. There is no question that important cultural changes are taking place. Languages spoken by handfuls of people are disappearing each year, but this process has been going on for centuries: it is how the mosaic of languages once spoken in France gave way to French and how the diverse peoples of China came to speak Chinese. This trend was at work long before the emergence of global communications, and it has positive as well as negative consequences. Like the movement from rural to urban settings, it is an inherent aspect of modernization.

In particular, since the deregulation of broadcasting, the spread of commercial advertising is thought to have encouraged the pursuit of materialistic desires and the accumulation of consumer products in poor societies, undermining spiritual values. This process is also charged with having opened the floodgates to a 'vast wasteland' of mindless American popular entertainment, encouraging people in traditional cultures to emulate the gratuitous violence and easygoing sexuality they see on the screen. For anti-globalists, who regard cultural diversity as under threat from these developments, it follows that the international community and national decision makers should implement policies designed to protect and regulate the cultural marketplace, by restricting the degree of foreign ownership of telecommunication and domestic media industries, regulating or limiting the importation of cultural products, regulating broadcasting and telecommunications in the public interest, and encouraging or subsidizing domestic creative industries, such as the performing arts, films, and public TV channels.

The debate about the need for cultural protectionism has been revived in the past decade, and new initiatives have been undertaken by multilateral agencies such as the European Union and UNESCO, although there is nothing new about these concerns. In 1973, Herbert Schiller argued that the disproportionate flow of information from Northern core to Southern periphery was a form of 'cultural imperialism' that eradicated other ways of thinking and living in developing societies and reinforced the influence of the Western powers and corporate capitalism.[18] During this era, Schiller and others accused the media of 'cultural imperialism,' and dependency theorists argued that journalists in developing societies were too reliant on imported media products and news wire services.[19] These issues fueled the heated UNESCO controversy that erupted in 1980, focusing attention on the North–South imbalance of communication flows and leading to the publication of the MacBride report.[20] The attempt to build a new world information order that would alter the concentration and commercialization of the media gave rise to concerns that its real purpose would be to facilitate state control of the media; the proposed development of a new world order became so controversial that it divided UNESCO and led the United States and the United Kingdom to leave the organization.

Concern about preserving and protecting cultural diversity from the global media is not limited to developing societies. Even within the European Union, protectionists led by the French have argued that the unrestricted flow of mass communications across national borders is bringing with it a homogenous European landscape dominated by American popular entertainment. This process is believed to have contributed to the extinction of small film industries and independent broadcasters, such as those in Italy, France, and Romania. Concern about the potentially damaging effects on cultural diversity if the transatlantic flow of entertainment products remains predominantly American has been especially prevalent in France.[21] A protectionist movement in Europe led to the 1989 EU Television without Borders directive, which required that EU member states reserve a majority of entertainment broadcast transmission time for programs of European origin.[22] To implement the directive, governments have imposed protectionist quotas on the proportion of non-European television entertainment and feature films that can be imported. In addition to enforcing legal regulations, many European countries have heavily subsidized their domestic visual and performing arts and audiovisual industries, and some have also limited the degree of overseas ownership of newspapers and broadcasting licenses. The Council of Europe's Recommendation on Measures to Promote Media Pluralism and article 151 EC of the Maastricht Treaty were also designed to encourage European broadcasters to ensure a certain amount of domestically produced programming. The impact of these legal instruments is conditioned by a context of increasing deregulation of the trade in goods and services and the telecommunication industry, which has expanded the number of private channels available in Europe, many of which rely on a diet of low-cost American television entertainment and movies.

In 2001, under UNESCO's leadership, the world's governments accepted the Universal Declaration on Cultural Diversity, which recognizes that cultural diversity reflects our common heritage and should be preserved as a source of exchange, innovation, and creativity.[23] According to the declaration, cultural diversity is as necessary as biodiversity is for nature. The convention sets forth an action plan with general guidelines that are to be implemented by member states in partnership with civil society. It defines culture broadly to cover not just art and literature but also lifestyles, ways of living together, value systems, traditions, and beliefs. It recognizes that freedom of expression and media freedom are necessary conditions for the flourishing of cultural diversity. Nevertheless, the declaration warns that, given globalization, market forces by themselves are insufficient to preserve and protect cultural diversity: 'In the face of current imbalances in flows and exchanges of cultural goods and services at the global level, it is necessary to reinforce international cooperation and solidarity aimed at enabling all countries, especially developing countries and countries in transition, to establish cultural industries that are viable and competitive at national and international level.'[24]

The action plan is cautious, however, about how the convention is best implemented, leaving it up to each state to determine what policies are appropriate for achieving a balance between securing rights to freedom of expression and protecting its cultural heritage. The convention specifies a number of steps – for example, fostering the sharing of knowledge and best practices about cultural diversity, supporting cultural industries in developing countries, and encouraging the preservation of a diversity of languages in cyberspace. More concretely, the action plan specifies that public service broadcasters play an important positive role in this process: 'Member states should encourage the production, safeguarding and dissemination of diversified contents in the media and global information networks and, to that end, promoting the role of public radio and television services in the development of audiovisual productions of good quality, in particular by fostering the establishment of cooperative mechanisms to facilitate their distribution.' Given the commitment of the United Nations to recognizing and strengthening human rights and freedom of expression, the Universal Declaration on Cultural Diversity does not explicitly favor more stringent protectionist measures, such as the use of trade barriers or broadcasting regulations that limit cultural imports or restrict foreign ownership of media industries. Spurred in part by this agreement, UNESCO has developed new initiatives designed to standardize and monitor international statistics related to the creative industries, including the production and distribution of feature films, newspapers, and radio and television broadcasting. This is a welcome development in an area that has often been neglected in the past and where international statistical series are often seriously out of date and incomplete.[25] And this perspective reflects genuine concerns: cultural diversity is precious, and it cannot be taken for granted, as is demonstrated by the thousands of languages that have disappeared from active use during the past century.

The Limits of the Evidence

The policy debates surrounding cultural globalization are based on conflicting claims about the alleged consequences of globalization, but these claims are rarely based on empirical data gleaned from public opinion. There is massive evidence that globalization *is* occurring – but relatively little examination of its actual impact on what people believe and value. The theoretical framework and the evidence presented in this study go farther than previous attempts to analyze the effects of cosmopolitan mass communications. Before summarizing and presenting our major findings, however, it is important that we acknowledge the limits of what is known about media effects and identify the next steps in this research agenda.

First, in seeking to understand the diverse drivers of public opinion, we took a parsimonious approach, focusing on the impact of the news media. It is conceivable that many other factors, not examined here, may also shape attitudes and values. A comprehensive explanation of civic engagement, for example, would incorporate a wide range of macrolevel institutional contexts, such as the role of electoral systems and patterns of party competition, mezzolevel factors such as the density and activities of civil society organizations and voluntary associations, and microlevel motivational attitudes and resources.[26] Similarly, assessing the strength of religiosity requires the analysis of existential security and human development in each society, as well as the multiplicity of beliefs, rituals, and practices found among the world's diverse faiths.[27] Parsimonious models have considerable advantages in their clarity and elegance, but the danger remains that important factors have been excluded that could help to explain patterns of cultural values. We introduced specific controls in this study to account for many of the most important characteristics of news users, but other controls could always be suggested, generating more complex interaction terms. More detailed cross-national, time-series, and case-study research can help us to delve more fully into each of the dimensions of cultural values and social attitudes that this book has compared.

This analysis focused primarily on the impact of cosmopolitan mass communication arising from the news media; we did not examine other information sources in any depth. It is clearly possible that other information sources, such as television and radio popular entertainment, novels and magazines, music videos and DVDs, feature films and documentaries, the performing and visual arts, design and applied arts, museums, and multiple and rapidly evolving online activities, have a greater impact. As pointed out in Chapter 3, diverse creative industries contribute to each society's cultural heritage. Cosmopolitan communications are also affected by the direct transfer of peoples and by international phone calls and e-mails. The fact that this study has nevertheless demonstrated significant effects of cosmopolitan mass communications suggests that we may have underestimated the potential cumulative effect of the growing interconnectedness of all types of information networks among societies. Comparisons of a broader and more diverse range of indicators of cross-cultural communication in all its forms in future public opinion surveys can build on this foundation and facilitate the analysis of these issues.

This study analyzed the cross-level effects of the national context and individual-level evidence of attitudes and values. We did not examine the potential impact of distinct ethnic, national, linguistic, or religious minority subcultures within nation-states, an important issue that is often framed in terms of 'glocalization,' where the local interacts directly with the global. This is likely to be a fruitful area of research, especially when the footprint of media markets extends beyond national borders – for example, when attitudes toward free markets and democracy conveyed by West German television reach the residents of Communist East Germany. Also important is the impact of the media in plural states; examples are the contrast in news coverage provided by different newspapers for Protestant and Catholic communities in Northern Ireland and the images of conflict shown on Palestinian and Israeli television. Additional detailed case-study comparisons focused on distinctive subcultures within nation-states would make an important contribution to future research, perhaps by aggregating successive waves of the Values Surveys to compare the effect of media use and changes in values on minority and majority populations living within common national borders.

This study also focused on the impact of relatively frequent exposure to news media without analyzing the contents of the media messages, which would be extremely complex in a study involving scores of countries. Thus, we do not know the extent to which people using the news media are exposed to information about local affairs within their own community, national events, or international news; nor do we know how much attention people are devoting to information at each of these levels. Research within specific countries and across member states of the European Union has linked systematic content analysis of information sources with surveys of public opinion, usually within a particular election campaign. More cross-national research along these lines could produce invaluable results.

Finally, interpreting the direction of causality linking use of the news media with the cultural attitudes, values, and practices examined in the research is inherently difficult. To some extent, the patterns documented in earlier chapters may arise from self-selection bias; the uses and gratification perspective suggests that people seek out media messages that are consistent with their prior preferences and values.[28] Those who are already interested in politics are more likely to tune into news programs, while others are more interested in and attentive to music, sports, and entertainment. But it also seems likely that this process is interactive rather than one-way, with repeated exposure to information from the mass media tending to reinforce values and attitudes. Cross-national panel survey data on media habits and social attitudes among the same respondents over time or experimental data under carefully controlled conditions would help to resolve these issues. Additional studies of mass communications and public opinion are needed to explore the complex questions concerning how we learn about different peoples and places, and how, in turn, this shapes our awareness, values, and behaviors, and thus the broader social culture.

The Firewall Theory of Conditional Effects

Having acknowledged these limitations, we need to ask which findings we can accept with a reasonable degree of confidence. In particular, to what extent is cultural diversity actually threatened – and to what extent does national diversity require protection against globalization of communications? The firewall thesis presented in this book suggests that distinctive identities, values, and ways of life in each society are more deeply rooted and resilient in the face of the impact of global media than is often claimed. We learn about the world and society from multiple sources of information, not just from the images and ideas conveyed on TV or in movies and newspapers. Simplistic 'stimulus–response' theories of 'hypodermic' media effects are now generally considered to be out of date in modern communication studies.[29] Writers such as Benedict Anderson have emphasized that national cultures and collective identities are powerfully shaped by common histories, shared languages, and religious traditions, which persist for centuries.[30] Similarly, socialization theory and research suggests that enduring beliefs and core values are acquired early in life from personal interactions with parents and family, teachers and spiritual authorities, and friends and neighbors in the local community, as well as directly from one's formative experiences, and that these values tend to persist throughout adulthood, despite the impact of mass communications.[31] Beliefs about the appropriate roles of women and men, attitudes toward the role of the state and markets, feelings about civic engagement, and beliefs about spiritual life are derived from multiple sources. The mass media is indeed one agent of socialization – and we have demonstrated that significant cultural effects *do* arise from frequent use of the news media. But the mass media changes the values of all societies, rich and poor. Culture in postindustrial societies is fluid rather than static, and it too evolves over time. A total ban on global mass media would not stop the evolution of cultural norms, and it is questionable whether it would be desirable to impose one.

The dissemination of images and ideas by the mass media is only part of a broader learning process by which values are acquired, and social psychological filters based on existing predispositions may restrict the acquisition of new ideas that go against deeply held beliefs and ingrained values, leading people to reject or reinterpret the meaning of cultural messages.[32] To summarize our findings, let us review the formal propositions that we outlined in Chapter 2 and consider to what extent they are supported by the evidence. Table 11.1, which provides a synopsis of the testable hypotheses at the heart of this book, shows variations by type of user, type of value, type of media, type of society, and change in values over time.

Type of User
Our first set of propositions predicted that individual use of the news media would differ by social sector, with those in the upper strata being heavier users than those in lower strata. This is not a controversial

TABLE 11.1. *Theoretical Propositions Investigated in the Study and Summary of the Results*

Primary and Secondary Propositions	Summary of Results
1. TYPE OF SOCIAL SECTOR	
H1.0: Use of the news media will differ by social sector.	Confirmed in Tables 4.3 and 4.4.
Chapter 4	
H1.1: Use of the news media will be greater among those who are well educated.	Confirmed in Tables 4.3 and 4.4.
H1.2: Use of the news media will be greater among high-income groups.	Confirmed in Tables 4.3 and 4.4.
H1.3: Use of the news media will be greater among those who are middle aged or older.	Not confirmed: In Table 4.4 use of the news media (especially the Internet) proved greater among the younger population.
H1.4: Use of the news media will be greater among men than women.	Conditional effects: In Table 4.3 the gender gap is reversed by level of economic development.
H1.5: Use of the news media will be greater among those who are fluent in English.	Confirmed in Tables 4.3 and 4.4.
2. TYPE OF VALUES	
H2.0: Individual news media use will encourage more modern cultural values and attitudes.	Confirmed.
H2.1: Individual exposure to the news media will foster more cosmopolitan orientations and tolerance of foreign lifestyles (*Chapter 6*).	Confirmed in Table 6.2.
H2.2: Individual exposure to the news media will encourage favorable attitudes toward global capitalism (*Chapter 7*).	Confirmed in Table 7.2.
H2.3: Individual exposure to the news media will shape more liberal and secular attitudes toward gender equality, sexuality, and religion (*Chapter 8*).	Confirmed in Table 8.3.
H2.4: Exposure to the news media will reinforce civic engagement (*Chapter 9*).	Confirmed in Table 9.3 with the proviso of no effect on democratic values.

Primary and Secondary Propositions	Summary of Results
3. TYPE OF MEDIA	
H3.0: The impact of cosmopolitan communications will vary by the type of media.	Confirmed.
Chapter 10	
H3.1: The impact of cosmopolitan communications will be strongest among regular users of the Internet and e-mail.	Confirmed in Table 10.3, except for the effect on economic values.
H3.2: The impact of cosmopolitan communications will be weaker among regular newspaper readers and TV news users.	Confirmed in Table 10.3, except for the impact on political engagement.
4. TYPE OF SOCIETY	
H4.0: The impact of mass media use on cultural values will be strongest in the most cosmopolitan societies today.	Confirmed, but the strength and direction of the cross-level impact vary by type of values.
Chapters 6–9	
H4.1: The impact of exposure to the mass media on cultural values will be strongest in societies most integrated into global markets and networks.	Confirmed, but the strength and direction of the cross-level impact vary by type of values.
H4.2: The impact of exposure to the mass media on cultural values will be strongest in societies with internal media freedom.	Confirmed, but the strength and direction of the cross-level impact vary by type of values.
H4.3: The impact of exposure to the mass media on cultural values will be strongest in societies where many people have widespread access to media technologies.	Confirmed, but the strength and direction of the cross-level impact vary by type of values.
5. CHANGE OVER TIME	
H5.0. Cultural convergence over time will be greatest among the most cosmopolitan societies.	
Chapter 10	
H5.1: The most cosmopolitan societies will display the greatest similarities in cultural values today.	Not confirmed.
H5.2: The most parochial societies will display the greatest divergence in cultural values today.	Not confirmed.
H5.3: Over time, growth in cosmopolitanism will reduce divergence among national cultures.	Not confirmed.

assumption, as a considerable body of research has shown that use of the news media is concentrated among the more educated segments of the population and those who have the cognitive skills, literacy, and background knowledge to make sense of news; it is similarly concentrated among high-income households and those who have the leisure time and means to buy equipment and access media services, such as pay-TV, satellite, and cable broadcasts, mobile phones with data services, and broadband Internet service providers. The digital divide in Internet access attracted considerable attention during the 1990s, but in fact it reflects broader and more enduring social and international disparities in access to mass media, including newspapers, radio, and television news.[33] Differences by gender and age have also been observed in patterns of media access and attention in the United States and Europe, leading to the proposition that use of the news media will be greater among men than women and among the middle-aged or older generation than among the younger generation. Finally, the prevalence of English-language Web sites and the predominance of English-speaking countries as exporters of audiovisual products and publications lead to the expectation that use of the news media will be greater among those who are fluent in English than among those who are not. These are all plausible propositions in the literature, which is based largely on research conducted in postindustrial societies.[34] We have tested whether these disparities persist today, and whether similar or even stronger information gaps exist in developing societies, in order to identify the most important controls to incorporate into the subsequent analysis of media effects.

Chapter 4 explored the evidence from the fifth wave of the WVS in 2005–2007 concerning which sectors of the population commonly use the news media – including newspapers, radio or TV news, the Internet, books, and magazines – in a wide range of contemporary societies. The evidence demonstrated, not surprisingly, the existence of major societal-level barriers to accessing information. More unexpectedly, cross-national comparisons of societal-level access to the Internet, telephones, television, and even radio indicate that disparities between rich and poor countries have been deepening, not diminishing, during recent decades. In addition, again confirming research reported in the literature, substantial information gaps remain among sectors and individuals *within* societies. The individual-level regression models in

Table 4.3 suggest that the primary drivers of media use for obtaining news and information about society and the world include the cognitive skills that come with education (H1.1); the resources required to purchase TVs, computers, and Internet access; and motivational attitude (H1.2). The profile by occupational class confirmed and reflected the income differentials. The news audience does not reflect the general population; there is a clear skew toward educated and affluent segments.

This imbalance varied by the type of media. Table 4.4 demonstrated that it is strongest among users of the Internet and newspapers, media with the highest demands for cognitive skills and literacy; the audience for radio or TV news is slightly broader, although still socially biased toward more affluent and educated social sectors. The age profile did not confirm our expectations, however; the younger generation proved significantly more likely to use the news media across all types of economies (H1.3). Further analysis broken down by type of media suggests that the inclusion of the Internet and e-mail as well as traditional news media was likely to have contributed to this pattern. Moreover, in developing nations, the younger generation is also generally more educated and literate than older populations. The traditional gender gap that we expected (H1.4) was reversed by type of economy, with women predominating in the news media audience in rich nations but men predominating in low-income societies. Those familiar with the English language also used the news media more than average (H1.5), as did those with the motivational attitudes of political interest and trust in the news media. Before we examine the impact of exposure to news on attitudes and values, we therefore need to control for the demographic and social characteristics of the audience.

Types of Values

The second set of propositions predicted that individual patterns of news media use would generate more modern cultural values (H2.0). What aspects of public opinion would we expect to change the most as a result of media exposure? Information about other peoples and places acquired from the global media can reasonably be expected to alter perceptions of territorial identities, by weakening the visceral appeal of nationalism, promoting understanding and tolerance of foreigners, and possibly generating support for the institutions and policies of global governance.[35] In the economic sphere, the convergence thesis emphasizes that exposure to the global media should strengthen support for the ideas and practices of market-driven capitalism, reflecting beliefs in a minimal role for the state, deregulation, privatization, and the importance of unfettered free trade competition. In this regard, Herman and McChesney regard the Western media as missionaries for global capitalism, reflecting the neoliberal Washington consensus on economic development advocated by the World Bank and International Monetary Fund.[36] Standardized brand images, mass advertising, and the marketing strategies of multinational corporations are the most obvious symbols of the homogenization of the world economy and they exemplify the ubiquity of major transnational corporations, whereby media companies such as Disney, CNN, and Google have become some of the best-known brands around the world. In the public sphere, the convergence thesis argues that exposure to news and information from the Western media should encourage the diffusion of the principles of liberal democracy in accordance with the values common in these societies, including the value of civic engagement. In terms of social and moral values, the culture reflected in popular entertainment and news journalism produced in the global North also often reinforces the relatively liberal ideas characteristic of postindustrial societies, so that exposure to the global media should lead to greater tolerance of nontraditional lifestyles and liberal sexual orientations, egalitarian attitudes toward the roles of men and women, and a secular and individualistic perspective on moral issues.

Chapter 6 confirmed Hypothesis 2.1: even after a battery of social controls for age, gender, education, and income was introduced, individual news media use was consistently associated with cosmopolitan orientations, measured by trust in people from other countries and faiths (Table 6.2), while simultaneously strengthening, not weakening, feelings of nationalism (Table 6.3). It is often assumed that there has to be a trade-off between identifying with one's own country and feeling part of a broader world community, as a zero-sum game, but it seems more accurate to understand modern identities as multiple and overlapping; people can feel simultaneously Scottish and European, Swedish and Scandinavian; they can consider themselves a resident of a particular city and a citizen of the world. The positive effect of media use on trust in outsiders was relatively strong as well as significant; it was slightly weaker than the effect of education but was similar to that of age.

Chapter 7 demonstrated that individual media use was indeed consistently linked with more capitalist economic values, as hypothesized (H2.2), whether measured by the values of individual success (Table 7.2) or of conservative economic attitudes (Table 7.3). Moreover, after age, use of the news media proved the most important social characteristic predicting support for the values of individual economic success, having a stronger impact than education, income, or gender.

Chapter 8 examined the impact of media use on support for liberal sexual and moral values. Given the pervasive depiction of sexuality and love, romantic relationships and marriage throughout the Western media, in everything from prime-time TV sitcoms and dramas to feature films and magazines, this could be expected to be important in shaping moral values. The evidence confirmed our expectation (H2.3) that individual use of the news media was significantly linked (Table 8.3) with more tolerant and liberal orientations toward sexual and moral values, to the disapproval of unethical standards in public life, to relatively secular orientations, to support for gender equality, and to liberal family values. The strength of the coefficients for media use varied across the different value scales, and they were usually weaker than similar effects arising from education, but in all cases the multivariate results proved statistically significant.

Finally, Chapter 9 examined the effects of the news media on civic engagement. Alternative predictions could be made on the basis of the literature, but we chose to test the virtuous circle thesis, which suggests that the acquisition of information and knowledge about public affairs and events from the news media encourages greater citizen awareness and involvement in the public sphere. We found (Table 9.3) that use of the news media was significantly and positively related to a range of indicators of civic engagement (H2.4), including confidence in institutions, membership in volunteer associations, activism expressed through protest politics, and citizen interest, although media use was not significantly linked to our indicators of support for democratic values. Despite arguments that the negative campaign coverage of the news media may alienate citizens, the evidence actually indicated that exposure to the news media in a wide range of societies is linked with *more* civic engagement, not less.

Type of Media

The third set of propositions predicted that the impact of cosmopolitan communications will vary by the type of media (H3.0). The cross-national evidence available from the WVS for examining this hypothesis is limited, given the wide range of sources and channels available today, but data does enable us to distinguish the impact of the Internet or e-mail from that of reading newspapers and watching or listening to radio or TV news. In particular, we assumed (H3.1) that the effects of exposure to cosmopolitan communications would be greater for users of the Internet or e-mail, as the medium without physical borders, compared with exposure to traditional news media. The effects were not expected to be strong, however, given the multiple sources of news and information, as well as the merging of sources across media platforms (such as listening to the radio, watching TV news, and reading papers online).

The evidence in Table 10.3 confirmed that in multivariate models, even after distinctive age, income, and educational profiles are controlled for, Internet users proved to be the most secular media user group, as well as the most liberal toward sexual morality and tolerance of sexual diversity, and the least nationalistic. Internet users were also more politically engaged than average, although slightly less so than newspaper and radio or TV users. In short, Internet users presented the most distinctive cultural profile, as expected, across four of the five dimensions under comparison.

Type of Society

The firewall theory posits that the impact of individual use of the mass media on cultural values will be strongest in the most cosmopolitan societies with open borders to the flow of information from abroad. Chapter 5 documented the existence of these firewalls and classified countries according to the Cosmopolitanism Index, based on levels of globalization, economic development, and media freedom. All of these indicators were strongly intercorrelated (Tables 5.1 and 5.2). Societies were ranked from the most isolated and parochial countries, such as Myanmar (Burma), Rwanda, Burundi, and Iran, through midlevel countries, such as Ghana, Brazil, and Turkey, to the most cosmopolitan and permeable nations, such as Sweden, Switzerland, and Luxembourg (Figure 5.6). The key issue is whether the effects of exposure to the news media on cultural values varied consistently in parochial and cosmopolitan societies.

The multilevel analysis confirmed that the Cosmopolitanism Index (and each of its components) was significantly associated with greater trust in outsiders (Table 6.2) and with less support for nationalism (Table 6.3). Most importantly, media use within cosmopolitan societies *reinforced* both of these effects.

When it came to comparing capitalist economic values, however, the Cosmopolitanism Index (and each of its separate components) was linked with *less* support for individual success values (Table 7.2) and less support for conservative economic values (Table 7.3), and again use of the news media in cosmopolitan societies strengthened these effects. The results suggest that use of the news media generally increased support for capitalist economic values, but the direct impact of this effect was reversed in the most globalized nations. Use of the news media generally tends to strengthen capitalist values, but the evidence indicates that this effect cannot be attributed to the role of the international media exporting consumer capitalism to developing nations. This interpretation is fully consistent with widespread evidence that the people of developing societies, which lack the basic conditions of security, stability, and prosperity, adhere more strongly to the values of material success and individual achievement than do the people of more affluent and secure societies, who place much stronger emphasis on self-expression and postmaterialist values.

In terms of social values, the multilevel models showed that higher values of the Cosmopolitanism Index were related to more liberal sexual and moral values, more secular orientations, and more egalitarian attitudes toward sex roles (Table 8.3). Here, however, the type of society did not predict feelings about appropriate ethical standards in public life or family values. The cross-level interaction effect for this dimension of values was also mixed, with the most consistent effects arising from media use in cosmopolitan societies, which reinforced liberal sexual and moral values. The cross-level effects on gender equality values proved negative, contrary to expectations. Overall, the analysis of how the type of society reinforces media use indicates that these effects are clearer and more consistent with respect to cosmopolitan orientations, such as feelings of national identity, than with respect to social values. The news media does have an important effect on social values, but many other factors, such as the imprint of religious traditions, seem more important in determining social attitudes and values than does the openness of societies to transnational information flows.

Proponents of soft power hope that the diffusion of information about democracy and human rights will encourage civic activism and adherence to these values around the world. Table 9.3 demonstrated that, by itself, use of the news media was indeed positively related to a wide range of indicators of civic engagement. The most significant effect was that of encouraging protest politics and democratic values in cosmopolitan societies. Why does individual news media use have no significant impact overall on democratic values, and yet emerge as significantly strengthening these values in cosmopolitan societies? One plausible reason is that under repressive regimes, which limit independent journalism and media pluralism, state control of the media can be used to limit public support for opposition reform movements and democratic principles. By contrast, in more open societies, the flow of Western news from abroad, as well as pluralism of outlets at home, can serve to strengthen positive attitudes toward democracy.

Change over Time

Finally, we examined whether there was any systematic evidence that national cultures had actually become increasingly similar during the past quarter of a century – especially the open cosmopolitan societies that were most subject to the potential forces of globalization. Trends over time in the successive waves of the WVS conducted since the early 1980s allowed us to test this proposition in 11 nations, for which a full set of time-series data is available from 1981 to 2006. The descriptive figures and the cross-national time-series regression analysis established two important findings. First, far from there being convergence over time, the values gap between parochial and cosmopolitan societies was maintained (in the case of liberal social values) or even widened (with feelings of nationalism and the strength of religiosity). This happened because culture in affluent postindustrial nations is not static, as the convergence thesis implicitly assumes; on the contrary, values and attitudes continue to evolve in these nations, as demonstrated in detail elsewhere, concerning religiosity and attitudes toward gender equality. Thus, the relative gap between types of societies has not been closing.[37] Moreover, even among postindustrial societies such as the

United States and Britain, Sweden and Germany, and Japan and South Korea, which are tightly interconnected through communication networks, trade flows, and economic interdependence, having the greatest share of cultural trade in audiovisual programs, there remain distinctive and persistent cultural differences that show no signs of disappearing. These societies do not share a monolithic Western culture toward which developing societies are converging. Instead, both developing societies and Western societies are changing in ways shaped by broad forces of modernization, while retaining distinctive national cultures. These cultures are not the same today as they were a generation ago, but it is by no means evident that all of the changes that have taken place are negative – they include a growing tolerance for gender equality and social diversity, and a growing emphasis on democracy and self-expression. And these changes seem to be due to the globalization of the media to only a limited extent.

The news media is an important agency of cultural values, reinforcing liberal sexual morals, cosmopolitan tolerance of other peoples, support for free markets, and strengthening civic engagement – as demonstrated throughout this book. But this does not imply convergence. This is true because the media is only one of the many factors that shape the trajectory of change in values; broad forces of modernization are reshaping people's values in all societies, rich and poor, and rich societies, which enjoy far more media access than poor societies, are experiencing more rapid cultural change than most developing societies.

As interconnections between societies gradually become denser and faster around the globe, their cultural impact is likely to increase. Yet we need to be cautious about exaggerating the consequences of cosmopolitan communications, for good or ill, because a series of firewalls persist that preserve the imprint of distinctive national cultures. In many countries in the 21st century, there continues to be a lack widespread literacy and even a reliable electricity supply – let alone TVs and broadband Internet. Others lack access to information from the outside world due to state control by highly repressive regimes. Cultural convergence over time has been predicted to result from more permeable borders – the crisscrossing of MTV, Google, and CNN – but instead the enduring imprint of distinctive historical traditions continues to be evident today. Even among open societies, Japan remains quite distinct from South Korea. Britain is not Germany. Sweden is not Spain. And despite an immense volume of cross-border flow, democratic political institutions, and shared languages, Canada is not the United States. Even within the member states of the European Union, despite the most heroic and ambitious attempt at economic and social integration in modern history, as well as 50 years of continuing efforts to develop a common European identity, distinct national identities and cultural practices do not appear to be dissolving. It seems even less likely that they will dissolve through exposure to the electronic media in less interdependent societies. The people of the world have come to share certain cultural icons and contemporary fashions, and increasing amounts of information and ideas about people and places, but this does not mean that they will lose their cultural heritage.

Technical Appendix A

Concepts and Measures

Variable	Definitions, Coding and Sources
Societal-level indicators	
Human Development Index	The Human Development Index (HDI) is based on longevity, as measured by life expectancy at birth; educational achievement; and standard of living, as measured by per capita GDP (purchasing power parity, $U.S.). *Source:* UNDP *Human Development Report*, various years.
Type of society	'Postindustrial societies' are defined as independent nation-states around the world with an HDI score of more than .900. 'Industrial societies' are classified as the nations with a moderate HDI (ranging from .740 to .899). 'Agrarian societies' are nations with lower levels of development (HDI of .739 or below). *Source:* UNDP *Human Development Report*, various years.
Type of economy	'High-income' economies are defined as the most affluent states around the world, with a mean per capita GDP of $15,000+. 'Medium-income' economies are classified as nations with a moderate per capita GDP of $2,000–14,999. 'Low-income' economies are those with a mean per capita GDP of $1,999 or less. All are measured in constant international dollars in purchasing power parity. *Source:* World Bank, World Development Indicators.
Per capita GDP	Measured in constant international dollars in purchasing power parity. *Source:* World Bank, World Development Indicators, various years.

(continued)

(continued)

Variable	Definitions, Coding and Sources
Level of democracy	The Gastil Index is a 7-point scale used by Freedom House to measure political rights and civil liberties every year. *Source:* Freedom House, various years; www.Freedomhouse.com.
Type of state	On the basis of the Freedom House Gastil Index, we define 'free' states as those with a Freedom House rating of 5.5–7.0. 'Partly free states' have Gastil Index ratings of 3.5–5.5. 'Not free states' have a Gastil Index rating of from 1.0 to 3.0; they include military-backed dictatorships, authoritarian states, elitist oligarchies, and absolute monarchies.
Media Freedom Index	This is based on the Freedom House Press Freedom Index, which measures how much the free flow of news is influenced by legal, political, and economic environments. The index is 100 points. Freedom House. 2007. Global Press Freedom, 2007. www.Freedomhouse.org. (and various years).
Globalization Index	The KOF Index of Globalization, 1970–2005. For methodological and technical details see http://globalization.kof.ethz.ch/. The 100-point index is constructed from a comprehensive range of two dozen variables, designed to gauge three dimensions: *social* globalization (the spread of personal contact, information flows, and cultural proximity); *economic* globalization (the actual long-distance flows of goods, investment capital, and commercial services, as well as restrictions through import barriers, taxes, and tariffs); and *political* globalization (measured by integration with international intergovernmental organizations, the number of embassies based in a country, and national engagement in UN peace missions).
Cosmopolitanism Index	The index is constructed by adding the standardized Media Freedom Index, the Globalization Index, and per capita GDP (for sources, see specific entries). The standardization means that each component is equally weighted.

Individual-level media and cultural indicators

Use of the media	'People use different sources to learn what is going on in their country and the world. For each of the following sources, please indicate whether you used it last week (1) or did not use it last week (0) to obtain information' (read out and code one answer for each):

	Used it last week	Did not use it last week
V223. Daily newspaper	1	0
V224. News broadcasts on radio or TV	1	0

Variable	Definitions, Coding and Sources

	V225. Printed magazines 1 0
	V226. In-depth reports 1 0
	      on radio or TV
	V227. Books 1 0
	V228. Internet, e-mail 1 0
	V229. Talk with friends 1 0
	      or colleagues
	Source: World Values Survey (2005–2007)

News media use scale	Based on the preceding item, this scale is calculated by summing the use of a daily newspaper, news broadcasts on radio or TV, printed magazines, books, and the Internet/e-mail, transformed into a 100-point scale. *Source:* World Values Survey (2005–2007).
Television use	E188 Q. 'Do you ever watch television? If yes, how much time do you often watch television during an average workday?' *Source:* World Values Survey (1981–2001).
Newspaper use	E187 Q. 'Do you regularly read a daily newspaper?' *Source:* World Values Survey (1981).
Confidence and trust in the media	V133–134. 'I am going to name a number of organizations. For each one, could you tell me how much confidence you have in them: is it a great deal of confidence (4), quite a lot of confidence (3), not very much confidence (2) or none at all (1)? (Read out and code one answer for each): The press. Television.' The 8-point media trust scale, where 'high' represents most confidence, combines both answers. *Source:* World Values Surveys.
Confidence in the UN and regional organizations	V146–147. 'I am going to name a number of organizations. For each one, could you tell me how much confidence you have in them: is it a great deal of confidence (4), quite a lot of confidence (3), not very much confidence (2) or none at all (1)? (Read out and code one answer for each): The United Nations. Regional organizations (such as the European Union).' The 8-point global institutional trust scale, where 'high' represents most confidence, combines both answers. *Source:* World Values Surveys.
Political interest	V95. 'How interested would you say you are in politics? Are you ...' Very interested (recoded 4), Somewhat interested (3), Not very interested (2), Not at all interested (1). *Source:* World Values Surveys.
Global and national identities	'People have different views about themselves and how they relate to the world. Using this card, would you tell me how strongly you agree or disagree with each of the following statements about how you see yourself?' (Read out and code one answer for each statement):

(continued)

(continued)

Variable	Definitions, Coding and Sources				
		Strongly agree	Agree	Disagree	Strongly disagree
	V210. I see myself as a world citizen.	1	2	3	4
	V211. I see myself as a member of my local community.	1	2	3	4
	V212. I see myself as a citizen of the [*French*]* nation.	1	2	3	4
	V213. I see myself as a citizen of the [*European Union*].**	1	2	3	4
	V214. I see myself as an autonomous individual.	1	2	3	4

* [Substitute your country's nationality for 'French.']
** [Substitute appropriate regional organization for 'European Union.']
Source: World Values Survey (2005–2007).

Variable	Definitions, Coding and Sources
Global governance	'Some people believe that certain kinds of problems could be better handled by the United Nations or regional organizations, such as the European Union, rather than by each national government separately. Others think that these problems should be left entirely to the national governments. I'm going to mention some problems. For each one, would you tell me whether you think that policies in this area should be decided by the national governments, by regional organizations, or by the United Nations?' (Read out and code one answer for each problem):

		National governments	Regional organizations	United Nations
	V179. Peacekeeping	1	2	3
	V180. Protection of the environment	1	2	3
	V181. Aid to developing countries	1	2	3
	V182. Refugees	1	2	3
	V183. Human rights	1	2	3

Variable	Definitions, Coding and Sources
National pride	V209. 'How proud are you to be [*French*]*?' Very proud (4); Quite proud (3); Not very proud (2); Not at all proud (1). *[Substitute nationality.] *Source:* World Values Surveys.

Variable	Definitions, Coding and Sources
Trust of foreigners	V130. 'I'd like to ask you how much you trust people from various groups. Could you tell me for each whether you trust people from this group completely, somewhat, not very much or not at all? People of another nationality.' *Source:* World Values Surveys.
Left–right ideology scale	V114. 'In political matters people talk of "the left" and "the right." How would you place your views on this scale, generally speaking?' The 10-point scale is coded from 1 = Most left to 10 = Most right. *Source:* World Values Surveys.
Type of religion	V184: 'Do you belong to a religious denomination?' [*If yes*] 'Which one?' Coded: No, not a member; Roman Catholic; Protestant; Orthodox (Russian/Greek/etc.); Jewish; Muslim; Hindu; Buddhist; Other. *Source:* World Values Surveys.
Type of predominant religion worldwide	The classification of the major religion (adhered to by the largest population) in all 193 states around the world is based on the Central Intelligence Agency, *The World Factbook, 2001* (Washington, DC: Central Intelligence Agency). *Source:* http://www.cia.gov/cia/publications/factbook.
Traditional vs. secular-rational values	The traditional values scale is measured by support of the following items: God is very important in respondent's life; It is more important for a child to learn obedience and religious faith than independence and determination; Autonomy Index; Abortion is never justifiable; Respondent has strong sense of national pride; Respondent favors respect for authority. In contrast, support for secular-rational values is measured by the opposite position on all of the above. *Source:* World Values Surveys.
Gender equality scale	The combined 100-point gender equality scale is based on the following 5 items: MENPOL Q118: 'On the whole, men make better political leaders than women do' ('agree' coded low); MENJOBS Q78: 'When jobs are scarce, men should have more right to a job than women' ('agree' coded low); BOYEDUC Q119: 'A university education is more important for a boy than a girl' ('agree' coded low); NEEDKID Q110: 'Do you think that a woman has to have children in order to be fulfilled or is this not necessary?' ('agree' coded low); SGLMUM Q112: 'If a woman wants to have a child as a single parent but she doesn't want to have a stable relationship with a man, do you approve or disapprove?' ('disapprove' coded low). *Source:* World Values Surveys.
Sexual liberalization scale	'Please tell me for each of the following statements whether you think it can always be justified (10), never be justified (1), or somewhere in between, using this card ... abortion, homosexuality, prostitution, divorce.' *Source:* World Values Surveys.

(continued)

(continued)

Variable	Definitions, Coding and Sources
Individual-level demographic and socioeconomic indicators	
Occupational class	Coded for the respondent's occupation. 'In which profession/occupation do you, or did you, work?' The scale has 4 categories: Professional/manager (1); Other non-manual (2); Skilled non-manual (3); Unskilled Manual Worker (4). *Source:* World Values Surveys.
Paid work status	V220. 'Are you employed now or not?' Coded full-time, part-time or self-employed (1), other (0). *Source:* World Values Surveys.
Education	V217. 'What is the highest educational level that you have ever attained?' Coded on a 9-point scale from no formal education (1) to university level with degree (9). *Source:* World Values Surveys.
Age	Age coded in continuous years derived from date of birth. *Source:* World Values Surveys.
Age group	Young = less than 30 years old; Middle aged = 30–59 years old; Older = 60 years and above. *Source:* World Values Surveys.
Cohort	Year of birth coded into 10-year cohorts: 1900–1916, 1917–1926, 1927–1936, 1947–1956, 1957–1966, 1967–1976, 1977–1984. *Source:* World Values Surveys.
Language	V222. 'What language do you normally speak at home?' Code: English = 1, other = 0. *Source:* World Values Surveys.
Urbanization	V255. Size of town (pop.). (1) Less than 2,000; (2) 2,000–5,000; (3) 5,000–10,000; (4) 10,000–20,000; (5) 20,000–50,000; (6) 50,000–100,000; (7) 100,000–500,000; (8) 500,000 and more. *Source:* World Values Surveys.
Household savings	V251. 'During the past year, did your family (read out and code one answer): (4) Save money; (3) Just get by; (2) Spend some savings; (1) Spend savings and borrow money.' *Source:* World Values Surveys.
Household income	V253. 'On this card is a scale of incomes on which 1 indicates the "lowest income decile" and 10 the "highest income decile" in your country. We would like to know in what group your household is. Please, specify the appropriate number, counting all wages, salaries, pensions, and other income.' (Code one number.) *Source:* World Values Surveys.
Education scale	V238. 'What is the highest educational level that you have attained?' [NOTE: If respondent indicates that s/he is a student, code highest level s/he expects to complete]: (1) No formal education; (2) Incomplete primary school; (3) Complete primary school; (4) Incomplete secondary school: technical/vocational

Variable	Definitions, Coding and Sources
	type; (5) Complete secondary school: technical/vocational type; (6) Incomplete secondary: university-preparatory type; (7) Complete secondary: university-preparatory type; (8) Some university-level education, without degree; (9) University-level education, with degree. *Source:* World Values Surveys.

Note: Full details of the World Values Survey code books and questionnaires can be found at www.worldvaluessurvey.com.

Technical Appendix B

List of Countries

TABLE B.1. *Sample Size of Nation-States Included in the World Values Survey, by Nation and Wave*

		Wave 1 1981–1984	Wave 2 1989–1993	Wave 3 1994–1999	Wave 4 1999–2004	Wave 5 2005–2007	Total
1	Albania	–	–	999	1,000	–	1,999
2	Algeria	–	–	–	1,282	–	1,282
3	Andorra	–	–	–	–	1,003	1,003
4	Argentina	1,005	1,002	1,079	1,280	1,002	5,368
5	Armenia	–	–	2,000	–	–	2,000
6	Australia	1,228	–	2,048	–	1,421	4,697
7	Austria	–	1,460	–	1,522	–	2,982
8	Azerbaijan	–	–	2,002	–	–	2,002
9	Bangladesh	–	–	1,525	1,500	–	3,025
10	Belarus	–	1,015	2,092	1,000	–	4,107
11	Belgium	1,145	2,792	–	1,912	–	5,849
12	Bosnia	–	–	800	800	–	1,600
13	Brazil	–	1,782	1,149	–	1,500	4,431
14	Britain	1,167	1,484	1,093	1,000	1,041	5,785
15	Bulgaria	–	1,034	1,072	1,000	1,001	4,107
16	Burkina Faso	–	–	–	–	1,534	1,534
17	Canada	1,254	1,730	–	1,931	2,148	7,063
18	Chile	–	1,500	1,000	1,200	1,000	4,700
19	China	–	1,000	1,500	1,000	2,015	5,515
20	Colombia	–	–	6,025	–	3,025	9,050
21	Croatia	–	–	1,196	1,003	–	2,199
22	Cyprus	–	–	–	–	1,050	1,050
23	Czech	–	3,033	1,147	1,908	–	6,088
24	Denmark	1,182	1,030	–	1,023	–	3,235
25	Dominican Republic	–	–	417	–	–	417

		Wave 1 1981–1984	Wave 2 1989–1993	Wave 3 1994–1999	Wave 4 1999–2004	Wave 5 2005–2007	Total
26	East Germany	–	1,336	1,009	999	1,076	4,420
27	Egypt	–	–	–	3,000	3,051	6,051
28	El Salvador	–	–	1,254	–	–	1,254
29	Estonia	–	1,008	1,021	1,005	–	3,034
30	Ethiopia	–	–	–	–	1,500	1,500
31	Finland	1,003	588	987	1,038	1,014	4,630
32	France	1,200	1,002	–	1,615	1,001	4,818
33	Georgia	–	–	2,008	–	–	2,008
34	Ghana	–	–	–	–	1,534	1,534
35	Greece	–	–	–	1,142	–	1,142
36	Guatemala	–	–	–	–	1,000	1,000
37	Hungary	1,464	999	650	1,000	–	4,113
38	Iceland	927	702	–	968	–	2,597
39	India	–	2,500	2,040	2,002	2,001	8,543
40	Indonesia	–	–	–	1,004	2,015	3,019
41	Iran	–	–	–	2,532	2,667	5,199
42	Iraq	–	–	–	2,325	2,701	5,026
43	Ireland	1,217	1,000	–	1,012	–	3,229
44	Israel	–	–	–	1,199	–	1,199
45	Italy	1,348	2,018	–	2,000	1,012	6,378
46	Japan	1,204	1,011	1,054	1,362	1,096	5,727
47	Jordan	–	–	–	1,223	1,200	2,423
48	Kyrgyzstan	–	–	–	1,043	–	1,043
49	Latvia	–	903	1,200	1,013	–	3,116
50	Lithuania	–	1,000	1,009	1,018	–	3,027
51	Luxembourg	–	–	–	1,211	–	1,211
52	Macedonia	–	–	995	1,055	–	2,050
53	Malaysia	–	–	–	–	1,201	1,201
54	Mali	–	–	–	–	1,534	1,534
55	Malta	467	393	–	1,002	–	1,862
56	Mexico	1,837	1,531	2,364	1,535	1,560	8,827
57	Moldova	–	–	984	1,008	1,046	3,038
58	Montenegro	–	–	240	1,060	–	1,300
59	Morocco	–	–	–	2,264	1,200	3,464
60	New Zealand	–	–	1,201	–	954	2,155
61	Netherlands	1,221	1,017	–	1,003	1,050	4,291
62	Nigeria	–	1,001	1,996	2,022	–	5,019
63	Norway	1,051	1,239	1,127	–	1,025	4,442
64	Pakistan	–	–	733	2,000	–	2,733
65	Peru	–	–	1,211	1,501	1,500	4,212
66	Philippines	–	–	1,200	1,200	–	2,400
67	Poland	–	1,920	1,153	1,095	1,000	5,168
68	Portugal	–	1,185	–	1,000	–	2,185

(continued)

TABLE B.1 *(continued)*

		Wave 1 1981–1984	Wave 2 1989–1993	Wave 3 1994–1999	Wave 4 1999–2004	Wave 5 2005–2007	Total
69	Romania	–	1,103	1,239	1,146	1,776	5,264
70	Russia	–	1,961	2,040	2,500	2,033	8,534
71	Rwanda	–	–	–	–	1,507	1,507
72	South Africa	1,596	2,736	2,935	3,000	2,988	13,255
73	South Korea	970	1,251	1,249	1,200	1,200	5,870
74	Saudi Arabia	–	–	–	1,502	–	1,502
75	Serbia	–	–	1,280	1,200	1,220	3,700
76	Singapore	–	–	–	1,512	–	1,512
77	Slovakia	–	1,602	1,095	1,331	–	4,028
78	Slovenia	–	1,035	1,007	1,006	1,037	4,085
79	Spain	2,303	4,147	1,211	2,409	1,200	11,270
80	Sweden	954	1,047	1,009	1,015	1,003	5,028
81	Switzerland	–	1,400	1,212	–	1,241	3,853
82	Taiwan	–	–	780	–	1,225	2,005
83	Tanzania	–	–	–	1,171	–	1,171
84	Thailand	–	–	–	–	1,534	1,534
85	Trinidad	–	–	–	–	1,002	1,002
86	Turkey	–	1,030	1,907	4,607	1,346	8,890
87	United States	2,325	1,839	1,542	1,200	2,742	9,648
88	Uganda	–	–	–	1,002	–	1,002
89	Ukraine	–	–	2,811	1,195	1,000	5,006
90	Uruguay	–	–	1,000	–	1,000	2,000
91	Venezuela	–	–	1,200	1,200	–	2,400
92	Vietnam	–	–	–	1,000	1,495	2,495
93	West Germany	1,305	2,101	1,017	1,037	988	6,448
94	Zambia	–	–	–	–	1,500	1,500
95	Zimbabwe	–	–	–	1,002	–	1,002
	Total sample	30,947	62,771	84,887	101,172	82,967	362,744
	Total nation-states	23	43	55	70	56	95

Note: Contemporary independent nation-states (83) excluding specific regional samples (e.g., Hong Kong, Northern Ireland, and Puerto Rico) except for East Germany and Montenegro (before independence).

TABLE B.2. *Periods of Change Before 2005, by Nation*

All Five Waves 1981–2005	Twenty-Five Years 1981 and 2005	Fifteen Years 1990 and 2005	Ten Years 1995 and 2005	Five Years 2000 and 2005
Argentina	Argentina	Argentina	Argentina	Argentina
Britain	Australia	Brazil	Australia	Britain
Finland	Britain	Britain	Brazil	Bulgaria
Japan	Canada	Bulgaria	Britain	Canada
Mexico	Finland	Canada	Bulgaria	Chile
South Africa	France	Chile	Chile	China
South Korea	Italy	China	China	Egypt
Spain	Japan	Finland	Colombia	Finland
Sweden	Mexico	France	Finland	France
United States	Netherlands	India	India	India
West Germany	Norway	Italy	Japan	Indonesia
–	South Africa	Japan	Mexico	Iran
–	South Korea	Mexico	Moldova	Iraq
–	Spain	Netherlands	New Zealand	Italy
–	Sweden	Norway	Norway	Japan
–	United States	Poland	Poland	Jordan
–	West Germany	Romania	Romania	Mexico
–	–	Russia	Russia	Moldova
–	–	Slovenia	Serbia	Serbia
–	–	South Africa	Slovenia	Morocco
–	–	South Korea	South Africa	Netherlands
–	–	Spain	South Korea	Peru
–	–	Sweden	Spain	Poland
–	–	Switzerland	Sweden	Romania
–	–	Turkey	Switzerland	Russia
–	–	United States	Taiwan	Slovenia
–	–	West Germany	Turkey	South Africa
–	–	–	United States	South Korea
–	–	–	Ukraine	Spain
–	–	–	Uruguay	Sweden
–	–	–	West Germany	Turkey
–	–	–		United States
–	–	–		Ukraine
–	–	–		Vietnam
–	–	–		West Germany
11 nations	17 nations	27 nations	31 nations	40 nations

Note: Contemporary independent nation-states (83) excluding specific regional samples (e.g., Hong Kong, Northern Ireland, and Puerto Rico), except for East Germany and Montenegro (before independence).

Technical Appendix C

Methods and Multilevel Regression Models

As not all readers may be familiar with the analytical methods used in this study, a brief note will help to clarify the techniques. The firewall theory developed in Chapters 1 and 2 predicts that individual use of the news media will have a *direct* effect on individual values. In addition, it predicts that a *cross-level interaction* effect will also be apparent, as external and internal barriers to information flows in each society will interact with individual patterns of news media use.

To operationalize these factors, the key models in the second section of the book involve measurement at two distinct levels. A representative sample of individual respondents (Level 1) is nested within national-level contexts (Level 2). The World Values Survey was conducted among a representative random sample of the adult population in each nation-state.

The danger of using ordinary least squares (OLS) regression for analysis is that the standard errors of the regression coefficients can be inaccurate for contextual and cross-level variables, because they overestimate the degrees of freedom, and therefore tests of significance can prove misleading. OLS models can attempt to control for national variations by using a pooled model including dummy variables for each country, but this becomes inefficient with the coverage of many nations. Alternatively, OLS models can be run with no pooling, where separate models are run for each nation or type of media environment, but this is also clumsy.

Given the use of multilevel data, hierarchical linear models (HLM) are most appropriate for analysis, including multilevel regression analysis.[1] The models in this study use restricted maximum likelihood techniques (REML) to estimate direct and cross-level effects for hierarchical data. Individual respondents are thus grouped into nation-states. Each nation-state has a different set of parameters for the random factors, allowing intercepts and slopes to vary by nation.[2]

Level 1 in our core models includes the following *individual-level* measures: male gender (0/1), household income using a 10-point scale, age (in years), the education scale, and the media use 5-point scale (or each of the separate dummy variables for use of newspapers, radio or TV, and the Internet).

Level 2 includes the following *national-level* variables: the standardized KOF Globalization Index, the standardized Freedom House Press Freedom Index, and the standardized level of economic development (per capita GDP [2006] in purchasing power parity). As each of these were highly intercorrelated ($R = .640$ and above), the standardized scores were combined in the Cosmopolitanism Index. Each component was equally weighted. In calculating the Cosmopolitanism Index, the appropriate year of these indices was matched to the closest year of the national survey.

Cross-level interactions are also included, as the effects of media use are expected to be moderated by the level of cosmopolitanism within each country. To measure the joint effects of media use at the individual level, while taking account of the environment at the national level, models include the Cosmopolitanism Index × media use.

All variables are described in Technical Appendix A and Table C.1. In SPSS 16.0 Mixed Models, the iterative REML algorithm was used for estimating parameters. In HLMs, as is customary, all independent variables were centered by subtracting the grand mean (which becomes zero). The standardized independent variables all have a standard deviation of 1.0. This process helps to guard against problems of collinearity in the independent variables in the OLS models. The dependent variables are all converted to 100-point scales for ease of comparison across tables. The independent variables were treated as fixed components, reflecting the weighted average for the slope across all groups, while 'nation' was treated as a random component, capturing the country variability in the slope. The strength of the beta coefficients (slopes)

TABLE C.1. *Description of the Core Independent Variables*

	N	Unstandardized			Standardized (z scores)		
		Min	Max	Mean	Min	Max	Mean
INDIVIDUAL LEVEL							
Demographic characteristics							
Age (years)	78,017	16	89	42	−1.55	2.86	.000
Male gender	78,320	0	1	.48	−.96	1.04	.000
Socioeconomic resources							
Household income scale	78,416	1	10	4.7	−1.67	2.42	.000
Education scale	77,822	1	9	5.3	−1.84	1.55	.000
Media use							
Media use 100-point scale	65,729	0	100	38.5	−1.16	1.85	.000
Read newspaper (0/1)	70,692	0	1	.57	−1.15	.86	.000
Use radio/TV news (0/1)	70,306	0	1	.88	−2.72	.37	.000
Use Internet/e-mail (0/1)	69,037	0	1	.29	−.65	1.53	.000
NATIONAL LEVEL							
External barriers: Globalization Index		0	100	62	−2.17	1.81	.000
Internal barriers: media freedom		0	100	58	−1.83	1.40	.000
Development: GDP per capita in PPP		$155	$40,947	$10,499	−.82	2.40	.000
Cosmopolitanism Index (Globalization + freedom + GDP)		−4.81	5.03	.010	−1.81	1.88	.000
CROSS-LEVEL INTERACTIONS							
Globalization × media use scale		0	9,002	2,606	−1.07	2.62	.000
Media freedom × media use scale		0	9,100	2,558	−1.01	2.58	.000
Cosmopolitanism Index × media use		−8.91	9.32	.95	−3.88	3.29	.000
Valid N listwise	61,513						

Source: World Values Survey (2005–2007).

can be interpreted intuitively as the degree of change in the dependent variable generated by a 1% change in each independent variable.

The treatment of missing data is also important. Mean substitution replaced missing data for individual-level income where this was omitted in the national surveys conducted in two countries (Argentina and Jordan). The country coverage of the KOF Globalization Index is skewed toward more developed societies, and some developing countries are omitted due to problems of missing data from official statistics. Accordingly, the regional mean was used to estimate the position for seven countries that were not included in the 2008 KOF Globalization Index (Andorra, Taiwan, Ethiopia, Moldova, Vietnam, Burkina Faso, and Serbia). Models were tested with and without these treatments to check that they did not have a substantial effect on the interpretation of the results.

The multilevel regression models used in this study usually generate small differences in the size of the slope coefficient (b) compared with the results of OLS models, but the average standard errors for Level 2 variables often tend to be slightly larger. The process is thus more rigorous and conservative, avoiding Type I errors (false positives, indicating that a statistically significant difference exists when, in truth, there is no statistical difference). The goodness-of-fit statistic in OLS is the adjusted R^2, where models with a higher coefficient indicate that it accounts for more of the variance. In the REML model, by contrast, Schwarz's Bayesian criterion (BIC) is used, where the model with the lower value has the best fit.

Table C.2 compares the results of using both the OLS and the REML models, where the 100-point trust in outsiders scale is used illustratively as the dependent variable. When the three components of the Cosmopolitanism Index were entered separately into the OLS model, severe problems of multicollinearity (using the indicators of tolerance and Variance Inflation factor) arose, making the coefficients unreliable and the signs inconsistent. The use of the combined Cosmopolitanism Index avoids potential problems of multicollinearity. Comparison of the estimates generated by the OLS and REML models in Table C.2 shows that most of the estimates of the slope and intercept are very similar. The main contrast is that the OLS model can inflate the appropriate degrees of freedom at the national level, whereas the REML model provides a more rigorous and conservative estimate of significance at the national level.

TABLE C.2. Comparison of OLS and Multilevel Regression Models Explaining Trust in Outsiders

	Model A: OLS Regression				Model B: REML Multilevel Regression		
	B	S.E.	Beta	Sig.	b	S.E.	Sig.
INDIVIDUAL LEVEL							
Demographic characteristics							
Age (years)	.975	.101	.041	.000	1.45	.099	.000
Gender (male = 1)	-.022	.094	-.000	.815	-.099	.090	.275
Socioeconomic resources							
Household income, 10-pt scale	.766	.101	.032	.000	.628	.101	.000
Education, 9-pt scale	1.345	.114	.055	.000	2.177	.119	.000
Media use							
Media use, 100-pt scale	1.488	.115	.062	.000	1.583	.112	.000
NATIONAL LEVEL							
Cosmopolitanism Index	2.405	.042	.257	.000	2.065	.459	.000
CROSS-LEVEL INTERACTIONS							
Cosmopolitanism × media use scale	.725	.038	.077	.000	.312	.039	.000
Constant	55.339				55.096		
Goodness of fit: adjusted R^2	.121						
Goodness of fit: Schwarz's BIC	56,413				493,479		
No. of respondents					55,090		
No. of nations	44				44		

Note: All independent variables have been standardized between 0 and 1 using mean centering (z-scores). Model A presents the results of OLS regression models, while Model B presents the results of REML multilevel regression models. The trust in outsiders (other nationalities and other religions) 100-point scale was the dependent variable. The 100-point media use scale combined use of newspapers, radio/TV, Internet, books, and magazines for information. Model A gives the unstandardized beta coefficients (*b*), the standard errors, the standardized beta coefficients, and their significance. The OLS models were checked by tolerance tests to ensure that they were free of multicollinearity problems. See Technical Appendix A for details about the measurement, coding, and construction of all variables. Significant coefficients are highlighted in bold.

Source: World Values Survey (2005–2007).

Both models confirm that, even with a battery of social controls, *media use at an individual level has a direct effect on trust in outsiders*. Each percentage point increase in the media use scale corresponds, on average, to a 1.5% increase in trust in outsiders when all independent variables are set equal to their grand mean values. Trust in outsiders is also significantly increased by age, income, and education (but not gender). The comparison of individual-level factors shows that media use had a stronger effect on trust in outsiders than any of the other individual-level factors.

At the national level, the REML model suggests that the Cosmopolitanism Index by itself has a very strong and significant effect on trust in outsiders; each percentage point increase in the Cosmopolitanism Index corresponds, on average, to a 2.0% increase in trust in outsiders when all independent variables are set equal to their grand mean values. The direct experience of living in a cosmopolitan society therefore generates more trust in outsiders than does use of the media alone.

Moreover, the models suggest that, over and above these effects, a cross-level interaction effect is also present: *the positive effect of media use on trust in outsiders is further increased in the most cosmopolitan societies*. As discussed in Chapter 6, the results of the analysis therefore confirm the firewall theory.

The estimates of covariance suggest that the national intercepts were significant and strong ($b = 65.9$, S.E.14.1, $p = .000$), capturing the variability in the trust in outsiders scale among countries.

Excluding the insignificant predictors generated the following equations. Subscript 1 refers to Level 1 (individual) and subscript 2 to Level 2 (national) variables.

Model A: OLS regression analysis without the interaction terms:

$$Y_{\text{trust}} = 55.339 + 975x_{\text{age 1}} + .766x_{\text{income 1}} + 1.345x_{\text{education 1}}$$
$$+ 1.488x_{\text{media use 1}} + 2.405x_{\text{cosmopolitanism 2}}$$
$$+ .725x_{\text{cosmopolitanism 2} \times \text{media use 1}}$$

Model B: REML multilevel regression analysis:

$$Y_{\text{trust}} = 55.096 + 1.45x_{\text{age 1}} + .628x_{\text{income 1}} + 2.177x_{\text{education 1}}$$
$$+ 1.583x_{\text{media use 1}} + 2.065x_{\text{cosmopolitanism 2}}$$
$$+ .426x_{\text{cosmopolitanism 2} \times \text{media use 1}}$$

Notes

Chapter 1: Is Cultural Diversity Under Threat?

1. Ross McDonald. 2004. 'Television, materialism and culture: An exploration of imported media and its implications for GNH.' *Journal of Bhutan Studies* 9: 68–89; Whalley J. Kezang. 2004. 'Telecommunications in the Land of the Thunder Dragon: Recent developments in Bhutan.' *Telecommunications Policy* 28 (11): 785–800; Shahid Akhtar and Jon Gregson. 2001. 'Internet technologies in the Himalayas: Lessons learned during the 1990s.' *Journal of Information Science* 27 (1): 9–17; Tashi Wangchuk. 2004. 'The middle path to democracy in the kingdom of Bhutan.' *Asian Survey* 44 (6): 836–855.
2. Cathy Scott-Clark and Adrian Levy. 2003. 'Fast forward into trouble.' *Guardian*, June 14.
3. Ibid.
4. Bhutan Information, Communication and Media Authority. Information Communications and Media Act 2006. Clause 26/2(g). http://www.bicma. gov.bt/.
5. For balanced overviews of the debate about globalization, see David Held, Anthony McGrew, David Goldblatt, and Jonathan Perraton. 1999. *Global Transformations: Politics, Economics, and Culture*, chapter 7. Stanford, CA: Stanford University Press; Anthony McGrew and David Held. Eds. 2007. *Globalization Theory: Approaches and Controversies*. Cambridge: Polity Press; David Held and Anthony McGrew. 2007. *Globalization/Anti-Globalization: Beyond the Great Divide*. Cambridge: Polity Press; Jens Bartelson. 2000. 'Three concepts of globalization.' *International Sociology* 15 (2): 180–196.
6. David Held, Anthony McGrew, David Goldblatt, and Jonathan Perraton. 1999. *Global Transformations: Politics, Economics, and Culture*, chapter 7. Stanford, CA: Stanford University Press.

7. For details, see Chapter 3.
8. See Ronald Inglehart and Christian Welzel. 2005. *Modernization, Cultural Change and Democracy*, chapter 2. Cambridge: Cambridge University Press.
9. William McNeill. 1986. *Polyethnicity and National Unity in World History*. Chicago: University of Chicago Press; Nayan Chanda. 2007. *Bound Together: How Traders, Preachers, Adventurers, and Warriors Shaped Globalization*. New Haven, CT: Yale University Press; Michael Lang. 2006. 'Globalization and its history.' *Journal of Modern History* 78 (4): 899–931.
10. It should be noted that networked computing and computer-mediated e-mail have existed for the scientific community since the early 1960s, but the number of users was very small, even in the United States. The birth of the Internet can be dated to the invention of the World Wide Web in 1990 and then the launch of Mosaic (1993), Netscape Navigator (1994), and Microsoft Internet Explorer (1995). For details, see Pippa Norris. 2001. *Digital Divide: Civic Engagement, Information Poverty and the Internet Worldwide*. Cambridge: Cambridge University Press.
11. See UNESCO's classification presented in Figure 3.1. The full range of the creative economy also includes international exchanges of performing arts (music, theater, dance, opera), visual arts (paintings, sculptures), heritage goods (crafts festivals, museums), creative services (architecture, advertising, research), and design (furniture, fashions), but these sectors are beyond the scope of this study.
12. For useful discussions of the concept, see Ulf Hannerz. 1990. 'Cosmopolitans and locals in world culture.' In *Global Culture: Nationalism, Globalization and Modernity*. Ed. Mike Featherstone. London: Sage; John Tomlinson. 1999. *Globalization and Culture*. Chicago: University of Chicago Press; Steven Vertovec and Robin Cohen. Eds. 2002. *Conceiving Cosmopolitanism: Theory, Context and Practice*. Oxford: Oxford University Press.
13. Robert Merton. 1957. *Social Theory and Social Structure*. Glencoe, IL: Free Press.
14. Daniele Archibugi and David Held. Eds. 1995. *Cosmopolitan Democracy: An Agenda for a New World Order*. Cambridge: Polity Press; David Held. 1995. *Democracy and the Global Order: From the Modern State to Cosmopolitan Governance*. Cambridge: Polity Press; Richard Falk. 1995. *On Humane Governance: Toward a New Global Politics*. Cambridge: Polity Press; Daniele Archibugi. 2008. *The Global Commonwealth of Citizens: Toward Cosmopolitan Democracy*. Princeton, NJ: Princeton University Press.
15. For studies of transnational television see, e.g., Jean K. Chalaby. Ed. 2005. *Transnational Television Worldwide: Towards a New Media Order*. London: I. B. Taurus; Khalil Rinnawi. 2006. *Instant Nationalism:*

McArabism, al-Jazeera and Transnational Media in the Arab World. Lanham, MD: University Press of America. For patterns of transnational media within Europe, see Council of Europe. 2004. *Transnational Media Concentrations in Europe.* Strasbourg: Council of Europe. http://www. coe.int/t/e/human_rights/media/AP-MD(2004)007-en.pdf.

16. For detailed accounts of the historical developments leading to deregulation, see, e.g., David Hesmondhalgh. 2007. *The Cultural Industries,* 2nd ed. London: Sage; Peter J. Humphrey. 1996. *Mass Media and Media Policy in Western Europe.* Manchester: University of Manchester Press; Open Society Institute. 2005. *Television Across Europe: Regulation, Policy and Independence.* Budapest: OSI; Monroe E. Price, Beata Rozumilowicz, and Stefaan G. Verhulst. Eds. 2001. *Media Reform: Democratizing Media, Democratizing the State.* London: Routledge; David Ward. 2007. *Television and Public Policy: Change and Continuity in an Era of Global Liberalization.* Mahwah, NJ: Lawrence Erlbaum.

17. Kerry Segrave. 1997. *American Films Abroad: Hollywood's Domination of the World's Movie Screens.* Jefferson, NC: McFarland.

18. Thomas L. McPhail. 2006. *Global Communication: Theories, Stakeholders, and Trends,* 2nd ed., chapter 5. Malden, MA: Blackwell.

19. Olivier Boyd-Barrett. 1980. *The International News Agencies.* London: Constable; William A. Hachten and James Scotton. 2006. *The World News Prism: Global Information in a Satellite Age.* Walden, MA: Blackwell; Thomas L. McPhail. 2006. *Global Communication: Theories, Stakeholders, and Trends,* 2nd ed., chapter 7. Malden, MA: Blackwell.

20. Jeremy Tunstall. 1977. *The Media Are American.* New York: Columbia University Press.

21. Pippa Norris. 2001. *Digital Divide: Civic Engagement, Information Poverty and the Internet Worldwide.* Cambridge: Cambridge University Press; Manuel Castells. 2000. *The Rise of the Network Society,* 2nd ed. Oxford: Blackwell.

22. Pippa Norris. 2001. *Digital Divide: Civic Engagement, Information Poverty and the Internet Worldwide.* Cambridge University Press.

23. There are numerous excellent overviews of these developments: see, e.g., Thomas L. McPhail. 2006. *Global Communication: Theories, Stakeholders, and Trends,* 2nd ed. Malden, MA: Blackwell.

24. See, e.g., Lee Artz and Yahya R. Kamalipour. Eds. 2007. *The Global Media: Trends in International Mass Media.* New York: Rowman and Littlefield; Chris Barker. 1997. *Global Television: An Introduction.* Oxford: Blackwell; Chris Barker. 1999. *Television, Globalization and Cultural Identities.* Philadelphia: Open University Press; Manuel Castells. 2004. *The Power of Identity,* 2nd ed. Oxford: Blackwell; Paula Chakravartty and Yuezhi Zhao. Eds. 2008. *Global Communications: Toward a Transcultural Political Economy.* Lanham, MD: Rowman and Littlefield; Anne Cooper-Chen. Ed. 2005. *Global Entertainment Media: Content,*

Audiences, Issues. Mahwah, NJ: Lawrence Erlbaum; Tyler Cowen. 2004.
Creative Destruction: How Globalization Is Changing the World's Cultures. Princeton, NJ: Princeton University Press.

25. Robert Holton. 2000. 'Globalization's cultural consequences.' *Annals of the American Academy of Political and Social Sciences* 570: 140–152; Frank Webster. 2006. *Theories of the Information Society,* 3rd ed. London: Routledge.

26. 'Cultural imperialism' has also been termed 'media imperialism' and 'electronic imperialism.' For the origins of the debate about this concept and the original advocates, see Johan Galtung and Mari Holmboe Ruge. 1965. 'The structure of foreign news.' *Journal of Peace Research* 2 (1): 64–91; Johan Galtung. 1971. 'A structural theory of imperialism.' *Journal of Peace Research* 8: 81–118; Johan Galtung. 1980. *The True Worlds.* New York: Free Press; Herbert J. Schiller. 1969. *Mass Communication and American Empire.* New York: A. M. Kelley; Herbert J. Schiller. 1976. *Communication and Cultural Domination.* White Plains, NY: International Arts and Sciences Press; Mustapha Masmoudi. 1981. 'The new world information order.' In *Crisis in International News: Policies and Prospects.* Ed. Jim Richstad and Michael A. Anderson. New York: Columbia University Press. For a critical account, see John Tomlinson. 1991. *Cultural Imperialism.* Baltimore: Johns Hopkins University Press.

27. For the origins of this debate see Johan Galtung and Mari Holmboe Ruge. 1965. 'The structure of foreign news.' *Journal of Peace Research* 2 (1): 64–91; Johan Galtung. 1971. 'A structural theory of imperialism.' *Journal of Peace Research,* 8: 81–118; Johan Galtung. 1980. *The True Worlds.* New York: Free Press; Herbert J. Schiller. 1969. *Mass Communication and American Empire.* New York: A. M. Kelley; Herbert J. Schiller. 1976. *Communication and Cultural Domination.* White Plains, NY: International Arts and Sciences Press; Mustapha Masmoudi. 1981. 'The new world information order.' In *Crisis in International News: Policies and Prospects.* Ed. Jim Richstad and Michael A. Anderson. New York: Columbia University Press. For critical accounts, see John Tomlinson. 1991. *Cultural Imperialism.* Baltimore: Johns Hopkins University Press; Peter Golding and Phil Harris. Eds. 1997. *Beyond Cultural Imperialism: Globalization, Communication and the New International Order.* London: Sage.

28. Thomas L. McPhail. 1983. *Electronic Colonialism: The Future of International Broadcasting and Communication,* p. 60. Beverly Hills, CA: Sage.

29. Tapio Varis. 1974. 'Global traffic in television.' *Journal of Communication* 241: 102–109; Tapio Varis. 1984. 'The international flow of television programs.' *Journal of Communication* 34 (1): 143–152; Tapio Varis. 1986. 'Trends in international television flows.' *International Political Science Review* 7: 235–249; Tapio Varis. 2002. 'The international flow of television programmes.' In *Television: Critical Concepts in Media and*

Cultural Studies. Ed. Toby Miller. New York: Routledge; Jeremy Tunstall. 1977. *The Media Are American.* New York: Columbia University Press.

30. Sean MacBride. 1980. *Many Voices, One World: Communication and Society Today and Tomorrow; Towards a New More Just and More Efficient World Information and Communication Order.* Paris: UNESCO, International Commission for the Study of Communication Problems; Hamid Mowlana. 1985. *International Flow of Information: A Global Report and Analysis.* Paris: UNESCO. For the background to the UNESCO debate and its consequences, see Thomas McPhail. 2006. *Global Communication: Theories, Stakeholders, and Trends,* 2nd ed., chapter 10. Malden, MA: Blackwell.

31. D. Howes. Ed. 1996. *Cross-Cultural Consumption: Global Markets, Local Realities.* London: Routledge; George Ritzer. 1993. *The McDonaldization of Society.* Newbury Park, CA: Pine Forge Press; George Ritzer and Allan Liska. 1997. 'McDisneyization.' In *Touring Cultures: Transformation of Travel and Theory.* Ed. C. Rojek and John Urry. London: Routledge; Tamar Liebes and Elihu Katz. 1993. *The Export of Meaning: Cross-Cultural Readings of Dallas.* Cambridge: Polity Press; Benjamin R. Barber. 1996. *Jihad vs. McWorld: How Globalism and Tribalism Are Reshaping the World.* New York: Ballantine Books.

32. Joseph S. Nye, Jr. 2004. *Soft Power: The Means to Success in World Politics.* New York: Public Affairs; Joseph S. Nye, Jr. 2008. 'Public diplomacy and soft power.' *Annals of the American Academy of Political and Social Science* 616: 94–109; Watanabe Yasushi and David L. McConnell. Eds. 2008. *Soft Power Superpowers: Cultural and National Assets of Japan and the United States.* New York: M. E. Sharpe.

33. David Rothkopf. 1997. 'In praise of cultural imperialism.' *Foreign Affairs* 107: 38–53.

34. UNESCO. 2001. *Universal Declaration of Cultural Diversity.* Paris: UNESCO. http://unesdoc.unesco.org/images/0012/001271/127160m.pdf. For a discussion, see Stephen Azzi. 2004. 'Negotiating cultural space in the global economy: The United States, UNESCO, and the convention on cultural diversity.' *International Journal* 60 (3): 765–784.

35. Jan Wouters and Bart De Meester. 2008. 'The UNESCO convention on cultural diversity and WTO law: A case study in fragmentation of international law.' *Journal of World Trade* 42 (1): 205–240; Christof B. Graber. 2006. 'The new UNESCO convention on cultural diversity: A counterbalance to the WTO? *Journal of International Economic Law* 9 (3): 553–574; M. Hahn. 2006. 'A clash of cultures? The UNESCO diversity convention and international trade law.' *Journal of International Economic Law* 9 (3): 515–552.

36. For the EU debates, see Mario Hirsch and Vibeke G. Petersen. 1998. 'European policy initiatives.' In *Media Policy: Convergence, Concentration and Commerce,* chapter 14. Ed. Denis McQuail and Karen Siune.

London: Sage; Mark Wheeler. 2004. 'Supranational regulation: Television and the European Union.' *European Journal of Communication* 19 (3): 349–369; Mira Burri-Nenova. 2007. 'The new audiovisual media services directive: Television without frontiers, television without cultural diversity.' *Common Market Law Review* 44: 1689–1725.

37. Roumeen Islam and Gianni Zanini. 2008. *World Trade Indicators, 2008: Benchmarking Policy and Performance.* Washington, DC: World Bank.

38. Michael G. Elasmar. Ed. 2003. *The Impact of International Television: A Paradigm Shift.* Mahwah, NJ: Lawrence Erlbaum.

39. For reviews of the literature, see William Ware and Michael Dupagne. 1994. 'Effects of U.S. television programs on foreign audiences: A meta-analysis.' *Journalism Quarterly* 71 (4): 947–959; Michael G. Elasmar and John E. Hunter. 1993. 'The impact of foreign TV on a domestic audience: A meta-analysis.' *Communication Yearbook* 20: 47–69; Michael G. Elasmar and John E. Hunter. 2003. 'A meta-analysis of cross-border effect studies.' In *The Impact of International Television: A Paradigm Shift.* Ed. Michael G. Elasmar. Mahwah, NJ: Lawrence Erlbaum.

40. See, e.g., Meic Pearse. 2004. *Why the Rest Hates the West: Understanding the Roots of Global Rage.* Downers Grove, IL: InterVarsity Press; Frank Louis Rusciano. 2006. *Global Rage after the Cold War.* New York: Palgrave Macmillan.

41. See, e.g., Meic Pearse. 2004. *Why the Rest Hates the West: Understanding the Roots of Global Rage.* Downers Grove, IL: InterVarsity Press.

42. Benjamin R. Barber. 1996. *Jihad vs. McWorld: How Globalism and Tribalism Are Reshaping the World.* New York: Ballantine Books; Thomas L. Friedman. 2000. *The Lexus and the Olive Tree: Understanding Globalization.* New York: Anchor Books; Thomas L. Friedman. 2007. *The World Is Flat: A Brief History of the Twenty-first Century.* New York: Picador / Farrar, Straus and Giroux.

43. Samuel Huntington. 1996. *The Clash of Civilizations and the Remaking of World Order.* New York: Simon & Schuster.

44. Daya Kishan Thussu. Ed. 1998. *Electronic Empires: Global Media and Local Resistance.* New York: Hodder Arnold.

45. Tomar Liebes and Elihu Katz. 1993. *The Export of Meaning: Cross-Cultural Readings of Dallas.* Cambridge: Polity Press.

46. Ernesto Zedillo. Ed. 2008. *The Future of Globalization: Explorations in Light of Recent Turbulence.* London: Routledge; Daniel Drache. 2008. *Defiant Publics: The Unprecedented Reach of the Global Citizen.* Cambridge: Polity Press.

47. http://www.incd.net/incden.html.

48. See, e.g., Marwan M. Kraidy. 2005. *Hybridity, or the Cultural Logic of Globalization.* Philadelphia: Temple University Press; Jan Nederveen Pieterse. 2003. *Globalization and Culture: Global Melange.* New York: Rowman and Littlefield.

49. Roland Robertson. 1992. *Globalization: Social Theory and Global Culture*. London: Sage; Eugene Eoyang. 2005. *Two-Way Mirrors: Cross-Cultural Studies in Glocalization*. Lanham, MD: Lexington Books; James Lull. 2000. *Media, Communication, Culture: A Global Approach*, 2nd ed. Cambridge: Polity Press; Jan Nederveen Pieterse. 2003. *Globalization and Culture: Global Melange*. New York: Rowman and Littlefield; Marwan M. Kraidy. 2005. *Hybridity, or the Cultural Logic of Globalization*. Philadelphia: Temple University Press.

50. For details about the surge in India's information technology industry, see Rafiq Dossani and Martin Kenney. 2007. 'The next wave of globalization: Relocating service provision to India.' *World Development* 35 (5): 772–791; NASSCOM. 2008. *Indian IT Industry Factsheet* (2008). http://www.nasscom.in/upload/5216/Strategic_Review_Feb2008.pdf.

51. Tyler Cowen. 2004. *Creative Destruction: How Globalization Is Changing the World's Cultures*. Princeton, NJ: Princeton University Press.

52. Terhi Rantanen. 2005. *The Media and Globalization*. London: Sage.

53. Anthony Giddens. 1990. *The Consequences of Modernity*. Cambridge: Polity Press.

54. Anthony Smith. 1995. 'Towards a global culture?' In *Global Culture*. Ed. Michael Featherstone. London: Sage.

55. Karl C. Kaltenthaler, Ronald D. Gelleny, and Stephen J. Ceccoli. 2004. 'Explaining citizen support for trade liberalization.' *International Studies Quarterly* 48 (4): 829–851; Martin S. Edwards. 2006. 'Public opinion regarding economic and cultural globalization: Evidence from a cross-national survey.' *Review of International Political Economy* 13 (4): 587–608.

56. Ronald Inglehart and Pippa Norris. 2003. *Rising Tide: Gender Equality and Cultural Change Around the World*. Cambridge: Cambridge University Press.

57. Pippa Norris and Ronald Inglehart. 2004. *Sacred and Secular: Politics and Religion Worldwide*. Cambridge: Cambridge University Press.

58. Caroline Pauwels and Jan Loisen. 2003. 'The WTO and the audiovisual sector: Economic free trade vs cultural horse trading?' *European Journal of Communication* 18 (3): 291–313; Mark Wheeler. 2004. 'Supranational regulation: Television and the European Union.' *European Journal of Communication* 19 (3): 349–369.

Chapter 2: Theoretical Framework

1. Stanely D. Brunn and Thomas R. Leinbach. Eds. 1991. *Collapsing Space and Time: Geographic Aspects of Communication and Information*. London: HarperCollins Academic.

2. UNCTAD. 2008. *Secretary-General's High Level Panel on the Creative Economy and Industries for Development*. Accra, Ghana: UN. TD

(XII)/BP/4 April 2008; UNESCO. 2005. *International Flows of Selected Cultural Goods and Services, 1994–2003*. Montreal: UNESCO Institute for Statistics.

3. European Audiovisual Observatory. 2007. *2007 Yearbook*. Strasbourg: Council of Europe.

4. Colin Hoskins and Rolf Mirius. 1988. 'Reasons for the U.S. domination of the international trade in television programmes.' *Media, Culture & Society* 10: 499–515; Kerry Segrave. 1997. *American Films Abroad: Hollywood's Domination of the World's Movie Screens*. Jefferson, NC: McFarland; Kerry Segrave. 1998. *American Television Abroad: Hollywood's Attempt to Dominate World Television*. London: McFarland; Melvyn Stokes and Richard Maltby. Eds. 2005. *Hollywood Abroad: Audiences and Cultural Exchange*. Berkeley: University of California Press; Michael Tracey and Wendy W. Redal. 1995. 'The new parochialism: The triumph of the populist in the flow of international television.' *Canadian Journal of Communication* 20: 343–365.

5. David Ward. 2007. *Television and Public Policy: Change and Continuity in an Era of Global Liberalization*. Mahwah, NJ: Lawrence Erlbaum; Richard Collins. 1998. *From Satellite to Single Market: New Communication Technology and European Public Services Television*. London: Routledge.

6. Dal Yong Jin. 2007. 'Transformation of the world television system under neo-liberal globalization, 1983 to 2003.' *Television and New Media* 8 (3): 179–196; Richard Collins. 1998. *From Satellite to Single Market: New Communication Technology and European Public Services Television*. London: Routledge.

7. Ben H. Bagdikian. 1997. *The Media Monopoly*. Boston: Beacon Press; Robert W. McChesney. 1999. *Rich Media, Poor Democracy: Communication Politics in Dubious Times*. Urbana: University of Illinois Press.

8. Council of Europe. 2004. *Transnational Media Concentrations in Europe*. Strasbourg: Council of Europe. http://www.coe.int/t/e/human_rights/media/AP-MD(2004)007_en.pdf.

9. David Bigman. 2007. *Globalization and the Least Developed Countries: Potentials and Pitfalls*. Cambridge: CABI.

10. UNESCO. The latest available year of all these estimates is 2005.

11. International Telecommunication Union. www.itu.int/ITU-D/ict/statistics/itc/graphs/fixed.jpg.

12. Trevor Haywood. 1995. *Info-Rich / Info-Poor: Access and Exchange in the Global Information Society*. London: Bowker-Saur; William Wresch. 1996. *Disconnected: Haves and Have-Nots in the Information Age*. New Brunswick, NJ: Rutgers University Press; Pippa Norris. 2001. *Digital Divide: Civic Engagement, Information Poverty and the Internet Worldwide*. Cambridge: Cambridge University Press; Liangzhi Yu. 2006. 'Understanding information inequality: Making sense of the literature of

the information and digital divides.' *Journal of Librarianship and Information Science* 38 (4): 229–252.

13. World Bank. 2007. *World Development Indicators, 2007*, tables 5.10 and 5.11. Washington DC: World Bank.

14. International Telecommunication Union. http://www.itu.int/ITU-D/ict/statistics/ict/index.html.

15. Georgette Wang, Anura Goonasekera, and Jan Servaes. Eds. 2000. *The New Communications Landscape: Demystifying Media Globalization.* London: Routledge.

16. For a discussion, see the collection of studies in Michael G. Elasmar. Ed. 2003. *The Impact of International Television: A Paradigm Shift.* Mahwah, NJ: Lawrence Erlbaum.

17. For an overview of socialization theory, see Joan E. Grusec and Paul D. Hastings. Eds. 2007. *Handbook of Socialization: Theory and Research.* New York: Guilford Press. For comparative studies, see Ronald Inglehart. 1997. *Modernization and Postmodernization: Cultural, Economic and Political Change in 43 Societies.* Princeton, NJ: Princeton University Press; Ronald Inglehart and Christian Welzel. 2005. *Modernization, Cultural Change and Democracy.* Cambridge: Cambridge University Press.

18. Preben Sepstrup. 1990. *Transnationalization of Television in Western Europe.* London: John Libbey. For the distinction between the program contents and the messages received and interpreted, see Tomar Liebes and Elihu Katz. 1993. *The Export of Meaning: Cross-Cultural Readings of Dallas.* Cambridge: Polity Press.

19. Walter Lippman. 1922. *Public Opinion.* New York: Macmillan; Harold Lasswell. 1971 [1927]. *Propaganda Techniques in World War I.* Cambridge, MA: MIT. Press. For a discussion, see Garth S. Jowett and Victoria O'Donnell. 2006. *Propaganda and Persuasion*, 4th ed. Thousand Oaks, CA: Sage.

20. Ian M. Rose. 1995. 'Barring foreigners from our airwaves: An anachronistic pothole on the global information highway.' *Columbia Law Review* 95: 1188.

21. For a comprehensive overview of alternative theories of mass communications, see Denis McQuail. 1994. *Mass Communication Theory*, 3rd ed. London: Sage.

22. Carl Iver Hovland, Arthur A. Lumsdaine, and Fred D. Sheffield. 1949. *Experiments on Mass Communication.* Princeton, NJ: Princeton University Press.

23. Elihu Katz and Paul F. Lazarsfeld. 1955. 'Images of the mass communications process.' In *Personal Influence: The Part Played by People in the Flow of Mass Communications.* Ed. Elihu Katz and Paul F. Lazarsfeld. Glencoe, IL: Free Press.

24. Steven H. Chaffee, L. Scott Ward, and Leonard P. Tipton. 1970. 'Mass communication and political socialization.' *Journalism Quarterly* 47 (4):

647; Charles Atkin and Walter Gantz. 1978. 'Television-news and political socialization.' *Public Opinion Quarterly* 42 (2): 183–198.

25. Jay G. Blumler and Elihu Katz. 1974. *The Uses of Mass Communications: Current Perspectives on Gratifications Research*. Beverly Hills, CA: Sage.

26. W. Russell Neuman, Marion R. Just, and Ann N. Crigler. 1992. *Common Knowledge: News and the Construction of Political Meaning*. Chicago: University of Chicago Press; Colleen Roach. 1997. 'Cultural imperialism and resistance in media theory and literary theory.' *Media, Culture & Society* 19: 47.

27. George Gerbner, Larry Gross, M. Jackson-Beeck, S. Jeffries-Fox, and Nancy Signorielli. 1993. 'Growing up with television: The cultivation perspective.' In *Media Effects: Advances in Theory and Research*. Ed. Jennings Bryant and Dolf Zillmann. Hillsdale, NJ: Lawrence Erlbaum.

28. See Michael G. Elasmar and Kathryn Bennett. 2003. 'The cultural imperialism paradigm revisited: Origin and evolution.' In *The Impact of International Television: A Paradigm Shift*. Ed. Michael G. Elasmar. Mahwah, NJ: Lawrence Erlbaum.

29. John Zaller. 1996. 'The myth of massive media impact revived: New support for a discredited idea.' In *Political Persuasion and Attitude Change*. Ed. Diana C. Mutz, Paul M. Sniderman, and Richard A. Brody. Ann Arbor: University of Michigan Press.

30. Bryant Jennings and Dolf Zillmann. Eds. 2002. *Media Effects: Advances in Theory and Research*, 2nd ed. Hillsdale, NJ: Lawrence Erlbaum; Glenn Sparks. 2005. *Media Effects Research: A Basic Overview*, 2nd ed. New York: Wadsworth. For agenda-setting theory, see Maxwell McCombs and Donald L. Shaw. 1972. 'The agenda-setting function of the mass media.' *Public Opinion Quarterly* 36: 176–185.

31. Jennings Bryant and Dolf Zillmann. Eds. 2002. *Media Effects: Advances in Theory and Research*. Mahwah, NJ: Lawrence Erlbaum; Eric Bucy. 2009. *Sourcebook for Political Communication Research: Methods, Measures, and Analytical Techniques*. New York: Routledge.

32. Michael Gurevitch and Jay Blumler. 1990. 'Comparative research: The extending frontier.' In *New Directions in Political Communication: A Resource Book*. Ed. David L. Swanson and Dan Nimmo. Newbury Park, CA: Sage.

33. Sophie Duchesne and André-Paul Frognier. 1995. 'Is there a European identity?' In *Public Opinion and Internationalized Governance*. Ed. Oskar Niedermayer and Richard Sinnott. Oxford: Oxford University Press; Angelika Scheuer. 1999. 'A political community?' In *Political Representation and Legitimacy in the European Union*. Ed. Hermann Schmitt and Jacques Thomassen. Oxford: Oxford University Press. See also Brian Nelson, David Roberts, and Walter Veit. Eds. 1992. *The Idea of Europe: Problems of National and Transnational Identity*. Oxford: Berg.

34. Wendy M. Rahn and Thomas J. Rudolph. 2001. 'National identities and the future of democracy.' In *Mediated Politics*. Ed. W. Lance Bennett

and Robert M. Enbtman. Cambridge: Cambridge University Press; Pippa Norris. 2001. 'Global governance and cosmopolitan citizens.' In *Governance in a Globalizing World*. Ed. Joseph S. Nye and John Donahue. Washington, DC: Brookings Institution Press.

35. Michael G. Elasmar and John E. Hunter. 1993. 'The impact of foreign TV on a domestic audience: A meta-analysis.' *Communication Yearbook 20*: 47–69; Michael Featherstone. Ed. 1990. *Global Culture: Nationalism, Globalism and Modernity*. London: Sage; Tamar Liebes and Elihu Katz. 1993. *The Export of Meaning: Cross-Cultural Readings of Dallas*. New York: Oxford University Press; Michael G. Elasmar and John E. Hunter. 2003. 'A meta-analysis of cross-border effect studies.' In *The Impact of International Television: A Paradigm Shift*. Ed. Michael G. Elasmar. Mahwah, NJ: Lawrence Erlbaum.

36. See contributions in Michael G. Elasmar. Ed. 2003. *The Impact of International Television: A Paradigm Shift*. Mahwah, NJ: Lawrence Erlbaum.

37. Ibid.

38. John Pimenta, Daniel Paolillo, and Daniel Prado. 2005. *Measuring Linguistic Diversity on the Internet*. Paris: UNESCO. See also regular estimates by Global Reach. http://global-reach.niz/globalstats.

39. Milton Rokeach. 1968. *Beliefs, Attitudes and Values*. San Fransisco: Jossey-Bass.

40. Herbert J. Schiller. 1969. *Mass Communication and American Empire*, Boulder, CO: Westview Press; Robert W. McChesney. 1999. *Rich Media, Poor Democracy: Communication Politics in Dubious Times*, chapter 2. Chicago: University of Illinois Press. See also Edward S. Herman and Robert W. McChesney. 1997. *The Global Media: The Missionaries of Global Capitalism*. Washington, DC: Cassell; Edward S. Herman. 1995. *Triumph of the Market: Essays on Economics, Politics, and the Media*. Boston: South End Press.

41. Ronald Deibert, John Palfrey, Rafal Rohozinski, and Jonathan Zittrain. 2008. *Access Denied: The Practice and Policy of Internet Filtering*. Cambridge, MA: MIT Press.

42. Hsiang Iris Chyi and George Sylvie. 2001. 'The medium is global, the content is not: The role of geography in online newspaper markets.' *Journal of Media Economics* 14 (4): 231–248; George Sylvie and Hsiang Iris Chyi. 2007. 'One product, two markets: How geography differentiates online newspaper audiences.' *Journalism & Mass Communication Quarterly* 84 (3): 562–581; Sammuel J. Best, Brian Chmielewski, and Brian S. Krueger. 2005. 'Selective exposure to online foreign news during the conflict with Iraq.' *Harvard International Journal of Press-Politics* 10 (4): 52–70.

43. Full methodological details about the World Values Surveys, including the questionnaires, sampling procedures, fieldwork procedures, principle investigators, and organization can be found at http://wvs.isr.umich.edu/wvs-samp.html.

44. These countries are ranked as equally 'free' according to the 2008 Freedom House assessments of political rights and civil liberties. Freedom House. 2008. *Freedom in the World*. www.freedomhouse.org.

45. Pippa Norris. 2001. *Digital Divide: Civic Engagement, Information Poverty and the Internet Worldwide*, chapter 3. Cambridge: Cambridge University Press.

46. Unfortunately the fifth wave of the survey does not allow us to disaggregate use of radio and television news, where we would expect to find some marked contrasts.

47. Karl Erik Gustafsson and Olof Hulten. 1997. 'Sweden.' In *The Media in Western Europe*. Ed. Bernt Stubbe Ostergaard. London: Sage.

48. Pippa Norris. 2000. *A Virtuous Circle: Political Communications in Post-Industrial Democracies*, chapter 4. Cambridge: Cambridge University Press.

49. Pippa Norris. 2001. *Digital Divide: Civic Engagement, Information Poverty and the Internet Worldwide*, chapter 3. Cambridge: Cambridge University Press.

50. See, e.g., The Pew Research Center for the People & the Press. August 2008. 'Key news audiences now blend online and traditional sources: Audience segments in a changing news environment.' http://people-press.org/report/444/news-media.

51. For a discussion of the advantages of mixed research designs, see Henry Brady and David Collier. 2004. *Rethinking Social Inquiry: Diverse Tools, Shared Standards*. New York: Rowman and Littlefield.

52. Robert Bickel. 2007. *Multilevel Analysis for Applied Research: It's Just Regression!* New York: Guilford Press.

53. James A. Stimson. 1985. 'Regression in time and space: A statistical essay.' *American Journal of Political Science* 29: 914–947; Cheng M. Hsiao. 1986. *Analysis of Panel Data*. Cambridge: Cambridge University Press; Sven E. Wilson and David M. Butler. 2007. 'A lot more to do: The sensitivity of time-series cross-section analyses to simple alternative specifications.' *Political Analysis* 15 (2): 101–123.

54. Nathaniel Beck and Jonathan Katz. 1995. 'What to do (and not to do) with time-series cross-section data.' *American Political Science Review* 89: 634–647; Nathaniel Beck and Jonathan Katz. 1996. 'Nuisance vs. substance: Specifying and estimating time-series cross-sectional models.' In *Political Analysis*. Ed. John Freeman. Ann Arbor: University of Michigan Press.

55. See Alexander L. George and Andrew Bennett. 2004. *Case Studies and Theory Development*. Cambridge, MA: MIT Press.

56. For a discussion of the potential problem of selection bias in comparative politics, see Barbara Geddes. 2003. *Paradigms and Sand Castles: Theory Building and Research Design in Comparative Politics*, chapter 3. Ann Arbor: University of Michigan Press; David Collier, James Mahoney, and

Jason Seawright. 2004. 'Claiming too much: Warnings about selection bias.' In *Rethinking Social Inquiry: Diverse Tools, Shared Standards.* Ed. Henry E. Brady and David Collier. Lanham, MD: Rowman and Littlefield.

Chapter 3: Markets

1. UNCTAD. 2008. *Secretary-General's High Level Panel on the Creative Economy and Industries for Development.* Accra, Ghana: UN. TD (XII)/BP/4 April 2008; UNESCO. 2005. *International Flows of Selected Cultural Goods and Services, 1994–2003.* Montreal: UNESCO Institute for Statistics.

2. Dal Yong Jin. 2007. 'Reinterpretation of cultural imperialism: Emerging domestic market vs. continuing US dominance.' *Media, Culture & Society* 29 (5): 753–777

3. Joseph S. Nye, Jr. 2002. *The Paradox of American Power*, chapter 3. New York: Oxford University Press.

4. Andrew Puddenphatt. 2007. *Defining Indicators of Media Development: Background Paper.* Paris: UNESCO.

5. Jacques Kayser. 1953. *One Week's News: Comparative Study of 17 Major Dailies for a Seven Day Period.* Paris: UNESCO; Tapio Varis. 1974. 'Global traffic in television.' *Journal of Communication* 241: 102–109; Tapio Varis. 1984. 'The international flow of television programs.' *Journal of Communication* 34 (1): 143–152; Tapio Varis. 1986. 'Trends in international television flows.' *International Political Science Review* 7: 235–249; Tapio Varis. 2002. 'The international flow of television programmes.' In *Television: Critical Concepts in Media and Cultural Studies.* Ed. Toby Miller. New York: Routledge; Francois Heinderyckx. 1993. 'Television news programmes in Western Europe: A comparative study.' *European Journal of Communication* 8: 425–450.

6. Els de Bens and Hedwig de Smaele. 2001. 'The inflow of American television fiction on European broadcasting channels revisited.' *European Journal of Communication* 16: 51–76.

7. Eurostat. 2007. *Cultural Statistics: 2007 Edition.* Brussels: Eurostat.

8. Robert McChesney. 1999. *Rich Media, Poor Democracy: Communication Politics in Dubious Times.* Urbana: University of Illinois Press.

9. PriceWaterhouseCoopers. 2008. *Global Entertainment and Media Outlook.* New York: PriceWaterhouseCoopers.

10. Stanley D. Brunn and Martin Dodge. 2001. 'Mapping the "worlds" of the World Wide Web: (Re)structuring global commerce through hyperlinks.' *American Behavioral Scientist* 44 (10): 1717–1739; George A. Barnett and Eunjung Sung. 2005. 'Culture and the structure of the international hyperlink network.' *Journal of Computer-Mediated Communication* 11 (1): 217–238; Lori Shumate and Michelle Dewitt. 2008. 'The North/South

divide in NGO hyperlink networks.' *Journal of Computer-Mediated Communication* 13 (2): 405–428.

11. UNESCO. 2005. *International Flows of Selected Cultural Goods and Services, 1994–2003*. Montreal: UNESCO Institute for Statistics.

12. Philip Ramsdale. Ed. 1999. *International Flows of Selected Cultural Goods, 1980–1998*. Paris: UNESCO Institute for Statistics.

13. UNESCO. 2005. *International Flows of Selected Cultural Goods and Services, 1994–2003*. Montreal: UNESCO Institute for Statistics.

14. Motion Picture Association. 2007. *2006 International Theatrical Market: Worldwide Market Research and Analysis*. http://www.mpaa.org/International%20Theatrical%20Snapshot.pdf.

15. UNCTAD. 2002. Quoted in UNESCO. 2005. *International Flows of Selected Cultural Goods and Services, 1994–2003*, p. 47. Montreal: UNESCO Institute for Statistics.

16. W. Wayne Fu. 2006. 'Concentration and homogenization of international movie sources: Examining foreign film import profiles.' *Journal of Communications* 56: 813–835; Kerry Segrave. 1997. *American Films Abroad: Hollywood's Domination of the World's Movie Screens*. Jefferson, NC: McFarland.

17. David Waterman and Krishna P. Jayakar. 2000. 'The competitive balance of the Italian and American film industries.' *European Journal of Communication* 15(4): 501–528.

18. European Audiovisual Observatory. 2007. *Yearbook 2007*. Strasbourg: Council of Europe.

19. Kaarle Nordenstreng and Tapio Varis. 1974. *Television Traffic: A One Way Street*. Reports and Papers on Mass Communication no. 70. Paris: UNESCO; Tapio Varis. 1974. 'Global traffic in television.' *Journal of Communication* 241: 102–109; Tapio Varis. 1984. 'The international flow of television programs.' *Journal of Communication* 34 (1): 143–152; Tapio Varis. 1986. 'Trends in international television flows.' *International Political Science Review* 7: 235–249; Peter Larsen. Ed. 1990. *Import/Export: International Flow of Television Fiction*. Paris: UNESCO; Tapio Varis. 2002. 'The international flow of television programmes.' In *Television: Critical Concepts in Media and Cultural Studies*. Ed. Toby Miller. New York: Routledge; Steven Wildman and Stephen E. Siwek. 1988. *International Trade in Films and Television Programs*. Cambridge, MA: Ballinger; Preben Sepstrup. 1990. *Transnationalization of Television in Western Europe*. London: John Libbey; Els de Bens and Hedwig de Smaele. 2001. 'The inflow of American television fiction on European broadcasting channels revisited.' *European Journal of Communication* 16: 51–76.

20. Colin Hoskins and Rolf Mirius. 1988. 'Reasons for the U.S. domination of the international trade in television programmes.' *Media, Culture & Society* 10: 499–515; Colin Hoskins, Stuart McFadyen, and Adam Finn. 1997. *Global Television and Film: An Introduction to the Economics of*

the Business. Oxford: Oxford University Press. There remains a debate about trends over time outside of the European Union, however; Straubhaar suggests that middle-income economies in Latin America and Asia became more independent of American imports during the 1980s. See Joseph D. Straubhaar. 1991. 'Beyond media imperialism: Asymmetrical interdependence and cultural proximity.' *Critical Studies in Mass Communication* 8: 39–59.

21. It should be noted that the original 1989 EU directive has been revised over the years to take account of technological developments in the audiovisual sector, and further proposals continue to be debated. See Europa. Summaries of Legislation. http://europa.eu/scadplus/leg/en/lvb/l24101.htm. See also Mark Wheeler. 2004. 'Supranational regulation: Television and the European Union.' *European Journal of Communication* 19 (3): 349–369.

22. European Audiovisual Observatory. 2007. *Yearbook 2007*. Strasbourg: Council of Europe.

23. Preben Sepstrup. 1990. *Transnationalization of Television in Western Europe*. London: John Libbey.

24. Peter Larsen. Ed. 1990. *Import/Export: International Flow of Television Fiction*. Paris: UNESCO; Michel Dupagne and David Waterman. 1998. 'Determinants of U.S. Television fiction imports in Western Europe.' *Journal of Broadcasting and Electronic Media* 42 (2): 208–220; Els de Bens and Hedwig de Smaele. 2001. 'The inflow of American television fiction on European broadcasting channels revisited.' *European Journal of Communication* 16: 51–76.

25. European Audiovisual Observatory. 2007. *Yearbook 2007*. Strasbourg: Council of Europe. See also Des Freedman. 2003. 'Who wants to be a millionaire? The politics of television exports.' *Information, Communication and Society*. 6 (1): 24–41.

26. Linda Lee Davis. 2003. 'Cultural proximity on the air in Ecuador: National, regional, television outperforms imported U.S. programming.' In *The Impact of International Television: A Paradigm Shift*. Ed. Michael G. Elasmar. Mahwah, NJ: Lawrence Erlbaum.

27. Michel Dupagne and David Waterman. 1998. 'Determinants of US television fiction imports in Western Europe.' *Journal of Broadcasting and Electronic Media* 42 (2): 208–220.

28. Kai Hafez. 2007. *The Myth of Media Globalization: Why Global Media Is Not Truly Globalized*. Cambridge: Polity Press.

29. Dal Yong Jin. 2007. 'Transformation of the world television system under neoliberal globalization, 1983 to 2003.' *Television and New Media* 8 (3): 179–196; David Ward. 2007. *Television and Public Policy: Change and Continuity in an Era of Global Liberalization*. Mahwah, NJ: Lawrence Erlbaum; Richard Collins. 1998. *From Satellite to Single Market: New Communication Technology and European Public Services Television*. London: Routledge.

30. Motion Picture Association. 2007. '2006 International Theatrical Market.' *Worldwide Market Research and Analysis*. http://www.mpaa.org/International%20Theatrical%20Snapshot.pdf.

31. Colin Hoskins and Rolf Mirius. 1988. 'Reasons for the U.S. domination of the international trade in television programmes.' *Media, Culture & Society* 10: 499–515; Kerry Segrave. 1997. *American Films Abroad: Hollywood's Domination of the World's Movie Screens*. Jefferson, NC: McFarland; Kerry Segrave. 1998. *American Television Abroad: Hollywood's Attempt to Dominate World Television*. London: McFarland; Melvyn Stokes and Richard Maltby. Eds. 2005. *Hollywood Abroad: Audiences and Cultural Exchange*. Berkeley: University of California Press; Michael Tracey and Wendy W. Redal. 1995. 'The new parochialism: The triumph of the populist in the flow of international television.' *Canadian Journal of Communication*, 20: 343–365.

32. Jeanette Steemers. 2004. *Selling Television: British Television in the Global Marketplace*. Berkeley: University of California Press; Paul Rixon. 2006. *American Television on British Screens: A Story of Cultural Interaction*. London: Palgrave.

33. http://www.newscorp.com.

34. Jean K. Chalaby. 2005. *Transnational Television Worldwide: Towards a New Media Order*. London: I. B. Tauris.

35. Jacques Kayser. 1953. *One Week's News: Comparative Study of 17 Major Dailies for a Seven Day Period* Paris: UNESCO; Wilbur Schramm. 1959. *One Day in the World's Press*. Stanford, CA: Stanford University Press; Wilbur Schramm. 1964. *Mass Media and National Development*. Stanford, CA: Stanford University Press; Johan Galtung and Mari Holmboe Ruge. 1965. 'The structure of foreign news.' *Journal of Peace Research* 1: 64–90.

36. Kaarle Nordenstreng and Tapio Varis. 1973. 'The non-homogeneity of the national state and the international flow of communication.' In *Communications Technology and Social Policy*. Ed. George Gerbner, Lawrence Gross, and W. Melody. New York: Wiley; Kaarle Nordenstreng and Tapio Varis. 1974. *Television Traffic: A One Way Street*. Reports and Papers on Mass Communication no. 70. Paris: UNESCO; Tapio Varis. 1974. 'Global traffic in television.' *Journal of Communication* 241: 102–109; Tapio Varis. 1984. 'The international flow of television programs.' *Journal of Communication* 34 (1): 143–152; Tapio Varis. 1986. 'Trends in international television flows.' *International Political Science Review* 7: 235–249; Tapio Varis. 1986. 'Trends in international television flows.' *International Political Science Review* 7: 235–249; Tapio Varis. 2002. 'The international flow of television programmes.' In *Television: Critical Concepts in Media and Cultural Studies*. Ed. Toby Miller. New York: Routledge.

37. Annabelle Sreberny-Mohammadi with Kaarle Nordenstreng, Robert Stevenson, and Frank Ugboajah. Eds. 1984. *Foreign News in the Media:*

International Reporting in Twenty-Nine Countries. Reports and Papers on Mass Communication no. 93. Paris: UNESCO; Robert L. Stevenson and Donald Lewis Shaw. Eds. 1984. *Foreign News and the New World Information Order.* Ames: Iowa State University Press; K. Kyloon Hur. 1984. 'A critical analysis of international news flow research.' Critical Studies in Mass Communication 1: 365–378; Scott M. Cutlip. 1954. 'Content and flow of AP news: From trunk to TTs to reader.' *Journalism Quarterly* 31: 434–446; Robert L. Bishop. 1975. 'How Reuters and AFP Coverage of Africa Compare.' *Journalism Quarterly* 52: 654–662; François Heinderyckx. 1993. 'Television news programmes in Western Europe: A comparative study.' *European Journal of Communication* 8: 425–450; Kaarle Nordenstreng and Tapio Varis. 1974. *Television Traffic: A One Way Street.* Reports and Papers on Mass Communication no. 70. Paris: UNESCO; Tapio Varis 1986. 'Trends in international television flows.' *International Political Science Review* 7: 235–249; Tapio Varis. 1984. 'The international flow of television programs.' *Journal of Communication* 34 (1): 143–152.

38. William H. Meyer. 1989. 'Global news flows: Dependency and neo-imperialism.' *Comparative Political Studies* 22 (3): 243–264; H. Denis Wu. 2000. 'Systematic determinants of international news coverage: A comparison of 38 countries.' *Journal of Communication* 50 (2): 110–130.

39. Council of Europe. 2004. *Transnational Media Concentrations in Europe.* Strasbourg: Council of Europe. http://www.coe.int/t/e/human_rights/media/AP-MD(2004)007_en.pdf.

40. http://www.newscorp.com/index.html.

41. http://www.bertelsmann.com.

42. Olivier Boyd-Barrett. 1980. *The International News Agencies.* London: Constable; Olivier Boyd-Barrett and Daya Kishan Thussu. 1992. *Contraflow in Global News: International and Regional News Exchange Mechanisms.* London: John Libby.

43. Associated Press. 2008. www.ap.org.

44. Associated Press. 2007. *Breaking News: How the Associated Press Has Covered War, Peace, and Everything Else.* Princeton, NJ: Princeton Architectural Press.

45. UNESCO. 2005. *International Flows of Selected Cultural Goods and Services, 1994–2003.* Montreal: UNESCO Institute for Statistics.

46. Ibid.

47. Pippa Norris. 2001. *Digital Divide: Civic Engagement, Information Poverty and the Internet Worldwide.* Cambridge: Cambridge University Press.

48. Albert Moran and Michael Keane. Eds. 2003. *Television Across Asia: Television Industries, Programme Formats and Globalization.* London: Taylor and Francis.

49. Lisa Parks. 2005. *Cultures in Orbit: Satellites and the Televisual.* Durham, NC: Duke University Press; Mamoun Fandy. 2007. *UnCivil War of*

Words: Media and Politics in the Arab World. New York: Praeger; Leo A. Gher and Hussein V. Amin. 1999. 'New and Old Media Access and Ownership in the Arab World.' *Gazette* 61 (1): 59–87.

50. Georgette Wang, Anura Goonasekera, and Jan Servaes. Eds. 2000. *The New Communications Landscape: Demystifying Media Globalization.* London: Routledge.

51. See, e.g., World Bank. 2006. *Information and Communications for Development: Global Trends and Policies.* Washington, DC: World Bank.

52. Stanley D. Brunn and Martin Dodge. 2001. 'Mapping the "worlds" of the World Wide Web: (Re)structuring global commerce through hyperlinks.' *American Behavioral Scientist* 44 (10): 1717–1739; George A. Barnett and Eunjung Sung. 2005. 'Culture and the structure of the international hyperlink network.' *Journal of Computer-Mediated Communication* 11 (1): 217–238; Lori Shumate and Michelle Dewitt. 2008. 'The North/South divide in NGO hyperlink networks.' *Journal of Computer-Mediated Communication* 13 (2): 405–428.

53. Global Reach. http://global-reach.biz/globstats/evol.html.

54. Dal Yong Jin. 2007. 'Reinterpretation of cultural imperialism: Emerging domestic market vs. continuing US dominance.' *Media, Culture & Society* 29 (5): 753–777.

55. Daniel Biltereyst and Philippe Meers. 2000. 'The international *telenovela* debate and the contra-flow argument: a reappraisal.' *Media, Culture & Society* 22 (4): 393; John Sinclair, Elizabeth Jacka, and Stuart Cunningham. Eds. 1996. *New Patterns in Global Television: Peripheral Vision.* Oxford: Oxford University Press.

Chapter 4: Poverty

1. See, e.g., the IREX report on the Media Sustainability Index for Mali, 2006–2007. http://www.irex.org/programs/MSI_Africa/2007/MSI07_mali.pdf. In 2007, the Press Freedom Worldwide Index of Reporters sans Frontières ranked Mali 52 highest out of 169 countries. http://www.rsf.org/article.php3?id_article=24025.

2. International Telecommunication Union. 2008. *Facts and Figures.* http://www.itu.int/ITU-D/connect/africa/2007/bgdmaterial/figures.html.

3. The Web site is www.tombouctou.net. The Mali Telecenter is a pilot project jointly funded by ITU, UNESCO, FAO, and WHO. For details, see http://www.itu.int/ITU-D/univ_access/pilots/.

4. International Telecommunication Union. 2008. *Facts and Figures.* http://www.itu.int/ITU-D/connect/africa/2007/bgdmaterial/figures.html.

5. http://www.irex.org/programs/MSI_Africa/2007/MSI07_mali.pdf. For comparison, Mali is about twice the physical size of Texas.

6. For details, see the SABC corporate Web site, http://www.sabc.co.za.

7. UNESCO. 2005. *International Flows of Selected Cultural Goods and Services, 1994–2003*. Montreal: UNESCO Institute for Statistics.

8. http://www.filmmaker.co.za/readarticle.php?article_id=3049.

9. World Economic Forum. 2007. *Global Information Technology Report, 2007–8*. http://www.insead.edu/v1/gitr/wef/main/home.cfm.

10. Goran Hyden, Michael Leslie, and Folu F. Ogundimu. Eds. 2002. *Media and Democracy in Africa*. Uppsala: Nordiska Afrikainstitutet; International Telecommunication Union. 2008. *African Telecommunication/ICT Indicators 2008: At a Crossroads*. Geneva: ITU.

11. UNDP. 2008. *The Human Development Report, 2007/8: Fighting Climate Change – Human Solidarity in a Divided World*. New York: UNDP / Oxford University Press. http://hdr.undp.org/en/humandev/.

12. Trevor Haywood. 1995. *Info-Rich – Info-Poor: Access and Exchange in the Global Information Society*. London: Bowker-Saur; William Wresch. 1996. *Disconnected: Haves and Have-Nots in the Information Age*. New Brunswick, NJ: Rutgers University Press; Pippa Norris. 2001. *Digital Divide: Civic Engagement, Information Poverty and the Internet Worldwide*. Cambridge: Cambridge University Press; Mark Warschauer. 2004. *Technology and Social Inclusion: Rethinking the Digital Divide*. Cambridge, MA: MIT Press; Jan A. G. M. Van Dijk. 2005. *The Deepening Divide: Inequality in the Information Society*. London: Sage.

13. Pippa Norris. 2001. *Digital Divide: Civic Engagement, Information Poverty and the Internet Worldwide*. Cambridge: Cambridge University Press; Wenhong Chen and Barry Wellman. 2004. 'The global digital divide: Within and between countries.' *IT and Society* 1: 39–45.

14. Mauro F. Guillen and Sandra L. Suarez. 2005. 'Explaining the global digital divide: Economic, political and sociological drivers of cross-national Internet use.' *Social Forces* 88 (4): 681–708.

15. For a discussion of the meaning of these concepts, see Jan A. G. M. Van Dijk. 2005. *The Deepening Divide: Inequality in the Information Society*. London: Sage.

16. Katie Hafner and Matthew Lyon. 1998. *Where Wizards Stay up Late: The Origins of the Internet*. New York: Simon & Schuster; Janet Abbate. 2000. *Inventing the Internet*. Cambridge, MA: MIT Press.

17. http://www.NUA.ie. The estimate of worldwide usage is for June 2000.

18. The ITU estimates that in 2007 there were 1.46 million Internet users. International Communications Union. 2007. *Key Global Telecom Indicators for the World Telecommunication Service Sector*. Geneva: ITU. http://www.itu.int/ITUD/ict/statistics/at_glance/KeyTelecom99.html.

19. Stephen L. Parente and Edward C. Prescott. 2002. *Barriers to Riches*. Cambridge, MA: MIT Press; World Bank. 2006. *Information and Communications for Development: Global Trends and Policies*. Washington, DC: World Bank; Eric Brousseau and Nicolas Curien. Eds. 2007. *Internet and Digital Economics*. Cambridge: Cambridge University Press; Marcus

Franda. 2002. *Launching into Cyberspace: Internet Development and Politics in Five World Regions.* Boulder, CO: Lynne Rienner.

20. World Bank. 2004. *World Development Report: Making Services Work for the Poor.* Washington, DC: World Bank; Shirin Madon. 2004. 'Evaluating the development impact of e-governance initiatives: An explanatory framework.' *Electronic Journal of Information System in Developing Countries* 20 (5).

21. Celia W. Dugger. 2000. 'Connecting rural India to the world.' *New York Times*, 28 May. http://www.nytimes.com/library/tech/yr/mo/biztech/articles/28india.html; Mitsuhiro Kagami, Masatsugu Tsuji, and Emanuele Giovannetti. Eds. 2004. *Information Technology Policy and the Digital Divide: Lessons for Developing Countries.* London: Edward Elgar.

22. Pippa Norris and Dieter Zinnbaue. 2002. *Giving Voice to the Voiceless: Good Governance, Human Development & Mass Communications,* UNDP Human Development Report Office (available at http://hdr.undp.org/docs/publications/background_papers/2002/Norris-Zinnbauer_2002.pdf).

23. United Nations Department of Economic and Social Affairs. 2003. *World Public Sector Report 2003: E-government at the Crossroads.* New York: United Nations.

24. Pippa Norris. 2001. *Digital Divide: Civic Engagement, Information Poverty and the Internet Worldwide.* Cambridge: Cambridge University Press.

25. UNESCO. 1998. *World Communication Report: The Media and Challenges of the New Technologies.* Paris: UNESCO.

26. UNDP. 1999. *Human Development Report 1999,* p. 63. New York: UNDP / Oxford University Press.

27. World Bank. 1999. *World Development Report: Knowledge and Development.* Washington, DC: World Bank; Francisco Rodriguez and Ernest J. Wilson III. 2000. 'Are poor countries losing the Information Revoluton?' The World Bank infoDev Working Paper Series. May. www.infoDev.org/library/wilsonrodriguez.doc.

28. Lisbon European Council. 2000. *An Agenda of Economic and Social Renewal for Europe,* pp. 23–24. European Commission, March. http://europa.eu.int.

29. See, e.g., the G8 Okinawa Charter on Global Information Society, 23 July 2000. http://www.g8kyushu-okinawa.go.jp/w/documents/it1.html.

30. There are numerous cases, but some of the best known include the GrameenPhone microcredit projects, which provide cell phones to villages in Bangladesh, and the One Laptop per Child initiative designed to produce $100 rugged, low-cost computers and educational software for children, led by Nicholas Negroponte at MIT. For details about GrameenPhone, see http://www.grameenphone.com. For the One Laptop per Child project, see http://laptop.org/. For a broader range of

cases and initaiatives, see Angathevar Baskaran and Mammo Muchie. Eds. 2006. *Bridging the Digital Divide: Innovation Systems for ICT in Brazil, China, India, Thailand and Southern Africa*. London: Adonis & Abbey.

31. WSIS. 2003. *Declaration of Principles*. Geneva: WSIS. http://www.itu. int/wsis/docs/geneva/official/dop.html.

32. Partnership on Measuring ICT for Development. 2008. *The Global Information Society: A Statistical View*. Santiago: United Nations.

33. Mark Warschauer. 2004. *Technology and Social Inclusion: Rethinking the Digital Divide*. Cambridge, MA: MIT Press.

34. Jeffrey James. 2008. 'Digital divide complacency: Misconceptions and dangers.' *Information Society* 24 (1): 54–61.

35. International Telecommunication Union. 2006. 'ICT and telecommunications in least developed countries: Midterm review for the decade 2001–2010.' http://www.itu.int/ITU-D/ldc/pdf/ICTand%20TELinLDC-e .pdf.

36. Trevor Haywood. 1995. *Info-Rich – Info-Poor: Access and Exchange in the Global Information Society*. London: Bowker-Saur; William Wresch. 1996. *Disconnected: Haves and Have-Nots in the Information Age*. New Brunswick, NJ: Rutgers University Press; Subbiah Arunachalam. 1999. 'Information and knowledge in the age of electronic communication: A developing country perspective.' *Journal of Information Science* 25 (6): 465–476.

37. Partnership on Measuring ICT for Development. 2008. *The Global Information Society: A Statistical View*. Santiago: United Nations.

38. For the problem arising from 'missing not at random' data, see Patrick E. McKnight, Katherine M. McKnight, Souraya Sidani, and Aurelio Jose Figueredo. 2007. *Missing Data: A Gentle Introduction*. New York: Guilford Press.

39. Andrew Puddenphatt. 2007. *Defining Indicators of Media Development: Background Paper*. Paris: UNESCO. http://portal.unesco.org/ci/en/ files/26032/12058560693media_indicators_framework_en.pdf/media_ indicators_framework_en.pdf.

40. World Economic Forum. 2007. *Global Information Technology Report, 2007–8*. http://www.insead.edu/v1/gitr/wef/main/home.cfm.

41. For a discussion, see Karine Barzilai-Nahon. 2006. 'Gaps and bits: Conceptualizing measurements for digital divide/s.' *Information Society* 22 (5): 269–278.

42. The Pew Internet and American Life Project. 1 January 2008. 'Increased use of video-sharing sites.' http://www.pewinternet.org/pdfs/Pew_ Videosharing_memo_Jan08.pdf.

43. Subscriber identity module (SIM) cards are issued by cellular service providers to charge calls to user's accounts. Ewan Sutherland. 2008. 'Counting mobile phones, SIM cards & customers.' LINK Centre. Available

from http://www.itu.int/ITU-D/ict/statistics/material/sutherland-mobile-numbers.pdf.

44. John Bongaarts. 2001. 'Household size and composition in the developing world in the 1990s.' *Population Studies* 55 (3): 263–279.

45. Wi-Max is important for development because it is a new 802.16 IEEE standard designed for point-to-point and point-to-multipoint wireless broadband access that is cheaper, smaller, simpler, and easier to use than any existing broadband option (such as DSL, cable, fiber, 3G wireless), and it bypasses the existing wired infrastructure and legacy service providers (i.e., the telephone and cable companies).

46. Jeffrey James. 2008. 'Digital divide complacency: Misconceptions and dangers.' *Information Society* 24 (1): 54–61.

47. EuroStat. 2007. 'Internet usage in 2007 households and individuals.' http://epp.eurostat.ec.europa.eu; for the EU policy background, see EuroActiv. http://www.euractiv.com/en/infosociety/bridging-digital-divide-eu-policies/article-132315.

48. See OECD. 2007. 'Communications in the emerging BRICS economies.' In *Communications Outlook, 2007*, chapter 9. Paris: OECD. Note that 'smart' phones are defined as a class of handsets with a mobile operating system such as Symbian, Microsoft OS, RIM, or Palm, currently exemplified by the iPhone, BlackBerry Curve, and Sony Ericsson's P990i or Nokia's E61, Moto Q, and Palm Treo 680. These typically combine some of the features of a PDA with a cell phone handset, such as a calendar, GPS navigator, document handling software, music player, and camera for photo or video capabilities. In 2006, the United States lagged behind some European countries in the adoption of smartphones. See http://telephia.com/html/Smartphonepress_release_template.html.

49. International Telecommunication Union. 2008. *Facts and Figures.* http://www.itu.int/ITU-D/connect/africa/2007/bgdmaterial/figures.html.

50. George A. Barnett and Young Choi. 1995. 'Physical distance and language as determinants of the international telecommunications network.' *International Political Science Review* 16: 249–265; George A. Barnett, T. Jacobson, Young Choi, and S. Sun-Miller. 1996. 'An examination of the international telecommunications network.' *Journal of International Communication* 32: 19–43; George A. Barnett. 2001. 'A longitudinal analysis of the international telecommunication network, 1978–1996.' *American Behavioral Scientist* 44: 1638–1655; George A. Barnett, Joseph T. G. Salisbury, C. Kim, and A. Langhorne. 1999. 'Globalization and international communication networks: An examination of monetary, telecommunications, and trade networks.' *Journal of International Communication.* 62: 7–49.

51. ITU World Telecommunications / ICT Indicators Database.

52. International Telecommunication Union. 2008. *World Summit on the Information Society Stocktaking, 2008.* Geneva: ITU. http://www.itu.int/wsis/stocktaking/index.html.

53. Nielsen Mobile. July 2008. *Critical Mass: The Worldwide State of the Mobile Web*. http://www.nielsenmobile.com/documents/CriticalMass.pdf.

54. Ewan Sutherland. 2008. *Counting Mobile Phones, SIM Cards & Customers*. LINK Centre. Available from http://www.itu.int/ITU-D/ict/statistics/material/sutherland-mobile-numbers.pdf.

55. International Telecommunication Union. 2008. *Facts and Figures*. Geneva: ITU. http://www.itu.int.

56. Phillip G. Tichenor, George A. Donohue, and Clarice Olien. 1970. 'Mass media flow and differential growth of knowledge.' *Public Opinion Quarterly* 34: 159–170. The concept has been applied in many studies; see, e.g., Thomas Holbrook. 2002. 'Presidential campaigns and the knowledge gap.' *Political Communication* 19: 437–454.

57. John Horrigan. 2008. 'Mobile access to data and information.' March. Washington, DC: Pew Internet and American Life Project. http://www.pewinternet.org/pdfs/PIP_Mobile.Data.Access.pdf. For an earlier study, see Scott L. Althaus and David Tewksbury, 2000. 'Patterns of Internet and traditional news media use in a networked community.' *Political Communication* 17 (1): 21–46.

58. Pippa Norris. 2000. *A Virtuous Circle: Political Communications in Post-Industrial Democracies*. Cambridge: Cambridge University Press.

59. NTIA. 2000. *Falling Through the Net*. Washington, D.C.: U.S. Department of Commerce. http://search.ntia.doc.gov/pdf/fttn00.pdf.

60. NTIA. 1999. *Falling Through the Net*. Washington, DC: U.S. Department of Commerce. www.ntia.doc.gov.ntiahome/fttn99; NTIA. 2000. *Falling Through the Net*. Washington, DC: U.S. Department of Commerce. http://search.ntia.doc.gov/pdf/fttn00.pdf.

61. Steven P. Martin. 2003. 'Is the digital divide really closing? A critique of inequality measurement in "A Nation Online."' *IT & Society* 1 (4): 1–13.

62. OECD. 2000. *Information Technology Outlook*, pp. 85–88. Paris: OECD. National studies summarized in this report have demonstrated variations in the use of PCs by income, education, and age and household size in Canada, Australia, and Finland. See also the Australian Bureau of Statistics. *Household Use of Information Technology, Australia*. http://www.abs.gov.au/ausstats. For a discussion, see also Brian D. Loader. Ed. 1998. *Cyberspace Divide: Equality, Agency and Policy in the Information Society*. London: Routledge.

63. David Resnick. 1998. 'Politics on the Internet: The normalization of cyberspace.' In *The Politics of Cyberspace*. Ed. Chris Toulouse and Timothy W. Luke. New York: Routledge; David Birdsell, Douglas Muzio, David Krane, and Amy Cottreau. 1998. 'Web users are looking more like America.' *Public Perspective* 9 (3): 33; Michael Margolis and David Resnick. 2000. *Politics as Usual: The Cyberspace 'Revolution.'* Thousand Oaks, CA: Sage.

64. The Pew Internet and American Life Project. 'Usage over time.' Consulted June 2008. http://www.pewinternet.org/trends.asp. See also Hioshi Ono and Madeline Zavodny. 2003. 'Gender and the Internet.' *Social Science Quarterly* 84: 111–121.

65. See, e.g., Hioshi Ono and Madeline Zavodny. 2007. 'Digital inequality: A five country comparison using micro-data.' *Social Science Research* 36: 1135–1155; Jan A. G. M. Van Dijk. 2005. *The Deepening Divide: Inequality in the Information Society*. London: Sage.

66. For a useful literature review, see Liangzhi Yu. 2006. 'Understanding information inequality: Making sense of the literature of the information and digital divides.' *Journal of Librarianship and Information Science* 38 (4): 229–252; Mauro F. Guillen and Sandra L. Suarez. 2005. 'Explaining the global digital divide: Economic, political and sociological drivers of cross-national Internet use.' *Social Forces* 88 (4): 681–708.

67. Liangzhi Yu. 2006. 'Understanding information inequality: Making sense of the literature of the information and digital divides.' *Journal of Librarianship and Information Science* 38 (4): 229–252.

68. See, e.g., Thomas Afullo. 2000. 'Global information and Africa: The telecommunications infrastructure for cyberspace.' *Library Management* 21 (4): 205–13; Mark Warschauer. 2004. *Technology and Social Inclusion: Rethinking the Digital Divide*. Cambridge, MA: MIT Press; Eszter Hargittai. 1999. 'Weaving the Western Web: Explaining differences in Internet connectivity among OECD countries.' *Telecommunications Policy* 23 (10–11): 701–718; Pippa Norris. 2001. *Digital Divide: Civic Engagement, Information Poverty and the Internet Worldwide*. Cambridge: Cambridge University Press; Mauro F. Guillen and Sandra L. Suarez. 2005. 'Explaining the global digital divide: Economic, political and sociological drivers of cross-national Internet use.' *Social Forces* 88 (4): 681–708.

69. Trevor Haywood. 1995. *Info-Rich – Info-Poor: Access and Exchange in the Global Information Society*. London: Bowker-Saur; William Wresch. 1996. *Disconnected: Haves and Have-Nots in the Information Age*. New Brunswick, NJ: Rutgers University Press.

70. For a discussion, see Pippa Norris. 2001. *Digital Divide: Civic Engagement, Information Poverty and the Internet Worldwide*. Cambridge: Cambridge University Press.

71. Central Statistical Agency. 2000. *Ethiopia Demographic and Health Survey, 2000*. Central Statistical Agency, Addis Abba, Ethiopia. http://www.measuredhs.com/pubs/pdf/FR118/00FrontMatter.pdf. Across sub-Saharan Africa, excluding Africa, about 5% of the rural population has an electricity supply. International Telecommunication Union. 'Measuring village ICT in Sub-Saharan Africa.' http://www.itu.int/ITUD/ict/statistics/material/Africa_Village_ICT_2007.pdf.

72. Reporters sans Frontières. 2006. *Annual World Press Freedom Index*. www.rsf.org.

73. Isaiah Berlin. 1958. *Two Concepts of Liberty: An Inaugural Lecture Delivered Before the University of Oxford on 31 October 1958*. Oxford: Clarendon Press.
74. International Telecommunication Union. 2008. *Facts and Figures*. Geneva: ITU. http://www.itu.int.
75. Ibid.
76. For more details, see Pippa Norris. 2001. *Digital Divide: Civic Engagement, Information Poverty and the Internet Worldwide*. Cambridge: Cambridge University Press; Mark Warschauer. 2004. *Technology and Social Inclusion: Rethinking the Digital Divide*. Cambridge, MA: MIT Press; Jan A. G. M. Van Dijk. 2005. *The Deepening Divide: Inequality in the Information Society*. London: Sage.

Chapter 5: Classifying Societies

1. UNCTAD. 2008. *Secretary-General's High Level Panel on the Creative Economy and Industries for Development*. Accra, Ghana: United Nations. TD (XII)/BP/4 April 2008; UNESCO. 2005. *International Flows of Selected Cultural Goods and Services, 1994–2003*. Montreal: UNESCO Institute for Statistics.
2. For the idea of cosmopolitanism, see Ulf Hannerz. 1990. 'Cosmopolitans and locals in world culture.' In *Global Culture: Nationalism, Globalization and Modernity*. Ed. Mike Featherstone. London: Sage; John Tomlinson. *Globalization and Culture*. Chicago: University of Chicago Press; Steven Vertovec and Robin Cohen. Eds. 2002. *Conceiving Cosmopolitanism: Theory, Context and Practice*. Oxford: Oxford University Press.
3. Axel Dreher, Noel Gaston, and Pim Martens. 2008. *Measuring Globalisation: Gauging Its Consequences*. New York: Springer. http://globalization.kof.ethz.ch/.
4. For more methodological details and results, see Freedom House. 2007. *Global Press Freedom, 2007*. www.freedomhouse.org. The IREX Media Sustainability Index provides another set of indicators (http://www.irex.org/resources/index.asp). The Media Sustainability Index benchmarks the conditions for independent media in a more limited range of countries across Europe, Eurasia, the Middle East, and North Africa. Unfortunately, the IREX index does not contain a sufficient number of cases worldwide to provide a further cross-check for this study.
5. Fredrick S. Siebert, Theodore Peterson, and Wilbur Schramm. 1956. *Four Theories of the Press*. Urbana: University of Illinois Press.
6. Pippa Norris. 2000. *A Virtuous Circle: Political Communications in Post-Industrial Democracies*. Cambridge: Cambridge University Press; Richard Gunther and Anthony Mughan. Eds. 2000. *Democracy and the Media: A Comparative Perspective*. Cambridge: Cambridge University Press.
7. Michael Schudson. 2002. 'The news media as political institutions.' *Annual Review of Political Science* 5: 249–269.

8. Denis McQuail. 1994. *Mass Communication Theory*, 3rd ed. London: Sage; Lee B. Becker, Tudor Vlad, and Nancy Nusser. 2007. 'An evaluation of press freedom indicators.' *International Communication Gazette* 69 (1): 5–28.

9. Daniel C. Hallin and Paolo Mancini. 2004. *Comparing Media Systems*. Cambridge: Cambridge University Press.

10. Denis McQuail. 1994. *Mass Communication Theory*, 3rd ed. London: Sage.

11. Richard Gunther and Anthony Mughan. Eds. 2000. *Democracy and the Media: A Comparative Perspective*. Cambridge: Cambridge University Press; Mary Kelly, Gianpietro Mazzoleni, and Denis McQuail. Eds. 2004. *The Media in Europe*. London: Sage; Frank Esser and Barbara Pfetsch. Eds. 2004. *Comparing Political Communication: Theories, Cases, and Challenges*. Cambridge: Cambridge University Press.

12. Goran Hyden, Michael Leslie, and Folu F. Ogundimu. Eds. 2002. *Media and Democracy in Africa*. Uppsala: Nordiska Afrikainstitutet; Katrin Voltmer. Ed. 2006. *Mass Media and Political Communication in New Democracies*. London: Routledge.

13. See the review by Andrew Puddenphatt. 2007. *Defining Indicators of Media Development: Background Paper*. Paris: UNESCO.

14. David Banisar. 2006. *Freedom of Information Around the World, 2006: A Global Survey of Access to Government Records Laws*. www. freedominfo.org; John M. Ackerman and Irma E. Sandoval-Ballesteros. 2006. 'The global explosion of freedom of information laws.' *Administrative Law Review* 581: 85–130.

15. Simeon Djankov, Caralee McLiesh, Tatiana Nenova, and Andrei Shleifer. 2003. 'Who owns the media?' *Journal of Law and Economics* 462 (3): 341–382.

16. See, e.g., Timothy Besley and Andrea Prat. 2006. 'Handcuffs for the grabbing hand? Media capture and government accountability.' *American Economic Review* 96 (3): 720–736; Aymo Brunetti and Beatrice Weder. 2003. 'A free press is bad news for corruption.' *Journal of Public Economics* 87: 1801–1824; Sebastian Freillea, M. Emranul Haque, and Richard Kneller. 2007. 'A contribution to the empirics of press freedom and corruption.' *Europäische Zeitschrift für politische Ökonomie* 23 (4): 838–862.

17. See note 4 to this chapter.

18. For details of the methodology and annual rankings, see Reporters sans Frontières. 2006. *Annual World Press Freedom Index*. www.rsf.org.

19. For details of the methodology and annual rankings, see ibid.

20. Lee B. Becker, Tudor Vlad, and Nancy Nusser. 2007. 'An evaluation of press freedom indicators.' *International Communication Gazette* 69 (1): 5–28. Moreover, Becker et al. found that IREX's Media Sustainability Index, covering 20 countries in 2001–2003, was also strongly correlated

($R = .72–.91$) with the Freedom House and the Reporters sans Frontières ratings. Only the Committee to Protect Journalist's tally of attacks on the press differed in their evaluations from the other three indices.

21. Further analysis revealed that replication of the core regression models in this study using the Reporters sans Frontières classification suggests that the results remain robust and consistent regardless of which measure of press freedom is used, which is hardly surprising given the strong intercorrelation of both measures.

22. Pippa Norris. 2008. *Driving Democracy: Do Power-Sharing Institutions Work?* chapter 4. Cambridge: Cambridge University Press.

23. David Held, Anthony McGrew, David Goldblatt, and Jonathan Perraton. 1999. *Global Transformations: Politics, Economics, and Culture.* Stanford, CA: Stanford University Press.

24. A. T. Kearney. 2007. 'The Globalization Index.' *Foreign Policy*, November/December. http://www.foreignpolicy.com/story/cms.php?story_id= 3995. More technical details and previous reports are available at: http://www.atkearney.com/main.taf?p=5,4,1,127.

25. For more details, see Axel Dreher, Noel Gaston, Noel, and Pim Martens. 2008. *Measuring Globalisation: Gauging Its Consequences.* New York: Springer. Axel Dreher. 2006. 'Does globalization affect growth?' *Applied Economics* 38 (10): 1091–1110. For methodological and technical details, see http://globalization.kof.ethz.ch/.

26. David Held, Anthony McGrew, David Goldblatt, and Jonathan Perraton. 1999. *Global Transformations: Politics, Economics, and Culture.* Stanford, CA: Stanford University Press.

27. David Dollar. 1992. 'Outward-oriented developing economies really do grow more rapidly: Evidence from 95 LDCs, 1976–1985.' *Economic Development and Cultural Change* 40: 523; David Dollar and Aart Kray. 2001. *Trade, Growth and Poverty.* Washington, DC: World Bank Discussion Paper; Axel Dreher. 2006. 'Does globalization affect growth?' *Applied Economics* 38 (10): 1091–1110; B. Stallings. 2007. 'The globalization of capital flows: Who benefits?' *Annals of the American Academy of Political and Social Science* 610: 202–216.

28. Jing Gu, John Humphrey, and Dirk Messner. 2008. 'Global governance and developing countries: The implications of the rise of China.' *World Development* 36: 274–292; Rafiq Dossani and Martin Kenney. 2007. 'The next wave of globalization: Relocating service provision to India.' *World Development* 35 (5): 772–791.

29. A. T. Kearney. 2007. 'The Globalization Index.' *Foreign Policy*, November/December. http://www.foreignpolicy.com/story/cms.php?story_id= 3995.

30. See, e.g., Kenneth A. Reinert. 2007. 'Ethiopia in the world economy: Trade, private capital flows, and migration.' *Africa Today* 53 (3): 65–89.

31. David Held, Anthony McGrew, David Goldblatt, and Jonathan Perraton. 1999. *Global Transformations: Politics, Economics, and Culture*, chapter 7. Stanford, CA: Stanford University Press.
32. See Werner A. Meier. 2004. 'Switzerland.' In *The Media in Europe: The Euromedia Handbook*. Ed. Mary Kelly, Gianpietro Mazzoleni, and Denis McQuail. London: Sage.
33. Eurodata-TV/European Audiovisual Observatory.
34. Reporters sans Frontières. 2006. *Worldwide Press Freedom Index 2006*. www.rsf.org.
35. Human Rights Watch. 2008. *Submission to the Human Rights Council*. April 7, 2008. http://hrw.org/english/docs/2008/04/11/global18513.htm.
36. Sean Jacobs. 2002. 'How good is the South African media for democracy? Mapping the South African public sphere after apartheid.' *African and Asian Studies* 1 (4): 279–302; Keyan Tomaselli. 2000. 'South African media, 1994–7: Globalizing via political economy.' In *De-Westernizing Media Studies*. Ed. James Curran and Myung Park. London: Routledge; Goran Hyden, Michael Leslie, and Folu F. Ogundimu. Eds. 2002. *Media and Democracy in Africa*. Uppsala: Nordiska Afrikainstitutet; Anton Harber. 2004. 'Reflections on journalism in the transition to democracy.' *Ethics & International Affairs* 18 (3): 79–87.
37. See, e.g., Gholam Khiabany and Annabelle Sreberny. 2001. 'The Iranian press and the continuing struggle over civil society, 1998–2000.' *Gazette* 63 (2–3): 203–223; Stanford D. Mukasa. 2003. 'Press and politics in Zimbabwe.' *African Studies Quarterly: The Online Journal of African Studies* 7 (2–3).
38. Reporters sans Frontières. 2007. *Syria Annual Report, 2007*. http://www.rsf.org/country-43.php3?id_mot=143&Valider=OK.
39. Joel Campagna. 2001. 'Press freedom reports: Stop signs.' Committee to Protect Journalists. http://www.cpj.org/Briefings/2001/Syria_sept01/Syria_sept01.html.
40. Human Rights Watch. http://hrw.org/english/docs/2007/10/08/syria17024.htm.
41. Freedom House. 2008. *Global Press Freedom, 2008*. http://www.freedomhouse.org/uploads/fop08/FOTP2008Tables.pdf.
42. Reporters sans Frontières. 2007. 'At least five journalists arrested in Rangoon, including Japanese daily's correspondent.' 30 September. http://www.rsf.org/article.php3?id_article=23837.
43. Committee to Protect Journalists. 2008. 'Foreign media clampdown spreads in China.' 19 March. http://www.cpj.org/news/2008/asia/china19mar08na.html; Committee to Protect Journalists. 2007. *Falling Short: As the China Olympics Approaches, China Falters on Press Freedom*. Committee to Protect Journalists. http://www.cpj.org/Briefings/2007/Falling_Short/China/index.html.
44. Leonard L. Chu. 1994. 'Continuity and change in China media reform.' *Journal of Communication* 44 (3): 4–21; Richard Cullen and Hua Ling

Fu. 1998. 'Seeking theory from experience: Media regulation in China.' *Democratization* 5: 155–78; Yuezhi Zhao. 1998. *Media, Market, and Democracy in China: Between the Party Line and the Bottom Line.* Urbana: University of Illinois Press; Jing Gu, John Humphrey, and Dirk Messner. 2008. 'Global governance and developing countries: The implications of the rise of China.' *World Development* 36: 274–292.

45. Shanthi Kalathil and Taylor C. Boas. 2001. *The Internet and State Control in Authoritarian Regimes: China, Cuba and the Counterrevolution.* Global Policy Program no. 21. Washington, DC: Carnegie Endowment for International Peace; John Palfrey, Jonathan Zittrain, Ron Deibert, and Rafal Rohozinski. 2008. *Access Denied: The Practice and Policy of Global Internet Filtering.* Cambridge, MA: MIT Press.

46. Ellen Mickiewicz. 1999. *Changing Channels: Television and the Struggle for Power in Russia.* Durham, NC: Duke University Press; Jonathan Becker. 2004. 'Lessons from Russia: A neo-authoritarian media system.' *European Journal of Communication* 19 (2): 139–163; Hedwig de Smaele. 2004. 'Limited access to information as a means of censorship in post-Communist Russia.' *Javnost – The Public* 11(2): 65–81; Anna Amelina. 2007. 'Evolution of the media and media control in post-Soviet Russia.' *Soziale Welt-Zeitschrift für Sozialwissenschaftliche Forschung und Praxis* 58 (2): 163; Christopher Walker. 2007. *Muzzling the Media: The return of censorship in the Commonwealth of Independent States.* Washington, DC: Freedom House. http://www.freedomhouse.org/uploads/press_release/muzzlingthemedia_15june07.pdf.

47. Rose Marie Beck and Frank Wittmann. Eds. 2004. *African Media Cultures: Transdisciplinary Perspectives.* Köln: Rüdiger Köppe Verlag; Goran Hyden, Michael Leslie, and Folu F. Ogundimu. Eds. 2002. *Media and Democracy in Africa.* Uppsala: Nordiska Afrikainstitutet.

48. UNDP. 2008. *Human Development Report, 2007/8: Fighting Climate Change – Human Solidarity in a Divided World,* table 1. New York: UNDP / Oxford University Press.

49. Fredrick S. Siebert, Theodore Peterson, and Wilbur Schramm. 1956. *Four Theories of the Press.* Urbana: University of Illinois Press.

50. Daniel C. Hallin and Paolo Mancini. 2004. *Comparing Media Systems.* Cambridge: Cambridge University Press.

51. See, e.g., Thomas L. Friedman. 2007. *The World Is Flat.* New York: Picador / Farrar, Straus and Giroux; Jagdish Bhagwati. 2007. *In Defence of Globalization.* New York: Oxford University Press.

Chapter 6: Citizens: National and Cosmopolitan Identities

1. Herbert J. Schiller. 1992. *Mass Communication and American Empire,* 2nd ed. Boulder, CO: Westview Press; Edward S. Herman and Robert W. McChesney. 1997. *The Global Media: The Missionaries of Global Capitalism.* Washington, DC: Cassell.

2. Joseph S. Nye, Jr. 2004. *Soft Power: The Means to Success in World Politics.* New York: Public Affairs; Joseph S. Nye, Jr. 2008. 'Public diplomacy and soft power.' *Annals of the American Academy of Political and Social Science* 616: 94–109.

3. D. Anable. 2006. 'The role of Georgia's media – and Western aid – in the Rose Revolution.' *Harvard International Journal of Press-Politics* 11 (3): 7–43.

4. Joan E. Grusec and Paul D. Hastings. 2007. (Eds). *Handbook of Socialization: Theory and Research.* New York: Guilford Press.

5. For a theoretical discussion of the debate, see David Held and Anthony McGrew. 2007. *Globalization/Anti-Globalization: Beyond the Great Divide*, chapter 3. Cambridge: Polity Press.

6. Ken'ichi Ohmae. 1995. *The End of the Nation State.* New York: Free Press.

7. See the overview of the literature provided by Jens Bartelson. 2000. 'Three concepts of globalization.' *International Sociology* 15(2): 180–196.

8. Anthony Giddens. 1990. *The Consequences of Modernity.* Cambridge: Polity Press.

9. David Held, Anthony McGrew, David Goldblatt, and Jonathan Perraton. 1999. *Global Transformations: Politics, Economics, and Culture*, chapter 7. Stanford, CA: Stanford University Press.

10. *Economist.* 18 October 2007. 'Lessons of the fall.' http://www.economist.com/displaystory.cfm?story_id=9988865.

11. Steffen Mau, Jan Mewes, and Ann Zimmernann. 2008. 'Cosmopolitan attitudes through transnational social practices?' *Global Networks* 8 (1): 1–24.

12. Paul Hirst and Grahame Thompson. 1996. *Globalization in Question: The International Economy and the Possibilities of Governance.* Cambridge: Polity Press.

13. Anthony Smith. 1995. 'Towards a global culture?' In *Global Culture.* Ed. Michael Featherstone. London: Sage.

14. Michael Mann. 1997. 'Has globalization ended the rise and rise of the nation-state?' *Review of International Political Economy* 4: 472.

15. David Hooson. 1994. *Geography and National Identity.* Oxford: Blackwell.

16. Manuel Castells. 2004. *The Power of Identity*, 2nd ed., p. 72. Oxford: Blackwell.

17. See Takashi Inoguchi and Ian Marsh. Eds. 2007. *Globalisation, Public Opinion and the State: Western Europe and East and Southeast Asia.* London: Routledge. For previous work by one of the authors, see Pippa Norris. 2001. 'Global governance and cosmopolitan citizens.' In *Governance in a Globalizing World.* Ed. Joseph S. Nye and John Donahue. Washington, DC: Brookings Institution Press; Pippa Norris. 2008. 'Confidence in the United Nations: Cosmopolitan and nationalistic attitudes.'

In *The Global System, Democracy and Values*. Ed. Yilmaz Esmer and Thorleif Pettersson. Uppsala: Uppsala University Press.

18. For a challenge to this view, however, emphasizing that the public sphere in Europe remains firmly national, see Philip Schlesinger. 2007. 'A cos mopolitan temptation.' *European Journal of Communication* 22 (4): 413–426.

19. S. Ciftci. 2005. 'Treaties, collective responses and the determinants of aggregate support for European integration.' *European Union Politics* 6 (4): 469–492.

20. Richard C. Eichenberg and Russell J. Dalton. 2007. 'Post-Maastricht blues: The transformation of citizen support for European integration, 1973–2004.' *Acta Politica* 42 (2–3): 128–152.

21. Sophie Duchesne and André-Paul Frognier. 1995. 'Is there a European identity?' In *Public Opinion and Internationalized Governance*. Ed. Oskar Niedermayer and Richard Sinnott. Oxford: Oxford University Press; Angelika Scheuer. 1999. 'A political community?' In *Political Representation and Legitimacy in the European Union*. Ed. Hermann Schmitt and Jacques Thomassen. Oxford: Oxford University Press; Thomas Risse. 2001. 'A European identity? Europeanization and the evolution of nation-state identities.' In *Transforming Europe*. Ed. Maria G. Cowles, James Caporaso, and Thomas Risse. Ithaca, NY: Cornell University Press. See also Brian Nelson, David Roberts, and Walter Veit. Eds. 1992. *The Idea of Europe: Problems of National and Transnational Identity*. Oxford: Berg; Lauren M. McLaren. 2005. *Identity, Interests and Attitudes to European Integration*. London: Palgrave Macmillan.

22. Liesbet Hooghe and Gary Marks. 2005. 'Calculation, community and cues: Public opinion on European integration.' *European Union Politics* 6 (4): 419–443; see also Lauren M. McLaren. 2005. *Identity, Interests and Attitudes to European Integration*. London: Palgrave Macmillan.

23. The most thorough empirical work on orientations within Europe from 1973 to 1990 using the Eurobarometer surveys can be found in Oskar Niedermayer and Richard Sinnott. 1995. *Public Opinion and Internationalized Governance*. Oxford: Oxford University Press. For more recent updates of trends see, e.g., European Commission. June 2008. *Eurobarometer 69: Public Opinion in the European Union. First Results* (fieldwork March–May 2008), http://ec.europa.eu/public_opinion/archives/eb/eb69/eb_69_first_en.pdf.

24. Pippa Norris. 2003. 'The political regime.' In *Political Representation and Legitimacy in the European Union*. Ed. Hermann Schmitt and Jacques Thomassen. Oxford: Oxford University Press. See also Mattei Dogan. 1994. 'The decline of nationalism within Western Europe.' *Comparative Politics* 23 (3): 281–305.

25. Geoffrey Evans. 1999. 'Europe: A new electoral cleavage?' In *Critical Elections: British Parties and Voters in Long-Term Perspective*.

Ed. Geoffrey Evans and Pippa Norris. London: Sage. Geoffrey Evans. 1998. 'How Britain views the EU.' In *British Social Attitudes: the 15th Report*. Ed. Roger Jowell et al. Aldershot: Dartmouth/SCPR.

26. Steffen Mau, Jan Mewes and Ann Zimmernann. 2008. 'Cosmopolitan attitudes through transnational social practices?' *Global Networks* 8 (1): 1–24.

27. Marcel Lubbers and Peer Scheepers. 2007. 'Explanations of political Euroscepticism at the individual, regional and national levels.' *European Societies* 9 (4): 643–669.

28. Jürgen Maier and Berthold Rittberger. 2008. 'Shifting Europe's boundaries: Mass media, public opinion and the enlargement of the EU.' *European Union Politics* 9 (2): 243–267.

29. Philip Evert. 1995. 'NATO, the European Community, and the United Nations.' In *Public Opinion and Internationalized Governance*. Ed. Oskar Niedermayer and Richard Sinnott. Oxford: Oxford University Press.

30. Pippa Norris. 2008. 'Confidence in the United Nations: Cosmopolitan and nationalistic attitudes.' In *The Global System, Democracy and Values*. Ed. Yilmaz Esmer and Thorleif Pettersson. Uppsala: Uppsala University Press.

31. Benjamin Page and Robert Shapiro. 1992. *The Rational Public: Fifty Years of Trends in American's Policy Preferences*. Chicago: University of Chicago Press; Richard Sobel. 2001. *The Impact of Public Opinion on American Foreign Policy Since Vietnam*. New York: Oxford University Press; Oli R. Holsti. 2004. *Public Opinion and American Foreign Policy*, rev. ed. Ann Arbor: University of Michigan Press; Edwards C. Luck. 1999. *Mixed Messages: American Politics and International Organizations, 1919–1999*. Washington, DC: Brookings Institution Press.

32. For example, the Pew Research Center for the People and the Press has carried out a dozen value surveys over the past two decades, and it reports that 90% of Americans have consistently agreed with the statement "I am very patriotic." See the Pew Research Center for the People and the Press. 2007. *Trends in Political Values and Core Attitudes: 1987–2007*. Washington, DC. http://people-press.org/reports/pdf/312.pdf.

33. Pippa Norris. 2008. 'Confidence in the United Nations: Cosmopolitan and nationalistic attitudes.' In *The Global System, Democracy and Values*. Ed. Yilmaz Esmer and Thorleif Pettersson. Uppsala: Uppsala University Press; Jai Kwan Jung. 2008. 'Growing supranational identities in a globalizing world? A multilevel analysis of the World Values Surveys.' *European Journal of Political Research* 47: 578–609.

34. Sam Schueth and John O'Laughlin. 2008. 'Belonging to the world: Cosmopolitanism in geographic contexts.' *Geoforum* 39 (2): 926–941; Jai Kwan Jung. 2008. 'Growing supranational identities in a globalizing world? A multilevel analysis of the World Values Surveys.' *European Journal of Political Research* 47: 578–609.

35. On Australia, see Ian Woodward, Zlato Skrbis, and Clive Bean. 2008. 'Attitudes towards globalization and cosmopolitanism: Cultural diversity, personal consumption and the national economy.' *British Journal of Sociology* 59 (2): 207–226. On Sweden, see Anna Olofsson and Susanna Ohman. 2007. 'Cosmopolitans and locals: An empirical investigation of transnationalism.' *Current Sociology* 55 (6): 877–895. On Britain, see James Tilley and Anthony Heath. 2007. 'The decline of British national pride.' *British Journal of Sociology* 58: 661–678.

36. Tilley and Heath. 2007. 'The decline of British national pride.' *British Journal of Sociology* 58: 661–678.

37. Jai Kwan Jung. 2008. 'Growing supranational identities in a globalizing world? A multilevel analysis of the World Values Surveys.' *European Journal of Political Research* 47: 578–609.

38. Ronald Inglehart and Pippa Norris. 2003. *Rising Tide: Gender Equality and Cultural Change Around the World.* Cambridge: Cambridge University Press; Ronald Inglehart and Christian Welzel. 2005. *Modernization, Cultural Change and Democracy.* Cambridge: Cambridge University Press.

39. There is an extensive theoretical literature on the concepts of nationalism and national identity. See, e.g., Michael Ignatieff. 1993. *Blood and Belonging.* London: Chatto and Windus; Benedict Anderson. 1996. *Imagined Communities: Reflections on the Origin and Spread of Nationalism.* London: Verso; Michael Billig. 1995. *Banal Nationalism.* London: Sage; Earnest Gellner. 1983. *Nations and Nationalism.* Oxford: Blackwell.

40. Anthony D. Smith. 1991. *National Identity*, chapter 7. London: Penguin.

41. For a discussion, see Ulrich Beck. 2006. *The Cosmopolitan Vision.* Cambridge: Polity Press; Ulrich Beck and Natan Sznaider. 2006. 'Unpacking cosmopolitanism for the humanities and social sciences: A research agenda.' *British Journal of Sociology* 57 (1): 1–23; Ulf Hannerz. 1990. 'Cosmopolitans and locals in world culture.' In *Global Culture: Nationalism, Globalization and Modernity.* Ed. Michael Featherstone. London: Sage.

42. Pew Global Surveys, http://pewglobal.org/; Chicago Council on Foreign Relations, http://www.ccfr.org/publications/opinion/main.html; World Public Opinion surveys, http://www.worldpublicopinion.org. See also Benjamin I. Page and Jason Barabas. 2000. 'Foreign policy gaps between citizens and leaders.' *International Studies Quarterly* 44: 339–364.

43. See, e.g., Andrew Kohut and Bruce Stokes. 2006. *America Against the World.* New York: Times Books; see also http://www.americans-world.org/index.cfm.

44. For studies based on the ISSP module on nationalism, see, e.g., Pippa Norris. 1999. 'Global communications and cultural identities.' *Harvard International Journal of Press-Politics* 4 (4): 1–7; Stefan Svallfors. 1999. 'National differences in national identities? An introduction to the International Social Survey Program.' In *Modern Society and Values: A*

Comparative Analysis Based on ISSP Project, pp. 3–14. Ed. Niko Tos, Peter P. Mohler, and Brina Malnar. Ljubljana: University of Ljubljana.

45. Richard Sinnott. 2006. 'An evaluation of the measurement of national, sub-national and supra-national identity in cross-national surveys.' *International Journal of Public Opinion Research* 18 (2): 211–223.

46. Victor Roudometof. 2005. 'Transnationalism, cosmopolitanism and glocalisation.' *Current Sociology* 53 (1): 113–135.

47. Anna Olofsson and Susanna Ohman. 2007. 'Cosmopolitans and locals: An empirical investigation of transnationalism.' *Current Sociology* 55 (6): 877–895.

48. Ian Woodward, Zlato Skrbis, and Clive Bean. 2008. 'Attitudes towards globalization and cosmopolitanism: Cultural diversity, personal consumption and the national economy.' *British Journal of Sociology* 59 (2): 207–226.

49. Sophie Duchesne and André-Paul Frognier. 1995. 'Is there a European identity?' In *Public Opinion and Internationalized Governance*. Ed. Oskar Niedermayer and Richard Sinnott. Oxford: Oxford University Press; Sam Schueth and John O'Laughlin. 2008. 'Belonging to the world: Cosmopolitanism in geographic contexts.' *Geoforum* 39 (2): 926–941.

50. Juan D. Medrano and Paula Gutierrez. 2001. 'Nested identities: National and European identities in Spain.' *Ethnic and Racial Studies* 24 (5): 753–778; James Rosenau. 2004. 'Emerging spaces, new places and old faces: Proliferating identities in a globalizing world.' In *Worlds on the Move: Globalization, Migration, and Cultural Security*. Ed. Jonathan Friedman and Shalini Randeria. London: I. B. Taurus.

51. It should be noted that the 2005–2007 wave of the WVS modified the coding scheme (see Technical Appendix A), replacing trade-off items with multiple choices, so that the results cannot be directly compared with previous versions of the questionnaire.

52. Exploratory models also included levels of urbanization and motivational attitudes, but these were removed from the final version of the analysis presented in this chapter on the grounds of parsimony and also because missing values for some variables sharply reduced the sample size.

53. Jai Kwan Jung. 2008. 'Growing supranational identities in a globalizing world? A multilevel analysis of the World Values Surveys.' *European Journal of Political Research* 47: 578–609.

54. See http://www.bbc.co.uk/info/purpose/public_purposes/communities.shtml.

55. Johannes Bardoel and Leen d'Haenens. 2008. 'Reinventing public service broadcasting in Europe: Prospects, promises and problems.' *Media, Culture & Society* 30 (3): 337–355.

56. For a broader discussion see, e.g., Pippa Norris. 2005. *Radical Right*. Cambridge: Cambridge University Press.

57. Robert D. Putnam. 2007. 'E pluribus unum: Diversity and community in the twenty-first century – the 2006 Johan Skytte Prize Lecture.' *Scandinavian Political Studies* 30 (2): 137–174.

58. Theodor W. Adorno, Else Fraenkel-Brunswick, David J. Levinson, and R. Nevitt Sanford. 1950. *The Authoritarian Personality.* New York: Harper and Row. For a discussion of the history and impact of this theory, see Martin Roiser and Carla Willig. 2002. 'The strange death of the authoritarian personality: 50 years of psychological and political debate.' *History of the Human Sciences* 15 (4): 71–96.

59. David Hooson. 1994. *Geography and National Identity.* Oxford: Blackwell.

60. Pia Knigge. 1998. 'The ecological correlates of right-wing extremism in Western Europe.' *European Journal of Political Research* 34: 249–79; Piero Ignazi. 2003. *Extreme Right Parties in Western Europe.* New York: Oxford University Press; Nonna Mayer and Pascal Perrineau. 1992. 'Why do they vote for Le Pen?' *European Journal of Political Research* 22 (1): 123–141; Hans-Georg Betz. 1994. *Radical Rightwing Populism in Western Europe.* New York: St. Martin's Press.

61. Benjamin I. Page and Jason Barabas. 2000. 'Foreign policy gaps between citizens and leaders.' *International Studies Quarterly* 44: 339–364.

62. Steffen Mau, Jan Mewes, and Ann Zimmernann. 2008. 'Cosmopolitan attitudes through transnational social practices?' *Global Networks* 8 (1): 1–24.

Chapter 7: Consumers: Economic Values

1. Martin Wolf. 2005. *Why Globalization Works.* New Haven, CT.: Yale University Press.

2. See David Held and Anthony McGrew. 2007. *Globalization/Antiglobalization: Beyond the Great Divide*, chapter 5. Cambridge: Polity Press; M. Lang. 2006. 'Globalization and its history.' *Journal of Modern History* 78 (4): 899–931.

3. Paul Collier. 2007. *The Bottom Billion*, chapter 6. Oxford: Oxford University Press; Joseph E. Stigletz. 2003. *Globalization and Its Discontents.* New York: W. W. Norton; Dani Rodrik. 2007. *One Economics, Many Recipes: Globalization, Institutions and Economic Growth.* Princeton, NJ: Princeton University Press.

4. Paul Collier. 2007. *The Bottom Billion*, chapter 6. Oxford: Oxford University Press; Joseph E. Stigletz. 2003. *Globalization and Its Discontents.* New York: W. W. Norton; Roumeen Islam and Gianni Zanini. 2008. *World Trade Indicators, 2008: Benchmarking Policy and Performance.* Washington, DC: World Bank.

5. Herbert J. Schiller. 1969. *Mass Communication and American Empire.* New York: A. M. Kelley; Herbert J. Schiller. 1992. *Mass Communication*

and American Empire, 2nd ed. Boulder, CO: Westview Press; Herbert J. Schiller. 1973. *Communication and Cultural Domination*. White Plains, NY: International Arts and Sciences Press. For a critical account, see John Tomlinson. 1991. *Cultural Imperialism*. Baltimore: Johns Hopkins University Press.

6. Herbert J. Schiller. 1992. *Mass Communication and American Empire*, 2nd ed., p. 36. Boulder, CO: Westview Press.

7. Ibid.

8. Robert W. McChesney. 1999. *Rich Media, Poor Democracy: Communication Politics in Dubious Times*, Urbana: University of Illinois Press. See also Edward S. Herman and Robert W. McChesney. 1997. *The Global Media: The Missionaries of Global Capitalism*. Washington, DC: Cassell; Edward S. Herman. 1995. *Triumph of the Market: Essays on Economics, Politics, and the Media*. Boston: South End Press.

9. Robin Andersen. 1995. *Consumer Culture*. Boulder, CO: Westview Press.

10. Ingrid Volkmer. 1999. *News in the Global Sphere: A Study of CNN and Its Impact on Global Communication*. Luton: University of Luton Press.

11. Joseph Nye, Jr. 2004. *Soft Power: The Means to Success in World Politics*. New York: Public Affairs.

12. D. Howes. Ed. 1996. *Cross-Cultural Consumption: Global Markets, Local Realities*. London: Routledge; George Ritzer. 1993. *The McDonaldization of Society*. Newbury Park, CA: Pine Forge Press; George Ritzer. 1996. 'Cultures and consumers: The McDonaldization thesis – Is expansion inevitable?' *International Sociology* 11: 291–308; George Ritzer and Allan Liska. 1997. 'McDisneyization.' In *Touring Cultures: Transformation of Travel and Theory*. Ed. C. Rojek and John Urry. London: Routledge; Benjamin R. Barber. 1996. *Jihad vs. McWorld: How Globalism and Tribalism Are Reshaping the World*. New York: Ballantine Books.

13. Joseph E. Stigletz. 2003. *Globalization and Its Discontents*. New York: W. W. Norton.

14. Barry K. Gills. 2002. *Globalization and the Politics of Resistance*. London: Palgrave Macmillan.

15. Karl C. Kaltenthaler, Ronald D. Gelleny, and Stephen J. Ceccoli. 2004. 'Explaining citizen support for trade liberalization.' *International Studies Quarterly* 48 (4): 829–851; Martin S. Edwards. 2006. 'Public opinion regarding economic and cultural globalization: Evidence from a cross-national survey.' *Review of International Political Economy* 13 (4): 587–608.

16. Kenneth F. Scheve and Matthew J. Slaughter. 2001. *Globalization and the Perceptions of American Workers*. Washington, DC: Institute for International Economics.

17. Anna Maria Mayda and Dani Rodrik. 2005. 'Why are some people (and countries) more protectionist than others?' *European Economic Review* 49: 1393–1430.

18. Anna Maria Mayda, Kevin H. O'Rourke, and Richard Sinnott. 2007. 'Risk, government and globalization: International survey evidence.' NBER Working Paper no. 13037. http://www.nber.org/papers/w13037.

19. Benjamin O. Fordham. 2008. 'Economic interests and public support for American global activism.' *International Organization* 62: 163–182.

20. Jan Duckett and William L. Miller. 2007. *The Open Economy and Its Enemies: Public Attitudes in East Asia and Eastern Europe*. Cambridge: Cambridge University Press.

21. See, e.g., Kenneth F. Scheve and Matthew J. Slaughter. 2001. *Globalization and the Perceptions of American Workers*. Washington, DC: Institute for International Economics; Anna Maria Mayda and Dani Rodrik. 2005. 'Why are some people (and countries) more protectionist than others?' *European Economic Review* 49: 1393–1430; Susan Stokes. 2001. *Public Support for Market Reforms in New Democracies*. Cambridge: Cambridge University Press; Lauren M. McLaren. 2005. *Identity, Interests and Attitudes to European Integration*. London: Palgrave Macmillan.

22. World Public Opinion. 15 April 2008. *Erosion of Support for Free Market System: Global Poll*. http://www.worldpublicopinion.org/pipa/articles/btglobalizationtradera/471.php?lb=btgl&pnt=471&nid=&id=.

23. BBC World Service Poll conducted between 31 October 2007 and 25 Janunary 2008 by GlobalScan together with the Program on International Policy Attitudes at the University of Maryland. http://www.worldpublicopinion.org/pipa/pdf/feb08/BBCEcon_Feb08_rpt.pdf.

24. Ian Woodward, Zlato Skrbis, and Clive Bean. 2008. 'Attitudes towards globalization and cosmopolitanism: Cultural diversity, personal consumption and the national economy.' *British Journal of Sociology* 59 (2): 207–226.

25. Michael Bratton and Robert Mattes. 2003. 'Support for economic reform? Popular attitudes in southern Africa.' *World Development* 31 (2): 303–323.

26. Ronald Inglehart. 1997. *Modernization and Postmodernization: Cultural, Economic and Political Change in 43 Societies*. Princeton, NJ: Princeton University Press; Shalom Schwartz. 2007. 'Value orientations: Measurement, antecedents and consequences across nations.' In *Measuring Attitudes Cross-Nationally: Lessons from the European Social Survey*. Ed. Roger Jowell, Caroline Roberts, Rory Fitzgerald, and Gillian Eva. London: Sage.

27. David M. Rankin. 2001. 'Identities, interests and imports.' *Political Behavior* 23: 351–76.

28. Richard Sinnott. 2000. 'Knowledge and the position of attitudes to a European foreign policy on the real-to-random continuum.' *International Journal of Public Opinion Research* 12 (2): 113–137.

29. Philip Converse. 1970. 'Attitudes and non-attitudes.' In *Quantitative Analysis of Social Problems*. Ed. E. R. Tufte. New York: Addison-Wesley.

30. John Zaller. 1992. *The Nature and Origins of Mass Public Opinion.* Cambridge: Cambridge University Press.

31. Hilde E. Nafstad, Rolv M. Blakar, and Erik Carlquist et al. 2007. 'Ideology and power: The influence of current neo-liberalism in society.' *Journal of Community & Applied Social Psychology* 17 (4): 313–327.

32. Shalom Schwartz. 2007. 'Value orientations: Measurement, antecedents and consequences across nations.' In *Measuring Attitudes Cross-Nationally: Lessons from the European Social Survey.* Ed. Roger Jowell, Caroline Roberts, Rory Fitzgerald, and Gillian Eva. London: Sage. The question is: 'Now I will briefly describe some people. Using this card, would you please indicate for each description whether that person is very much like you, like you, somewhat like you, not like you, or not at all like you.' The Schwartz items then present a series of 10 brief descriptions.

Chapter 8: Morality: Traditional Values, Sexuality, Gender Equality, and Religiosity

1. George Gerbner, Lawrence Gross, M. Morgan, and Nancy Signorielli. 1994. 'Growing up with television: The cultivation perspective.' In *Media Effects: Advances in Theory and Research.* Ed. Jennings Bryant and Dolf Zillman. Hillsdale, NJ: Erlbaum.

2. Nancy L. Buerkel-Rothfuss and Sandra Mayes, 1981. 'Soap opera viewing: The cultivation effect.' *Journal of Communication* 31: 108–115.

3. Victor Strasburger and Edward Donnerstein. 1999. 'Children, adolescents, and the media: Issues and solutions.' *Pediatrics* 103: 129–139.

4. Dale Kunkel, Keren Eyal, and Edward Donnerstein et al. 2007. 'Sexual socialization messages on entertainment television: Comparing content trends, 1997–2002.' *Media Psychology* 9 (3): 595–622.

5. Margaret Duffy and Michael Gotcher. 1996. 'Crucial advice on how to get the guy: The rhetorical vision of power and seduction in the teen magazine.' *Journal of Communication Inquiry* 20: 32–48; Joseph E. Scott. 1986. 'An updated longitudinal content analysis of sex references in mass circulation magazines.' *Journal of Sex Research* 22: 385–392.

6. Jana Bufkin and Sarah Eschholz. 2000. 'Images of sex and rape: A content analysis of popular film.' *Violence Against Women* 6: 1317–1344.

7. Richard L. Baxter, Cynthia De Riemer, Ann Landini, Larry Leslie, and Michael W. Singletary. 1985. 'A content analysis of music videos.' *Journal of Broadcasting and Electronic Media* 29: 333–340.

8. Tom Reichert, Jacqueline Lambiase, Susan Morgan, Meta Carstarphen, and Susan Zavoina. 1999. 'Cheesecake and beefcake: No matter how you slice it, sexual explicitness in advertising continues to increase.' *Journalism and Mass Communication Quarterly* 76: 7–20.

9. Jason Carroll, Laura Padilla-Walker, and Larry Nelson. 2008. 'Generation XXX: Pornography acceptance and use among emerging adults.' *Journal of Adolescent Research* 23 (1): 6–30; Janice Wolak, Kimberly

Mitchell, and David Finkelhor. 2007. 'Unwanted and wanted exposure to online pornography in a national sample of youth Internet users.' *Pediatrics* 119 (2): 247–257.

10. Jerry Ropelato. 2008. *Internet Pornography Statistics*. http://internet-filter-review.toptenreviews.com/internet-pornography-statistics.html #anchor4.

11. Sandra Hofferth and John Sandberg. 2001. 'How American children spend their time.' *Journal of Marriage and the Family* 63: 295–308.

12. James Lull and Stephen Hinerman. Eds. 1998. *Media Scandals*. New York: Columbia University Press; John B. Thompson. 2000. *Political Scandal: Power and Visibility in the Media Age*. Cambridge: Polity Press.

13. Pippa Norris. Ed. 1997. *Women, Media, and Politics*. New York: Oxford University Press; Laura Castañeda and Shannon B. Campbell. Eds. 2006. *News and Sexuality: Media Portraits of Diversity*. Thousand Oaks, CA: Sage.

14. Pippa Norris. Ed. 1997. *Women, Media, and Politics*. New York: Oxford University Press; Paula Poindexter, Sharon Meraz, and Amy Schmitz Weiss. 2007. *Women, Men, and News: Divided and Disconnected in the News Media Landscape*. Mahwah, NJ: Lawrence Erlbaum.

15. Stewart M. Hoover and Lynn Schofield Clark. 2002. *Practicing Religion in the Age of the Media*. New York: Columbia University Press; Stewart M. Hoover. 2006. *Religion in the Media Age*. New York: Routledge; Birgit Meyer and Annelies Moors. 2005. *Religion, Media, and the Public Sphere*. Bloomington: University of Indiana Press; Hent de Vries and Samuel Weber. Eds. 2001. *Religion and Media*. Stanford, CA: Stanford University Press.

16. Claire H. Badaracco. Ed. 2004. *Quoting God: How Media Shape Ideas about Religion and Culture*. Waco, TX: Baylor University Press.

17. Yaman Akdeniz. 2008. *Internet Child Pornography and the Law: National and International Responses*. Burlington, VT: Ashgate; Eric M. Barendt. 2005. *Freedom of Speech*, 2nd ed. New York: Oxford University Press.

18. David S. Silverman. 2007. *You Can't Air That: Four Cases of Controversy and Censorship in American Television Programming*. Syracuse, NY: University of Syracuse Press; Julia Bauder. Ed. 2007. *Censorship*. Detroit: Greenhaven Press; Jane Arthurs. 2004. *Television and Sexuality: Regulation and the Politics of Taste*. Buckingham: Open University Press.

19. Ronald Diebert, John Palfrey, Rafel Rohozinski, and Jonathan Zittrain. 2008. *Access Denied*. Cambridge, MA: MIT Press.

20. L. Monique Ward. 2003. 'Understanding the role of entertainment media in the sexual socialization of American youth: A review of empirical research.' *Developmental Review* 23 (3): 347–388.

21. Jeanne Steele and Jane Brown. 1995. 'Adolescent room culture: Studying media in the context of everyday life.' *Journal of Youth and Adolescence* 24: 551–576.

22. Myna German. 2007. *The Paper and the Pew: How Religion Shapes Media Choice*. Landham, MD: University Press of America.

23. Pippa Norris and Ronald Inglehart. 2004. *Sacred and Secular: Religion and Politics Worldwide*. Cambridge: Cambridge University Press.

24. Ronald Inglehart and Pippa Norris. 2003. *Rising Tide: Gender Equality and Cultural Change Around the World*. Cambridge: Cambridge University Press.

25. Pippa Norris and Ronald Inglehart. 2004. *Sacred and Secular: Religion and Politics Worldwide*. Cambridge: Cambridge University Press; Ronald Inglehart and Pippa Norris. 2003. *Rising Tide: Gender Equality and Cultural Change Around the World*. Cambridge: Cambridge University Press.

26. George Gerbner, Lawrence Gross, M. Morgan, and Nancy Signorielli. 1994. 'Growing up with television: The cultivation perspective.' In *Media Effects: Advances in Theory and Research*. Ed. Jennings Bryant and Dolf Zillman. Hillsdale, NJ: Erlbaum.

27. Jay Blumler and Elihu Katz. 1974. *The Uses of Mass Communication*. Thousand Oaks, CA: Sage.

Chapter 9: Activists: Civic Engagement

1. For a review, see Pippa Norris. 2008. *Driving Democracy: Do Power-Sharing Institutions Work?* Cambridge: Cambridge University Press.

2. Seymour Martin Lipset. 1959. 'Some social requisites of democracy: Economic development and political legitimacy.' *American Political Science Review* 53: 69–105. See also Seymour Martin Lipset. 1960. *Political Man: The Social Basis of Politics*. New York: Doubleday; Seymour Martin Lipset, Kyoung-Ryung Seong, and John Charles Torres. 1993. 'A comparative analysis of the social requisites of democracy.' *International Social Science Journal* 45 (2): 154–175; Seymour Martin Lipset and Jason M. Lakin. 2004. *The Democratic Century*. Norman: University of Oklahoma Press.

3. Dankwart Rustow. 1970. 'Transitions to democracy.' *Comparative Politics* 2: 337–63.

4. J. Krieckhaus. 2004. 'The regime debate revisited: A sensitivity analysis of democracy's economic effect.' *British Journal of Political Science* 34 (4): 635–655.

5. Robert W. Jackman. 1973. 'On the relation of economic development and democratic performance.' *American Journal of Political Science* 17: 611–21; Kenneth A. Bollen. 1979. 'Political democracy and the timing of development.' *American Sociological Review* 44: 572–587; Kenneth A. Bollen. 1983. 'World system position, dependency and democracy: The cross-national evidence.' *American Sociological Review* 48: 468–479; Kenneth A. Bollen and Robert W. Jackman. 1985. 'Political democracy and the size distribution of income.' *American Sociological Review* 50:

438–458; Gregory C. Brunk, Gregory A. Caldeira, and Michael S. Lewis-Beck. 1987. 'Capitalism, socialism, and democracy: An empirical inquiry.' *European Journal of Political Research* 15: 459–70; Evelyne Huber, Dietrich Rueschmeyer, and John D. Stephens. 1993. 'The impact of economic development on democracy.' *Journal of Economic Perspectives* 7 (3): 71–85; Ross E. Burkhart and Michael S. Lewis-Beck. 1994. 'Comparative democracy: The economic development thesis.' *American Political Science Review* 88: 903–910; John F. Helliwell. 1994. 'Empirical linkages between democracy and economic growth.' *British Journal of Political Science* 24 (2): 225–48; Tatu Vanhanen. 1997. *Prospects for Democracy: A Study of 172 Countries.* New York: Routledge; Robert J. Barro. 1999. 'Determinants of democracy.' *Journal of Political Economy* 107 (6): 158–183; Adam Przeworski, Michael E. Alvarez, José Antonio Cheibub, and Fernando Limongi. 2000. *Democracy and Development: Political Institutions and Well-Being in the World, 1950–1990.* Cambridge: Cambridge University Press; Seymour Martin Lipset, Kyoung-Ryung Seong, and John Charles Torres. 1993. 'A comparative analysis of the social requisites of democracy.' *International Social Science Journal* 45 (2): 154–175; Seymour Martin Lipset and Jason M. Lakin. 2004. *The Democratic Century.* Norman: University of Oklahoma Press.

6. Pippa Norris. 2008. *Driving Democracy: Do Power-Sharing Institutions Work?* chapter 4. Cambridge: Cambridge University Press.

7. Richard Gunther and Anthony Mughan. Eds. 2000. *Democracy and the Media: A Comparative Perspective.* Cambridge: Cambridge University Press; Katrin Voltmer. Ed. 2006. *Mass Media and Political Communication in New Democracies.* London: Routledge.

8. Pippa Norris. 2008. *Driving Democracy: Do Power-Sharing Institutions Work?* chapter 8. Cambridge: Cambridge University Press.

9. Adam Przeworski, Michael E. Alvarez, José Antonio Cheibub, and Fernando Limongi. 2000. *Democracy and Development: Political Institutions and Well-Being in the World, 1950–1990.* Cambridge: Cambridge University Press.

10. Ronald Inglehart and Christopher Welzel. 2003. 'Political culture and democracy: Analyzing cross-level linkages.' *Comparative Politics* 36 (1): 61; Ronald Inglehart and Christian Welzel. 2005. *Modernization, Cultural Change and Democracy.* Cambridge: Cambridge University Press.

11. Torsten Perrson and Guido Tabellini. 2003. *The Economic Effects of Constitutions.* Cambridge, MA: MIT Press.

12. Robert D. Putnam. 1995. 'Tuning in, tuning out: The strange disappearance of social capital in America.' *PS: Political Science and Politics* 28 (December): 664–683.

13. Kurt Lang and Gladys Lang. 1966. 'The mass media and voting.' In *Reader in Public Opinion and Communication.* Ed. Bernard Berelson and M. Janowitz. New York: Free Press.

14. Michael Robinson. 1976. 'Public affairs television and the growth of political malaise: The case of "the selling of the President."' *American Political Science Review* 70 (3): 409–432.

15. Lee Becker, Idowu A. Sobowale, and William Casey, Jr. 1979. 'Newspaper and television dependencies: Effects on evaluations of public officials.' *Journal of Broadcasting* 23 (4): 465–475; Lee Becker and D. Charles Whitney. 1980. 'Effects of media dependencies: Audience assessment of government.' *Communication Research* 7 (1): 95–120; Jack McLeod, Jane D. Brown, Lee B. Becker, and Dean A. Ziemke. 1977. 'Decline and fall at the White House: A longitudinal analysis of communication effects.' *Communication Research* 4: 3–22; Arthur Miller, Edie H. Goldenberg, and Lutz Erbring. 1979. 'Set-type politics: The impact of newspapers on public confidence.' *American Political Science Review* 73: 67–84.

16. Neil Postman. 1985. *Entertaining Ourselves to Death*. New York: Viking.

17. Roderick Hart. 1994. *Seducing America*. New York: Oxford University Press; Roderick Hart. 1996. 'Easy citizenship: Television's curious legacy.' In *The Media and Politics*. Ed. Kathleen Hall Jamieson. *Annals of the American Academy of Political and Social Science*, vol. 546.

18. George Gerbner and Larry Gross. 1976. 'Living with television: The violence profile.' *Journal of Communication* 16 (2): 173–199; George Gerbner, Larry Gross, Michael Morgan, and Nancy Signorielli. 1982. 'Charting the mainstream: Television's contribution to political orientations.' *Journal of Communication* 32 (2): 100–27; George Gerbner, Larry Gross, Michael Morgan, and Nancy Signorielli. 1984. 'Political correlates of television viewing.' *Public Opinion Quarterly* 48 (1): 283–300; George Gerbner. 1990. 'Advancing on the path of righteousness.' In *Cultivation Analysis: New Directions in Media Effects Research*. Ed. N. Signorielli and M. Morgan. Newbury Park, CA: Sage.

19. See Robert D. Putnam. 1995. 'Tuning in, tuning out: The strange disappearance of social capital in America.' *PS: Political Science and Politics* 28 (December): 664–83; Pippa Norris. 1996. 'Does television erode social capital? A reply to Putnam.' *P.S.: Political Science and Politics* 29 (3); Robert D. Putnam. 2000. *Bowling Alone*. New York: Simon & Schuster.

20. Michael Crozier, Samuel P. Huntington, and Joji Watanuki. 1975. *The Crisis of Democracy*. New York: New York University Press.

21. Jay G. Blumler and Michael Gurevitch. 1995. *The Crisis of Public Communication*. London: Longman. See also Jay Blumler. 1990. 'Elections, the media and the modern publicity process.' In *Public Communication: The New Imperatives*. Ed. M. Ferguson. London: Sage; Jay G. Blumler. 1997. 'Origins of the crisis of communication for citizenship.' *Political Communication*, 14 (4): 395–404.

22. Pippa Norris, John Curtice, David Sanders, Margaret Scammell, and Holli Semetko. 1999. *On Message*. London: Sage; Kenneth Newton. 1997. 'Politics and the news media: Mobilisation or videomalaise?' In *British Social*

Attitudes: the 14th Report, 1997/8. Ed. Roger Jowell, John Curtice, Alison Park, Katarina Thomson, and Lindsay Brook. Aldershot: Ashgate; Kenneth Newton. 1999. 'Mass media effects: Mobilization or media malaise?' *British Journal of Political Science* 29: 577–599; Sonia Livingstone and Tim Markham. 2008. 'The contribution of media consumption to civic participation.' *British Journal of Sociology* 59 (2) : 351–371.

23. Christina Holtz-Bacha. 1990. 'Videomalaise revisited: Media exposure and political alienation in West Germany.' *European Journal of Communication* 5: 73–85; Marc Hooghe. 2002. 'Watching television and civic engagement: Disentangling the effects of time, programs, and stations.' *Harvard International Journal of Press-Politics* 7: 84; Claes H. de Vreese and Hajo Boomgaarden. 2006. 'News, political knowledge and participation: The differential effects of news media exposure on political knowledge and participation.' *Acta Politica* 41 (4): 317–341.

24. Stephen Earl Bennett, Staci L. Rhine, Richard S. Flickinger, and Linda L. M. Bennett. 1999. 'Videomalaise revisited: Reconsidering the relation between the public's view of the media and trust in government.' *Harvard International Journal of Press-Politics* 4 (4): 8–23.

25. Pippa Norris. 2000. *A Virtuous Circle: Political Communications in Post-Industrial Democracies*. Cambridge: Cambridge University Press; Pippa Norris. 2000. 'Television and civic malaise.' In *What's Troubling the Trilateral Democracies*. Ed. Susan J. Pharr and Robert D. Putnam. Princeton, NJ: Princeton University Press.

26. David Easton. 1975. 'A reassessment of the concept of political support.' *British Journal of Political Science* 5: 435–457.

27. Pippa Norris. Ed. 1998. *Critical Citizens: Global Support for Democratic Government*. New York: Oxford University Press.

28. Russell Dalton. 2003. *Democratic Challenges, Democratic Choices*. New York: Oxford University Press.

29. Pippa Norris. Ed. 1998. *Critical Citizens: Global Support for Democratic Government*. New York: Oxford University Press.

30. For comparative studies see, e.g., Robert D. Putnam. Ed. 2002. *Democracy in Flux*. Oxford: Oxford University Press; Marc Hooghe and Dietlind Stolle. Eds. 2003. *Generating Social Capital: Civil Society and Institutions in Comparative Perspective*. New York: Palgrave Macmillan; Jan Willem Van Deth. Ed. 1997. *Private Groups and Public Life: Social Participation, Voluntary Associations and Political Involvement in Representative Democracies*. London: Routledge.

31. Robert D. Putnam, 2000. *Bowling Alone*. New York: Simon & Schuster; Robert D. Putnam. Ed. 2002. *Democracy in Flux*. Oxford: Oxford University Press.

32. Samuel Barnes and Max Kaase. 1979. *Political Action: Mass Participation in Five Western Democracies*. Beverley Hills, CA: Sage. See also Alan Marsh. 1977. *Protest and Political Consciousness*. Beverly Hills, CA:

Sage; Charles Adrian and David A. Apter. 1995. *Political Protest and Social Change: Analyzing Politics.* New York: New York University Press.

33. Similar results were reported in Peter Van Aelst and Stefaan Walgrave. 2001. 'Who is that (wo)man in the street? From the normalization of protest to the normalization of the protester.' *European Journal of Political Research* 39: 461–486; Pippa Norris, Stefaan Walgrave, and Peter Van Aelst. 2004. 'Who demonstrates? Anti-state rebels, conventional participants, or everyone?' *Comparative Politics* 37 (2): 189–206.

34. Pippa Norris and Ronald Inglehart. 2005. 'Gendering social capital: Bowling in women's leagues?' In *Gender and Social Capital.* Ed. Brenda O'Neill. New York: Routledge.

35. Ronald Inglehart and Pippa Norris. 2003. *Rising Tide: Gender Equality and Cultural Change Around the World.* Cambridge: Cambridge University Press.

36. Sidney Verba, Norman H. Nie, and Jae-on Kim. 1971. *The Modes of Democratic Participation: A Cross-National Analysis.* Beverley Hill, CA: Sage; Sidney Verba and Norman Nie. 1972. *Participation in America: Social Equality and Political Participation.* New York: HarperCollins; Sidney Verba, Norman Nie, and Jae-on Kim. 1978. *Participation and Political Equality: A Seven-Nation Comparison.* Cambridge: Cambridge University Press.

37. Pippa Norris. Ed. 1998. *Critical Citizens: Global Support for Democratic Government.* New York: Oxford University Press.

38. See Pippa Norris. Ed. 2009. *The Roles of the News Media in the Governing Reform Agenda.* Washington, DC: World Bank.

39. Pippa Norris. 2000. *A Virtuous Circle: Political Communications in Post-Industrial Democracies.* Cambridge: Cambridge University Press.

Chapter 10: Cultural Convergence over Time?

1. Herbert J. Schiller. 1973. *Communication and Cultural Domination.* White Plains, NY: International Arts and Sciences Press; Thomas L. McPhail. 1983. *Electronic Colonialism: The Future of International Broadcasting and Communication.* Beverly Hills, CA: Sage; David Howes. Ed. 1996. *Cross-Cultural Consumption: Global Markets, Local Realities.* London: Routledge; George Ritzer. 1993. *The McDonaldization of Society.* Newbury Park, CA: Pine Forge Press; George Ritzer and Allan Liska. 1997. 'McDisneyization.' In *Touring Cultures: Transformation of Travel and Theory.* Ed. C. Rojek and John Urry. London: Routledge; Benjamin R. Barber. 1996. *Jihad vs. McWorld: How Globalism and Tribalism Are Reshaping the World.* New York: Ballantine Books.

2. Alexander Stephan. 2007. *The Americanization of Europe: Culture, Diplomacy, and Anti-Americanism after 1945.* New York: Berghahn Books; Mark Wheeler. 2004. 'Supranational regulation: Television and

the European Union.' *European Journal of Communication* 19(3): 349–369; Mira Burri-Nenova. 2007. 'The new audiovisual media services directive: Television without frontiers, television without cultural diversity.' *Common Market Law Review* 44: 1689–1725.

3. Pippa Norris and Ronald Inglehart. 2004. *Sacred and Secular: Politics and Religion Worldwide.* Cambridge: Cambridge University Press.

4. Ronald Inglehart and Wayne E. Baker. 2000. 'Modernization, globalization and the persistence of tradition: Empirical evidence from 65 Societies.' *American Sociological Review.* 65: 19–55.

5. Pippa Norris and Ronald Inglehart. 2004. *Sacred and Secular: Politics and Religion Worldwide.* Cambridge: Cambridge University Press.

6. Ibid.

7. Ted Gerard Jelen and Clyde Wilcox. Eds. 2002. *Religion and Politics in Comparative Perspective: The One, the Few and the Many.* Cambridge: Cambridge University Press.

8. Ronald Inglehart and Pippa Norris. 2003. *Rising Tide: Gender Equality and Cultural Change Around the World.* Cambridge: Cambridge University Press.

9. Ronald Inglehart and Christian Welzel. 2005. *Modernization, Cultural Change and Democracy.* Cambridge: Cambridge University Press; John Scott. 1998. 'Changing attitudes to sexual morality: A cross-national comparison.' *Sociology: Journal of the British Sociological Association* 32 (4): 815–845.

10. Ted Gerard Jelen and Clyde Wilcox. 2003. 'Causes and consequences of public attitudes toward abortion: A review and research agenda.' *Political Research Quarterly* 56 (4): 489–500.

11. Pippa Norris. 2002. *Democratic Phoenix: Political Activism Worldwide.* Cambridge: Cambridge University Press.

12. Robert W. McChesney. 1999. *Rich Media, Poor Democracy: Communication Politics in Dubious Times.* Urbana: University of Illinois Press.

13. James A. Stimson. 1985. 'Regression in time and space: A statistical essay.' *American Journal of Political Science* 29: 914–947; Cheng M. Hsiao. 1986. *Analysis of Panel Data.* Cambridge: Cambridge University Press.

14. Nathaniel Beck and Jonathan Katz. 1995. 'What to do (and not to do) with time-series cross-section data.' *American Political Science Review* 89: 634–647; Nathaniel Beck and Jonathan Katz. 1996. 'Nuisance vs. substance: Specifying and estimating time-series cross-sectional models.' In *Political Analysis.* Ed. John Freeman. Ann Arbor: University of Michigan Press. Beck and Katz argue that for time-series cross-sectional datasets, feasible generalized least squares approaches that estimate the error process with an AR1 model are less accurate and efficient than ordinary least squares with panel-corrected standard errors. To double-check the robustness of the specification, models were run using both methods, and the choice did not affect the substantive interpretation of the results.

15. See Sven E. Wilson and David M. Butler. 2007. 'A lot more to do: The sensitivity of time-series cross-section analyses to simple alternative specifications.' *Political Analysis* 15 (2): 101–123.

16. Cheng M. Hsaio. 1986. *Analysis of Panel Data*. Cambridge: Cambridge University Press.

17. Nathaniel Beck and Jonathan Katz. 1995. 'What to do (and not to do) with time-series cross-section data.' *American Political Science Review* 89: 634–647.

18. Ronald Inglehart and Christian Welzel. 2005. *Modernization, Cultural Change and Democracy*, p. 133. Cambridge: Cambridge University Press.

19. Pippa Norris and Ronald Inglehart. 2004. *Sacred and Secular: Politics and Religion Worldwide*. Cambridge: Cambridge University Press.

20. Ronald Inglehart and Pippa Norris. 2003. *Rising Tide: Gender Equality and Cultural Change Around the World*. Cambridge: Cambridge University Press.

21. Ronald Inglehart. 1997. *Modernization and Postmodernization: Cultural, Economic and Political Change in 43 Societies*. Princeton, NJ: Princeton University Press; Ronald Inglehart and Christian Welzel. 2005. *Modernization, Cultural Change and Democracy*. Cambridge: Cambridge University Press.

Chapter 11: The Implications for Cultural Policies

1. Michael G. Elasmar. Ed. 2003. *The Impact of International Television: A Paradigm Shift*. Mahwah, NJ: Lawrence Erlbaum.

2. Robert Holton. 2000. 'Globalization's cultural consequences.' *Annals of the American Academy of Political and Social Sciences* 570: 140–152.

3. For a discussion, see Trevor Haywood. 1995. *Info-Rich – Info-Poor: Access and Exchange in the Global Information Society*. London: Bowker-Saur; William Wresch. 1996. *Disconnected: Haves and Have-Nots in the Information Age*. New Brunswick, NJ: Rutgers University Press; Benjamin R. Barber. 1996. *Jihad vs. McWorld: How Globalism and Tribalism Are Reshaping the World*. New York: Ballantine Books; David Held, Anthony McGrew, David Goldblatt, and Jonathan Perraton. 1999. *Global Transformations: Politics, Economics, and Culture*, chapter 7. Stanford, CA: Stanford University Press.

4. United Nations. 2005. *2005 World Summit Outcome. Resolution 60/1 Adopted by the United Nations General Assembly*. http://daccess-ods.un.org/TMP/2663872.html.

5. For a discussion, see chapter 2 in Manuel Castells. 2004. *The Power of Identity*, 2nd ed. Oxford: Blackwell.

6. Benjamin R. Barber. 1996. *Jihad vs. McWorld: How Globalism and Tribalism Are Reshaping the World*. New York: Ballantine Books.

7. Meic Pearse. 2004. *Why the Rest Hates the West: Understanding the Roots of Global Rage*. Downers Grove, IL: InterVarsity Press; Frank Louis

Rusciano. 2006. *Global Rage after the Cold War*. New York: Palgrave Macmillan.

8. http://www.slowfood.com/; Benjamin Shepard and Ronald Hayduk. Eds. 2002. *From ACT UP to the WTO: Urban Protest and Community Building in the Era of Globalization*. London: Verso.

9. According to the 2001 Census, for example, in the London boroughs of Wembley, Hyde Park, and Southall West, almost half the population has settled from abroad. Nor is this simply a matter of the traditional Caribbean, Indian, Pakistani, and Bangladeshi immigrant communities; almost as many Germans live in London as in Bonn, and more Americans live in London than in Syracuse, Dayton, or Tallahassee. See http://news.bbc.co.uk/2/shared/spl/hi/uk/05/born_abroad/html/overview.stm.

10. David Held and Anthony McGrew. 2007. *Globalization/Anti-Globalization: Beyond the Great Divide*. Cambridge: Polity Press.

11. See, e.g., the arguments presented by Martin Wolf. 2005. *Why Globalization Works*, 2nd ed. New Haven, CT: Yale University Press; Jagdish Bhagwati. 2007. *In Defense of Globalization*. Oxford: Oxford University Press.

12. For a recent summary of the literature, see Taylor Boas, T. Dunning, and J. Bussell. 2005. 'Will the digital revolution revolutionize development? Drawing together the debate.' *Studies in Comparative International Development* 40 (2): 95–110. See also Surendra J. Patel. Ed. 1993–1995. *Technological Transformation in the Third World*, 5 vols. Aldershot: Avebury; David J. Jeremy. 1992. *The Transfer of International Technology: Europe, Japan and the USA in the Twentieth Century*. Aldershot: Edward Elgar; Nathan Rosenberg and Claudio Frischtak. Ed. 1985. *International Technology Transfer: Concepts, Methods and Comparisons*. New York: Praeger; David Charles and Jeremy Howells. 1992. *Technology Transfer in Europe*. London: Belhaven Press; Manas Chatterji. 1990. *Technology Transfer in the Developing Countries*. New York: St. Martin's Press; S. R. Melkote. 1991. *Communication for Development in the Third World: Theory and Practice*. Newbury Park, CA: Sage.

13. Barry James. Ed. 2006. *Media Development and Poverty Eradication*. Paris: UNESCO; Roumeen Islam. Ed. 2002. *The Right to Tell: The Role of Mass Media in Economic Development*. Washington, DC: World Bank.

14. A substantial literature has developed on the role of ICTs for e-governance, public administration, and democracy. For recent overviews, see Donald F. Norris. Ed. 2007. *Current Issues and Trends in e-Government Research*. Hershey, PA: Cybertech; Viktor Mayer-Schönberger and David Lazer. Eds. 2007. *Governance and Information Technology: From Electronic Government to Information Government*. Cambridge, MA: MIT Press.

15. Timothy Besley and Roger Burgess. 2002. 'The political economy of government responsiveness: Theory and evidence from India.' *Quarterly Journal of Economics* 117 (4): 1415–1451; Timothy Besley and Andrea

Prat. 2006. 'Handcuffs for the grabbing hand? Media capture and government accountability.' *American Economic Review* 96 (3): 720–736; Aymo Brunetti and Beatrice Weder. 2003. 'A free press is bad news for corruption.' *Journal of Public Economics* 87 (7–8): 1801–1824; D. Fell. 2005. 'Political and media liberalization and political corruption in Taiwan.' *China Quarterly* (184): 875–893.

16. Douglas A. Van Belle, A. Cooper Drury, and Richard Stuart Olson. 2005. 'The CNN effect, geo-strategic motives and the politics of U.S. foreign disaster assistance.' *Journal of Politics*; Douglas A. Van Belle, Jean-Sébastien Rioux, and David M. Potter. 2004. *Media, Bureaucracies, and Foreign Aid: A Comparative Analysis of the United States, the United Kingdom, Canada, France and Japan.* New York: Palgrave Macmillan; Douglas A. Van Belle. 2000. *Press Freedom and Global Politics.* Westport, CT: Praeger; Kristen A. Swain. 2003. 'Proximity and power factors in Western coverage of the sub-Saharan AIDS crisis.' *Journalism & Mass Communication Quarterly* 80 (1): 145–165.

17. Daya Kishan Thussu. 2006. *International Communication: Continuity and Change.* New York: Hodder Arnold.

18. Herbert J. Schiller. 1973. *Communication and Cultural Domination.* White Plains, NY: International Arts and Sciences Press.

19. Ibid.; Johan Galtung. 1979. 'A structural theory of imperialism.' In *Transnational Corporations and World Order.* Ed. G. Modelski. San Fransisco: W. H. Freeman; Johan Galtung. 1980. *The True Worlds.* New York: Free Press; M. Masmoudi. 1981. 'The new world information order.' In *Crisis in International News: Policies and Prospects.* Ed. Jim Richstad and Michael A. Anderson. New York: Columbia University Press.

20. Sean MacBride. 1980. *Many Voices, One World: Communication and Society Today and Tomorrow; Towards a New More Just and More Efficient World Information and Communication Order.* Paris: UNESCO, International Commission for the Study of Communication Problems; Hamid Mowlana. 1985. *International Flow of Information: A Global Report and Analysis.* Paris: UNESCO.

21. Alexander Stephan. 2007. *The Americanization of Europe: Culture, Diplomacy, and Anti-Americanism after 1945.* New York: Berghahn Books.

22. David L. Looseley. 1997. *The Politics of Fun: Cultural Policy and Debate in Contemporary France.* Oxford: Berg; Christian Thomsen. Ed. 1989. *Cultural Transfer or Electronic Imperialism.* Heidelberg: Carl Winter.

23. UNESCO. 2001. *Universal Declaration of Cultural Diversity.* Paris: UNESCO. http://unesdoc.unesco.org/images/0012/001271/127160m.pdf.

24. Ibid., article 10.

25. See UNESCO Institute for Statistics. http://www.uis.unesco.org/ev.php?URL_ID=5830&URL_DO=DO_TOPIC&URL_SECTION=201.

26. Pippa Norris. 2003. *Democratic Phoenix*. Cambridge: Cambridge University Press.

27. Pippa Norris and Ronald Inglehart. 2004. *Sacred and Secular: Politics and Religion Worldwide*. Cambridge: Cambridge University Press.

28. Jay G. Blumler and Elihu Katz. 1974. *The Uses of Mass Communications: Current Perspectives on Gratifications Research*. Beverly Hills, CA: Sage.

29. Jennings Bryant and Dolf Zillmann. Eds. 2002. *Media Effects: Advances in Theory and Research*. Mahwah, NJ: Lawrence Erlbaum.

30. Benedict Anderson. 1996. *Imagined Communities: Reflections on the Origin and Spread of Nationalism*. London: Verso.

31. Joan E. Grusec and Paul D. Hastings. Eds. 2007. *Handbook of Socialization: Theory and Research*. New York: Guilford Press.

32. Tamar Liebes and Elihu Katz. 1993. *The Export of Meaning: Cross-Cultural Readings of Dallas*. Cambridge: Polity Press.

33. Pippa Norris. 2001. *Digital Divide: Civic Engagement, Information Poverty and the Internet Worldwide*. Cambridge: Cambridge University Press.

34. Pippa Norris. 2000. *A Virtuous Circle: Political Communications in Post-Industrial Democracies*. Cambridge: Cambridge University Press.

35. Michael Mann. 1997. 'Has globalization ended the rise and rise of the nation-state?' *Review of International Political Economy* 4 (3): 472–496; Manuel Castells. 2004. *The Power of Identity*, 2nd ed. Oxford: Blackwell.

36. Edward S. Herman and Robert W. McChesney. 1997. *The Global Media: The Missionaries of Global Capitalism*. Washington, DC: Cassell.

37. Ronald Inglehart and Pippa Norris. 2003. *Rising Tide: Gender Equality and Cultural Change Around the World*. Cambridge: Cambridge University Press; Pippa Norris and Ronald Inglehart. 2004. *Sacred and Secular: Politics and Religion Worldwide*. Cambridge: Cambridge University Press.

Technical Appendix C: Methods and Multilevel Regression Models

1. Robert Bickel. 2007. *Multilevel Analysis for Applied Research: It's Just Regression!* New York: Guilford Press.

2. Stephen W. Raudenbush and Anthony Bryk. 2002. *Hierarchical Linear Models*, 2nd ed. Thousand Oaks, CA: Sage; Andrew Gelman and Jennifer Hill. 2007. *Data Analysis Using Regression and Multilevel/Hierarchical Models*. Cambridge: Cambridge University Press.

Select Bibliography

Abbate, Janet. 2000. *Inventing the Internet*. Cambridge, MA: MIT Press.

Ackerman, John M., and Irma E. Sandoval-Ballesteros. 2006. 'The global explosion of freedom of information laws.' *Administrative Law Review* 581: 85–130.

Adorno, Theodor W., Else Fraenkel-Brunswick, David J. Levinson, and R. Nevitt Sanford. 1950. *The Authoritarian Personality*. New York: Harper and Row.

Afullo, Thomas. 2000. 'Global information and Africa: The telecommunications infrastructure for cyberspace.' *Library Management* 21 (4): 205–213.

Akdeniz, Yaman. 2008. *Internet Child Pornography and the Law: National and International Responses*. Burlington, VT: Ashgate.

Akhtar, Shahid, and Jon Gregson. 2001. 'Internet technologies in the Himalayas: Lessons learned during the 1990s.' *Journal of Information Science* 27 (1): 9–17.

Althaus, Scott L., and David Tewksbury. 2000. 'Patterns of Internet and traditional news media use in a networked community.' *Political Communication* 17 (1): 21–46.

Amelina, Anna. 2007. 'Evolution of the media and media control in post-Soviet Russia.' *Soziale Welt-Zeitschrift für Sozialwissenschaftliche Forschung und Praxis* 58 (2): 163ff.

Anable, David. 2006. 'The role of Georgia's media – and Western aid – in the Rose Revolution.' *Harvard International Journal of Press-Politics* 11 (3): 7–43.

Andersen, Robin. 1995. *Consumer Culture*. Boulder, CO: Westview Press.

Anderson, Benedict. 1996. *Imagined Communities: Reflections on the Origin and Spread of Nationalism*. London: Verso.

Archibugi, Daniele. 2008. *The Global Commonwealth of Citizens: Toward Cosmopolitan Democracy*. Princeton, NJ: Princeton University Press.

Archibugi, Daniele, and David Held (Eds.). 1995. *Cosmopolitan Democracy: An Agenda for a New World Order*. Cambridge: Polity Press.

Arthurs, Jane. 2004. *Television and Sexuality: Regulation and the Politics of Taste*. Buckingham: Open University Press.

Artz, Lee, and Yahya R. Kamalipour (Eds.). 2007. *The Media Globe: Trends in International Mass Media*. Lanham, MD: Rowman and Littlefield.

Arunachalam, Subbiah. 1999. 'Information and knowledge in the age of electronic communication: A developing country perspective.' *Journal of Information Science* 25 (6): 465–476.

Associated Press. 2007. *Breaking News: How the Associated Press Has Covered War, Peace, and Everything Else*. Princeton, NJ: Princeton Architectural Press.

Atkin, Charles, and Walter Gantz. 1978. 'Television news and political socialization.' *Public Opinion Quarterly* 42 (2): 183–198.

Ayish, Muhammad I. 2002. 'Political communication on Arab world television: Evolving patterns.' *Political Communication* 19 (2): 137–154.

Azzi, Stephen. 2004. 'Negotiating cultural space in the global economy: The United States, UNESCO, and the convention on cultural diversity.' *International Journal* 60 (3): 765–784.

Badaracco, Claire H. (Ed.). 2004. *Quoting God: How Media Shape Ideas about Religion and Culture*. Waco, TX: Baylor University Press.

Bagdikian, Ben H. 1997. *The Media Monopoly*. Boston, MA: Beacon Press.

Banisar, David. 2006. *Freedom of Information Around the World, 2006: A Global Survey of Access to Government Records Laws*. www.freedominfo.org.

Banks, Arthur S. 2007. *Cross-National Time-Series Data Archive (CNTS), 1815–2007*. Binghamton, NY: Databanks International.

Barber, Benjamin R. 1996. *Jihad vs. McWorld: How Globalism and Tribalism Are Reshaping the World*. New York: Ballantine Books.

Bardoel, Johannes, and Leen D'Haenens. 2008. 'Reinventing public service broadcasting in Europe: Prospects, promises and problems.' *Media, Culture & Society* 30 (3): 337–355.

Barendt, Eric M. 2005. *Freedom of Speech*. 2nd ed. New York: Oxford University Press.

Barker, Chris. 1997. *Global Television: An Introduction*. Oxford: Blackwell.

Barker, Chris. 1999. *Television, Globalization and Cultural Identities*. Philadelphia: Open University Press.

Barnett, George A. 2001. 'A longitudinal analysis of the international telecommunication network, 1978–1996.' *American Behavioral Scientist* 44: 1638–1655.

Barnett, George A., Bum Chon, and Devan Rosen. 2001. 'The structure of international Internet flows in cyberspace.' *NETCOM: Network and Communication Studies* 151 (2): 61–80.

Barnett, George A., and Eunjung Sung. 2005. 'Culture and the structure of the international hyperlink network.' *Journal of Computer-Mediated Communication* 11 (1): 217–238.

Barnett, George A., and Joseph G. T. Salisbury. 1996. 'Communication and globalization: A longitudinal analysis of the international telecommunication network.' *Journal of World System Research* 216: 1–17.

Barnett, George A., Joseph G. T. Salisbury, C. Kim, and A. Langhorne. 1999. 'Globalization and international communication networks: An examination of monetary, telecommunications, and trade networks.' *Journal of International Communication* 62: 7–49.

Barnett, George A., T. Jacobson, Young Choi, and S. Sun-Miller. 1996. 'An examination of the international telecommunications network.' *Journal of International Communication* 32: 19–43.

Barnett, George A., and Young Choi. 1995. 'Physical distance and language as determinants of the international telecommunications network.' *International Political Science Review* 16: 249–265.

Bartelson, Jens. 2000. 'Three concepts of globalization.' *International Sociology* 15 (2): 180–196.

Barzilai-Nahon, Karine. 2006. 'Gaps and bits: Conceptualizing measurements for digital divide/s.' *Information Society* 22 (5): 269–278.

Baskaran, Angathevar, and Mammo Muchie (Eds.). 2006. *Bridging the Digital Divide: Innovation Systems for ICT in Brazil, China, India, Thailand and Southern Africa*. London: Adonis & Abbey.

Bauder, Julia (Ed.). 2007. *Censorship*. Detroit: Greenhaven Press.

Bauman, Zygmunt. 1998. *Globalization: The Human Consequences*. New York: Columbia University Press.

Baxter, Richard L., Cynthia De Riemer, Ann Landini, Larry Leslie, and Michael W. Singletary. 1985. 'A content analysis of music videos.' *Journal of Broadcasting and Electronic Media* 29: 333–340.

Beck, Nathaniel, and Jonathan Katz. 1995. 'What to do (and not to do) with time-series cross-section data.' *American Political Science Review* 89: 634–647.

Beck, Nathaniel, and Jonathan Katz. 1996. 'Nuisance vs. substance: Specifying and estimating time-series cross-sectional models.' In John Freeman (Ed.). *Political Analysis*. Ann Arbor: University of Michigan Press.

Beck, Rose Marie, and Frank Wittmann (Eds.). 2004. *African Media Cultures: Transdisciplinary Perspectives*. Köln: Rüdiger Köppe Verlag.

Beck, Ulrich. 2006. *The Cosmopolitan Vision*. Cambridge: Polity Press.

Beck, Ulrich, and Natan Sznaider. 2006. 'Unpacking Cosmopolitanism for the Humanities and Social Sciences: A Research Agenda.' *British Journal of Sociology* 57 (1): 1–23.

Becker, Jonathan. 2004. 'Lessons from Russia: A neo-authoritarian media system.' *European Journal of Communication* 19 (2): 139–163.

Becker, Lee B., Tudor Vlad, and Nancy Nusser. 2007. 'An evaluation of press freedom indicators.' *International Communication Gazette* 69 (1): 5–28.

Benhamou, Françoise, and Stéphanie Peltier. 2007. 'How should cultural diversity be measured? An application using the French publishing industry.' *Journal of Cultural Economics* 31: 85–107.

Berlin, Isaiah. 1958. *Two Concepts of Liberty, an Inaugural Lecture Delivered Before the University of Oxford on 31 October 1958.* Oxford: Clarendon Press.

Besley, Timothy, and Andrea Prat. 2006. 'Handcuffs for the grabbing hand? Media capture and government accountability.' *American Economic Review* 96 (3): 720–736.

Besley, Timothy, and Roger Burgess. 2002. 'The political economy of government responsiveness: Theory and evidence from India.' *Quarterly Journal of Economics* 117 (4): 1415–1451.

Best, Samuel J., Brian Chmielewski, and Brian S. Krueger. 2005. 'Selective exposure to online foreign news during the conflict with Iraq.' *Harvard International Journal of Press-Politics* 10 (4): 52–70.

Betz, Hans-Georg. 1994. *Radical Rightwing Populism in Western Europe.* New York: St. Martin's Press.

Bhagwati, Jagdish. 2007. *In Defence of Globalization.* New York: Oxford University Press.

Bickel, Robert. 2007. *Multilevel Analysis for Applied Research: It's Just Regression!* New York: Guilford Press.

Bigman, David. 2007. *Globalization and the Least Developed Countries: Potentials and Pitfalls.* Cambridge, MA: CABI.

Billig, Michael. 1995. *Banal Nationalism.* London: Sage.

Biltereyst, Daniel, and Philippe Meers. 2000. 'The international telenovela debate and the contra-flow argument: A reappraisal.' *Media, Culture & Society* 22 (4): 393.

Birdsell, David, Douglas Muzio, David Krane, and Amy Cottreau. 1998. 'Web users are looking more like America.' *Public Perspective* 9 (3): 33.

Bishop, Robert L. 1975. 'How Reuters and AFP coverage of Africa compare.' *Journalism Quarterly* 52: 654–662.

Blankson, Isaac A., and Patrick D. Murphy (Eds.). 2007. *Negotiating Democracy: Media Tranformations in Emerging Democracies.* Albany: State University of New York Press.

Blumler, Jay G., and Elihu Katz. 1974. *The Uses of Mass Communications: Current Perspectives on Gratifications Research.* Beverly Hills, CA: Sage.

Bongaarts, John. 2001. 'Household size and composition in the developing world in the 1990s.' *Population Studies* 55 (3): 263–279.

Boyd-Barrett, Olivier. 1977. 'Media imperialism: Towards an international framework for an analysis of media systems.' In James Curran, Michael Gurevitch, and J. Woollacott (Eds.). *Mass Communication and Society,* pp. 116–135. London: Edward Arnold in association with Open University Press.

Boyd-Barrett, Olivier. 1980. *The International News Agencies*. London: Constable.

Boyd-Barrett, Olivier, and Daya Kishan Thussu. 1992. *Contraflow in Global News: International and Regional News Exchange Mechanisms*. London: John Libbey.

Boyd-Barrett, Olivier, and Daya Kishan Thussu. 1993. 'NWIO strategies and media imperialism: The case of regional news exchange.' In Kaarle Nordenstreng and Herbert Schiller (Eds.). *Beyond National Sovereignty: International Communication in the 1990s*, pp. 177–192. Norwood, NJ: Ablex.

Brady, David, Jason Beckfield, and Wei Zhao. 2007. 'The consequences of economic globalization for affluent democracies.' *Annual Review of Sociology* 33: 313–334.

Brady, Henry, and David Collier. 2004. *Rethinking Social Inquiry: Diverse Tools, Shared Standards*. New York: Rowman and Littlefield.

Bratton, Michael, and Robert Mattes. 2003. 'Support for economic reform? Popular attitudes in southern Africa.' *World Development* 31 (2): 303–323.

Brophy, Peter, and Edward Halpin. 1999. 'Through the Net to freedom: Information, the Internet and human rights.' *Journal of Information Science* 25 (5): 351–364.

Brousseau, Eric, and Nicolas Curien (Eds.). 2007. *Internet and Digital Economics*. Cambridge: Cambridge University Press.

Brunetti, Aymo, and Beatrice Weder. 2003. 'A free press is bad news for corruption.' *Journal of Public Economics* 87: 1801–1824.

Brunn, Stanley D., and Martin Dodge. 2001. 'Mapping the "worlds" of the World Wide Web: (Re)structuring global commerce through hyperlinks.' *American Behavioral Scientist* 44 (10): 1717–1739.

Brunn, Stanley D., and Thomas R. Leinbach (Eds.). 1991. *Collapsing Space and Time: Geographic Aspects of Communication and Information*. London: HarperCollins Academic.

Bryant, Jennings, and Dolf Zillmann (Eds.). 2002. *Media Effects: Advances in Theory and Research*. Mahwah, NJ: Lawrence Erlbaum.

Bucy, Eric. 2009. *Sourcebook for Political Communication Research: Methods, Measures, and Analytical Techniques*. New York: Routledge.

Buerkel-Rothfuss, Nancy L., and Sandra Mayes, 1981. 'Soap opera viewing: The cultivation effect.' *Journal of Communication* 31: 108–115.

Bufkin, Jana, and Sarah Eschholz. 2000. 'Images of sex and rape: A content analysis of popular film.' *Violence Against Women* 6: 1317–1344.

Bull, Benedicte, and Desmond McNeill. 2007. *Development Issues in Global Governance: Public–Private Partnerships and Market Multilateralism*. New York: Routledge.

Burri-Nenova, Mira. 2007. 'The new audiovisual media services directive: Television without frontiers, television without cultural diversity.' *Common Market Law Review* 44: 1689–1725.

Carroll, Jason, Laura Padilla-Walker, and Larry Nelson et al. 2008. 'Generation XXX: Pornography acceptance and use among emerging adults.' *Journal of Adolescent Research* 23 (1): 6–30.

Cassidy, William P. 2005. 'Variations on a theme: The professional role conceptions of print and online newspaper journalists.' *Journalism and Mass Communication Quarterly* 82 (2): 264–280.

Castañeda, Laura, and Shannon B. Campbell (Eds.). 2006. *News and Sexuality: Media Portraits of Diversity*. Thousand Oaks, CA: Sage.

Castells, Manuel. 2000. 'Materials for an exploratory theory of the network society.' *British Journal of Sociology* 514: 5–24.

Castells, Manuel. 2000. *The Rise of the Network Society*. 2nd ed. Oxford: Blackwell.

Castells, Manuel. 2004. *The Power of Identity*. 2nd ed. Oxford: Blackwell.

Chaffee, Steven H., L. Scott Ward, and Leonard P. Tipton. 1970. 'Mass communication and political socialization.' *Journalism Quarterly* 47 (4): 647.

Chakravarty, Paula, and Katharine Sarikakis. 2006. *Media Policy and Globalization*. Edinburgh: Edinburgh University Press.

Chakravartty, Paula, and Yuezhi Zhao (Eds.). 2008. *Global Communications: Toward a Transcultural Political Economy*. Lanham, MD: Rowman and Littlefield.

Chalaby, Jean K. (Ed.). 2005. *Transnational Television Worldwide: Towards a New Media Order*. London: I. B. Tauris.

Chan, J. M., Pan Zhongdang, and Lee Francis L. F. 2004. 'Professional aspirations and job satisfaction: Chinese journalists at a time of change in the media.' *Journalism and Mass Communication Quarterly* 81 (2): 254–273.

Chanda, Nayan. 2007. *Bound Together: How Traders, Preachers, Adventurers, and Warriors Shaped Globalization*. New Haven, CT: Yale University Press.

Chang, Tsan-Kuo. 1998. 'All countries not created equal to be news: World system and international communication.' *Communication Research* 25 (5): 528–563.

Charles, Jeff, Larry Shore, and Rusty Todd. 1979. 'The *New York Times* coverage of equatorial and lower Africa.' *Journal of Communication* 29 (2): 148–155.

Chase-Dunn, Christopher, and Peter Grimes. 1995. 'World systems analysis.' *Annual Review of Sociology* 21: 387–417.

Chen, Wenhong, and Barry Wellman. 2004. 'The global digital divide: Within and between countries.' *IT and Society* 1: 39–45.

Chowdhury, Shyamal K. 2004. 'The effect of democracy and press freedom on corruption: An empirical test.' *Economics Letters* 85 (1): 93–101.

Chu, Leonard L. 1994. 'Continuity and change in China media reform.' *Journal of Communication* 44 (3): 4–21.

Chyi, Hsiang Iris, and George Sylvie. 2001. 'The medium is global, the content is not: The role of geography in online newspaper markets.' *Journal of Media Economics* 14 (4): 231–248.

Ciftci, Sabri. 2005. 'Treaties, collective responses and the determinants of aggregate support for European integration.' *European Union Politics* 6 (4): 469–492.

Clayman, Steven, and Ann Reisner. 1998. 'Gate-keeping in action: Editorial conferences and assessments of newsworthiness.' *American Sociological Review* 63 (2): 178–199.

Cohen, Bernard C. 1963. *The Press and Foreign Policy*. Princeton, NJ: Princeton University Press.

Collier, David, James Mahoney, and Jason Seawright. 2004. 'Claiming too much: Warnings about selection bias.' In Henry E. Brady and David Collier (Eds.). *Rethinking Social Inquiry: Diverse Tools, Shared Standards*. Lanham, MD: Rowman and Littlefield.

Collier, Paul. 2007. *The Bottom Billion*, chapter 6. Oxford: Oxford University Press.

Collins, Richard. 1998. *From Satellite to Single Market: New Communication Technology and European Public Services Television*. London: Routledge.

Converse, Philip. 1970. 'Attitudes and non-attitudes.' In Edward R. Tufte (Ed.). *The Quantitative Analysis of Social Problems*. New York: Addison-Wesley.

Cooper-Chen, Anne (Ed.). 2005. *Global Entertainment Media: Content, Audiences, Issues*. Mahwah, NJ: Lawrence Erlbaum.

Corneo, Giacomo. 2005. 'Media capture in a democracy: The role of wealth concentration.' *European Journal of Political Economy* 213: 37–58.

Corrocher, Nicoletta. 2002. 'Measuring the digital divide: A framework for the analysis of cross-country differences.' *Journal of Information Technology* 17: 9.

Council of Europe. 2004. *Transnational Media Concentrations in Europe*. Strasbourg: Council of Europe. http://www.coe.int/t/e/human_rights/media/AP-MD(2004)007_en.pdf.

Cowen, Tyler. 2004. *Creative Destruction: How Globalization Is Changing the World's Cultures*. Princeton, NJ: Princeton University Press.

Cullen, Richard, and Hua Ling Fu. 1998. 'Seeking theory from experience: Media regulation in China.' *Democratization* 5: 155–78.

Cunningham, Stuart, and Elizabeth Jacka. 1996. *Australian Television and International Mediascapes*, pp. 3–47. Cambridge: Cambridge University Press.

Curran, James, and Myung Park (Eds.). 2000. *De-Westernizing Media Studies*. London: Routledge.

Cutlip, Scott M. 1954. 'Content and flow of AP news: From trunk to TTs to reader.' *Journalism Quarterly* 31: 434–446.

Damm, Jens, and Simona Thomas (Eds.). 2006. *Chinese Cyberspace: Technological Changes and Political Effects.* New York: Routledge.

Davis, Richard. 1999. *The Web of Politics.* New York: Oxford University Press.

Davis, Richard, and Diana Owen. 1998. *New Media and American Politics.* New York: Oxford University Press.

de Bens, Els, and Hedwig de Smaele. 2001. 'The inflow of American television fiction on European broadcasting channels revisited.' *European Journal of Communication* 16: 51–76.

de Jong, Wilma, Martin Shaw, and Neil Stammers (Eds.). 2005. *Global Activism, Global Media.* London: Pluto Press.

de Smaele, Hedwig. 2004. 'Limited access to information as a means of censorship in post-Communist Russia.' *Javnost – The Public* 11 (2): 65–81.

de Verneil, A. J. 1977. 'A correlation analysis of international newspaper coverage and international economic, communication, and demographic relationships.' *Communication Yearbook* 1: 307–317. New Brunswick, NJ: International Communication Association.

de Vries, Hent, and Samuel Weber (Eds.). 2001. *Religion and Media.* Stanford, CA: Stanford University Press.

Deibert, Ronald, John Palfrey, Rafal Rohozinski, and Jonathan Zittrain. 2008. *Access Denied: The Practice and Policy of Global Internet Filtering.* Cambridge, MA: MIT Press.

Deuze, Mark. 2002. 'National news cultures: A comparison of Dutch, German, British, Australian, and U.S. journalists.' *Journalism and Mass Communication Quarterly* 79 (1): 134–149.

Djankov, Simeon, Caralee McLiesh, Tatiana Nenova, and Andrei Shleifer. 2003. 'Who owns the media?' *Journal of Law and Economics* 462 (3): 341–382.

Dogan, Mattei. 1994. 'The decline of nationalism within Western Europe.' *Comparative Politics* 23 (3): 281–305.

Dollar, David. 1992. 'Outward-oriented developing economies really do grow more rapidly: Evidence from 95 LDCs, 1976–1985.' *Economic Development and Cultural Change* 40: 523.

Dollar, David, and Aart Kray. 2001. *Trade, Growth and Poverty.* Washington, DC: World Bank Discussion Paper.

Donald, Stephanie Hemelryk, Michael Keane, and Yin Hong (Eds.). 2002. *Media in China: Consumption, Content and Crisis.* London: Routledge.

Donsbach, Wolfgang. 1995. 'Lapdogs, watchdogs, and junkyard dogs.' *Media Studies Journal* 94: 17–30.

Donsbach, Wolfgang, and Thomas E. Patterson. 2004. 'Political news journalists: Partisanship, professionalism, and political roles in five countries.'

In Frank Esser and Barbara Pfetsch (Eds.). *Comparing Political Communication: Theories, Cases, and Challenges*, pp. 251–270. Cambridge: Cambridge University Press.

Dossani, Rafiq, and Martin Kenney. 2007. 'The next wave of globalization: Relocating service provision to India.' *World Development* 35 (5): 772–791.

Douglas, Susan J. 1987. *Inventing American Broadcasting, 1899–1922*. Baltimore: Johns Hopkins University Press.

Drache, Daniel. 2008. *Defiant Publics: The Unprecedented Reach of the Global Citizen*. Cambridge: Polity Press.

Dreher, Axel. 2006. 'Does globalization affect growth?' *Applied Economics* 38 (10): 1091–1110.

Dreher, Axel, Noel Gaston, and Pim Martens. 2008. *Measuring Globalisation: Gauging Its Consequences*. New York: Springer. http://globalization.kof.ethz.ch/.

Duchesne, Sophie, and André-Paul Frognier. 1995. 'Is there a European identity?' In Oskar Niedermayer and Richard Sinnott (Eds.). *Public Opinion and Internationalized Governance*. Oxford: Oxford University Press.

Duckett, Jan, and William L. Miller. 2007. *The Open Economy and Its Enemies: Public Attitudes in East Asia and Eastern Europe*. Cambridge: Cambridge University Press.

Duffy, Margaret, and Michael Gotcher. 1996. 'Crucial advice on how to get the guy: The rhetorical vision of power and seduction in the teen magazine.' *Journal of Communication Inquiry* 20: 32–48.

Dugger, Celia W. 2000. 'Connecting rural India to the world.' *New York Times*, 28 May.

Dupagne, Michel, and David Waterman. 1998. 'Determinants of US television fiction imports in Western Europe.' *Journal of Broadcasting and Electronic Media* 42 (2): 208–220.

Dupree, J. D. 1971. 'International communication: View from "a window on the world."' *Gazette* 17: 224–235.

Dutton, William H. 1999. 'The web of technology and people: Challenges for economic and social research.' *Prometheus* 17 (1): 5–20.

Dutton, William H. 1999. *Society on the Line: Information Politics in the Digital Age*. Oxford: Oxford University Press.

Dutton, William H. (Ed.) 1996. *Information and Communication Technologies*. Oxford: Oxford University Press.

Dutton, William H., Jay Blumler, and Kenneth L. Kraemer (Eds.). 1987. *Wired Cities: Shaping the Future of Communications*. Boston: G. K. Hall.

Dyczok, Marta. 2006. 'Was Kuchma's censorship effective? Mass media in Ukraine before 2004.' *Europe–Asia Studies* 58 (2): 215–238.

Edwards, Martin S. 2006. 'Public opinion regarding economic and cultural globalization: Evidence from a cross-national survey.' *Review of International Political Economy* 13 (4): 587–608.

Eichenberg, Richard C., and Russell J. Dalton. 2007. 'Post-Maastricht blues: The transformation of citizen support for European integration, 1973–2004.' *Acta Politica* 42 (2–3): 128–152.

Eickelman, Dale F., and Jon W. Anderson (Eds.). 2003. *New Media in the Muslim World: The Emerging Public Sphere*. Bloomington: Indiana University Press.

Elasmar, Michael G. (Ed.). 2003. *The Impact of International Television: A Paradigm Shift*. Mahwah, NJ: Lawrence Erlbaum.

Elasmar, Michael G., and John E. Hunter. 1993. 'The impact of foreign TV on a domestic audience: A meta-analysis.' *Communication Yearbook* 20: 47–69. New Brunswick, NJ: International Communication Association.

Elasmar, Michael G., and John E. Hunter. 2003. 'A meta-analysis of cross-border effect studies.' In Michael G. Elasmar (Ed.). *The Impact of International Television: A Paradigm Shift*. Mahwah, NJ: Lawrence Erlbaum.

Elasmar, Michael G. and Kathryn Bennett. 2003. 'The cultural imperialism paradigm revisited: Origin and evolution.' In Michael G. Elasmar (Ed.). *The Impact of International Television: A Paradigm Shift*. Mahwah, NJ: Lawrence Erlbaum.

Enli, Gunn Sara. 2007. 'Gate-keeping in the new media age: A case study of the selection of text-messages in a current affairs programme.' *Javnost – The Public* 14 (2): 47–61.

Eoyang, Eugene. 2005. *Two-Way Mirrors: Cross-Cultural Studies in Glocalization*. Lanham, MD: Lexington Books.

Esser, Frank, and Barbara Pfetsch (Eds.). 2004. *Comparing Political Communication: Theories, Cases, and Challenges*. Cambridge: Cambridge University Press.

European Audiovisual Observatory. 2007. *Yearbook 2007: Cinema, Television, Video and Multimedia in Europe*. Strasbourg: Council of Europe.

Eurostat. 2007. *Cultural Statistics: 2007 edition*. Brussels: Eurostat.

Evans, Geoffrey. 1998. 'How Britain views the EU.' In Roger Jowell et al. (Eds.). *British Social Attitudes: The 15th Report*. Aldershot: Dartmouth/SCPR.

Evans, Geoffrey. 1999. 'Europe: A new electoral cleavage?' In Geoffrey Evans and Pippa Norris (Eds.). *Critical Elections: British Parties and Voters in Long-Term Perspective*. London: Sage.

Everard, Jerry. 2000. *Virtual States: The Internet and the Boundaries of the Nation-State*. London: Routledge.

Evert, Philip. 1995. 'NATO, the European Community, and the United Nations.' In Oskar Niedermayer and Richard Sinnott (Eds.). *Public Opinion and Internationalized Governance*. Oxford: Oxford University Press.

Falk, Richard. 1995. *On Humane Governance: Toward a New Global Politics*. Cambridge: Polity Press.

Fandy, Mamoun. 1999. 'Cyber-resistance: Saudi opposition between global-ization and localization.' *Comparative Studies in Society and History* 41 (1): 124–147.

Fandy, Mamoun. 2007. *UnCivil War of Words: Media and Politics in the Arab World*. Westport, CT: Praeger Security International.

Featherstone, Michael (Ed.). 1990. *Global Culture: Nationalism, Globalism and Modernity*. London: Sage.

Feigenbaum, Harvey B. 2007. 'Hegemony or diversity in film and television? The United States, Europe and Japan.' *Pacific Review* 20: 371–396.

Flew, Terry. 2007. *Understanding Global Media*. New York: Palgrave Macmillan.

Fordham, Benjamin O. 2008. 'Economic interests and public support for American global activism.' *International Organization* 62: 163–182.

Franda, Marcus. 2002. *Launching into Cyberspace: Internet Development and Politics in Five World Regions*. Boulder, CO: Lynne Rienner.

Fraser, Matthew. 2005. *Weapons of Mass Distraction: Soft Power and American Empire*. New York: Thomas Dunne Books.

Frederick, Howard H. 1993. *Global Communication and International Relations*. Belmont, CA: Wadsworth.

Freedman, Des. 2003. 'Who wants to be a millionaire? The politics of television exports.' *Information, Communication and Society* 6 (1): 24–41.

Freillea, Sebastian, M. Emranul Haque, and Richard Kneller. 2007. 'A contribution to the empirics of press freedom and corruption.' *Europäische Zeitschrift für politische Ökonomie* 23 (4): 838–862.

Friedman, Thomas L. 2000. *The Lexus and the Olive Tree: Understanding Globalization*. New York: Anchor Books.

Friedman, Thomas L. 2007. *The World Is Flat: A Brief History of the Twenty-first Century*. New York: Picador / Farrar, Straus and Giroux.

Fu, W. Wayne. 2006. 'Concentration and homogenization of international movie sources: Examining foreign film import profiles.' *Journal of Communications* 56: 813–835.

Galperin, Hernan. 1999. 'Cultural industries policy in regional trade agreements: The cases of NAFTA, the European Union and MERCOSUR.' *Media, Culture & Society* 21 (5): 627–648.

Galtung, Johan. 1971. 'A structural theory of imperialism.' *Journal of Peace Research* 8: 81–118.

Galtung, Johan. 1980. *The True Worlds: A Transnational Perspective*. New York: Free Press.

Galtung, Johan, and Mari Holmboe Ruge. 1965. 'The structure of foreign news.' *Journal of Peace Research* 2 (1): 64–91.

Galtung, Johan, and Richard C. Vincent. 1992. *Global Glasnost: Toward a New World Information and Communication Order*. Cresskill, NJ: Hampton Press.

Gans, Herbert J. 1979. *Deciding What's News: A Study of "CBS Evening News," "NBC Nightly News," Newsweek, and Time*. New York: Pantheon Books.

Geddes, Barbara. 2003. *Paradigms and Sand Castles: Theory Building and Research Design in Comparative Politics*, chapter 3. Ann Arbor: University of Michigan Press.

Gellner, Ernest. 1983. *Nations and Nationalism*. Oxford: Blackwell.

Gelman, Andrew, and Jennifer Hill. 2007. *Data Analysis Using Regression and Multilevel/Hierarchical Models*. Cambridge: Cambridge University Press.

Gentz, Natascha, and Stefan Kramer (Eds.). 2006. *Globalization, Cultural Identities, and Media Representations*. New York: State University of New York Press.

George, Alexander L., and Andrew Bennett. 2004. *Case Studies and Theory Development*. Cambridge, MA: MIT Press.

Gerbner, George, and George Marvanyi. 1977. 'The many worlds of the world's press.' *Journal of Communication* 27 (1): 52–66.

Gerbner, George, Lawrence Gross, Michael Morgan, and Nancy Signorielli. 1994. 'Growing up with television: The cultivation perspective.' In Jennings Bryant and Dolf Zillman (Eds.). *Media Effects: Advances in Theory and Research*, pp. 17–41. Hillsdale, NJ: Lawrence Erlbaum.

Gerbner, George, and Marsha Siefert (Eds.). 1984. *World Communications: A Handbook*. New York: Longman.

German, Myna. 2007. *The Paper and the Pew: How Religion Shapes Media Choice*. Landam, MD: University Press of America.

Gher, Leo A., and Hussein V. Amin. 1999. 'New and old media access and ownership in the Arab world.' *Gazette* 61 (1): 59–87.

Giddens, Anthony. 1990. *The Consequences of Modernity*. Cambridge: Polity Press in association with Basil Blackwell.

Giddens, Anthony. 2002. *Runaway World: How Globalisation Is Reshaping Our Lives*. London: Profile.

Gills, Barry K. 2002. *Globalization and the Politics of Resistance*. London: Palgrave Macmillan.

Ginneken, Jaap van. 1998. *Understanding Global News: A Critical Introduction*. London: Sage.

Global Reach. Various years. Number of Internet users by language. http://global-reach.biz/globalstats.

Golding, Peter, and Phil Harris. 1997. *Beyond Cultural Imperialism: Globalization, Communication and the New International Order*. London: Sage.

Golding, Philip. 1977. 'Media professionalism in the Third World: The transfer of an ideology.' In James Curran, Michael Gurevitch, and J. Woollacott (Eds.). *Mass Communication and Society*, pp. 291–308. London: Edward Arnold in association with Open University Press.

Graber, Christoph B. 2006. 'The new UNESCO convention on cultural diversity: A counterbalance to the WTO?' *Journal of International Economic Law* 9 (3): 553–574.

Graber, Doris. 2003. 'The media and democracy: Beyond myths and stereotypes.' *Annual Review of Political Science* 6: 139–160.

Grainge, Paul. 2008. *Brand Hollywood: Selling Entertainment in a Global Media Age*. New York: Routledge.

Grusec, Joan E., and Paul D. Hastings (Eds.). 2007. *Handbook of Socialization: Theory and Research*. New York: Guilford Press.

Gu, Jing, John Humphrey, and Dirk Messner. 2008. 'Global governance and developing countries: The implications of the rise of China.' *World Development* 36: 274–292.

Guillen, Mauro F., and Sandra L. Suarez. 2005. 'Explaining the global digital divide: Economic, political and sociological drivers of cross-national Internet use.' *Social Forces* 88 (4): 681–708.

Gunther, Albert C., Yah-Huei Hong, and Lulu Rodriquez. 1994. 'Balancing trust in media and trust in government during political change in Taiwan.' *Journalism Quarterly* 71 (3): 628–636.

Gunther, Richard, and Anthony Mughan (Eds.). 2000. *Democracy and the Media: A Comparative Perspective*. Cambridge: Cambridge University Press.

Gunther, Richard, José Ramon Montero, and Hans-Jurgen Puhle. 2007. *Democracy, Intermediation, and Voting on Four Continents*. Oxford: Oxford University Press.

Gurevitch, Michael, and Jay Blumler. 1990. 'Comparative research: The extending frontier.' In David L. Swanson and Dan Nimmo (Eds.). *New Directions in Political Communication: A Resource Book*. Newbury Park, CA: Sage.

Gustafsson, Karl Erik, and Olof Hulten. 1997. 'Sweden.' In Bernt Stubbe Ostergaard (Eds.). *The Media in Western Europe*. London: Sage.

Haarhuis, Carolien K., and René Torenvlied. 2006. 'Dimensions and alignments in the African anti-corruption debate.' *Acta Politica* 41 (1): 41–67.

Hachten, William A., and James Scotton. 2006. *The World News Prism: Global Information in a Satellite Age*. Malden, MA: Blackwell.

Hafez, Kai. 2007. *The Myth of Media Globalization: Why Global Media Is Not Truly Globalized*. Cambridge: Polity Press.

Hafner, Katie, and Matthew Lyon. 1998. *Where Wizards Stay up Late: The Origins of the Internet*. New York: Simon & Schuster.

Hague, Barry, and Brian Loader. 1999. *Digital Democracy: Discourse and Decision-Making in the Information Age*. London: Routledge.

Hahn, M. 2006. 'A clash of cultures? The UNESCO diversity convention and international trade law.' *Journal of International Economic Law* 9 (3): 515–552.

Hallin, Daniel C., and Paolo Mancini. 2004. *Comparing Media Systems: Three Models of Media and Politics*. Cambridge: Cambridge University Press.

Hanitzsch, Thomas. 2005. 'Journalists in Indonesia: Educated but timid watchdogs.' *Journalism Studies* 6: 493–508.

Hannerz, Ulf. 1990. 'Cosmopolitans and locals in world culture.' In Mike Featherstone (Ed.). *Global Culture: Nationalism, Globalization and Modernity*. London: Sage.

Hannerz, Ulf. 1992. *Cultural Complexity*. New York: Columbia University Press.

Harber, Anton. 2004. 'Reflections on journalism in the transition to democracy.' *Ethics & International Affairs* 18 (3): 79–87.

Hargittai, Eszter. 1999. 'Weaving the Western Web: Explaining differences in Internet connectivity among OECD Countries.' *Telecommunications Policy* 23 (10–11): 701–718.

Haynes, R. D., Jr. 1984. 'Test of Galtung's theory of structural imperialism.' In Robert L. Stevenson and Donald Lewis Shaw (Eds.). *Foreign News and the New World Information Order*, pp. 200–216. Ames: Iowa State University Press.

Haywood, Trevor. 1995. *Info-Rich – Info-Poor: Access and Exchange in the Global Information Society*. London: Bowker-Saur.

Hedley, R. Alan. 1998. 'Technological diffusion or cultural imperialism: Measuring the information revolution.' *International Journal of Comparative Sociology* 39 (2): 198–212.

Heinderyckx, François. 1993. 'Television news programmes in Western Europe: A comparative study.' *European Journal of Communication* 8: 425–450.

Held, David. 1995. *Democracy and the Global Order: From the Modern State to Cosmopolitan Governance*. Cambridge: Polity Press.

Held, David, and Anthony McGrew. 2007. *Globalization/Anti-Globalization: Beyond the Great Divide*. Cambridge: Polity Press.

Held, David, Anthony McGrew, David Goldblatt, and Jonathan Perraton. 1999. *Global Transformations: Politics, Economics, and Culture*, chapter 7. Stanford, CA: Stanford University Press.

Held, David, and Henrietta L. Moore. 2008. *Cultural Politics in a Global Age: Uncertainty, Solidarity and Innovation*. Oxford: Oneworld.

Helms, Ludger. 2006. 'The changing parameters of political control in Western Europe.' *Parliamentary Affairs* 59 (1): 78–97.

Hendy, David. 2000. *Radio in the Global Age*. Oxford: Polity Press.

Herman, Edwards S. 1995. *Triumph of the Market: Essays on Economics, Politics, and the Media*. Boston, MA: South End Press.

Herman, Edward S., and Noam Chomsky. 1988. *Manufacturing Consent: The Political Economy of the Mass Media*. New York: Pantheon Books.

Herman, Edward S., and Robert W. McChesney. 1997. *The Global Media: The New Missionaries of Corporate Capitalism*. Washington, DC: Cassell.

Herron, Erik S. 1999. 'Democratization and the development of information regimes: The Internet in Eurasia and the Baltics.' *Problems of Post-Communism* 46 (4): 56–68.

Herrscher, Roberto. 2002. 'A universal code of journalism ethics: Problems, limitations, and proposals.' *Journal of Mass Media Ethics* 17: 277–289.

Herscovitz, Heloiza G. 2004. 'Brazilian journalists' perceptions of media roles, ethics, and foreign influences on Brazilian journalism.' *Journalism Studies* 51: 71–86.

Hesmondhalgh, David. 2007. *The Cultural Industries.* 2nd ed. London: Sage.

Hill, Kevin A., and John E. Hughes. 1998. *Cyberpolitics: Citizen Activism in the Age of the Internet.* Lanham, MD: Rowan and Littlefield.

Hirsch, Mario, and Vibeke G. Petersen. 1998. 'European policy initiatives.' In Denis McQuail and Karen Siune (Eds.). *Media Policy: Convergence, Concentration and Commerce*, chapter 14. London: Sage.

Hirst, Paul, and Grahame Thompson. 1996. *Globalization in Question: The International Economy and the Possibilities of Governance.* Cambridge: Polity Press.

Hoff, Jens, Ivan Horrocks, and Pieter Tops. 2000. *Democratic Governance and New Technology: Technologically Mediated Innovations in Political Practice in Western Europe.* London: Routledge.

Hofferth, Sandra, and John Sandberg. 2001. 'How American children spend their time.' *Journal of Marriage and the Family* 63: 295–308.

Holbrook, Thomas. 2002. 'Presidential campaigns and the knowledge gap.' *Political Communication* 19: 437–454.

Hollifield, C. Ann, Lee B. Becker, and Tudor Vlad. 2006. 'The effects of political, economic and organizational factors on the performance of broadcast media in developing countries.' Presented to the Political Communication Research Section of the International Association for Media and Communication Research, Cairo, Egypt, July 2006.

Holsti, Oli R. 2004. *Public Opinion and American Foreign Policy.* Rev. ed. Ann Arbor: University of Michigan Press.

Holton, Robert. 2000. 'Globalization's cultural consequences.' *Annals of the American Academy of Political and Social Sciences* 570: 140–152.

Holtz-Bacha, Christina. 2007. 'Freedom of the press: Is a worldwide comparison possible?' Paper for the conference *Measuring Press Freedom*, Annenberg School of Communication, University of Pennsylvania.

Hooghe, Liesbet, and Gary Marks. 2005. 'Calculation, community and cues: Public opinion on European integration.' *European Union Politics* 6 (4): 419–443.

Hooson, David. 1994. *Geography and National Identity.* Oxford: Blackwell.

Hoover, Stewart M. 2006. *Religion in the Media Age.* New York: Routledge.

Hoover, Stewart M., and Lynn Schofield Clark. 2002. *Practicing Religion in the Age of the Media.* New York: Columbia University Press.

Horrigan, John. 2008. *Mobile Access to Data and Information*. Washington, DC: Pew Internet and American Life Project.

Hoskins, Colin, and Rolf Mirius. 1988. 'Reasons for the U.S. domination of the international trade in television programmes.' *Media, Culture & Society* 10: 499–515.

Hoskins, Colin, Stuart McFadyen, and Adam Finn. 1997. *Global Television and Film: An Introduction to the Economics of the Business*. Oxford: Oxford University Press.

Hovland, Carl Iver, Arthur A. Lumsdaine, and Fred D. Sheffield. 1949. *Experiments on Mass Communication*. Princeton, NJ: Princeton University Press.

Howes, David (Ed.). 1996. *Cross-Cultural Consumption: Global Markets, Local Realities*. London: Routledge.

Hsiao, Cheng M. 1986. *Analysis of Panel Data*. Cambridge: Cambridge University Press.

Humphrey, Peter J. 1996. *Mass Media and Media Policy in Western Europe*. Manchester: University of Manchester Press.

Huntington, Samuel. 1996. *The Clash of Civilizations and the Remaking of World Order*. New York: Simon & Schuster.

Hur, K. Kyloon. 1984. 'A critical analysis of international news flow research.' *Critical Studies in Mass Communication* 1: 365–378.

Hyden, Goran, Michael Leslie, and Folu F. Ogundimu (Eds.). 2002. *Media and Democracy in Africa*. Uppsala: Nordiska Afrikainstitutet.

Ignatieff, Michael. 1993. *Blood and Belonging*. Toronto: Viking.

Ignazi, Piero. 2003. *Extreme Right Parties in Western Europe*. New York: Oxford University Press.

Inglehart, Ronald. 1995. *Value Change on Six Continents*. Ann Arbor: University of Michigan Press.

Inglehart, Ronald. 1997. *Modernization and Postmodernization: Cultural, Economic and Political Change in 43 Societies*. Princeton, NJ: Princeton University Press.

Inglehart, Ronald. 1998. *Human Values and Beliefs: A Cross-Cultural Sourcebook*. Ann Arbor: University of Michigan Press.

Inglehart, Ronald. 2004. *Human Beliefs and Values: A Cross-Cultural Sourcebook Based on the 1999–2002 Values Surveys*. Mexico City: Siglo XXI.

Inglehart, Ronald, and Christian Welzel. 2005. *Modernization, Cultural Change and Democracy*. Cambridge: Cambridge University Press.

Inglehart, Ronald, and Pippa Norris. 2003. *Rising Tide: Gender Equality and Cultural Change Around the World*. Cambridge: Cambridge University Press.

Inoguchi, Takashi, and Ian Marsh (Eds.). 2007. *Globalisation, Public Opinion and the State: Western Europe and East and Southeast Asia*. London: Routledge.

International Telecommunication Union. Annual since 1975. *World Telecommunication/ICT Development Report*. Geneva: ITU.

International Telecommunication Union. 2007. *Key Global Telecom Indicators for the World Telecommunication Service Sector.* Geneva: ITU.

International Telecommunication Union. 2008. *Facts and Figures.* Geneva: ITU.

Iosifidis, Petros, Jeanette Steemers, and Mark Wheeler. 2005. *European Television Industries.* London: BFI.

Islam, Roumeen. 2003. *Do More Transparent Governments Govern Better?* Washington, DC: World Bank.

Islam, Roumeen (Ed). 2002. *The Right to Tell: The Role of Mass Media in Economic Development.* Washington, DC: World Bank.

Islam, Roumeen, and Gianni Zanini. 2008. *World Trade Indicators, 2008: Benchmarking Policy and Performance.* Washington, DC: World Bank.

Jacobs, Sean. 2002. 'How good is the South African media for democracy? Mapping the South African public sphere after apartheid.' *African and Asian Studies* 1 (4): 279–302.

Jakubowicz, Karol. 2001. 'Rude awakening: Social and media change in Central and Eastern Europe.' *Javnost – The Public* 8 (4): 59–80.

Jakubowicz, Karol. 2004. 'Ideas in our heads: Introduction of PSB as part of media system change in Central and Eastern Europe.' *European Journal of Communication* 19 (1): 53–74.

James, Barry (Eds.). 2006. *Media Development and Poverty Eradication.* Paris: UNESCO.

James, Jeffrey. 2008. 'Digital divide complacency: Misconceptions and dangers.' *Information Society* 24 (1): 54–61.

Janowitz, Morris. 1975. 'Professional models in journalism: The gatekeeper and the advocate.' *Journalism Quarterly* 52: 618–626.

Jennings, Bryant, and Dolf Zillmann (Eds.). 2002. *Media Effects: Advances in Theory and Research.* 2nd ed. Hillsdale, NJ: Lawrence Erlbaum.

Jin, Dal Yong. 2007. 'Reinterpretation of cultural imperialism: Emerging domestic market vs. continuing US dominance.' *Media, Culture & Society* 29 (5): 753–771.

Jin, Dal Yong. 2007. 'Transformation of the world television system under neoliberal globalization, 1983 to 2003.' *Television and New Media* 8 (3): 179–196.

Johnson, Melissa A. 1997. 'Predicting news flow from Mexico.' *Journalism and Mass Communication Quarterly,* 74 (2): 315–330.

Jowett, Garth S., and Victoria O'Donnell. 2006. *Propaganda and Persuasion.* 4th ed. Thousand Oaks, CA: Sage.

Jung, Jai Kwan. 2008. 'Growing supranational identities in a globalizing world? A multilevel analysis of the World Values Surveys.' *European Journal of Political Research* 47: 578–609.

Kagami, Mitsuhiro, Masatsugu Tsuji, and Emanuele Giovannetti (Eds.). 2004. *Information Technology Policy and the Digital Divide: Lessons for Developing Countries.* Northhampton, MA: Edward Elgar.

Kalathil, Shanthi, and Taylor C. Boas. 2001. *The Internet and State Control in Authoritarian Regimes: China, Cuba and the Counterrevolution.* Global Policy Program no. 21. Washington, DC: Carnegie Endowment for International Peace.

Kaltenthaler, Karl C., Ronald D. Gelleny, and Stephen J. Ceccoli. 2004. 'Explaining citizen support for trade liberalization.' *International Studies Quarterly* 48 (4): 829–851.

Kamalipour, Yahya R. (Ed.). 2007. *Global Communication.* 2nd ed. Belmont, CA: Wadsworth.

Kareil, Herbert, and Lynn Rosenvall. 1984. 'Factors influencing international news flow.' *Journalism Quarterly* 61: 509–516.

Katsirea, Irini. 2007. 'Audiovisual media services without frontiers implementing the rules.' *Common Market Law Review* 44: 1837–1839.

Katz, Elihu, and Paul F. Lazarsfeld. 1955. 'Images of the mass communications process.' In Katz Elihu and Paul F. Lazarsfeld (Eds.). *Personal Influence: The Part Played by People in the Flow of Mass Communications*, pp. 15–42. Glencoe, IL: Free Press.

Kayser, Jacques. 1953. *One Week's News: Comparative Study of 17 Major Dailies for a Seven Day Period.* Paris: UNESCO.

Keefer, Philip. 2007. 'Clientelism, credibility, and the policy choices of young democracies.' *American Journal of Political Science* 51 (4): 804–821.

Kelly, Mary, Gianpietro Mazzoleni, and Denis McQuail (Eds.). 2004. *The Media in Europe.* London: Sage.

Kezang, Whalley J. 2004. 'Telecommunications in the Land of the Thunder Dragon: Recent developments in Bhutan.' *Telecommunications Policy* 28 (11): 785–800.

Khiabany, Gholam, and Annabelle Sreberny. 2001. 'The Iranian press and the continuing struggle over civil society, 1998–2000.' *Gazette* 63 (2–3): 203–223.

Kick, Edward, and Byron Davis. 2001. 'World-system structure and change: An analysis of global networks and economic growth across two time periods.' *American Behavioral Scientist* 44: 1561–1578.

Kiiski, Sampsa, and Matti Pohjola. 2002. 'Cross-country diffusion of the Internet.' *Information Economics and Policy* 14 (2): 297–310.

Kim, Kyungmo, and George A. Barnett. 1996. 'The determinants of international news flow: A network analysis.' *Communication Research* 23 (3): 323–352.

Kim, Kyungmo, and George A. Barnett. 2000. 'The structure of the international telecommunications regime in transition: A network analysis of international organizations.' *International Interactions* 261: 91–127.

Kitley, Philip (Eds.). 2003. *Television, Regulation, and Civil Society in Asia.* London: Routledge.

Knigge, Pia. 1998. 'The ecological correlates of right-wing extremism in Western Europe.' *European Journal of Political Research* 34: 249–279.

Kocher, Renate. 1986. 'Bloodhounds or missionaries: Role definitions of German and British journalists.' *European Journal of Communication* 11: 43–64.

Kohut, Andrew, and Bruce Stokes. 2006. *America Against the World*. New York: Times Books.

Kraidy, Marwan M. 2005. *Hybridity, or the Cultural Logic of Globalization*. Philadelphia: Temple University Press.

Kunkel, Dale, Keren Eyal, and Edward Donnerstein et al. 2007. 'Sexual socialization messages on entertainment television: Comparing content trends, 1997–2002.' *Media Psychology* 9 (3): 595–622.

Lang, Michael. 2006. 'Globalization and its history.' *Journal of Modern History* 78 (4): 899–931.

Larsen, Peter (Ed.). 1990. *Import/Export: International Flow of Television Fiction*. Paris: UNESCO.

Larson, James F. 1979. 'International affairs coverage on U.S. network television.' *Journal of Communication* 29 (2): 136–147.

Larson, James F. 1984. *Television's Window on the World: International Affairs Coverage on the U.S. Networks*. Norwood, NJ: Ablex.

Lasswell, Harold. 1971 [1927]. *Propaganda Techniques in World War I*. Cambridge, MA: MIT Press.

Lawson, Chappel. 2002. *Building the Fourth Estate: Democratisation and the Rise of a Free Press in Mexico*. Berkeley: University of California Press.

Lee, C.-C. 2001. 'Servants of the state or the market? Media and journalists in China.' In Jeremy Tunstall (Ed.). *Media Occupations and Professions: A Reader*, pp. 240–252. New York: Oxford University Press.

Lee Davis, Linda. 2003. 'Cultural proximity on the air in Ecuador: National, regional, television outperforms imported U.S. programming.' In Michael G. Elasmar (Ed.). *The Impact of International Television: A Paradigm Shift*, pp. 111–131. Mahwah, NJ: Lawrence Erlbaum.

Liebes, Tamar, and Elihu Katz. 1993. *The Export of Meaning: Cross-Cultural Readings of Dallas*. Cambridge: Polity Press.

Lippman, Walter. 1922. *Public Opinion*. New York: Macmillan.

Loader, Brian D. (Ed.). 1998. *Cyberspace Divide: Equality, Agency and Policy in the Information Society*. London: Routledge.

Lubbers, Marcel, and Peer Scheepers. 2007. 'Explanations of political Euroscepticism at the individual, regional and national levels.' *European Societies* 9 (4): 643–669.

Luck, Edwards C. 1999. *Mixed Messages: American Politics and International Organizations, 1919–1999*. Washington, DC: Brookings Institution Press.

Lull, James. 2000. *Media, Communication, Culture: A Global Approach*. 2nd ed. New York: Cambridge University Press.

Lull, James, and Stephen Hinerman (Eds.). 1998. *Media Scandals*. New York: Columbia University Press.

MacBride, Sean. 1980. *Many Voices, One World: Communication and Society Today and Tomorrow; Towards a New More Just and More Efficient World Information and Communication Order.* Paris: UNESCO, International Commission for the Study of Communication Problems.

Madon, Shirin. 2004. 'Evaluating the development impact of e-governance initiatives: An explanatory framework.' *Electronic Journal of Information System in Developing Countries* 20 (5).

Maier, Jürgen, and Berthold Rittberger. 2008. 'Shifting Europe's boundaries: Mass media, public opinion and the enlargement of the EU.' *European Union Politics* 9 (2): 243–267.

Mankekar, D. R. 1981. *Whose Freedom? Whose Order? A Plea for a New International Information Order by Third World.* Delhi: Clarion Books.

Mann, Michael. 1997. 'Has globalization ended the rise and rise of the nation-state?' *Review of International Political Economy* 4 (3): 472–496.

Maor, Moshe. 2004. 'Feeling the heat? Anticorruption mechanisms in comparative perspective.' *Governance* 17 (1): 1–28.

Margolis, Michael, and David Resnick. 2000. *Politics as Usual: The Cyberspace 'Revolution.'* Thousand Oaks, CA: Sage.

Martin Steven P. 2003. 'Is the digital divide really closing? A critique of inequality measurement in "A Nation Online."' *IT & Society* 1 (4): 1–13.

Masmoudi, Mustapha. 1981. 'The new world information order.' In Jim Richstad and Michael A. Anderson (Eds.). *Crisis in International News: Policies and Prospects.* New York: Columbia University Press.

Masterton, Murray (Ed.). 1996. *Asian Values in Journalism.* Singapore: AMIC.

Matei, Sorin A. 2006. 'Globalization and heterogenization: Cultural and civilizational clustering in telecommunicative space, 1989–1999.' *Telematics and Informatics* 23: 316–331.

Mau, Steffen, Jan Mewes, and Ann Zimmernann. 2008. 'Cosmopolitan attitudes through transnational social practices?' *Global Networks* 8 (1): 1–24.

Mayda, Anna Maria, and Dani Rodrik. 2005. 'Why are some people (and countries) more protectionist than others?' *European Economic Review* 49: 1393–1430.

Mayda, Anna Maria, Kevin H. O'Rourke, and Richard Sinnott. 2007. 'Risk, government and globalization: International survey evidence.' NBER Working Paper no. 13037.

Mayer, Nonna, and Pascal Perrineau. 1992. 'Why do they vote for Le Pen?' *European Journal of Political Research* 22 (1): 123–141.

Mayer-Schönberger, Viktor, and David Lazer (Eds.) 2007. *Governance and Information Technology: From Electronic Government to Information Government.* Cambridge, MA: MIT Press.

McChesney, Robert W. 1999. *Rich Media, Poor Democracy: Communication Politics in Dubious Times.* Urbana: University of Illinois Press.

McChesney, Robert W. 2008. *Communication Revolution: Critical Junctures and the Future of Media.* New York: New Press.

McCombs, Maxwell, and Donald L. Shaw. 1972. 'The agenda-setting function of the mass media.' *Public Opinion Quarterly* 36: 176–185.

McDonald, Ross. 2004. 'Television, materialism and culture: An exploration of imported media and its implications for GNH.' *Journal of Bhutan Studies* 9: 68–89.

McGrew, Anthony, and David Held (Eds.). 2007. *Globalization Theory: Approaches and Controversies.* Cambridge: Polity Press.

McKnight, Patrick E., Katherine M. McKnight, Souraya Sidani, and Aurelio Jose Figueredo. 2007. *Missing Data: A Gentle Introduction.* New York: Guilford Press.

McLaren, Lauren M. 2005. *Identity, Interests and Attitudes to European Integration.* London: Palgrave Macmillan.

McNair, Brian. 2006. *Cultural Chaos: Journalism, News and Power in a Globalised World.* London: Routledge.

McNeill, William. 1986. *Polyethnicity and National Unity in World History.* Chicago: University of Chicago Press.

McPhail, Thomas. L. 1983. *Electronic Colonialism: The Future of International Broadcasting and Communication.* Beverly Hills, CA: Sage.

McPhail, Thomas L. 2006. *Global Communication: Theories, Stakeholders, and Trends.* 2nd ed. Malden, MA: Blackwell.

McQuail, Denis. 1994. *Mass Communication Theory.* 3rd ed. London: Sage.

McQuail, Denis, and Karen Siune. 1998. *Media Policy: Convergence, Concentration and Commerce.* London: Sage.

Medrano, Juan D., and Paula Gutierrez. 2001. 'Nested identities: National and European identities in Spain.' *Ethnic and Racial Studies* 24 (5): 753–778.

Medved, Michael. 1992. *Hollywood vs. America: Popular Culture and the War on Traditional Values.* London: HarperCollins.

Meier, Werner A. 2004. 'Switzerland.' In Mary Kelly, Gianpietro Mazzoleni, and Denis McQuail (Eds.). *The Media in Europe: The Euromedia Handbook.* London: Sage.

Melkote, Srinivas R., and H. Leslie Steeves. 2001. *Communication for Development in the Third World: Theory and Practice for Empowerment.* London: Sage.

Merton, Robert. 1957. *Social Theory and Social Structure.* Glencoe, IL: Free Press.

Meyen, Michael, and William Hillman. 2003. 'Communication needs and media change: The introduction of television in East and West Germany.' *European Journal of Communication* 18 (4): 455–476.

Meyer, Birgit, and Annelies Moors. 2005. *Religion, Media, and the Public Sphere.* Bloomington: University of Indiana Press.

Meyer, William H. 1988. *Transnational Media and Third World Development: The Structure and Impact of Imperialism*. Westport, CT: Greenwood.

Meyer, William H. 1989. 'Global news flows: Dependency and neo-imperialism.' *Comparative Political Studies* 22 (3): 243–264.

Meyer, William. H. 2000. 'Globalization: Sources and effects on national states and societies.' *International Sociology* 15 (2): 233–248.

Mickiewicz, Ellen. 1999. *Changing Channels: Television and the Struggle for Power in Russia*. Durham, NC: Duke University Press.

Milner, Helen V. 2006. 'The digital divide: The role of political institutions in technology diffusion.' *Comparative Political Studies* 39 (2): 176–199.

Mody, Bella (Ed). 2003. *International and Development Communication: A 21st-Century Perspective*. London: Sage.

Mohammadi, Ali (Ed.). 1997. *International Communication and Globalization: A Critical Introduction*. London: Sage.

Mollison, Thomas. 1998. 'Television broadcasting leads Romania's march toward an open, democratic society.' *Journal of Broadcasting and Electronic Media* 42 (1): 128–141.

Monge, Peter, and Noshir S. Contractor. 2003. *Theories of Communication Networks*. New York: Oxford University Press.

Monge, Peter, and Sorin A. Matei. 2004. 'The role of the global telecommunications network in bridging economic and political divides, 1989 to 1999.' *Journal of Communication* 54: 511–531.

Moran, Albert, and Michael Keane (Eds.). 2003. *Television Across Asia: Television Industries, Programme Formats and Globalization*. London: Taylor and Francis.

Morris, Nancy, and Silvio Waisbord (Eds.). 2001. *Media and Globalization*. Lanham, MD: Rowman and Littlefield.

Mowlana, Hamid. 1985. *International Flow of Information: A Global Report and Analysis*. Paris: UNESCO.

Mukasa, Stanford D. 2003. 'Press and politics in Zimbabwe.' *African Studies Quarterly: The Online Journal of African Studies* 7 (2–3).

Mullainathan, Sendhil, and Andrei Shleifer. 2005. 'The market for news.' *American Economic Review* 95 (4): 1031–1053.

Muthyala, John. 2008. 'Whose world is flat? Mapping the globalization of information technology.' *New Global Studies* 2 (1): 3.

Mwesige, Peter G. 2004. 'Disseminators, advocates, and watchdogs: A profile of Ugandan journalists in the new millennium.' *Journalism* 51: 69–96.

Nacos, Brigitte Lebens. 2008. *Terrorism and Counterterrorism: Understanding Threats and Responses in the Post-9/11 World*. 2nd ed. New York: Pearson Longman.

Nafstad, Hilde E., Rolv M. Blakar, and Erik Carlquist et al. 2007. 'Ideology and power: The influence of current neo-liberalism in society.' *Journal of Community & Applied Social Psychology* 17 (4): 313–327.

Negrine, Ralph, and Stylianos Papathanassopoulos. 1990. *The Internationalisation of Television*. London: Pinter.

Nelson, Brian, David Roberts, and Walter Veit (Eds.). 1992. *The Idea of Europe: Problems of National and Transnational Identity*. New York: Berg.

Neuman, W. Russell, Marion R. Just, and Ann N. Crigler. 1992. *Common Knowledge: News and the Construction of Political Meaning*. Chicago: University of Chicago Press.

Ni, Y. Y. 1995. 'State media relations under authoritarian regimes in South-Korea and Taiwan.' *Issues and Studies* 31 (10): 99–118.

Niedermayer, Oskar, and Richard Sinnott. 1995. *Public Opinion and Internationalized Governance*. Oxford: Oxford University Press.

Nisbet, Erik C., Matthew C. Nisbet, Dietram Scheufele, and James E. Shanahan. 2004. 'Public diplomacy, television news, and Muslim opinion.' *Harvard International Journal of Press-Politics* 9 (2): 11–37.

Nissen, Christian S. (Ed.). 2007. *Making a Difference: Public Service Broadcasting in the European Media Landscape*. Bloomington: Indiana University Press.

Nnaemeka, Tony, and Jim Richstad. 1980. 'Structured relations and foreign news flow in the Pacific region.' *Gazette* 26: 235–258.

Noam, Eli. 1991. *Television in Europe*. New York: Oxford University Press.

Nordenstreng, Kaarle, and Tapio Varis. 1973. 'The non-homogeneity of the national state and the international flow of communication.' In George Gerbner, Lawrence Gross, and W. Melody (Eds.). *Communications Technology and Social Policy*. New York: Wiley.

Nordenstreng, Kaarle, and Tapio Varis. 1974. *Television Traffic: A One Way Street*. Reports and Papers on Mass Communication no. 70. Paris: UNESCO.

Norris, Donald F. (Ed.). 2007. *Current Issues and Trends in e-Government Research*. Hershey, PA: Cybertech Publishers.

Norris, Pippa. 1996. 'The restless searchlight: Network news framing of the post cold-war world.' *Political Communication* 12 (4): 357–370.

Norris, Pippa. 1999. 'Global communications and cultural identities.' *Harvard International Journal of Press Politics* 4 (4): 1–7.

Norris, Pippa. 2000. *A Virtuous Circle: Political Communications in Post-Industrial Democracies*. Cambridge: Cambridge University Press.

Norris, Pippa. 2001. 'Global governance and cosmopolitan citizens.' In Joseph S. Nye and John Donahue (Eds.). *Governance in a Globalizing World*, pp. 155–177. Washington, DC: Brookings Institution Press.

Norris, Pippa. 2001. *Digital Divide: Civic Engagement, Information Poverty and the Internet Worldwide*. Cambridge: Cambridge University Press.

Norris, Pippa. 2003. 'The political regime.' In Hermann Schmitt and Jacques Thomassen (Eds.). *Political Representation and Legitimacy in the European Union*. Oxford: Oxford University Press.

Norris, Pippa. 2004. 'Global political communication.' In Frank Esser and Barbara Pfetsch (Eds.). *Comparing Political Communication: Theories, Cases and Challenges*, pp. 115–150. Cambridge: Cambridge University Press.

Norris, Pippa. 2005. *Radical Right*. Cambridge: Cambridge University Press.

Norris, Pippa. 2008. 'Confidence in the United Nations: Cosmopolitan and nationalistic attitudes.' In Yilmaz Esmer and Thorleif Pettersson (Eds.). *The Global System, Democracy and Values*. Uppsala: Uppsala University Press.

Norris, Pippa. 2008. *Driving Democracy: Do Power-Sharing Institutions Work?* Cambridge: Cambridge University Press.

Norris, Pippa (Ed). 1997. *Women, Media, and Politics*. New York: Oxford University Press.

Norris, Pippa, and Dieter Zinnbauer. 2002. 'Giving voice to the voiceless: Good governance, human development and mass communications.' Human Development Report Office Occasional Paper 2002/11. Cambridge, MA: UNDP.

Norris, Pippa, and Ronald Inglehart. 2004. *Sacred and Secular: Politics and Religion Worldwide*. Cambridge: Cambridge University Press.

Norris, Pippa, and Ronald Inglehart. 2008. 'Silencing Dissent.' Paper available at www.pippanorris.com.

Nye, Jr., Joseph S. 2002. *The Paradox of American Power*. New York: Oxford University Press.

Nye, Jr., Joseph S. 2004. *Soft Power: The Means to Success in World Politics*. New York: Public Affairs.

Nye, Jr., Joseph S. 2008. 'Public diplomacy and soft power.' *Annals of the American Academy of Political and Social Science* 616: 94–109.

Ognianova, Ekaterina, and Byron Scott. 1997. 'Milton's paradox: The market-place of ideas in post-Communist Bulgaria.' *European Journal of Communication* 12 (3): 369–390.

Ogunyemi, Olatunji. 2006. 'The appeal of African broadcast web sites to African diasporas: A case study of the United Kingdom.' *Journal of Black Studies* 36 (3): 334–352.

Ohmae, Ken'ichi. 1995. *The End of the Nation State*. New York: Free Press.

Olofsson, Anna, and Susanna Ohman. 2007. 'Cosmopolitans and locals: An empirical investigation of transnationalism.' *Current Sociology* 55 (6): 877–895.

Olsen Gorm R., Nils Carstensen, and Kristian Hoyen. 2003. 'Humanitarian crises: What determines the level of emergency assistance? Media coverage, donor interests and the aid business.' *Disasters* 27 (2): 109–126.

Ono, Hioshi, and Madeline Zavodny. 2003. 'Gender and the Internet.' *Social Science Quarterly* 84: 111–121.

Ono, Hiroshi, and Madeline Zavodny. 2007. 'Digital inequality: A five country comparison using microdata.' *Social Science Research* 36 (3): 1135–1155.

Open Society Institute. 2005. *Television Across Europe: Regulation, Policy and Independence*. Budapest: OSI.

Ornebring, Henrik. 2003. 'Televising the public sphere: Forty years of current affairs debate programmes on Swedish television.' *European Journal of Communication* 18 (4): 501–527.

Page, Benjamin I., and Jason Barabas. 2000. 'Foreign policy gaps between citizens and leaders.' *International Studies Quarterly* 44: 339–364.

Page, Benjamin, and Robert Shapiro. 1992. *The Rational Public: Fifty Years of Trends in American's Policy Preferences*. Chicago: University of Chicago Press.

Paletz, David L., and Karol Jakubowicz. (Eds.). 2003. *Business as Usual: Continuity and Change in Central and Eastern European Media*. Cresskill, NJ: Hampton Press.

Palfrey, John, Jonathan Zittrain, Ron Deibert, and Rafal Rohozinski. 2008. *Access Denied: The Practice and Policy of Global Internet Filtering*. Cambridge, MA: MIT Press.

Pan, Zhongdang, and Joseph M. Chan. 2003. 'Shifting journalistic paradigms: How China's journalists assess "media exemplars."' *Communication Research* 30 (6): 649–682.

Papathanassopoulos, Stylianos. 2002. *European Television in the Digital Age*. Cambridge: Polity Press.

Parente, Stephen L., and Edward C. Prescott. 2002. *Barriers to Riches*. Cambridge, MA: MIT Press.

Parks, Lisa. 2005. *Cultures in Orbit: Satellites and the Televisual*. Durham, NC: Duke University Press.

Partnership on Measuring ICT for Development. 2008. *The Global Information Society: A Statistical View*. Santiago: United Nations.

Pasti, Svetlana. 2005. 'Two generations of contemporary Russian journalists.' *European Journal of Communication* 20 (1): 89–115.

Pauwels, Caroline, and Jan Loisen. 2003. 'The WTO and the audiovisual sector: Economic free trade vs. cultural horse trading?' *European Journal of Communication* 18 (3): 291–313.

Pearse, Meic. 2004. *Why the Rest Hates the West: Understanding the Roots of Global Rage*. Downers Grove, IL: InterVarsity Press.

Pieterse, Jan Nederveen. 2003. *Globalization and Culture: Global Melange*. Lanham, MD: Rowman and Littlefield.

Pimenta, John, Daniel Paolillo, and Daniel Prado. 2005. *Measuring Linguistic Diversity on the Internet*. Paris: UNESCO.

Poindexter, Paula, Sharon Meraz, and Amy Schmitz Weiss. 2007. *Women, Men, and News: Divided and Disconnected in the News Media Landscape*. New York: Routledge.

Price, Monroe E. 2002. *Media and Sovereignty: The Global Information Revolution and Its Challenge to State Power*. Cambridge, MA: MIT Press.

Price, Monroe E., Beata Rozumilowicz, and Stefaan G. Verhulst (Eds.). 2001. *Media Reform: Democratizing Media, Democratizing the State*. London: Routledge.

PriceWaterhouseCoopers. 2008. *Global Entertainment and Media Outlook*. New York: PriceWaterhouseCoopers.

Puddenphatt, Andrew. 2007. *Defining Indicators of Media Development: Background Paper.* Paris: UNESCO.

Putnam, Robert D. 2007. 'E pluribus unum: Diversity and community in the twenty-first century – the 2006 Johan Skytte Prize Lecture.' *Scandinavian Political Studies* 30 (2): 137–174.

Quester, George. H. 1990. *The International Politics of Television.* Lexington MA: Lexington Books.

Rahn, Wendy M., and Thomas J. Rudolph. 2001. 'National identities and the future of democracy.' In W. Lance Bennett and Robert M. Enbtman (Eds.). *Mediated Politics.* Cambridge: Cambridge University Press.

Ramaprasad, Jyotika. 2001. 'A profile of journalists in post-independence Tanzania.' *Gazette* 63: 539–556.

Ramaprasad, Jyotika, and James D. Kelly. 2003. 'Reporting the news from the world's rooftop: A survey of Nepalese journalists.' *Gazette* 65: 291–315.

Ramaprasad, Jyotika, and Naila Hamdy. 2006. 'Functions of Egyptian journalists: Perceived importance and actual performance.' *International Communication Gazette* 68 (2): 167–185.

Ramaprasad, Jyotika, and Shafiqur Rahman. 2006. 'Tradition with a twist: A survey of Bangladeshi journalists.' *International Communication Gazette* 682: 148–165.

Ramos, Howard, James Ron, and Oskar N. T. Thoms. 2007. 'Shaping the Northern media's human rights coverage, 1986–2000.' *Journal of Peace Research* 44 (4): 385–406.

Ramsdale, Philip (Ed). 1999. *International Flows of Selected Cultural Goods, 1980–1998.* Paris: UNESCO Institute for Statistics.

Rankin, David M. 2001. 'Identities, interests and imports.' *Political Behavior* 23: 351–76.

Rantanen, Terhi. 2005. *The Media and Globalization.* London: Sage.

Raudenbush, Stephen W., and Anthony Bryk. 2002. *Hierarchical Linear Models.* 2nd ed. Thousand Oaks, CA: Sage.

Reichert, Tom, Jacqueline Lambiase, Susan Morgan, Meta Carstarphen, and Susan Zavoina. 1999. 'Cheesecake and beefcake: No matter how you slice it, sexual explicitness in advertising continues to increase.' *Journalism and Mass Communication Quarterly* 76: 7–20.

Reinert, Kenneth A. 2007. 'Ethiopia in the world economy: Trade, private capital flows, and migration.' *Africa Today* 53 (3): 65–89.

Resnick, David. 1998. 'Politics on the Internet: The normalization of cyberspace.' In Chris Toulouse and Timothy W. Luke (Eds.). *The Politics of Cyberspace.* New York: Routledge.

Rinnawi, Khalil. 2006. *Instant Nationalism: McArabism, al-Jazeera and Transnational Media in the Arab World.* Lanham, MD: University Press of America.

Risse, Thomas. 2001. 'A European identity? Europeanization and the evolution of nation-state identities.' In Maria G. Cowles, James Caporaso, and

Thomas Risse (Eds.). *Transforming Europe*. Ithaca, NY: Cornell University Press.

Ritzer, George. 1993. *The McDonaldization of Society*. Newbury Park, CA: Pine Forge Press.

Ritzer, George. 1996. 'Cultures and consumers: The McDonaldization thesis – Is expansion inevitable?' *International Sociology* 11: 291–308.

Ritzer, George, and Allan Liska. 1997. 'McDisneyization.' In Chris Rojek and John Urry (Eds.). *Touring Cultures: Transformation of Travel and Theory*. London: Routledge.

Rixon, Paul. 2006. *American Television on British Screens: A Story of Cultural interaction*. London: Palgrave Macmillan.

Roach, Colleen. 1997. 'Cultural imperialism and resistance in media theory and literary theory.' *Media, Culture & Society* 19: 47.

Roberts, Alasdair. 2006. *Blacked Out: Government Secrecy in the Information Age*. Cambridge: Cambridge University Press.

Robertson, Roland. 1992. *Globalization: Social Theory and Global Culture*. London: Sage.

Robinson, Joch G., and Vernone M. Sparkes. 1976. 'International news in the Canadian and American press: A comparative news flow study.' *Gazette* 22: 203–218.

Rodrik, Dani. 2007. *One Economics, Many Recipes: Globalization, Institutions and Economic Growth*. Princeton, NJ: Princeton University Press.

Roiser, Martin, and Carla Willig. 2002. 'The strange death of the authoritarian personality: 50 years of psychological and political debate.' *History of the Human Sciences* 15 (4): 71–96.

Rokeach, Milton. 1968. *Beliefs, Attitudes and Values*. San Fransisco: Jossey-Bass.

Rose, Ian M. 1995. 'Barring foreigners from our airwaves: An anachronistic pothole on the global information highway.' *Columbia Law Review* 95: 1188.

Rosenau, James. 2004. 'Emerging spaces, new places and old faces: Proliferating identities in a globalizing world.' In Jonathan Friedman and Shalini Randeria (Eds.). *Worlds on the Move: Globalization, Migration, and Cultural Security*. London: I. B. Taurus.

Rosenberg, Justin. 2000. *The Follies of Globalization Theory*. London: Verso.

Rothkopf, David. 1997. 'In praise of cultural imperialism.' *Foreign Affairs* 107: 38–53.

Roudometof, Victor. 2005. 'Transnationalism, cosmopolitanism and glocalisation.' *Current Sociology* 53 (1): 113–135.

Rozanova Julia. 2006. 'Behind the screen: The role of state–TV relationships in Russia, 1990–2000.' *Canadian Review of Sociology and Anthropology* 43 (2): 185–203.

Rugh, William A. 2004. *Arab Mass Media: Newspapers, Radio, and Television in Arab Politics*. Westport, CT: Praeger.

Rusciano, Frank Louis. 2006. *Global Rage after the Cold War*. New York: Palgrave Macmillan.

Sakr, Naomi. 2001. *Satellite Realms: Transnational Television, Globalization and the Middle East*. London: I. B. Tauris.

Sani, Mohd A. M. 2005. 'Media freedom in Malaysia.' *Journal of Contemporary Asia* 35 (3): 341–367.

Scheuer, Angelika. 1999. 'A political community?' In Hermann Schmitt and Jacques Thomassen (Eds.). *Political Representation and Legitimacy in the European Union*. Oxford: Oxford University Press.

Scheve, Kenneth F., and Matthew J. Slaughter. 2001. *Globalization and the Perceptions of American Workers*. Washington, DC: Institute for International Economics.

Schiller, Herbert J. 1969. *Mass Communication and American Empire*. New York: A. M. Kelley.

Schiller, Herbert J. 1973. *Communication and Cultural Domination*. White Plains, NY: International Arts and Science Press.

Schlesinger, Philip. 2007. 'A cosmopolitan temptation.' *European Journal of Communication* 22 (4): 413–426.

Schmitt-Beck, Rudig, and Katrin Voltmer. 2007. 'The mass media in third-wave democracies: Gravediggers or seedsmen of democratic consolidation?' In Richard Gunther, José Ramon Montero, and Hans-Jürgen Puhle (Eds.). *Democracy, Intermediation, and Voting in Four Continents*, pp. 75–134. Oxford: Oxford University Press.

Schramm, Wilbur. 1964. *Mass Media and National Development: The Role of Information in Developing Countries*. Stanford, CA: Stanford University Press.

Schramm, Wilbur. 1959. *One Day in the World's Press: Fourteen Great Newspapers on a Day of Crisis*. Stanford, CA: Stanford University Press.

Schueth, Sam, and John O'Laughlin. 2008. 'Belonging to the world: Cosmopolitanism in geographic contexts.' *Geoforum* 39 (2): 926–941.

Schwartz, Shalom. 2007. 'Value orientations: Measurement, antecedents and consequences across nations.' In Roger Jowell, Caroline Roberts, Rory Fitzgerald, and Gillian Eva (Eds.). *Measuring Attitudes Cross-Nationally: Lessons from the European Social Survey*. London: Sage.

Scott, Joseph E. 1986. 'An updated longitudinal content analysis of sex references in mass circulation magazines.' *Journal of Sex Research* 22: 385–392.

Scott-Clark, Cathy, and Adrian Levy. 2003. 'Fast forward into trouble.' *Guardian*, June 14.

Scriven, Michael, and Emily Roberts (Eds.). 2003. *Group Identities on French and British Television*. New York: Berghahn Books.

Segrave, Kerry. 1998. *American Television Abroad: Hollywood's Attempt to Dominate World Television*. London: McFarland.

Segrave, Kerry. 1997. *American Films Abroad: Hollywood's Domination of the World's Movie Screens*. Jefferson, NC: McFarland.

Semetko, Holli A., Joanne B. Brzinski, David Weaver, and Lars Willnat. 1992. 'TV news and U.S. public opinion about foreign countries: The impact of exposure and attention.' *International Journal of Public Opinion Research* 4 (1): 18–36.

Sen, Amartya. 1984. *Poverty and Famines*. Oxford: Oxford University Press.

Sen, Amartya. 1999. *Development as Freedom*. New York: Alfred Knopf.

Sepstrup, Preben. 1990. *Transnationalization of Television in Western Europe*. London: John Libbey.

Shah, Hemant. 1996. 'Modernization, marginalization, and emancipation: Toward a normative model of journalism and national development.' *Communication Theory* 62 (2): 143–166.

Shoemaker, Pamela J. 1997. 'A new gatekeeping model.' In Daniel Berkowitz (Ed.). *Social Meanings of News: A Text-Reader*. Thousand Oaks, CA: Sage.

Shoemaker, Pamela J., and Akiba A. Cohen. 2006. *News Around the World: Content, Practitioners, and the Public*. New York: Routledge.

Shoemaker, Pamela J., and Stephen D. Reese. 1991. *Mediating the Message: Theories of Influences on Mass Media Content*. New York: Longman.

Shumate, Lori, and Michelle Dewitt. 2008. 'The North/South divide in NGO hyperlink networks.' *Journal of Computer-Mediated Communication* 13 (2): 405–428.

Siebert, Fredrick S., Theodore Peterson, and Wilbur Schramm. 1956. *Four Theories of the Press*. Urbana: University of Illinois Press.

Silverman, David S. 2007. *You Can't Air That: Four Cases of Controversy and Censorship in American Television Programming*. Syracuse, NY: University of Syracuse Press.

Sinclair, John, Elizabeth Jacka, and Stuart Cunningham (Eds.). 1996. *New Patterns in Global Television: Peripheral Vision*. Oxford: Oxford University Press.

Sinnott, Richard. 2000. 'Knowledge and the position of attitudes to a European foreign policy on the real-to-random continuum.' *International Journal of Public Opinion Research* 12 (2): 113–137.

Sinnott, Richard. 2006. 'An evaluation of the measurement of national, sub-national and supranational identity in cross-national surveys.' *International Journal of Public Opinion Research* 18 (2): 211–223.

Skelton, Tracey, and Tim Allen (Eds.). 1999. *Culture and Global Change*. New York: Routledge.

Skolkay, Andrej. 1998. 'Professionalization of post-communist journalists.' *Sociologia* 30 (3): 311–336.

Skurnik, W. A. E. 1981. 'Foreign news coverage in six African newspapers: The potency of national interests.' *Gazette* 28: 117–130.

Slaatta, Toore. 2006. 'Europeanisation and the news media: Issues and research imperatives.' *Javnost – The Public* 13 (1): 7–23.

Smith, Anthony. 1995. 'Towards a global culture?' In Michael Featherstone (Ed.). *Global Culture*. London: Sage.

Sobel, Richard. 2001. *The Impact of Public Opinion on American Foreign Policy Since Vietnam*. New York: Oxford University Press.

Soloski, John. 1989. 'News reporting and professionalism: Some constraints on the reporting of the news.' *Media, Culture, and Society* 11 (2): 207–228.

Sparks, Colin, and Anna Reading. 1994. 'Understanding media change in East-Central-Europe.' *Media, Culture & Society* 16 (2): 243–270.

Sparks, Glenn. 2005. *Media Effects Research: A Basic Overview*. 2nd ed. New York: Wadsworth.

Sreberny-Mohammadi, Annabelle. 1991. 'The global and the local in international communications.' In James Curran and Michael Gurevitch (Eds.). *Mass Media and Society*, pp. 118–138. New York: Routledge.

Sreberny-Mohammadi, Annabelle, with Kaarle Nordenstreng, Robert Stevenson, and Frank Ugboajah (Eds.). 1985. *Foreign News in the Media: International Reporting in Twenty-Nine Countries*. Reports and Papers on Mass Communication no. 93. Paris: UNESCO.

Stallings, Barbara. 2007. 'The globalization of capital flows: Who benefits?' *Annals of the American Academy of Political and Social Science* 610: 202–216.

Stanton, Richard. 2007. *All News Is Local: The Failure of the Media to Reflect World Events in a Globalized Age*. Jefferson, NC: McFarland.

Steele, Jeanne, and Jane Brown. 1995. 'Adolescent room culture: Studying media in the context of everyday life.' *Journal of Youth and Adolescence* 24: 551–576.

Steemers, Jeanette. 2004. *Selling Television: British Television in the Global Marketplace*. Berkeley: University of California Press.

Steinmueller, Edward. 2001. 'ICTs and the possibilities for leapfrogging by developing countries.' *International Labour Review* 140: 193–210.

Stephan, Alexander. 2007. *The Americanization of Europe: Culture, Diplomacy, and Anti-Americanism after 1945*. New York: Berghahn Books.

Stevenson, Robert L. 1988. *Communication, Development and the Third World: The Global Politics of Information*. New York: Longman.

Stevenson, Robert L. 1994. *Global Communications in the 21st Century*. New York: Longman.

Stevenson, Robert L., and Donald Lewis Shaw (Eds.). 1984. *Foreign News and the New World Information Order*. Ames: Iowa State University Press.

Stigletz, Joseph E. 2003. *Globalization and Its Discontents*. New York: W. W. Norton.

Stimson, James A. 1985. 'Regression in time and space: A statistical essay.' *American Journal of Political Science* 29: 914–947.

Stokes, Melvyn, and Richard Maltby (Eds.). 2005. *Hollywood Abroad: Audiences and Cultural Exchange*. Berkeley: University of California Press.

Stokes, Susan. 2001. *Public Support for Market Reforms in New Democracies*. Cambridge: Cambridge University Press.

Strasburger, Victor, and Edward Donnerstein. 1999. 'Children, adolescents, and the media: Issues and solutions.' *Pediatrics* 103: 129–139.

Straubhaar, Joseph D. 1991. 'Beyond media imperialism: Asymmetrical interdependence and cultural proximity.' *Critical Studies in Mass Communication* 8: 39.

Straubhaar, Joseph D. 2007. *World Television: From Global to Local.* London: Sage.

Stromberg, David. 2001. 'Mass media and public policy.' *European Economic Review* 45 (4–6): 652–663.

Stromberg, David. 2007. 'Natural disasters, economic development, and humanitarian aid.' *Journal of Economic Perspectives* 21 (3): 199–222.

Svallfors, Stefan. 1999. 'National differences in national identities? An introduction to the International Social Survey Program.' In Niko Tos, Peter P. Mohler, and Brina Malnar (Eds.). *Modern Society and Values: A Comparative Analysis Based on ISSP Project*, pp. 3–14. Ljubljana: University of Ljubljana.

Swain, Kristen A. 2003. 'Proximity and power factors in Western coverage of the sub-Saharan AIDS crisis.' *Journalism and Mass Communication Quarterly* 80 (1): 145–165.

Sylvie, George, and Hsiang Iris Chyi. 2007. 'One product, two markets: How geography differentiates online newspaper audiences.' *Journalism & Mass Communication Quarterly* 84 (3): 562–581.

Taylor, Matthew. 2000. 'Media relations in Bosnia: A role for public relations in building civil society.' *Public Relations Review* 26 (1): 1–14.

Tettey, Wisdom. 2001. 'The media and democratization in Africa: Contributions, constraints and concerns of the private press.' *Media, Culture & Society* 231: 5–31.

Tettey, Wisdom. 2002. *The Media, Accountability and Civic Engagement in Africa.* Human Development Report Office Occasional Paper. New York: UNDP.

Tettey, Wisdom. 2006. 'The politics of media accountability in Africa: An examination of mechanisms and institutions.' *International Communication Gazette* 68 (3): 229–248.

Thomas, Amos Owen. 2005. *Imagi-Nations and Borderless Television: Media, Culture & Politics across Asia.* New Dehli: Sage.

Thomas, Hanitzsch. 2007. 'Deconstructing journalism culture: Toward a universal theory.' *Communication Theory* 17 (4): 367–385.

Thompson, John B. 2000. *Political Scandal: Power and Visibility in the Media Age.* Cambridge: Polity Press.

Thomsen, Christian (Ed.). 1989. *Cultural Transfer or Electronic Imperialism?* Heidelberg: Carl Winter Universitatsverlag.

Thorn, Hakan. 2007. 'Social movements, the media and the emergence of a global public sphere: From anti-apartheid to global justice.' *Current Sociology* 55: 896–918.

Thussu, Daya Kishan. 2006. *International Communication: Continuity and Change.* New York: Hodder Arnold.

Thussu, Daya Kishan. 2006. *Media on the Move: Global Flow and Contra-Flow.* New York: Routledge.

Thussu, Daya Kishan. 2007. 'The "Murdochization" of news? The case of Star TV in India.' *Media, Culture & Society* 29 (4): 593–611.

Thussu, Daya Kishan (Ed). 1998. *Electronic Empires: Global Media and Local Resistance.* New York: Hodder Arnold.

Tichenor, Phillip J., George A. Donohue, and Clarice Olien. 1970. 'Mass media flow and differential growth of knowledge.' *Public Opinion Quarterly* 34: 159–170.

Tilley, James, and Anthony Heath. 2007. 'The decline of British national pride.' *British Journal of Sociology* 58: 661–678.

Tomaselli, Keyan. 2000. 'South African media, 1994–7: Globalizing via political economy.' In James Curran and Myung Park (Eds.). *De-Westernizing Media Studies.* London: Routledge.

Tomlinson, John. 1991. *Cultural Imperialism.* Baltimore: Johns Hopkins University Press.

Tomlinson, John. 1999. *Globalization and Culture.* Chicago: University of Chicago Press.

Tracey, Michael, and Wendy W. Redal. 1995. 'The new parochialism: The triumph of the populist in the flow of international television.' *Canadian Journal of Communication* 20: 343–365.

Tsai, Ming-Chang. 2007. 'Does globalization affect human well-being? *Social Indicators Research* 81 (1): 103–126.

Tunstall, Jeremy. 1977. *The Media Are American.* New York: Columbia University Press.

UNCTAD. 2008. *Secretary-General's High Level Panel on the Creative Economy and Industries for Development.* Accra, Ghana: UN. TD (XII)/BP/4 April 2008.

UNDP. 1999. *Human Development Report, 1999.* New York: UNDP/Oxford University Press.

UNDP. 2008. *Human Development Report, 2007/8: Fighting Climate Change – Human Solidarity in a Divided World.* New York: UNDP/Oxford University Press.

UNESCO. 1998. *World Communication Report: The Media and Challenges of the New Technologies.* Paris: UNESCO.

UNESCO. 2005. *International Flows of Selected Cultural Goods and Services, 1994–2003.* Montreal: UNESCO Institute for Statistics.

United Nations. 2006. *Comtrade Yearbook.* http://comtrade.un.org.

United Nations Department of Economic and Social Affairs. 2003. *World Public Sector Report 2003: e-Government at the Crossroads.* New York: United Nations.

Vaidya, Samarth. 2005. 'Corruption in the media's gaze.' *European Journal of Political Economy* 213: 667–687.

Van Belle, Douglas. 2000. *Press Freedom and Global Politics*. Westport, CT: Praeger.

Van Belle, Douglas, A. Cooper Drury, and Richard Stuart Olson. 2005. 'The CNN effect, geo-strategic motives and the politics of U.S. foreign disaster assistance.' *Journal of Politics* 67 (2): 454–473.

Van Belle, Douglas, Jean-Sébastien Rioux, and David M. Potter. 2004. *Media, Bureaucracies, and Foreign Aid: A Comparative Analysis of the United States, the United Kingdom, Canada, France and Japan*. New York: Palgrave Macmillan.

Van Dijk, Jan A. G. M. 2005. *The Deepening Divide: Inequality in the Information Society*. London: Sage.

Van Rossem, Roman. 1996. 'The world system paradigm as general theory of development: A cross-national test.' *American Sociological Review* 61: 508–527.

Varis, Tapio. 1974. 'Global traffic in television.' *Journal of Communication* 241: 102–109.

Varis, Tapio. 1984. 'The International Flow of Television Programs.' *Journal of Communication* 34 (1): 143–152.

Varis, Tapio. 1986. 'Trends in international television flows.' *International Political Science Review* 7: 235–249.

Varis, Tapio. 2002. 'The international flow of television programmes.' In Toby Miller (Ed.). *Television: Critical Concepts in Media and Cultural Studies*, pp. 72–77. New York: Routledge.

Vertovec, Steven, and Robin Cohen (Eds.). 2002. *Conceiving Cosmopolitanism: Theory, Context and Practice*. Oxford: Oxford University Press.

Volkmer, Ingrid. 1999. *News in the Global Sphere: A Study of CNN and Its Impact on Global Communication*. Luton: University of Luton Press.

Voltmer, Katrin. 2000. 'Constructing political reality in Russia–Izvestiya: Between old and new journalistic practices.' *European Journal of Communication* 15 (4): 469–500.

Voltmer, Katrin (Ed.). 2006. *Mass Media and Political Communication in New Democracies*. London: Routledge.

Waisbord, Silvio. 1994. 'Knocking on newsroom doors: Press and political scandals in Argentina.' *Political Communication* 111: 19–34.

Waisbord, Silvio. 2000. *Watchdog Journalism in South America: News, Accountability, and Democracy*. New York: Columbia University Press.

Waisbord, Silvio. 2004. 'Scandals, media, and citizenship in contemporary Argentina.' *American Behavioral Scientist* 47 (8): 1072–1098.

Waisbord, Silvio (Ed.). 2001. *Media and Globalization: Why the State Matters*. Lanham, MD: Rowan and Littlefield.

Walker, Christopher. 2007. *Muzzling the Media: The Return of Censorship in the Commonwealth of Independent States.* Washington, DC: Freedom House.

Wallerstein, Immanuel. 1976. *The Modern World System.* New York: Academic Press.

Wang, Georgette, Anura Goonasekera, and Jan Servaes (Eds.). 2000. *The New Communications Landscape: Demystifying Media Globalization.* London: Routledge.

Wangchuk, Tashi. 2004. 'The middle path to democracy in the kingdom of Bhutan.' *Asian Survey* 44 (6): 836–855.

Wanta, Wayne, Guy Golan, and Cheolhan Lee. 2004. 'Agenda setting and international news: Media influence on public perceptions of foreign nations.' *Journalism and Mass Communication Quarterly* 81 (2): 364–377.

Ward, David. 2007. *Television and Public Policy: Change and Continuity in an Era of Global Liberalization.* Mahwah, NJ: Lawrence Erlbaum.

Ward, L. Monique. 2003. 'Understanding the role of entertainment media in the sexual socialization of American youth: A review of empirical research.' *Developmental Review* 23 (3): 347–388.

Ware, William, and Michel Dupagne. 1994. 'Effects of U.S. television programs on foreign audiences: A meta-analysis.' *Journalism Quarterly* 71 (4): 947–959.

Warnock, Kitty, Emrys Schoemaker, and Mark Wilson. 1997. *The Case for Communication in Sustainable Development.* London: Panos.

Warschauer, Mark. 2004. *Technology and Social Inclusion: Rethinking the Digital Divide.* Cambridge, MA: MIT Press.

Wasko, Janet, and Mary Erickson (Eds.). 2008. *Cross-Border Cultural Production: Economic Runaway or Globalization?* Amherst, NY: Cambria Press.

Waterman, David, and Krishna P. Jayakar. 2000. 'The competitive balance of the Italian and American film industries.' *European Journal of Communication* 15 (4): 501–528.

Weaver, David (Ed.). 1998. *The Global Journalist: News People Around the World.* Cresskill, NJ: Hampton Press.

Weaver, David, and G. Cleveland Wilhoit. 1994. 'Daily newspaper journalists in the 1990s.' *Newspaper Research Journal* 15: 2–21.

Weaver, David, and G. Cleveland Wilhoit. 1996. *The American Journalist in the 1990s: U.S. News People at the End of an Era.* Mahwah, NJ: Lawrence Erlbaum.

Webster, Frank. 2006. Theories *of the Information Society.* 3rd ed. London: Routledge.

Wheeler, Mark. 2000. 'Globalization of the communications marketplace.' *Harvard International Journal of Press-Politics* 5 (3): 27–44.

Wheeler, Mark. 2000. 'Research note: The "undeclared war," part II – The European Union's consultation process for the new round of the General

Agreement on Trading Services / World Trade Organization on audiovisual services.' *European Journal of Communication* 15 (2): 253–262.

Wheeler, Mark. 2004. 'Supranational regulation: Television and the European Union.' *European Journal of Communication* 19 (3): 349–369.

White, James D. 2005. *Global Media: The Television Revolution in Asia.* New York: Routledge.

Wieten, Jan, Graham Murdoch, and Peter Dahlgren (Eds.). 2000. *Television Across Europe.* London: Sage.

Wildman, Steven, and Stephen E. Siwek. 1988. *International Trade in Films and Television Programs.* Cambridge, MA: Ballinger.

Wiley, Stephen B. C. 2004. 'Rethinking nationality in the context of globalization.' *Communication Theory* 14 (1): 78–96.

Wilhelm, Anthony G. 2006. *Digital Nation: Toward an Inclusive Information Society.* Cambridge, MA: MIT Press.

Wilkinson, Kenton T. 2004. 'Language difference and communication policy in the information age.' *Information Society* 20 (3): 217–229.

Wilson, Sven E., and David M. Butler. 2007. 'A lot more to do: The sensitivity of time-series cross-section analyses to simple alternative specifications.' *Political Analysis* 15 (2): 101–123.

Wintrobe, Ronald. 1998. *The Information Revolution and Developing Countries.* Cambridge, MA: MIT Press.

Wolak, Janis, Kimberly Mitchell, and David Finkelhor. 2007. 'Unwanted and wanted exposure to online pornography in a national sample of youth Internet users.' *Pediatrics* 119 (2): 247–257.

Wolf, Martin. 2005. *Why Globalization Works.* New Haven, CT: Yale University Press.

Wolfsfeld, Gadi. *Media and Paths to Peace.* Cambridge: Cambridge University Press.

Woods, Joshua. 2007. 'Democracy and the press: A comparative analysis of pluralism in the international print media.' *Social Science Journal* 44 (2): 213–230.

Woodward, Ian, Zlato Skrbis, and Clive Bean. 2008. 'Attitudes towards globalization and cosmopolitanism: Cultural diversity, personal consumption and the national economy.' *British Journal of Sociology* 59 (2): 207–226.

World Association of Newspapers. Annual 1989–2007. *World Press Trends.* Paris: Zenith Media.

World Bank. 1999. *World Development Report: Knowledge and Development.* Washington, DC: World Bank.

World Bank. 2004. *World Development Report: Making Services Work for the Poor.* Washington, DC: World Bank.

World Bank. 2006. *Information and Communications for Development: Global Trends and Policies.* Washington, DC: World Bank.

World Bank. 2007. *World Development Indicators, 2007.* Washington, DC: World Bank.

Wouters, Jan, and Bart DeMeester. 2008. 'The UNESCO convention on cultural diversity and WTO law: A case study in fragmentation of international law.' *Journal of World Trade* 42 (1): 205–240.

Wresch, William. 1996. *Disconnected: Haves and Have-Nots in the Information Age.* New Brunswick, NJ: Rutgers University Press.

Wu, H. Denis. 1998. 'Investigating the determinants of international news flow: A meta-analysis.' *Gazette* 60 (6): 490–510.

Wu, H. Denis. 2000. 'Systematic determinants of international news coverage: A comparison of 38 countries.' *Journal of Communication* 50 (2): 110–130.

Wu, Wei, et al. 1995. 'Professional roles of Russian and U.S. journalists: A comparative study.' *Journalism and Mass Communication Quarterly*, 73: 534–548.

Xiaoge, Xu. 2005. *Demystifying Asian Values in Journalism.* Singapore: Marshall Cavendish.

Xiaoming, Hao, and Sunanda K. Datta-Ray (Eds.). 2006. *Issues and Challenges in Asian Journalism.* Singapore: Marshall Cavendish.

Yartey, Charles Amo. 2008. 'Financial development, the structure of capital markets, and the global digital divide.' *Information Economics and Policy* 20 (2): 208–227.

Yasushi, Watanabe, and David L. McConnell (Eds.). 2008. *Soft Power Superpowers: Cultural and National Assets of Japan and the United States.* New York: M. E. Sharpe.

Yu, Liangzhi. 2006. 'Understanding information inequality: Making sense of the literature of the information and digital divides.' *Journal of Librarianship and Information Science* 38 (4): 229–252.

Zaller, John. 1992. *The Nature and Origins of Mass Public Opinion.* Cambridge: Cambridge University Press.

Zaller, John. 1996. 'The myth of massive media impact revived: New support for a discredited idea.' In Diana C. Mutz, Paul M. Sniderman, and Richard A. Brody (Eds.). *Political Persuasion and Attitude Change*, pp. 17–78. Ann Arbor: University of Michigan Press.

Zayani, Mohamed. Ed. 2005. *The Al Jazeera Phenomenon: Critical Perspectives on New Arab Media.* Boulder, CO: Paradigm.

Zedillo, Ernesto (Ed.). 2008. *The Future of Globalization: Explorations in Light of Recent Turbulence.* New York: Routledge.

Zhao, Yuezhi. 1998. *Media, Market, and Democracy in China: Between the Party Line and the Bottom Line.* Urbana: University of Illinois Press.

Index